after fellini

after fellini

National Cinema in the Postmodern Age

Millicent Marcus

THE JOHNS HOPKINS UNIVERSITY PRESS | BALTIMORE AND LONDON

The Johns Hopkins University Press
2715 North Charles Street
Baltimore, Maryland 21218-4363
www.press.jhu.edu

Library of Congress
Cataloging-in-Publication Data
Marcus, Millicent Joy.
After Fellini : national cinema in the
postmodern age / Millicent Marcus
p.   cm.
Includes bibliographical references and index.
ISBN 0-8018-6847-5 (pbk.)
1. Motion pictures—Italy.   I. Title.
PN1993.5.I88 M283 2002
791.43′0945—dc21
2001002201

A catalog record for this book is available
from the British Library.

To the memory of Sydney Marcus
dolcissimo padre

Contents

Acknowledgments   ix

Introduction   3

Looking Back

1 National Identity by Means of Montage
   in Roberto Rossellini's *Paisan* | 15

2 Luchino Visconti's *Bellissima:*
   The Diva, the Mirror, and the Screen | 39

Italy by Displacement

3 Bernardo Bertolucci's *The Last Emperor:* Powerless in Peking | 61

4 *Mediterraneo* and the "Minimal Utopias" of Gabriele Salvatores | 76

5 From Salazar's Lisbon to Mussolini's Rome by Way of France in
   Roberto Faenza's *Pereira Declares* | 94

Family as Political Allegory

6 Francesco Rosi's *Three Brothers:* After the Diaspora | 115

7 The Alternative Family of Ricky Tognazzi's *La scorta* | 138

8 The Gaze of Innocence:
   Lost and Found in Gianni Amelio's *Stolen Children* | 154

Postmodernism; or, the Death of Cinema?

9 *Ginger and Fred:* Fellini after Fellini | 181

10 Giuseppe Tornatore's *Cinema Paradiso* and the
Art of Nostalgia | 199

11 From Conscience to Hyperconsciousness in
Maurizio Nichetti's *The Icicle Thief* | 214

12 Postmodern Pastiche, the *Sceneggiata,* and the View of the
Mafia from Below in Roberta Torre's *To Die for Tano* | 234

The Return of the Referent

13 Filming the Text of Witness: Francesco Rosi's *The Truce* | 253

14 The Seriousness of Humor in Roberto Benigni's
Life Is Beautiful | 268

15 *Caro diario* and the Cinematic Body of Nanni Moretti | 285

Appendix: Plot Summaries and Credits | 301
Notes | 321
Bibliography | 355
Videography | 365
Index | 367

Acknowledgments

Not until I had finished the essay on *Life Is Beautiful* did I realize how important the memory of my father was to my engagement with Italian cinema. His wartime reminiscences, especially his account of the landing at Normandy, have woven themselves into my own images of World War II and have led to my fascination with Liberation history as it has been interpreted reverentially, but also critically, in the films of the neorealists and their heirs. So it is Sydney Marcus whom I wish to acknowledge here as the "first cause" of all that has led to the writing of this book.

A number of others have offered invaluable aid in a more concrete sense. Thanks to Umberto Brazzini, the Mediateca Regionale Toscana in Florence remains the most user-friendly video archive and film library in which I have ever had the good fortune to work. Robert Cargni, projectionist of the International House of Philadelphia and Italophile extraordinaire, has supplied me with a steady stream of insider knowledge and materials on the current state of Italian film production. Nicola Gentili, administrative coordinator of the Center for Italian Studies and the Program in Film Studies at the University of Pennsylvania, as well as director of the Film Project at the International House, has been a marvelous organizer of events that have brought Italian films and filmmakers to campus, providing me with first-hand information about the subjects of this study. My colleague in Italian at the University of Pennsylvania, Victoria Kirkham, has been an extremely important source of intellectual inspiration and personal encouragement—our many informal conversations over lunch have enriched and enlivened the thinking that went into this book. In writing the introduction, I was tremendously helped by the wealth of second-ary texts with which I was supplied by Lino Miccichè, who has been unstinting in support of my scholarship over the years. I am also extremely grateful to Peter Bondanella, Gaetana Marrone-Puglia, and Ben Lawton for reading and commenting on these pages.

Thanks to a fellowship from the University Research Institute of the University of Texas at Austin, I was able to take off a semester from teaching—a leave that allowed me to generate considerable momentum in the early stages of my research. I am also deeply indebted to the Johns Hopkins University Press, whose enthusiasm for the project dates back to its very inception in 1995. Maura Burnett, the current humanities editor, has squired me through the final phase of manuscript preparation with the greatest skill, and it is thanks to her that the book finally found its title. My copy editor, Dennis Marshall, is to be especially commended for his expertise, professionalism, patience, cheerfulness, and profound engagement in the task at hand. Mary Corliss, director of the Film Stills Archive of the Museum of Modern Art, and Francesco Rosi were of great service in helping me acquire most of the photographs published in these pages.

Some of the chapters in the book are expanded versions of essays or parts of articles published in other scholarly venues. These include "Rossellini's *Paisà:* National Identity by Means of Montage," *Italian Quarterly* 37, issue in honor of Vittore Branca (winter/fall 2000): 295-302; "A Corridor with a View: Florence through the Eyes of Rossellini," *Forum Italicum* 33, issue in memory of Gian-Paolo Biasin and Giovanni Cecchetti (spring 1999): 161-68; "Visconti's *Bellissima:* The Diva, the Mirror, and the Screen," *Italian Culture* 17, issue in honor of Gregory Lucente (1999): 9-17; "Bertolucci's *Last Emperor* and the Case for National Cinema," *Romance Languages Annual* 1 (1989): 45-51; "Beyond *cinema politico:* Family as Political Allegory in *Three Brothers,*" in *Poet of Civic Courage: The Films of Francesco Rosi,* ed. Carlo Testa (Wiltshire, U.K.: Flick Books, 1996), 116-37; "Who Owns Film Studies?" *Romance Languages Annual* 5 (1993): 241-44; "Palimpsest versus Pastiche: Revisiting Neorealism in the 1990s," *Annali d'italianistica* 17 (1999): 61-68; "'Me lo dici babbo che gioco è?': The Serious Humor of *La vita è bella,*" *Italica* 77 (summer 2000): 153-70; and "*Caro diario* and the Cinematic Body of Nanni Moretti," *Italica* 73 (summer 1996): 233-47.

Finally, I would like to thank my husband, Robert Hill, and my children, Jacob and Lucy, who have lived with this project for longer than I'm sure they would have cared to. For them, the new Italian cinema toward which this book aspires could not come too soon.

after fellini

Introduction

"Last Fall, as Federico Fellini's coffin was lying in state in a Cinecittà studio," wrote Daniel Singer in January 1994, "people were really mourning the virtual death of Italian cinema."[1] Singer was hardly alone in interpreting the maestro's departure as something more than the demise of a beloved and highly gifted individual. As the last of the great postwar auteurs (Rossellini, Visconti, De Sica, and Pasolini had died in the 1970s, and Antonioni had been struck with a debilitating illness in 1985), Fellini stood for the entire age of brilliant signature filmmaking that gave Italian directors a disproportionate place in the international pantheon. Typical of such filmmakers as Renoir, Bergman, Bunuel, Kurosawa, Ozu, Ray, and Welles, according to Clive James, was the impulse to get "the whole of their country's life" into each film, or as Alan Cowell wrote, to "define the nation's self image, at home and abroad."[2] Biographer Tullio Kezich summed it up when he pronounced Fellini the "absolute Master of a certain kind of filmmaking *alla grande e all'italiana*."[3]

What emerges from these testaments to Fellini's place in the collective imaginary is his function as signifier, as synedoche, as *uomo-simbolo* (man-symbol), whose very mention conjures up associations of plenitude, of unfettered creativity, of personal reinvention, that made his films cultural events of the first order. To name Fellini, then, is to invoke that period when cinema occupied a position of cultural primacy—when films were seen as foundational acts, as socially defining exercises, as interventions in the life of the country. In short, Fellini stands for a time when filmmaking mattered.

This generational factor provides the most powerful measure of the "afterness" of contemporary Italian cinema, coming as it does in the wake of the great postwar auteurist developments that extended from the mid-1940s to the late 1970s. Coinciding with the disappearance of an entire generation of auteurs is the waning of the ideological and generic impulses that fueled the revolutionary achievement of their successors: Rosi, Petri, Bertolucci, Bellocchio, Ferreri, the Tavianis, Wertmuller, Cavani, and Scola. The discrediting of the Left, with the terrorist extremism of the *anni di piombo* (years of lead) and the fall of Communism, brought an end to the political engagement that drove so much of the realist cinema and its generic offshoots in the postwar years. *Cinema politico,* the sequel to neorealism in the '60s and '70s, ceded to the ideological torpor of the '80s, while the *commedia all'italiana,* with its withering critique of social mores as the country moved from *Il Boom* to the Berlusconi age, lost its sting.[4]

Domestic box-office statistics reflected the cinema's cultural marginalization in those years, with ticket sales falling off by 94 percent over the period from 1975 to 1996.[5] Contributing to this *cine-disastro*—or *cinecido,* as Lino Miccichè called it—was the media war triggered by the deregulation of the airwaves in 1976.[6] This meant the end of the rigorous state monopoly of television (previously limited to the three channels run by RAI—the Italian national broadcast network) and the immediate proliferation of private stations, whose ravenous appetite for film broadcasting dealt a crushing blow to the box office. So sudden and so total was the process of deregulation that it sent Italy on a televisual binge, as the nation gorged itself on an indiscriminate diet of any and all available offerings. Commenting later on Italy's decision to legalize private broadcasting, Fava and Viganò wrote, "Passing suddenly from a stern monopoly to a brazen liberty, without apparent rules . . . [the country has experienced] an overdose of the small screen that has no equal in Europe or perhaps the world."[7] Giorgio Gosetti, in more benign terms, called the television-saturated Italy of the 1980s an "audiovisual laboratory" of the most unique sort. "That was because of the explosion of private television stations and the ensuing battles between public and private broadcasting, things that went hand in hand with two, interconnected, interdependent phenomena. First, the shutting down of film theaters, second, the popularity of films aired on television and the definitive success of cinema *for* television, which got started in the 1970s."[8]

But the box-office debacle hid a far more disturbing story—that of television infiltration into all mass media,[9] changing the way in which cinema was conceived by its makers ("who got used to the comfortable idea that cinema could be packaged in boxes and in that form could always find a consumer")[10] and received by the general public, whose "horizon of expectations" had been lowered by prolonged exposure to the emanations of the small screen.[11] As if domestic programming were not debilitating enough, the deregulated Italian airwaves, in their frenzy to fill up their broadcasting schedules, resorted to massive importation of American sitcoms, soap operas, and action shows, creating a television culture that was not only trivial and artificial, but borrowed. A constant diet of *Happy Days, Dallas,* and *Bay Watch* conspired to "deprive a generation of its own imaginary," according to Sandro Bernardi, exchanging its indigenous dreams and utopias for ersatz ones from abroad.[12]

The deregulation of television thus operated a seismic shift in the Italian cultural terrain, moving cinema away from the epicenter of the collective imagination and replacing it with what has commonly been called *videocrazia*.[13] No longer the fulcrum of cultural debate, cinema forfeited its determining role in the shaping of mass desires.[14] The medium's loss of cultural prestige and its relegation to the status of filler material for television had tremendous consequences for the structuring of the new popular imaginary from which the cinema was deposed. If the public of the 1980s and 1990s was, according to Brunetta, "conditioned by the televised vision of the cinema, now devoid of cinematic memory and culture for which the televisual language is the mother tongue and the cinematographic is the foreign or adopted language,"[15] it would behoove us to examine the nature of that mother tongue and its relationship to the previous vernacular that has since been rendered "foreign."

In the simplest terms, the difference between the televisual *lingua materna* and the cinematic *lingua straniera* might be understood as the difference between simulation and mimesis, between a signifying system that ignores or subverts its referential function and one that points toward an external signified whose very representation in art makes moral and cognitive claims on viewers' attention. The fact that neorealism and its offshoots aspired to this second kind of representation—

whether we call it cinema's "civic function" (Peter Bondanella), its "record of a country's history as it unfolds" (Giorgio Gosetti), its tendency to register, "for better or for worse, the progress of Italian society" (Ettore Scola)[16]—made postwar filmmakers the foremost custodians of what I would like to call the Italian "national story." I do not mean this in a narrow, patriotic sense, but in terms of the filmmakers' insistence that this cinema refer, on some interpretive level, to the collective life of the country, be it through social satire, critical realism, or melodrama and family chronicle.

With the ascendancy of television, Italy exchanged her referential *lingua materna* for that of simulation. In a culture saturated with images whose consumption had come to take the place of primary experience, the relationship between signs and referents, between signifiers and signifieds, had weakened to the point of exhaustion. *Simulation,* which is defined as "pretense, feigning, false resemblance,"[17] derives from *simulacrum,* the copy that has the power to supplant the original and to erase the difference between the real and its image. "It is no longer a question of imitation, nor of reduplication, nor even of parody," writes Baudrillard in *Simulations.* "It is rather a question of substituting signs of the real for the real itself." Baudrillard opposes the flattening operations of the simulacrum to traditional notions of mimesis, based as the latter are on "the dialectical capacity of representations as a visible and intelligible mediation of the real."[18] In collapsing the distance between copy and original, Baudrillard's simulacra partake of the depthlessness that Jameson identifies as one of the foremost attributes of postmodernism. Of particular relevance is Jameson's claim for the dismantling of "the semiotic opposition between signifier and signified"[19] that resides at the heart of simulation and that explains the postmodern withering of reference.

In its wanton plundering of images from the world of lived experience, its promiscuous mixture of programming registers (commercials, game shows, talk shows, soap operas, sitcoms, news reports, sports events, educational broadcasts, etc.), television removes its signs from any meaningful anchoring in their original historical, social, or cultural contexts and turns them into simulations. On the small screen, in random juxtaposition with whatever shows precede or follow or whatever simultaneous broadcasts allow for channel surfing across programs, televisual signs are stripped of cognitive or moral value and given new meaning only in that they relate to other signs in the signifying chain. The small screen becomes a hermetically sealed universe, self-enclosed and indifferent to the moral claims of the world beyond its confines.

How has the Italian cinema responded to the usurpation of its cultural primacy and its mimetic calling by this medium of simulation? Much of the 1980s cinema turned inward, withdrawing into the recesses of the domestic space in a "claustrophilia" well documented by Mario Sesti. This cinema showed a marked preference for the suburbs, renounced narrative agency, ceased to foreground personal style,[20] and fell back on the most retrograde of comedic formulas for success—formulas inspired and abetted by television.[21] Such cinema occupied the middle and the lower rungs of national production, providing an oversupply of what Miccichè called "unexportable and often invisible little films, cute films, and trash." The few 1980s films at the "narrow qualitative top"[22] of this hierarchy are among the subjects of analysis in this book. Products of the medium's struggle against the televisual trend toward simulation, they illustrate its successful creation of a hybrid language that both absorbs and transcends its small-screen competitor.[23]

But it would be wrong to consider the entire interval from 1980 to the present as one extended period of decline. In fact, the late 1980s and the entire decade of the 1990s witnessed a gradual and steady rebuilding of Italian film culture. Sated and even repelled by the degenerating level of television offerings, spectators abandoned the small screen in droves.[24] New movie theaters and multiplexes opened, and the number of domestic films being produced annually displayed a healthy increase.[25] Italian films earned Oscars at an impressive rate, beginning in the late '80s with *The Last Emperor* (1987), *Mediterraneo* (1988), and *Cinema Paradiso* (1989) and continuing with the near-winning, near-Italian *Il postino* (1996) and the triumphant *Life Is Beautiful* (1999). The ranks of auteurs, so sadly depleted by the deaths of the postwar masters, have been replenished by a new generation of author-directors (Amelio, Tornatore, Salvatores) and a new breed of filmmakers who combine the roles of author-director with that of lead actor (Nichetti, Benigni, Moretti, Verdone).

Film scholarship and criticism of the 1980s and 1990s, with some notable exceptions,[26] has chosen to focus on the half-empty portion of the glass, reciting the usual litany of "lacks" and scolding the current generation for failing to produce a new nouvelle vague on the order of the other great cinematic revolutions (what Sesti calls "strong models"). But the expectation that a cinematic revival must always follow the paradigms of earlier avant-gardes—"authorial originality, displacements and transformations of language, psychic, social, and ideological urgency of messages"[27]—fails to take into account the vastly altered cultural context within which the current cinema must operate. It is a terrain scarred by media wars that force the cinema into a disadvantaged, adversarial position with respect to a monolithic and all-consuming video culture.

To preserve its integrity, film must engage in a continuous struggle to carve out and maintain an autonomous signifying field—a field that in the postwar "glory days" involved a morally engaged, if aesthetically self-conscious, telling of the national story. In this age of postmodern simulation, the cinema's vocation for reference instead requires deliberate strategies of resistance or reinvention. Critical holdovers from an earlier era blind viewers to the fact that our present moment might harbor a different kind of newness, that originality and revival might be taking diverse and unexpected forms in the current cultural climate against which the cinema is struggling to define itself. And it is the critic's task to play midwife to this process by identifying the signs of renewal, reinforcing them, and helping cultivate within the viewing public an appropriate level of receptivity.[28]

Mario Sesti's plea for a new critical adequacy to the altered conditions of the '80s and '90s finds one possible response in Vito Zagarrio's resurrection of the cinema/film dichotomy.[29] No longer understood in semiotic terms as the difference between the general code and the individual message, the cinema/film duality comes to mean the distinction between "a functioning industry, a series of apparatuses, laws, an idea of the market, a possibility of programming, a cohort of producers, an appropriate relationship with television networks, etc."[30] and individual *films* that manage to transcend the adverse institutional conditions facing the medium as a whole. Sesti himself interprets the cinema/film dichotomy in strictly medialogical terms, noting the new promiscuity with which films themselves have become available anywhere, anytime, to anyone to be consumed in isolation via television broadcasts, video rentals, and so forth, and opposing that to *the idea of cinema* as a public event and mass spectacle, staged in a theater, capable of shaping the collective imaginary in powerful and enduring ways.[31] For the purposes of my own study, the cinema/film dichotomy will take the form of a detailed, molecular approach to individual films whose richness and seriousness serve to challenge the dismissive attitude that critics and scholars have harbored toward the Italian industry in general during this time. In other words, the whole is less than the sum of its parts, and the parts merit our most serious critical attention if we are to identify and reward the tendencies that could contribute to a revitalized cinematic culture in years to come.

The films I have selected for inclusion in this study do not amount to a movement, a school, or even a tendency—the cinema of the '80s and '90s lacks such unifying characteristics.[32] In their absence, members of the film community gathering in Pesaro in 1988 issued a manifesto entitled *Per un cinema-cinema,* in which they adopted the metaphor of the archipelago to signify the isolated pockets of creativity that defined the contemporary state of the medium. What resulted was the map of a fragmented film industry "whose different individual routes cluster like islands in an archipelago."[33] In this study, I will attempt to navigate that archipelago, stopping on various islands (as does Nanni Moretti in the middle chapter of *Caro diario,* but with less cynical results) to examine what they bring to the map as a whole. This critical voyage has no pretensions to thoroughness, but it hopes to make up in depth and detail what it may lack in expanse.[34] In fact, this book may be read as a partial answer to Mario Sesti's call for a close examination of an overlooked body (or better, archipelago) of works.[35]

The dearth of scholarship on the Italian cinema of the '80s and '90s in the English-speaking world is a special concern of this study. Such scholarly neglect is due, in part, to the maddening inaccessibility of "primary texts." The problem lies in the vagaries of the film distribution system that has supplied ever-dwindling inventories of Italian films to the United States and has inordinate power to determine the image of the national cinema situation from abroad. Within academic settings, where subtitled videos are required for most teaching and screening purposes, the selection is even more meager. Because I believe that access to primary texts is an important corollary of a project such as mine,

I have chosen films that, for the most part, are available in English-subtitled videos (though some, of British provenance, can be found only in PAL format).[36] Along with the signers of the Pesaro manifesto, then, I seek in this book to "legitimize the new cinema, so often easily criticized and disparaged and that often, instead, finds itself representing Italy in the major festivals, despite the structural conditions that we know so well and that make of every film a small miracle of production." It is to a representative sample of such "miracles" that the current study is devoted. (Synopses and credits of the films discussed can be found in the book's appendix.)

In an attempt to construct a model against which contemporary film practice can be measured, I begin by looking back at two classics of the immediate postwar period. Rossellini's *Paisan* (1946) stands as a powerful example of filmmaking as a foundational act, as a building of national consciousness out of the ravages of Fascism and war. But Rossellini's insistence on historical representation is counterbalanced by an equally intense awareness that *Paisan* is a filmic artifact, a complex aesthetic construction that transcends its documentary or didactic scope. It is Rossellini's supreme achievement in *Paisan* to bring the film's referential and aesthetic impulses into perfect alignment in the forging of a new identity for the postwar cinematic medium. In Visconti's *Bellissima* (1951), which foregrounds issues of artifice and spectacle, the admirable balance achieved in neorealist aesthetics is torn asunder. Visconti nevertheless insists on the cinema's cognitive and moral accountability through the medium's exposé of its own powers of illusion. *Paisan* and *Bellissima* thus serve as examples of a cinema that is "answerable" to an external referent and that insists on the centrality of its position within postwar cultural discourse.

If the cinema of social reference had to go underground in the age of simulation, a number of filmmakers did their best to unearth it, telling the national story by deflection, allegory, or proxy. Thus "Italy by displacement" may be said to describe Bertolucci's relationship to Chinese history in *The Last Emperor* (1988), Salvatores' use of the Greek island setting in *Mediterraneo* (1991), and Faenza's perspective on Portugal in *Pereira Declares* (1995). For Bertolucci, staging the demise of imperial China allows him to vent his own anxieties and disappointments about revolutionary politics at home; for Salvatores, the Greek island on which a band of soldiers is marooned in 1941 offers a pretext for the exploration of a cherished utopian dream; while for Faenza, Salazar's Lisbon serves as a thinly veiled version of Mussolini's Rome of the late 1930s.

The family unit, both in its traditional configuration and in unexpectedly reconstituted forms, serves as a vehicle for social allegory in Rosi's *Three Brothers* (1981), Amelio's *Stolen Children* (1992), and Tognazzi's *La scorta* (1992). In Rosi's film, the death of the rural Italian mother occasions the return home of her sons, scattered throughout urban Italy in a reenactment of the demographic and cultural shifts of the postwar terrain. Amidst the dissolution of contemporary, industrialized urban life, Amelio's carabiniere and two "stolen children" form a miraculous family unit for the brief duration of a journey from Milan to Sicily in search of a mythic homeland. In Tognazzi's *La scorta,* the Mafia regime that rules Trapani meets its counterpart in the utopian family formed by a trial judge and his heroic cadre of bodyguards.

Films that directly face the specter of cinematic demise or that confront television's challenge to the medium by inventing a new, hybrid sign through contamination and pastiche are included in the book's fourth part, "Postmodernism; or, the Death of Cinema?" In Tornatore's *Cinema Paradiso* (1988), nostalgia for bygone youth, for an impossible rootedness, for romance and family, blends with memories of a filmic paradise-lost in the local movie house of a prevideo age. Postmodern anxiety about the death of the medium in a losing battle with television is the subject of two films: Fellini's *Ginger and Fred* (1985), in which an elderly vaudeville couple performs a tap-dance routine on an immensely vulgar and ersatz TV show, and Nichetti's *The Icicle Thief* (1989), whose neorealist film-within-a-film is held hostage to a commercial. Roberta Torre's *To Die for Tano* (1997) combines the conventions of musical comedy, eyewitness news, silent movies, MTV, and the Neapolitan sceneggiata in her spoof of the Mafia investigation genre.

The final section of the book includes films whose testimonial function heralds a double return, both to the social referent and to the moral accountability of neorealism. I speak of the newly emergent "cinema of witness," which has taken as its subject the Holocaust—in the case of Rosi's *The Truce* (1997) and Benigni's *Life Is Beautiful* (1998)—or one man's struggle with mortal illness—in Moretti's *Caro diario* (1993). As a sign of Italy's urgent, contemporary need to come to terms with Holocaust history, Rosi's film adapts Primo Levi's memoir in ways that reflect back on the national quest for renewal in the wake of World War II, and the cinema's place in such a process. Equally committed to the task of Holocaust witness, but by diametrically opposed means, *Life Is Beautiful* blends humor with Pirandellian seriousness in its transformation of genocide into child's play. Moretti's *Caro diario* (1993), although chronologically not the last film of those discussed here, provides a fitting conclusion to this study in its onscreen use of the body as metaphor for both the Italian body politic and the body of films produced in Italy during the '80s and '90s. Moretti's cinematic diary, which contains, among other things, documentary footage from his own chemotherapy session, brings closure to the traditions of national reference and aesthetic self-consciousness by insisting that the body on screen, once a generational and meta-cinematic signifier, is now strictly his own. It is appropriate that Moretti's "cine-diary" of personal witness, announcing a radical departure for the medium as it enters its second century of life, should have come out in the very year of Fellini's death, signaling that the end of the era personified by the quintessential auteur is also very much a new beginning.

looking back

1

National Identity by Means of Montage in Roberto Rossellini's *Paisan*

Nowhere in postwar Italian cinema are the twin tendencies to national reference and aesthetic self-consciousness brought into more perfect balance than in Roberto Rossellini's *Paisan* (1946).[1] While *Open City* (1945) served as an auspicious point of origin, with the reconquest of Rome by the boy activists heralding the postwar rebirth of the country, and with scattered hints throughout the film of an awareness that a new cinematic language was being forged, *Paisan* brings both tendencies to a higher level of development. At its most obvious, the juxtaposition of six short stories that cover the map from Sicily to the Po Valley enables Rossellini literally to encompass the entire nation in his film, rather than resort to a synecdochal relationship between Rome and Italy that blurs regional distinctions and perpetuates the historiographically suspect fiction of national unity.[2] As a heuristic device, the episode film allows Rossellini to explore various phases of the Liberation process, from the landing itself (Sicily), to the effects of an American military occupation (Naples, Rome), to partisan activities behind the lines—either awaiting the inexplicably delayed British advance (Florence) or in concert with the OSS having been cut off by Allied command (Po Valley).

The national referent of *Paisan,* however, is an extremely problematic one, as Peter Brunette has eloquently argued.[3] Though bound by the documentary film technique of a map with a narrative voice-over that provides the glue of historical continuity and geographical progression, this gimmick is so contrived and so external to the stories that it calls into question the very unity it allegedly proclaims.[4] The six discrete stories—each one a minifilm with its own distinct genre, visual style, and soundtrack—announce, instead, the irreconcilable regional differences that underwrite their respective narrative and audio-visual identities.[5] Thus, the episodic structure of *Paisan* is itself mimetic—signifying, in the uneasy relationship between the embedded stories and the historic framework, the problems inherent in the concept of Italian national unity imposed from above on a terrain fractured by regional differences.[6] In making a film that testifies to the difficulties of constructing Italian national identity as that identity takes shape in the aftermath of Fascism and war, Rossellini's work establishes the formative link between the neorealist cinema and the newly emergent collective consciousness of the country.

In addition to its geographic and temporal inclusiveness, *Paisan* supersedes *Open City* as a film of national reference in its specifically cinematic approach to the problem of unity-in-diversity.[7] In *Paisan*, Rossellini makes the medium-specific technique of montage the paradigm for a national unity predicated on difference. The film suggests that fragmentation and disjunction, when acknowledged and understood, paradoxically provide the energy to move forward in time and space, furnishing a dynamic model for a history of true liberation from a discredited past. Though montage is often equated with editing in general, for our purposes the term will be taken to mean an *obtrusive* process by which disparate elements are juxtaposed to form a composite whole. This practice stands in sharp contrast to Hollywood continuity editing, which "naturalizes" its operations through a code so familiar that viewers are unaware of the cuts and links between adjacent shots.[8] *Montage,* as I will be using it, emphasizes discontinuity, rupture, the discreteness of its constituent parts, and calls upon the viewer actively to collaborate in the making of meaning. "Montage, in its artistic and literary applications," claims Alexandra Wettlaufer, "relies on a deconstructive aesthetic, which produces a constructive experience in its audience . . . montage allows, even forces, the reader of the visual or verbal text to synthesize meaning from its disparate pieces. The assembly, which constitutes part of its very definition, can only take place when the work of art is experienced, for the integration of the sequentially juxtaposed parts may only take place in the mind of the perceiving audience."[9]

As a model for the construction of a national discourse, then, the Italy of *Paisan* is composed in the viewers' minds. The various fragments emerging from the six regional stories assemble themselves into a national whole only at the end of the film, and that whole becomes a creation of the audience, which actively integrates its disparate parts as the film reaches closure. Almost in defiance of the map and authoritative voice-over that had imposed a unity on the film so artificial and contrived as to lose all credibility, the cohesion achieved through montage emerges naturally from the accumulation of episodes according to Pudovkin's constructive principles.[10] It is a unity in which the audience collaborates through the act of interpretation, exemplifying the kind of democratic consent needed to produce a viable political order. But this is not to argue that Rossellini's national unity is consigned to the purely utopian realm of art, for to do so would be to deny the activist ambitions of the neorealists: their belief in the power of film to intervene in social reality, their commitment to the convergence of the cinematic signifier and its national referent. The image of Italian unity engendered in the minds of viewers of *Paisan* through the cinematic technique of montage can be seen as a performative one, both testifying to the possibility of such a unity and striving to instill in the audience the desire to bring about its realization.

The montage of short stories that make up *Paisan* enables Rossellini to exercise his predilection for peak moments of narration and to dispense with the demands of conventional dramatic structure. "The dramatic progression is limited to the minimum required for the understanding and intelligibility of the story," explains Gianni Rondolino. "Freer in improvising single scenes without having to come to terms with 'narrativity,' Rossellini was able to indulge his need to observe without preconceptions and to document with extraordinary intellectual and sentimental openness."[11] While the minimalism of Rossellini's narrative technique makes considerable intellectual demands on the viewers, who must fill in the gaps and infer principles of linkage, it simultaneously shortchanges them emotionally. This occurs because spectators are not allowed enough time for a climactic death or devastating epiphany to sink in before the map and authoritative voice-over of history return to propel them onward.[12] Such relentless pacing can be seen as itself mimetic, enacting history's inexorable progress, which neither speeds up nor slows down to accommodate the personal stories of its protagonists. Instead, that history catches and holds us in its current, like the swiftly moving waters of the Po as it pulls the partisan's body downstream in the final episode of *Paisan*.[13]

Because montage relies upon the heterogeneity of its constituent parts, it would behoove us to analyze in some detail what is distinctive about each episode—in narrative, visual, and auditory terms—as well as what contrasts are established between the six embedded stories and the documentary framework surrounding them.[14] From the very outset of *Paisan*, the discrepancy between macrohistory and microhistory, between the annals of the Allied advance and the intimate stories of individuals caught in its wake, is an ironic one.[15] The film begins with documentary footage of exploding bombs, fleets of ships, and a spectacular landing on the beachhead of Licata, accompanied by the voice-over announcement that "on the night of July 10, 1943, the Allied fleet opened fire against the southern coast of Sicily. Twelve hours later, the first great Allied landing on the European continent had begun" (165).

With this opening, *Paisan* appropriates the heroic tone of a monumental history that has already run its course, that knows that victory awaits the Allied forces and that reads such certainty back into the initial moments of the campaign. This celebratory framework, however, encloses a series of stories that call into question the givens of monumental history, for these fictions are set in a narrative present that cannot benefit from the confidence born of triumphant historical retrospection. Thus, from the macrolevel of armies and navies storming the beachhead of Licata, of epic certainties on a sweeping scale, the film descends to the microlevel of a knot of soldiers, plagued by fear and ineptitude, straggling up a path into a town, where they are mistaken for Germans by the local Fascist leader, Luca.[16] The effusive welcome that we would expect the townspeople to accord their "liberators" after the celebratory tone of the newsreel preface to the film is not forthcoming, and the Sicilians greet the new military incursion with anxiety: a woman fears for the safety of her son, stationed at Licata, and Carmela is preoccupied about the fate of her father and brother who have disappeared. The interminable wake for a dead woman being held in the church where the townspeople seek refuge can be generalized to describe the psychological and political condition of this entire community as it lives out this brief and bewildering interregnum in the shadow of death.

The title *Paisan,* meaning *countryman* in the narrowest geographic sense, in which *country* is understood to mean village or district, receives its first, and most cynical definition, in this scene, as Tony Mascali's ancestral ties to the nearby town of Gela are cast into doubt. "There aren't any Mascali's in Gela" Luca announces. "He's not from Gela. They come here and tell a pack of lies, and they want you to believe them" (172). It is, of course, in the Fascist leader's interests to deny that members of the Allied forces could have any personal link to the land they are "invading." In so doing, he calls into question the U.S. strategy of assigning Italian Americans to the Fifth Army, as if their mere presence would bridge the cultural abyss between the troops and the indigenous population. Paradoxically, the one GI to achieve a breakthrough in communication is not Tony but the decidedly monolingual, monocultural Joe from Jersey, whose irreducible Americanness is announced by the fact that his geographic provenance has come to replace his last name. In the initial episode of the film, then, the designation *Paisan* reveals its semantic instability, its openness to ideological, even military, appropriation, and its susceptibility to ever-changing meanings that will accommodate the shifting nature of Italian American relations as the Allies make their way north.

It is Joe from Jersey who sets the terms for that evolution in the "vocabulary list" he recites to Carmela when they are left alone after the other GIs leave to patrol for mines. "Look, *paisan, spaghetti, bambina, mangiare, Mussolini, tout de suite, c'est la guerre*—that's it. Oh yes, and Carmela! Now how about you? Is your English any better than my Italian?" (186-87). This pastiche of terms, of course, is what Joe would have learned on the streets of Jersey City, and would have associated, vaguely, with things European. By putting *paisan* first on the list, he both privileges it and reduces it to the level of those stereotypic terms associated with Italian immigrant culture in the United States. As a form of greeting used by natives of the same Italian town when they encounter each other abroad, the salutation is a way of forging a bond of familiarity and comfort in the midst of an alien culture. One of the many ironies of Rossellini's title is the way in which the term reverses geographic direction, returning to Italy with Italian Americans who now try to reconnect with their culture of origin. But to do so the Italian Americans must overcome their own degree of assimilation into, and identification with, the New World.

By invoking such cultural clichés, Joe from Jersey brings into play all of the assumptions on which stereotypic thinking is based—assumptions of otherness, of antithesis, of rigid categorization. In fact, Joe's pedagogy is based primarily on antitheses—boy/girl, blond/dark, fantasy/reality, here/there. But the didactic tone soon gives way to reverie, as Joe turns inward and yields to his nostalgia, "You know, I can almost imagine I'm home. It's quiet at night like this where I come from" (187). Joe's words are, at first, incomprehensible to Carmela until he resorts to a pantomime of milking cows to explain that he works for the dairy industry. It is at this point that Carmela begins to speak with great animation, pouring out her own childhood memories about riding a cow with her cousins at her uncle's farm. And despite all the barriers of language and culture, of childhoods led on separate sides of the world, Carmela and Joe communicate a shared nostalgia, a longing for a pastoral past—be it in rural New Jersey or rural Sicily—that allows them to break through their separateness (fig. 1). This is an intensely delicate interlude in which defenses have been set aside and enough trust established that these private spaces of idyllic memory can be explored together.

The couple's moment of psychological intimacy is not devoid of romance. When Carmela experiences a twinge of jealousy at seeing a photograph of Joe's sister, whom she mistakes for his wife, the man feels compelled to illuminate his face with a cigarette lighter to show a sibling resemblance. The flicker of light is all it takes to attract German gunfire, and Joe is killed for his momentary surrender to the normal dynamics of courtship. In a wartime context, Rossellini is telling us, the boy-meets-girl scenario can have fatal consequences—the natural impulses of burgeoning desire are a luxury that World War II combatants can ill afford.[17] The very light used to dispel Carmela's jealousy and advance the couple's relationship is the light that makes Joe a fixed target for Nazi gunfire—the light that snuffs out his life. But Carmela has not forgotten Joe's vocabulary lesson and the power of naming to establish a bond. When she finds that the wounded soldier has died, her response is simply to utter his name, to reconfirm the connection that had raised Joe above the level of sameness to which she consigns Americans, Germans, Fascists, "all you people with guns! You're all [alike]!" (184-85).[18] In naming him, in proclaiming his identity in the

FIGURE 1 | Joe from Jersey (Robert Van Loon) and Carmela (Carmela Sazio) share a breakthrough moment of communication during an impromptu language lesson in the Sicilian episode of *Paisan*. Courtesy of the Museum of Modern Art/Film Stills Archive.

context of wrongful death, Carmela must act according to her own personal code of honor[19] and avenge this man who had succeeded in becoming a human being to her, and in so doing had confirmed her own humanity. With the Americans' misunderstanding of Carmela's sacrifice for Joe, she is literally unnamed, condemned as the "dirty little Eyetie" who has reverted to type.

But Rossellini does not surrender to the futility of these sacrifices, as Robert Warshow has suggested.[20] The American GIs might "unname" Carmela, and her heroic gesture may be consigned to oblivion within the narrative of the episode, but Rossellini's film gives her back her name and bears witness to her act. And the delicate breakthrough moment of communication—a moment that neither of them will long survive—offers the first hint of the cumulative power that Rossellini's title will achieve by the end of the film.

This moving, memorialist conclusion to the Sicilian episode could hardly have been predicted from its parodic opening. "Hey, Junior, remember Frankenstein?" quips the sergeant as he sizes up the ancient watchtower where the action will unfold. "This reminds me of the old mill there!" "It does, now that you mention it," concurs Junior. "What a place for a murder!" (177). Indeed, the nocturnal time frame, the dark murky atmosphere of the tower, the sense of pervasive danger lurking under trapdoors ("Hey! Any witches or stiffs down here?" [181] Joe prophetically jokes), the paucity of characters, the long lulls in action that allow for a slow build-up of tensions, all conspire to make the sergeant's allusion to genre films seem less parodic than prescriptive.[21] And indeed, the prophecy of murder finds threefold fulfillment in the deaths of an American, a German, and an Italian, though the agency is hardly supernatural.

In keeping with the contrastive principles of montage, the second episode constitutes a radical change in tone, visual style, and narrative genre from its predecessor. Set in broad daylight in a teeming area of downtown Naples, this story has a cluttered, carnivalesque quality that allies it with the commedia dell'arte tradition of stock characters, slapstick antics, and brash theatricality. In the opening shots of the episode, Rossellini's camera presents Naples as a fairground or circus, featuring a series of tent-like booths, a fire-eating display, an acrobatic demonstration, and a game of leapfrog before introducing us to the two main characters: the African American MP Joe and the *scugnizzo* (street urchin) Pasquale. There is nothing to set these two apart from their context. They are simply one more amusing sideshow to observe, one more example of the inversion of hierarchies and the defiance of social order that Bakhtin ascribes to the carnival world. Naples becomes a hyperbolic theater for the staging of spectacle, an extension of the puppet show that Joe and Pasquale visit to escape detection by the man the scugnizzo has just cheated. Unable to distinguish between reality and fantasy, the drunken Joe storms the stage to intervene on the side of the Moors, who are being defeated by the forces of Charlemagne.[22] "To arms, to arms, Christians," shouts the puppeteer, "to war against the black Saracen" (208), adds the second. "God summons us," continues the first. "We seek not riches and gold. Justice and civilization. Death to the Moors," adds a third. The elevated rhetoric of holy war involving high-minded ideals of justice, faith, and manifest destiny sets up a Manichaean opposition between the forces of light and darkness that will be subverted by successive levels of representation throughout this episode (see table 1).

In addition to light/dark imagery, body size serves as an important signifier throughout this episode. Not only is Joe too big for the puppet stage, he is too big for Naples, towering over the native populace in his drunkenness like a perpetually leaning tower. The soldier is out of proportion with the surrounding space, just as the American values of heroism that he embodies are inappropriate, indeed obstructionist, in a world where survival is the only "good." But as his drunken euphoria wears off, Joe realizes how small he really is in the American scheme of things, and like Joe from Jersey he reaches deep into himself to convey an inner world that touches his Italian companion and establishes them as *paesani*. The scugnizzo cannot possibly understand the words of "Nobody Knows the Troubles I've Seen," but the lament and the longing for redemption have obviously reached the boy and moved him to the ultimate act of friendship that his circumstances will allow—to warn Joe of the impending theft of his boots.

If the Naples sequence plays off the conventions of commedia dell'arte—with the broad physicality of the actions (like so many *lazzi,* or gags), the incongruity between the huge black body in military regalia and the tiny white one in "borrowed" garb, and the concentric circles of stages—then the ending marks an abrupt change of genre. All the clowning, the superficiality, and the stock characterization of the previous action comes to a sudden halt as Joe surveys the squalid interior of the cave that houses Pasquale and so many other persons displaced by the bombing of Naples (fig. 2). Suddenly and belatedly, Joe shares the realization that Pasquale had gained, if only in an inchoate and subconscious way, from the drunken man's performance of the negro spiritual. Joe at last understands that for Pasquale, as for himself, "home" is a sentimental fiction that circumstances (in the child's case, the devastations of war; in his own case, racially induced poverty) have rendered inoperative.[23] Whereas Carmela and Joe from Jersey had been bound by a nostalgia for the idea of home as a privileged space of childhood, innocence, and pastoral withdrawal, Joe and Pasquale are united by the absence of such a space, both as a physical entity and as a mechanism of psychological grounding. Though racial, cultural, and experiential worlds apart, Joe and Pasquale are *paesani* in the displaced persons' camp

TABLE 1

Levels of Representation in the Puppet Show Scene

Holy War on the Puppet Stage

BLACK	WHITE
Saracens	Christians
bad	good
infidels	believers
losers	winners

World War II in Europe

BLACK	WHITE
American MPs	Nazis
good	bad
liberators	oppressors
winners	losers

The Survival War of Liberated Naples

BLACK	WHITE
American MPs	native populace
bad	good
oppressors	oppressed
winners	losers

Class War in America

BLACK	WHITE
underclass	elite
good	bad
oppressed	oppressors
losers	winners

FIGURE 2 | American MP Joe (Dots Johnson) escorts the thieving Pasquale (Alfonsino Pasca) to his "home" in a cave outside Naples and realizes how much his own marginalized social position resembles that of the orphaned street kid. Courtesy of the Museum of Modern Art/Film Stills Archive.

of the permanently marginalized, of those who, by virtue of ethnicity and class, must remain in the caves and shacks that surround the centers of true social belonging.

Because the Florentine sequence of *Paisan* has attracted relatively little scholarly scrutiny and because, elsewhere, I have devoted considerable critical attention to the film's Roman episode,[24] I dwell on Florence at some length in these pages. Implicit in any photographic treatment of that city is a conventional visual regime epitomized in the celebrated Merchant-Ivory adaptation of E. M. Forster's *Room with a View* (1985), which, for convenience, I establish here as the polar opposite of Rossellini's gaze in *Paisan*. The kind of visual connoisseurship experienced from a room with a view implies mastery, separation, subject/object relations that are fixed and hierarchical, a perspective that is frontal, unobstructed, fully possessed of the visual field. The room with a view turns Florence into a museum—a series of static images of monuments and works of art, outside time, removed from the space of historical contingency, to be consumed by the tourist whose illusion of omniscience and control remains unchallenged.

Rossellini inscribes this tourist gaze in the Florentine episode of *Paisan* as two British officers contemplate the architectural beauties of the historic urban center from the safety of Boboli gardens in the already liberated south of the city. "The baptistry's the one near the church. It was built at a later date," observes one of the soldiers. "I once saw a picture of the doors of the baptistry—rather like those of Salisbury Cathedral" (266), quips the second. Though in and of itself this exchange is innocuous, arising naturally out of the confrontation between educated foreigners and the splendors of monumental Florence, the wartime context renders these comments frivolous to the point of inanity. But the bitter humor of this exchange does not hide its dire implications—the British officers' sight-seeing takes the place of the kind of military reconnaissance that could save the city, just as the Allied failure to advance has left the partisans to confront the Nazi-Fascist threat on their own.[25] For Rossellini, this tourist gaze—sedentary, distant, and safe—translates into visual terms a precise moral condition—a cowardly and reprehensible nonengagement in the world.

Binoculars play an important role in defining the British officers' spectatorship, providing the long-distance vision that keeps them far from the embattled downtown, while allowing them to enjoy its architectural treasures. By contrast, the urgency of Massimo's attempt to cross the Arno and join his family only heightens our impatience with the soldiers' inertia. When Massimo asks to borrow the binoculars, it is because he wants to glean a very different kind of information from them—not art-historical but military data about the battle that threatens the very existence of the monuments the sight-seers so admire. Appropriately, neither Massimo's dialogue nor Rossellini's camera complies with the British officers' point of view. When asked to identify a certain bell tower, Massimo does not deign to oblige them, although it is clear that he knows the answer. Appropriately, Rossellini's camera refuses to give us the obvious view through the binoculars (we could expect a double-iris shot focusing on the Badia tower, for example), so as not to align our gaze with that of the two observers whose detachment threatens the very survival of Florence.[26] In this gaze of non-intervention, Rossellini sets up a foil for his ethics of commitment, suggesting how cinema itself, as a medium of vision, can serve both as a way of knowing, and, more importantly, a way of morally engaging in the world.

Later, there will be another character who uses binoculars to reverse the passive spectatorship of the British. This is a retired major from World War I (the "real war") whose binocular-enhanced gaze, along with his auditory knowledge of artillery fire, enables him to pinpoint the location of German troops and pass on the intelligence to partisan command.[27] Unlike the self-protective British officers who observe from the safety of the south bank, the major is perched high on a rooftop terrace in the downtown area, arousing the understandable fears of his wife. He grudgingly agrees to wear his helmet (to protect himself from sunstroke, he explains). Coming out of retirement to support the partisan cause, risking exposure to the very artillery whose sound and location he so expertly identifies, this major, in his use of binoculars, sets a standard of "committed spectatorship" diametrically opposed to that of the British voyeurs.

What makes the Florentine episode so cinematically powerful, establishing it as the most revolutionary of the episodes in *Paisan* with respect to visual style (pace André Bazin, who makes this claim for the Po Valley sequence)[28] is Rossellini's systematic subversion of the touristic, consumerist, idealizing, and dehistoricizing gaze to which this city is so often subjected. Though we do see some of Florence's most glorious "trademark" monuments—the Duomo, Piazza della Signoria, Palazzo Pitti, Ponte Vecchio—the camera captured them only fleetingly, in passing, as if they were merely incidental to the Liberation drama un-

FIGURE 3 | Massimo (Renzo Avanzo) and Harriet (Harriet White) have no time to savor the view from the upper story of the Uffizi; they have just crossed the Arno through the Vasari corridor, a passageway unknown to Nazi occupying troops. Courtesy of the Museum of Modern Art/Film Stills Archive.

folding in its streets. In tracking Harriet and Massimo through the Vasari corridor and the Uffizi, Rossellini showed items of statuary crated up, barely visible, just as the embattled city itself had been trussed up and ballasted to withstand the onslaughts of war. Racing through this cityscape, the protagonists constantly deflected interest from the monuments to the treachery of their passage among them. "Look, that's the way we came" (272), Massimo told Harriet as he pointed out the Ponte Vecchio from the windows of the Uffizi in a shot that entirely subordinated the picturesqueness of the view to the anxiety of the moment and the urgent need to pass on (fig. 3). In filming the tower of the Palazzo Vecchio, a sign that the protagonists had successfully completed their crossing of the Arno, the camera refused to luxuriate in this emblem of Florentine sovereignty. Instead, Rossellini immediately panned down to the street, which the Germans ominously patrolled, as the inevitable huge motorcycle careened to a halt in the midst of the Uffizi esplanade. When Massimo called Harriet's attention to the spectacle, it was not the Palazzo Vecchio that he pointed out, but the military threat from below. "Look, the Germans" (273). Using a visual withholding strategy that negated the touristic view, Rossellini's camera filmed only a fragment of the Duomo, flanked by the baptistry, on one side, and Giotto's bell tower, on the other, showing us at close range what the British officers had examined through the safety of their binoculars. But Rossellini's lens was far more focused on the German motorcycle and patrol maneuvers than on their monumental surroundings. As Harriet and Massimo ascended the rooftop where the major was observing artillery operations, we were given an overhead shot like the views offered to tourists through the narrow slits that perforate the walls of Giotto's bell tower. But there could be no lingering on the city as it miraculously unfolded below us.

This highly mobilized camera, whose speed of movement is synchronized both to his protagonists' hurried flight and to the urgent rhythms of the musical score, turns Florence into a dynamic, unfamiliar, and uncomfortable space. It would be no exaggeration to claim that Rossellini's visual strategy *alone* tells us all we need to know about the Florentine Liberation campaign: this city-museum has become a battlefield. "Nowhere else in *Paisan* does Rossellini's camera capture so perfectly the sense of a historic event," claims Bondanella. "The three earlier episodes clearly juxtaposed the main story line of their episodes to the newsreel clips preceding them, but here with his highly mobile camera, the grainy film he uses, everything seems to be filmed as if it were actually unfolding before us as historical and film time merge together."[29]

This historic corridor, providing not only spatial passage between two halves of a divided city but temporal passage back to a Renaissance past fraught with political and artistic significance, stands, by synecdoche, for Florence itself in this episode of *Paisan*. No longer a static space of aesthetic contemplation where a European elite can enhance its cultural credentials, Florence has become a passageway, a space to be traversed, both for pressing personal reasons (Massimo must reach his family; Harriet must join Il Lupo) and for strategic, military ones. The term *passare* is used constantly throughout the episode—in fact, the entire episode can be read as a series of *passaggi:* there is the slow, funereal *passaggio* of the Red Cross procession transporting a corpse; the dragging of the newly caught Fascist snipers to execution;[30] and even the *passaggio* of the demijohn of water from one street corner to another in the first shot ever directed by Fellini. But most important is the *passaggio* of Harriet across the city—an excursion that implies the metaphoric journey from ignorance to tragic knowledge.[31] This cognitive *passaggio* takes place in incremental steps as she learns (1) that Guido is the legendary partisan leader Il Lupo; (2) that he has been wounded; and (3) in a sequence full of tragic incident (Massimo makes it home, the snipers are summarily executed, a partisan is fatally wounded and dies in Harriet's arms), that Guido is dead.

It is important that Guido remain unrepresented in the film—that he hover in the phantomatic background of the plot, unrealized and forever unattained. This means that we know him only from a mythic distance, in the same way that the Florentines experience their "legendary leader," whose clandestine operations both keep him out of sight and elevate him to the level of hero and savior. By consigning Guido to the shadows, Rossellini maintains his character's generic quality—the cultured man who sheds his aura of privilege to join in the struggle, like Manfredi in *Open City,* whose three names made the question of a singular identity problematic and ultimately irrelevant.

Though the Florentine episode has the structure of a quest, there is the hint of an alternative plot of considerable interest to our argument—a suppressed *Room with a View* scenario lurks in the narrative prehistory of Harriet. In her exchange with a wounded partisan early in the episode, we learn that Harriet is not new to Florence—she had spent several years there and had made many friends, among them the well-known painter Guido Lombardi. Judging by the intensity of her desire to rejoin him, we infer that their bond was more than one of discipleship or mere acquaintance. From this minimal exposition, we can construct a fairly conventional story line—Harriet was either studying abroad or traveling on her own European Grand Tour, fell in love with Florence, Florentine art, and one Florentine painter in particular who personified it all. We can imagine the potent blend of amorous and cultural awakening that Harriet experienced in her room with a view as she lived out the timeless tourist romance against the fixed and perfect backdrop of the Lungarno.

But in Rossellini's film, that fixed and perfect backdrop becomes a mobilized and militarized foreground. The room in which lovers tarry, drinking in the beauty of the panorama outside the window, becomes a corridor through which a man and a woman race in frantic flight from the forces of history. For them, the monuments are mere distractions, if not outright threats, whose hulking masses could hide German patrols waiting to apprehend them, or whose roofs could harbor Fascist sharpshooters, all too happy to empty their cartridges on random passers-by.

The conversion of Florence from museum to battlefield is the master trope from which a number of other conversions follow.[32] In terms of narrative genre, tourist romance gives way to militarized quest, necessitating important transformations in their respective casts of characters. Harriet, the American traveler enamored of Florentine culture and of one particularly cultured Florentine, becomes a Red Cross nurse committed to the cause of liberation. Guido Lombardi gives up the paintbrush for the rifle to become the partisan leader Lupo, whose name reveals the need to relinquish high culture and descend to the jungle operations of guerrilla war. Guido's paintbrush-turned-rifle is analogous to Rossellini's camera, which records the city's architectural treasures only to convert them into something else—the mise-en-scène for committed action. By choosing a city that offers itself up as the quintessential object of aesthetic contemplation and transforming the static gaze of the connoisseur into the mobilized witness of the participant, Rossellini makes vision a powerful metaphor for the moral engagement that defines the cinema of neorealism.

The insertion of the episode scripted by Fellini of the monastery of Savignano di Romagna—serene, reflective, and at times mildly humorous—in between the frantic race through Florence and the desolate drama played out on the waters and the banks of the Po serves the contrastive principles of montage. If the surrounding two episodes set themselves squarely in the midst of battle, the monastery offers a welcome respite from it, a quiet parenthesis in the ongoing syntax of war. The monastery's exemption from history, its position outside time, is in fact the explicit subject of Chaplain Martin's first comment upon entering its confines. "You know, I can't help thinking that by the time this monastery was built, why, America hadn't even been discovered yet . . . an immense wilderness! These walls, these olive trees, that church bell were already here. This time, this time of the evening five hundred years ago—everything had the same soft color" (292). Martin's statement testifies not only to the vintage of this structure but also to its stasis. No matter what upheavals take place in the valley of historical change, in this hilltop retreat evening will register its same soft colors, day after day, as time follows the sun's diurnal rhythms and natural cycles, not man's violent pursuit of an elusive progress.

This peeling away of the layers of time prepares us for the generic basis of the narration—a basis that goes far, I think, toward explaining the interpretive problems that this episode, more than any other in *Paisan,* has insistently raised. The miracles mentioned throughout the dialogue,[33] the monastic setting, the occurrence of a number of deus ex machina events (the sudden arrival of a peasant couple with an offering of livestock; the American GIs' cornucopia of canned goods), and the visual clues all hint strongly at the hagiographic basis of this narration. Early on in the episode, the dialogue hints at the nature of the miracle to come. When the Protestant and Jewish chaplains fail to make the sign of the cross, Martin jokes, "Those two are very bad. He's Protestant, and he's a Jew" (306). While Martin's moralizing is facetious, his Italian hosts take him seriously. For them, the non-Catholics are indeed "very bad," and the rest of the episode is dedicated to the monks' efforts to convert the plot into that of a miracle tale. The fact that the episode takes place entirely within the walls of the monastery (fig. 4) and never enacts the kind of religious immersion in secular life that Don Pietro embodied in *Open City,* suggests that the narrative remains within the generic confines of the miracle tale, even as it parodies that genre. Thus, Martin's own moment of breakthrough consciousness, his instance of true communion with the monks, may represent the fulfillment of the *paisan* theme in this episode, but it shows that the miracle has misfired. Martin may indeed be profoundly moved by the monks' sacrifice, but he will not go on to proselytize to his fellow chaplains, who remain, due to the language barrier, oblivious to the Italians' reasons for fasting. But this parody of the miracle tale is not meant to disparage its traditional source material; on the contrary, like all parodies, this one is double-voiced, at once celebrating the older art form and acknowledging its obsolescence in a contemporary culture that can no longer accommodate it.[34] Through parody, this episode can have it

FIGURE 4 | The three army chaplains (Elmer Feldman, William Tubbs, and Nowell Jones) are welcomed into the monastery dining hall in the fifth episode of *Paisan*. Courtesy of the Museum of Modern Art/Film Stills Archive.

both ways, indulging in nostalgia for a time of "humility, simplicity, and pure faith" (316) while admitting that, in today's world, such orthodoxies have no place.

The quiet and serene fifth episode provides both a stylistic relief from the clutter and noise of the rest of *Paisan* and a narrative content that reflects on that stylistic choice of temporary withdrawal from the wartime context. "I think one can really be in peace with his Lord without removing himself from the world. After all, it was created for us. The world is our parish" (305), Chaplain Jones had remarked early in the episode, echoing the partisan leader's argument in *Open City* when Don Pietro offered to give refuge to Manfredi in a monastery: "I know, Father, but there are only a few of us, and if everybody goes into monasteries . . ." (38). It is precisely this withdrawal that Martin celebrates in his closing speech: "I've found here that peace of mind I'd lost in the horrors and the trials of war, a beautiful, moving lesson of humility, simplicity, and pure faith" (315–16). On the level of ideology, these two pronouncements are entirely irreconcilable, and each is presented in a way that makes powerful claims on our sympathies—Jones's commentary is in keeping with Rossellini's career-long crusade for moral engagement, for a Christian humanist commitment to right action in the world. At the same time, Martin's speech is privileged by its climactic position and by all the cinematic apparatus that surrounds it: a mise-en-scène redolent of Leonardo's *Last Supper*,[35] a musical commentary designed to maximize the emotional impact of the words, and the generic mechanism of the miracle tale itself. All this leads us to expect that the speech will become a *speech act,* performing the very miracle so devoutly desired by the monastic community.

The considerable interpretive discomfort caused by the coexistence of two such contradictory positions has given rise to various solutions, the most obvious of which is to read the final speech as irony.[36] But I tend to agree with Peter Brunette, who argues for the undecidability of the interpretation, proposing that "a better reading might be to admit that the irreconcilable interpretations cannot, in fact, be reconciled, despite the uncomfortable lack of closure that results."[37] Montage, which has governed the interrelations between episodes in geographic, narrative, and stylistic terms, now seems to be operative even within a given episode on the level of ideology. Open-endedness, heterogeneity, and disjunction all conspire to destabilize this episode, whose generic associations with the miracle tale, and whose seeming distinction from the other episodes of *Paisan,* had promised to make it the least problematic of them all.

The sojourn at the monastery, despite its interpretive difficulties, provides a surface calm that is shattered by the opening image of the film's Po Valley episode. "Every film I make interests me for a particular scene, perhaps for a finale I already have in mind. . . . And when I made *Paisan,* I had in mind the last part with the corpses floating on water slowly being carried down the River Po with labels bearing the word 'Partisan' on them. The river had those corpses in it for months. Often several would be found on the same day."[38] With this statement, the filmmaker invites us to read all of *Paisan* as a reaction to this spectacle, as Rossellini's attempt to purge himself of its hold on his imagination. All of *Paisan* could be seen as an attempt to retrieve that corpse from the relentless current of the Po, to counteract the body's powerlessness by intervening, as Dale and Cigolani do, at great personal risk to them-

FIGURE 5 | The term *partigiano* receives its final and most solemn meaning in this hasty rite of burial toward the end of *Paisan*. Courtesy of the Museum of Modern Art/Film Stills Archive.

selves and to their cause. The entire film could be seen as the attempt to reverse the Nazi-Fascist use of that body as spectacle, as an exemplary punishment to deter any bystanders from the acts of resistance that led to such public abuse of a corpse.

What Dale and Cigolani do (and, by extension, what all of *Paisan* does) is radically to subvert the relationship established by the Nazi Fascists between the placard reading *Partigiano,* and the image of the dead body floating below it. For the enemy forces, *Partigiano* is a caption—a condensation into one word of a narrative of exemplary punishment and of implicit threat. In this caption, *Partigiano* signifies bandit, transgressor, outlaw—one who defies the rules of Nazi-Fascist authority and has therefore abdicated any claim to human dignity or respect. By intervening, by seizing the body from the relentless current of the Po and giving it decent burial, Dale and Cigolani commit an act of *pietas* that confers dignity on the dead and that, in anthropological terms, stands as one of the defining marks of human civilization (fig. 5). Though they cannot give the body a name, they can give it an identity—one that involves a subversive resignification of the Nazi-Fascist caption. Planting the placard at the head of the hastily dug grave, the OSS men and partisans radically realign the relationship between the sign and the body, turning the term of opprobrium into encomium, converting an exemplary punishment into a consecration.

In burying and labeling this victim as they do, Dale and Cigolani have created an epitaph, literally a writing on a tomb, that looks both backward and forward, retroactively endowing earlier episodes of *Paisan* with a memorialist function and anticipating the film's tragic ending. Though none of the characters within the narrative of the Sicilian episode knew of Carmela's sacrifice, we do, and the film gives her the burial and the epitaph that history had denied her. The unnamed partisan who dies in Harriet's arms may not have achieved the legendary stature of Il Lupo, but his death is represented on screen, whereas the hero's is not. The episode writes this unnamed man's epitaph, as it does for all those unsung fighters whose deaths make them equal (*uguali,* to use the term from the Italian dialogue) to their legendary leader.[39] For the terrified partisan ("no one will know how I died" [347]),[40] awaiting death by drowning with his comrades as the body of Cigolani hangs from a gibbet above them, *Paisan* provides burial and epitaph. And finally for Dale, who rushes forward to protest the execution of the partisans and is shot when he could have sought refuge in the international law that protects prisoners of war, *Paisan* offers a memorial.

Critics who read the juxtaposition of these deaths with the voice-over announcement that "this happened in the winter of 1944. At the beginning of spring, the war was over" (348) as bitterly defeatist,[41] fail to acknowledge the literary context in which Rossellini's film is situated. As epitaph, as a writing on a tomb, *Paisan* takes its place in a memorialist tradition crowned by Ugo Foscolo's *Dei sepolchri*. In Foscolo's verses, cemeteries are read as signifiers of a heroic engagement with life, forging continuity with a humanist past and inspiring a future of *impegno civile* (civic commitment), much like the link that the neorealists sought to establish between the ideals of the Resistance and the postwar rebirth of a nation.

The commemorative impulse underlying *Paisan,* the desire to write epitaphs that testify to the lives and acts on which the new postwar national identity can be built, finds its most powerful, emblematic expression in Dale's and Cigolani's burial of the executed partigiano. Their strategy of reappropriation, of converting the caption from one of punitive admonition to eulogy, contains, in germinal form, the film's evolving relationship to its own title. When Joe first mentioned *paisan* in his vocabulary list, the term harked back to what he must have heard in Jersey City, where Italian immigrants would have been subject to the most reductive and degrading of ethnic stereotypes. He brings this preconception to his encounter with Carmela in the "haunted tower" of the Sicilian coast, but for a miraculous moment the cultural divide is overcome, only to be reopened by the misunderstood sacrifice of "that dirty little Eyetie" (201). In another miraculous instance of connectedness, an African American military policeman drunkenly reveals the troubles he's seen to a Neapolitan street urchin whom the soldier condescendingly calls *paisan,* little realizing how accurately the term describes their shared status as social outcasts. To become a paisan of the city of Florence in Rossellini's film, Harriet had to undergo a conversion similar to that reflected in the urban space itself, once static and tourist-oriented, now a mobilized, militarized passageway for history's march to liberation.

Two episodes, those of Rome and Savignano di Romagna, present incomplete or asymmetrical relationships between potential paesani. The romantic connection between Francesca and Fred, established on the day of Rome's liberation, is renewed only partially when the GI fails to recognize the girl who now, six months later, has resorted to prostitution. In the monastery sequence, only a one-way understanding is forged when Chaplain Martin accepts the monks' sacrifice—itself based on a bias that remains in place.

The highest realization of the paisan theme is achieved in the final sequence, where distinctions break down entirely, and Dale consciously chooses to share the tragic destiny of his Italian comrades rather than avail himself of the protections due to legitimate prisoners of war. From the "half contemptuous slang for Italians,"[42] testifying to the kind of cultural barriers to which thinking in stereotypes always leads, *paisan* has come to mean the highest bond of human solidarity—a bond transcending differences of language, culture, race, and nationality in a common commitment to liberation.

The original subject for *Paisan* stipulated an ending in the Val d'Aosta, whose mountain setting near the northern border would have symbolized the apotheosis of the partisan cause as well as providing geographic closure to the film.[43] Rossellini's decision to conclude instead with the Po Valley sequence has both medium-specific and autobiographical logic. Since this was where he sojourned as a child, the area around Porto Tolle was a familiar and evocative space.[44] But the signifying possibilities of the river are many, including its association with historical progress and with the cinema itself as a technology that makes *kine,* or movement, its very medium of expression. Dale and Cigolani's retrieval of the corpse from the fast-moving current of the Po, their attempt to bring the body to rest and remove it from the relentless flow of Nazi-Fascist signification, enacts the new relationship that Rossellini hoped to establish between cinema and national history. The image of a floating corpse, buoyed by a life preserver whose function is ghoulishly perverted to keep the dead body in public view, is a spectacle staged for a precise rhetorical purpose—to coerce the audience into a highly prejudicial reading of its caption. Rossellini undoes this spectacle by rewriting the meaning of the caption, making it an epitaph in the noblest commemorative tradition of Italian letters. In this disruption of Nazi spectacle and its reappropriation for the cause of the Resistance, *Paisan* suggests the way in which cinema can intervene to redirect the flow of postwar of Italian history.[45]

If Rossellini uses the Po as the master trope that retroactively organizes *Paisan* into a moving image of Liberation history, this is not to deny the difference of the landscape through which the river flows, nor to proclaim the inevitability of the course it runs. Like montage, which juxtaposes disparate elements to form a composite whole, the forward movement of *Paisan* is predicated on difference, discontinuity, and rupture, forcing the viewer to acknowledge the gaps and the conflicts involved in the forging of national identity. And just as Dale and Cigolani can intervene in the river's flow to change its signifying power, so, too, can the filmmaker, through a conscious and strategic arrangement of the elements of montage, create a representation of postwar Italian history that acknowledges its difficulties and disjunctions, but that nonetheless invests viewers with the power to affect its course.

2

Luchino Visconti's *Bellissima*

THE DIVA, THE MIRROR, AND THE SCREEN

A combination of historical circumstance and cultural preparedness enabled the first neorealists to make films conceived as foundational acts, as concrete interventions in the forging of a new national identity after the devastations of Fascism and war. In so doing, these filmmakers were able to achieve an admirable balance of referential and aesthetic concerns, in which the impulse to document the newly evolving postwar order developed in tandem with a self-conscious quest for a cinematic vehicle adequate to its representation. Once the revolutionary promise of the Resistance had met with the disappointments of the 1948 electoral rout and the conservative retrenchment of the 1950s, however, neorealism's political/aesthetic unity would be shattered. Thus, when Luchino Visconti abandoned the neorealist epic vision of *La terra trema* (1948) for the intimist portrait of a starstruck Roman matron in *Bellissima* (1951), the break between the cinema of national reference and that of aesthetic self-consciousness seemed complete. For Lino Miccichè, in fact, *Bellissima* signals "the end of the 'poetics' of neorealism . . . the sunset of a cinematographic utopia that saw film, for several seasons, as one of the epicenters of the social and political struggle between old and new . . . [the demise] of the illusion that cinema was something distinct from the realm of illusion."[1]

And yet, despite Visconti's withdrawal from the epic arena of neorealism, with its engagement in the world-historical issues of war, liberation, unemployment, and class struggle, I would argue that *Bellissima* does not mark a renunciation of neorealist social commitment so much as a redirection of it.[2] Though the neorealist unity of political and aesthetic concerns is severed in *Bellissima* at the expense of the former, Vis-

| 39

conti's commentary on the consciousness-raising power of the medium has important implications for the cinema of national reference. In his critique of mainstream production and his plea for a cinema that transcends its basis in illusionism and escape, Visconti seeks to purge the industry of its regressive tendencies and prepare the way for a return to a medium of true national-popular renewal.

Though not enthralled by Zavattini's original subject for *Bellissima*,[3] Visconti warmed to the idea when he learned that Anna Magnani had been cast as the lead, for she would allow him to build a self-conscious reflection on the workings of *divismo* (stardom) and the power of spectacle into the very structure of his film.

> After I had to give up on filming *Cronache di poveri amanti* and *La Carrozza del Santissimo Sacramento,* Salvo D'Angelo proposed that I do a subject by Zavattini. I had wanted to make a film with Magnani for a long time, and since she was in fact to play the lead in *Bellissima,* I accepted. I was interested in working with an authentic "character," with whom many more interior and meaningful things could be expressed. And I was also interested in knowing what relationship would be born between myself as director and the "diva" Magnani. The result was very felicitous.[4]

Though the personal results were not very felicitous for Magnani, who fell madly in love with Visconti, producing tension, storminess, and quarreling behind the scenes, the professional results were indeed fortunate. The working partnership of Visconti and Magnani yielded a running commentary, at one remove from the literal level of the narrative, on the relationship between diva and auteur—a commentary that I will label, for want of a more elegant term, *meta-performative*. Throughout *Bellissima* we are made conscious, by a number of devices, that Maddalena Cecconi, who has displaced all her own thwarted acting ambitions onto her daughter, is being played by the diva who is precisely what her character aspires to become. When Maddalena primps before a mirror and conjures up a glamourous image of herself while at the same time explaining to her daughter that acting is "pretending to be someone else," the viewers are invited to consider that this "someone else" is indeed Magnani. The flesh-and-blood actress shown in the mirror is both the alfa and the omega of Maddalena's onscreen character, the creator and the goal of all her wish-fulfillment fantasies.[5] In this crucial reflection on the art of acting, Visconti creates a dizzying specularity, linking the literal to the meta-performative level of *Bellissima* in a way that asks us to interpret the entire film as a mirror of Magnani's divismo.[6]

To do so, we must turn back six years to the performance that established once and for all Magnani's definitive onscreen persona—the role of Sor Pina in Rossellini's *Open City* (1945). Though she had made her debut in the cinema as early as 1934 in Nunzio Malasomma's *La cieca di Sorrento,* it was the role of Pina that was to fix Magnani in the public mind. The actress would be forever identified with the vital, tough, tender-hearted, generous, earthy, and deeply principled *popolana* (woman of the people) whose execution by Nazi machine-gun fire as she ran after the truck carrying off her fiancé Francesco was to become the visual trademark of neorealism. Visconti's strategy in *Bellissima,* however, is not to accept this received stereotype of Magnani but to have the actress reinvent it on screen,[7] both through a long process of character development and through individual scenes of improvisation.

In ideological terms, the character of Maddalena begins far below the level of Pina, whose political function in *Open City* is to organize the neighborhood women to rebel against the Nazi occupation and who is ready to sacrifice her safety and her life for the partisan cause. When she says of her frivolous sister Lauretta, a music-hall performer who does not disdain to sleep with the occasional Fritz, "she's not bad, just stupid," Pina could be speaking about the very character Magnani will play in *Bellissima,* who will do anything in her pursuit of social mobility and vicarious stardom.[8] But by the end of *Bellissima,* Maddalena has undergone a conversion that allows her to achieve the moral stature of Pina, thanks to a change that Visconti worked into Zavattini's original story. In its initial form, *Bellissima* was to have ended with Blasetti's rejection of Maria, making the Cecconi family's exclusion from the world of cinematic glamour an external fact, a social given as inexorable and final as the Ricci family's exclusion from middle-class stability in Zavattini's script for *Bicycle Thief.* By having Maria accepted for the part, and then letting Maddalena make the decision to turn down the contract, Visconti completely transforms the Zavattini story from just another example of social defeat to one of moral growth leading to triumphant personal agency.

The institutional mechanisms that vanquished the Cecconis in Zavattini's story are thus internalized in Maddalena, who uses her newly won knowledge of the industry's corruption to form the moral judgment on which the peripeteia is based. When Maddalena storms into the screening room to confront Blasetti with his callousness and unhands the various henchmen who try to restrain her, the actress's physical movements evoke memories of Pina's attempt to break away from the Nazi guards in order to follow Francesco. Whereas Pina came to us as a character whose moral consciousness was fully formed and activated by the events of World War II, Maddalena is a product of a postwar society whose primary concerns are show business and soccer, forcing her to begin from an ideological ground zero in her difficult ascent to enlightenment. The ideological distance between Pina and Maddalena at the beginning of their respective films is thus a measure of the decline in Italy's collective political consciousness, from the heightened level reached during the Resistance years to the torpor of the 1950s.

There is another way in which Visconti allows Magnani to reinvent her onscreen persona, and that is through improvisation. A technique that has always formed an important part of Visconti's directorial repertoire ("to give my actors the greatest charge of truth, I always leave a wide margin, of repartee and of action, before and after a scene that I actually need"),[9] improvisation served two specific functions in the filming of *Bellissima*: first, it freed Visconti from ironclad adherence to a script for which he had little sympathy; second, it allowed him to exploit his diva's talent for spontaneous inventiveness and receptivity to her immediate environment.[10] Visconti's habit of turning on the camera in advance of the required action so that the actress could warm up her improvisational "engine" is particularly evident in the scenes of Maddalena's rounds as a nurse who gives injections to a clientele of both the very sick and the merely "run down." In the latter category is an especially fat, lazy, cigarette-smoking patient whose need for dietary supplements is questionable at best and who provides the occasion for considerable wisecracking and gestural humor on Magnani's part. The scene opens as Maddalena prepares the syringe in the bathroom adjacent to the "sick" room. From here, the chatter flows so naturally that it seems as if Visconti had simply turned on his camera in mid banter, though what we know about the filmmaker's technique suggests that a good deal of footage must have been shot before Magnani had hit her improvisational stride. "This method," Visconti explains, "functions perfectly with Magnani, who, coming in from the cold, would never succeed in finding such felicitous dialogue."[11]

Playing to Magnani's improvisational strengths means that the camera must be subservient to the diva's onscreen presence, taking its cues from her as it "trails" the actress in a variation on the neorealist technique of *pedinamento*. It is Magnani, then, who directs the camera, creating a visual style that can best be described as "internal montage,"[12] replacing explicit cuts and splices with subtle shifts of angle and distance in response to the progress of the actress through a given space. In an earlier scene, set in Maddalena's kitchen, the cinematic apparatus is completely subordinate to the diva's movements as she rails against the invasion of the "starving" acting teacher Tilde Sperlanzoni, who has helped herself to three raw eggs and ordered her hostess to fix her a cup of coffee with "lots of sugar." Though forced by the dictates of decorum to obey the commands of her domineering guest, Maddalena reasserts her authority by taking complete control of her domestic space (and the camera). Moving from stove to cabinet to ironing table in obedience to the internal rhythms of her own monologue, Maddalena utters a seamless flow of words that are matched by the uncut flow of images on the celluloid strip.

If, on the meta-performative level, *Bellissima* is about the relationship between diva and auteur, then it would behoove us to consider another, much shorter film that Visconti dedicated to Anna Magnani and to her distinct brand of divismo.[13] Two years after the release of *Bellissima*, Visconti shot an episode entitled "Anna" for the anthology *Siamo donne* (1953), whose contributors also included Roberto Rossellini, Alfredo Guarini, Luigi Zampa, and Gianni Franciolini.[14] All five episodes involve a diva who tells a story from her private life—a story that, with one exception, illustrates the conflict between *essere donna* and *essere attrice* ("being a woman" and "being an actress"). The exceptional case is that of Magnani, whose *essere attrice* is shown to be a natural consequence of her *essere donna*.[15] The episode is set in 1943, ten years prior to its filming, in the period when Magnani still performed in music halls, and it revolves around a quarrel between the diva and a cab driver on the way to the theater. When the driver insists on charging a supplemental fee for Magnani's pet dachshund, the actress rebels on the grounds that hers is a lapdog and therefore entitled to ride free of charge. After having persuaded an entire barracks of carabinieri that her pet adheres to the dictionary definition for exempt animals, the actress arrives late at the theater, pays the cab driver an exorbitant fare for having driven her all over Rome to prove her point, and ends by performing a song that enchants the theatrical public.

This apparently simple anecdote is, in truth, a complex and multi-leveled staging of Magnani's divismo. First of all, the episode offers a micro-genealogy of her career, beginning with her origins in vaudeville and retracing the unusual itinerary that led her to fame as the female personification of neorealism in the 1940s. "Magnani," Visconti had explained in the interview with Michele Gandin in 1951, "has an acting style full of popular instinct that has nothing to do with the professional theater."[16] According to Visconti, the diva's vaudeville origins protected her from the sclerotic tendencies of traditionally trained actors, allowing her to establish close contact with the mass public to which the filmmaker himself aspired after the box-office failure of *La terra trema* (1948). At the same time, the actress demonstrates the professionalism that Visconti admired in all the arts, and whose absence, especially in some examples of neorealism, he was known to regret. Highly professional, yet able to enter into a dialogic relationship with her audience, expert, yet far from the canons of the conventional theater, Magnani occupies a middle ground between the extremes of Tilde Sperlanzoni, the acting teacher of *Bellissima*, and Iris, the nonprofessional who had enjoyed ephemeral fame during the last years of neorealism.[17] It is this fusion of professionalism and "popular instinct" that resides at the core of the Magnani myth and that gives the impression of a dynamic continuity between the public and private life of the diva. "To the eyes of the spectators and readers of fan magazines," wrote Francesco Bolzoni, "person and character end up coinciding,"[18] and Visconti's episode can be interpreted as a critical investigation of that convergence.

On the surface, the episode reveals how the diva's success on stage derives from her identity in private life, characterized by a spontaneous theatricality and a predisposition to witty banter that enables her to amuse and delight the crowd of carabinieri.[19] Magnani's natural histrionics work to transform every space she occupies into a stage and every person she encounters into a straight man. Visconti himself commented on the diva's ability to elicit the innate theatricality even of the non-professionals with whom she collaborated. "She knows how to put herself at the level of others, and, in a certain way, she knows how to bring others up to hers."[20] It is her tendency to convert every location into a theater that justifies Visconti's metaphoric vision of Rome as a series of stages in *Bellissima,* including the radio studio that broadcasts Donizetti's *Elixir of Love,* the variety show and cinema in the courtyard of Maddalena's tenement, the stairwell in which so many family dramas are publicly enacted, the circus that serves as background to the protagonist's conversion, and finally Cinecittà itself, the master stage on which the hopes and dreams of the populace are played out.[21]

If the myth of the diva in "Anna" is rooted in the fusion of public and private identities, Visconti examines Magnani's public persona with a critical eye, revealing how constructed and studied is the *essere donna* of this *attrice.* "Now it's my turn," the diva explains in voice-over to introduce her episode of *Siamo donne.* "I'm sure that if I don't tell the story of a quarrel, you'll be disappointed. Isn't that so? I don't know why, but every now and then, when Magnani is mentioned, I hear the comment 'Leave her be. She'll talk back to you.'" Aware of audience expectations that she does not want to disappoint, the actress reveals that her divismo is based on a contract established with her public—a contract that must be renewed through regular performances both on stage and off. Consisting of fragments gleaned both from cinematic roles (Pina's insistence on following Francesco in the Nazi roundup, for example) and from real-life events (the plate of spaghetti thrown in Rossellini's face at a restaurant upon his return from a phone conversation with rival Ingrid Bergman), Magnani's divismo offers an image of impulsive, restless, and passionate femininity. In Magnani's case, the public and private merge to become an integral part of the myth, a trademark, a signatory rite that offers a liberating example to women and a challenge to men to defend their sexual primacy.

In "Anna," Visconti inverts the terms of Magnani's myth. It is not the private self that nourishes the actress's public persona, but rather the *es-*

FIGURE 6 | Playing himself as the director of the film within the film, Alessandro Blasetti is the real star of this mise-en-scène. Courtesy of the Museum of Modern Art/Film Stills Archive.

sere attrice that gives birth to the *essere donna*. Accordingly, diva and woman both emerge as expressions of Magnani's genius for inventing and publicly projecting a powerful image of self. For Visconti, the question of an authentic, private biographical essence is relegated to the unknowable: the mystery and privacy of the human being Anna Magnani remain intact. In an approach to identity that we could label poststructuralist, Visconti reveals that the Anna of his title will remain always a signifier, a mask, whose referent or signified is located beyond the confines of representation. Or, in the most cynical of readings, the sign of divismo refers only to itself, in the hermetically sealed universe of spectacle that the diva, in turn, both reflects and defines.[22]

If the vaudeville routine at the end of "Anna" constitutes the true staging of Magnani's celebrity, we can consider her divismo to be artisanal in its intimate connection with popular culture and its genuinely homespun nature. Magnani, in this episode, presents herself as the authentic product of a personal *bottega* (workshop) that finds its raw materials in her own life story as well as in the humus of the Roman working class. In *Bellissima,* this homegrown divismo is played off against the industrial model embodied by the filmmaker-within-the-film, Alessandro Blasetti, who is himself presented as a full-fledged *divo,* introduced on screen with fanfare and constantly surrounded by a swarm of lackeys, sycophants, and women who faint at the mere sound of his voice. When Blasetti ascends to the stage to begin auditions for "the prettiest [girl] child in Rome," it is obvious that he is the real star of the show,[23] the focus of the cinematic apparatus both within the fiction of *Bellissima* and in Visconti's representation of it (fig. 6). Filmed without dialogue, to an increasingly carnivalized musical accompaniment, the sequence is shot from an overhead camera that tracks Blasetti as he makes his way through the surging crowd of mothers, shakes hands, caresses babies, and poses for publicity stills. Once on stage, Blasetti becomes the center of the mise-en-scène as technicians swirl around him and the soundtrack reaches a babelic pitch. Grabbing the microphone, he demands silence and imposes order on the unruly mass, which immediately surrenders to his sovereign control.[24]

Having Blasetti play himself in the film serves a number of signifying purposes, not the least of which is to blur the distinction between person and *personaggio,* or character. In so doing, Blasetti stands at one end of a spectrum of relations between actors and characters extending from absolute identity (the director and his assistant Glori play themselves) through close association (Liliana Mancini, the discarded actress of two Castellani movies, plays Iris, a slightly modified version of her biographical self), to absolute difference (Walter Chiari, popular actor, plays a Cinecittà parasite). But Blasetti's function in *Bellissima* is also film-historical: as the enormously successful director of the 1930s–1950s whose name became synonymous with high-quality mainstream production, Blasetti personifies the Italian cinema *as industry* during those years. Much of Visconti's satire is organized around Blasetti, who is presented as an all-powerful Third World potentate (he even wears African safari garb) and whose film-within-the-film, ominously entitled *Today, Tomorrow, Never,* exemplifies the industry's most regressive tendencies. Any doubts as to the film's maudlin sentimentality and formulaic plot are dispelled by this summary offered by the photographer's wife: "She says she's leaving him, he wants to kill her, and all the while the child dances and leaps for joy around the birthday cake on the table."

Visconti's satire extends beyond Blasetti to include all of Cinecittà, whose very name (Cinema City) reveals its pretensions to create an alternative metropolis, a glamourous, romantic escape from the everyday life of *la città*. The irony is that Cinecittà reinscribes within its borders all of the banality and decay of the world it so boldly promises to replace. Even in visual terms, Cinecittà is a colossal disappointment, abounding in dilapidated structures that could as easily be unrepaired war ruins as the rear view of movie sets. The inner workings of Cinecittà mirror the shabbiness and decrepitude of its external appearance—corruption and sleaze are the norms that determine who gains access to the wielders of power. Within the fiction of *Bellissima,* these norms are embodied in the Cinecittà hustler Alberto Annovazzi, himself a victim of maternal overdrive who reenacts his own impossible quest for approval by promoting his clients' equally impossible dreams of stardom, at a price.

Far from correcting the sins of the outside world, then, Cinecittà isolates and magnifies them. In the lobby awaiting the second round of tryouts, the mothers of the prospective starlets run through the gamut of political options, from utopian solidarity (let's protest the injustice of a corrupt and fraudulent selection process) to individualistic influence peddling (whom do I know who has pull?), in a reenactment of Italy's historical fall from the optimism of the immediate postwar period to the cynicism and ideological slippage of the 1950s retrenchment.

To further demystify Cinecittà, Visconti presents the Italian industry as totally reliant on borrowed glamour. The stars who are constantly invoked (Montgomery Clift, Burt Lancaster, Lana Turner, Betty Grable, Greta Garbo, Maureen O'Hara, and the never-mentioned but always emulated Shirley Temple) and the films alluded to (Howard Hawks's *Red River* [1948], screened in the outdoor-movie scene, and Herman J. Mankiewicz's *A Woman's Secret* [1949], advertized on a poster outside the movie theater where Annovazzi acquires his Lambretta) are all Hollywood imports. Though these references point to the concrete economic circumstance of American domination of European film markets, they also set up a kind of relay of glamour, whereby Italian aspirants to stardom seek approval by an indigenous industry that itself aspires to a model of glamour from abroad.

Imported or not, this glamour has a narcotic effect on Maddalena, for whom it promises release from the limits of her domestic condition. "Let's go to the movies tonight," she begs Spartaco upon her return from Cinecittà, eager to prolong the euphoria of her first contact with this privileged order of existence and loathe to reenter the drudgery of her lower-class Prenestino life. Visconti intensifies this need for escape by adding a sociological element to Maddalena's aspirations. In the original subject by Zavattini, Maddalena was to play a bourgeoise matron, living in the Annibaliano neighborhood and affluent enough to be able to afford a maid. By down-classing Maddalena, Visconti establishes a bipolar social environment, oscillating between the Prenestino tenement, teeming with overweight housewives (*le balene* [whales], as Spartaco calls them) and soccer-crazed men, on the one hand, and Cinecittà, frequented by sleek, perfectly groomed bourgeois women with the material and cultural means to propel their daughters to stardom, on the other.[25] Maddalena occupies an anomalous middle ground between these two worlds. Though the apartment house is clearly her element—as her joyous circulation up and down the stairwell, in semiundress, brandishing a hyperdermic and trading quips with the women and children at each level, suggests—Maddalena has powerful impulses to social mobility. That she does *not* belong to the gaggle of bourgeois mothers storming the gates of Cinecittà is made clear by the mise-en-scène the minute she appears on screen. Dressed in traditional black garb—whereas the other mothers are brightly and fashionably clothed—Maddalena separates herself immediately from the other women in order to seek her lost child. Maria's straying is a sure sign that she, too, is out of her element among these exquisitely manicured and highly coached middle-class daughters, for she would much rather muddy herself in a pond than join the other aspiring Shirley Temples in their ascent to stardom.

Unlike Rossellini or De Sica, Visconti does not sentimentalize the proletariat in *Bellissima,* but he does betray a fascination for the relentlessly public, performative nature of tenement life.[26] The omnipresent stairwell (which significantly will be replaced by the more private elevator, signifier of upward mobility, in the new house of the Cecconis) is a staging area, a conduit of information, and a theater for the performance of Maddalena's public persona. The congested space of the tenement means that family life is routinely performed for an audience of neighbors, be it the quarrel that distracts the spectators of the movie being shown in the courtyard or Maddalena's triumphant defense of her ambitions before a jury of *balene*.

Visconti's interest in the public enactment of private passions lies at the heart of his generic preference for melodrama, which, understood etymologically as "drama set to music," explains the filmmaker's career-long passion for opera. Not only did this love lead Visconti to direct a number of operas but it also conditioned his approach to filmmaking in a number of ways. The very structure of *Bellissima* may be said to be operatic, given the centrality of Maddalena (the functional equivalent of the dramatic soprano) and how she is played off against a series of choruses: the "whale women" of the housing project, the middle-class, stage-door mothers, and the Cinecittà flunkies. Or she is presented in duet with individual characters who serve as foils to her, notably Spartaco and Annovazzi. Operatic importance is accorded to sound in general in *Bellissima,* since Visconti was the only director at the time to record direct sound, refusing the technique of postsynchronization that was used even by his neorealist contemporaries. Thus we constantly hear ambient sound, distracting sound, contaminating sound: the outdoor movie competes with family quarrels and characters shout at cross-purposes in a cacophony that provides the acoustic equivalent to the physical congestion of working-class urban life.[27]

But the most important function of opera in *Bellissima* is intertextual. Just as Verdi's *Trovatore* introduced *Senso* (1954) and provided the heroic counterplot against which all the subsequent action of the film would be measured and found wanting, Donizetti's *Elisir d'amore* opens *Bellissima* and provides a running critique of the role of cinema in Italian collective thought. During the title sequence of *Bellissima,* we hear a radio broadcast of Donizetti's act 2, scene 4, in which the village women have just learned that the male protagonist of the opera, Nemorino, has inherited a fortune from his rich uncle. *"Non fate strepito"* (Don't make a commotion) warns the chorus, while visually Visconti cuts from the radio station to crowds of mothers storming the barricades of Cinecittà, making the very commotion that the singers advise against.

In setting up this dialogue between opera text and film action, Visconti establishes right from the very start the admonitory function of the older art form and the failure to heed that admonition on the part of the newer medium. A more urgent warning is issued in the second Donizettian allusion when Blasetti makes his grand entrance to the strains of the "Theme of the Charlatan," originally composed for the quack Dr. Dulcamara as he peddles his elixir of love.[28] The operatic reference also creates a subterranean link between Maddalena's livelihood and Blasetti's. As a nurse who earns an income by administering cures that are not always medically indicated, Maddalena is herself a pedlar of illusions, an exploiter of public gullibility who, in turn, uses her proceeds to invest in the cinema's illusory promise of fame and fortune. In a final Donizettian recall, Visconti uses the lyrics *"quanto è bella, quanto è cara"* (How pretty, how dear she is) for the soundtrack of the very last frames of the film: a shot of Maria, who is finally allowed to sleep peacefully, released from the stranglehold of her mother's ambitions. Maria no longer has to be *bellissima,* nor *la più bella bambina di Roma.* It is enough for her to be *bella,* without superlatives of an absolute or relative sort. At this point, we can say that the film has finally paid heed to the operatic text, taking seriously its warning against uncritical acceptance of the illusions peddled by the charlatans of mass spectacle.

Maddalena is finally able to break the enchantment of the elixir, thanks to the epiphany that she experiences in a screening room toward the end of the film. It is here that the technique of cinematic projection exposes and remedies the process of psychological projection that had characterized the mother/daughter relationship up to this point. Throughout *Bellissima,* Maddalena has refused to accord her daughter the slightest trace of autonomous selfhood—the child has been dragged around like a rag doll from morning to night, her needs for sleep, nourishment, and even medicine routinely overlooked in the mother's frenzy to meet the entrance requirements for the middle class. Ballet lessons, photography shoots, and dress measurings take the place of true nurturance as Maddalena deceives herself into thinking that she is promoting her daughter's interests by pushing her own agenda for vicarious stardom.

Visconti exposes Maddalena's self-serving notions of motherhood

FIGURE 7 | In a multilevel scene of visual and psychological self-reflexivity, Maddalena (Anna Magnani) speculates on what it means to be an actress. Courtesy of the Museum of Modern Art/Film Stills Archive.

by reversing the gender roles in the Cecconi household, making the virile Spartaco into a far more maternal figure than his wayward wife. When we first see Spartaco onscreen, he is worried about the whereabouts of Maddalena and Maria, and symmetrically at the film's end, he is unable to concentrate on the contract because he is again preoccupied about his missing wife and child. He is constantly scolding Maddalena for taking their daughter around at all hours, is concerned (and rightly so) that the girl has not been properly fed—to his query about whether or not Maria had eaten that evening, the answer is, "Do you think I'm starving her? I bought her a caffè latte and two rolls!" It is Spartaco who undresses the child, tucks her into bed, and promises her a treat (as unnutritious as her meager supper, but at least more age-appropriate) of ice cream. Most important in establishing the reversal by the Cecconis of stereotypical gender roles is the fact that while Maddalena dreams of fame in the outside world, Spartaco wants nothing more than a new house—an enlarged and improved space of domesticity. Thus, within the psychological economy of the Cecconis, it is Spartaco who embodies the nesting instinct, with all its concomitant values of stability, nurturing, and familial order. Maddalena, on the other hand, wants to affirm her being-in-the-world, to experience social mobility, to compete for whatever resources of fame, recognition, and material reward her environment has to offer.

But to comprehend Maddalena's parental failure fully, we must return to the mirror scene, for it is there that the narcissistic basis of the mother/child relationship is exposed. Until now, Maddalena's vision of the world has been a strictly utilitarian one: when she looks at Maria, it is only to see if the child needs tidying up or other corrective attentions, just as, when she looks at Annovazzi or Tilde Sperlanzoni, it is to take their measure and determine if these parasites might nonetheless promote her interests. In the mirror scene, her gaze, for the first time, is more pensive and abstract, as she contemplates her image in the glass, brushes her hair, and strikes a glamourous pose. "What is acting, really?" she thinks out loud. "If I believed myself to be someone else? If I pretended to be another . . . then I'm acting." During the course of this monologue, the image that she beholds in the mirror is her ideal self, the glamourous actress she longs to be but whom her life circumstances have placed out of reach (fig. 7). Turning away from her reflection and toward Maria, Maddalena exclaims, "You see, *you* can act, too," making explicit the transfer of her ambitions to the child, who is now engulfed in the shadow that her mother's advancing form casts upon her in the mise-en-scène.[29] "You're my daughter. You, yes *you*, can be an actress. I could have, too, if I had wanted." As Maddalena recites these lines, she busies herself with her daughter's hair, tries out various styles, and finally brushes it straight back *"come sta mamma"* (like mommy wears it), establishing the specularity of this mother/daughter rapport. At last, the utilitarian gaze that Maddalena has directed at Maria gives way to a look of pure love. "Sei carina, sei bella" (You're cute, you're pretty), she observes, as the soundtrack swells with the all-too-appropriate strains of Donizetti's *quant'è bella* motif.

It is important to note that the mirrors in Maddalena's dressing area are two: a large, frontal glass, on the wall before her, and a smaller one, angled to the left, standing on top of the bureau. This multiplication of mirrors functions not only to reveal the principle of doubling on which narcissistic identification is based but also to reinforce the psychoanalytic claim for the analogy between the mirror and the screen. In Christian Metz's terms, the cinematic signifier is the sum of a chain of mirror effects, of surfaces that receive and reflect back images, from the photosensitive emulsion of film stock in the camera to the celluloid strip in the projector, to the screen of the theater, to the retina of the spectator's eye.[30] Both Metz and Laura Mulvey[31] argue that the cinema situation replicates what Jacques Lacan has termed the mirror phase—the moment of development between the age of six months and eighteen months when the child first grasps that the image reflected in the mirror is her own.[32] But since this is the stage when the child's physical skills lag far behind her motor ambitions, she will endow the mirror image with those qualities of competence and wholeness that she feels she so woefully lacks. The resulting combination of recognition ("that image is me") and simultaneous misrecognition ("that image is my better self") lays the groundwork for two processes: the emergence of the ego, and the ability to identify with others in later life. This second process sets in motion "the dialectic that will henceforth link the I to socially elaborated situations," according to Lacan. "It is this moment which decisively tips the whole of human knowledge into mediatization through desire of the other."

Because the mirror phase involves identification with an image, understood etymologically as *imago,* or effigy, likeness, copy, Lacan insists on locating this development in the realm of the imaginary, in the preoedipal, prelinguistic sphere of primary processes. "This jubilant assumption of his specular image by the child at the *infans* stage, still sunk in his motor incapacity and nurseling dependence, would seem to exhibit in an exemplary situation the symbolic matrix in which the I is precipitated in primordial form, before it is objectified in the dialectic of identification with the other, and before language restores to it, in the universal, its function as subject."[33] If, as Metz and Mulvey claim, the cinema reactivates the experience of the mirror phase, plunging us back "like the child again, in a sub-motor or hyper perceptive state, prey to the imaginary, to the double,"[34] this insight explains the oneiric condition in which Maddalena finds herself as she watches the outdoor screening of *Red River* midway into *Bellissima.*[35] In this scene, Maddalena has obviously entered a trance-like state when, in a willful rejection of the dividing line between the phantasmagoric and the real, she insists that the images onscreen "are not fables."[36]

More interesting than Maddalena's credulity, however, is her cinema-induced resistance to Spartaco's sexual advances. He has come to the courtyard to coax her into leaving the movie and going to bed. When she objects, "Spartaco, you don't understand me. Look at those beautiful places. Look where we live," Maddalena opposes her fascination with the screen to the requirements of conjugal love. Her libidinal investment in the film-viewing experience precludes libidinal enactments in everyday life. It is significant that the film's denouement hinges precisely on the resolution of this conflict in favor of marital sex. As husband and wife embrace in the final scene of *Bellissima,* Maddalena suffers a momentary relapse at the sound of Burt Lancaster's voice, which wafts into their bedroom from the courtyard theater. When Spartaco reacts angrily, Maddalena recoups by saying it was only a joke, and reconfirms her preference for the concrete pleasures of the marriage bed over her libidinized identifications with the silver screen.[37]

When read in Lacanian terms, the mirror scene contains the key both to Maddalena's psychology and Magnani's divismo. Gazing at her reflection in the looking glass, primping and posing to make that image ever more glamourous as she fantasizes about the acting career she never had, Maddalena both recognizes herself yet sees the image as the more accomplished individual she longed to become. Acting, the art of pretending to be someone else, would have let her embrace that "better" self, enabling her to remedy the split between consciousness and image that has left her so frustrated and incomplete. Clinging to this belief, Maddalena has remained in a state of arrested development, caught up in the process of narcissistic identification that keeps her hostage to the imaginary and will not let her progress to a mature recognition of others as autonomous beings with their own distinct consciousness and needs.

To get beyond the mirror phase, to transcend infantile narcissism, is to use the process of *misrecognition,* of perceiving the image to be a better self, as a step on the road to intersubjectivity.[38] In Laura Mulvey's analysis, the child's perception of her mirror image as superior "projects this body outside itself as an ego ideal, the alienated subject which, reintrojected as an ego ideal, prepares the way for identification with others in the future."[39] Refusing to relinquish the belief that through acting she will be able to heal the split in her being and reappropriate her better self, Maddalena cannot make the transition to the next phase in her psychic development. She cannot acknowledge the link between the ideal image in the mirror and an autonomous other with whom she can some day identify and relate. Thus when she turns from the looking glass to confront Maria with her thwarted dreams, her daughter simply becomes another mirror, a surface onto which Maddalena will displace her frustrated desire to embrace an ego ideal through acting. In this way Maddalena fits the pattern of the immature mothers cited in Christine Olden's psychoanalytic study of empathy, where the parent/child fusion of identity enabled the mothers "vicariously to gratify their own frustrated instinctual needs by virtue of projecting themselves onto the child."[40] Maria will never function as a separate, autonomous subject for Maddalena as long as the woman remains trapped in the realm of the imaginary, unable to detach the ideal image in the mirror from her own dreams of fulfillment and wholeness. And the cinema is her willing accomplice, both at the level of the narrative of *Bellissima,* which is set in motion by Maddalena's desire for vicarious stardom, and at the level of deep psychological mechanisms mobilized by the medium, which "quite apart from the extraneous similarities between screen and mirror" according to Mulvey, "has structures of fascination strong enough to . . . [recall] the pre-subjective moment of image recognition."[41]

Visconti's genius in *Bellissima* is to turn the cinematic apparatus back on itself, to use its structures of fascination in order to expose and remedy the processes that have held Maddalena so long in their thrall. This occurs in the projection booth toward the end of the film where the mirror has been replaced by the screen and Maddalena is made to see, both physically and intellectually, the results of what she has been doing to her daughter all along.[42] It would be no exaggeration to claim that the crisis of *Bellissima* hinges on a psychocinematic pun, where the technological and emotional meanings of projection come together to expose the abuses of cinematic enchantment.

Of utmost importance is the fact that Maddalena and Maria are not the only viewers at the screening. Concealed in the projection booth, mother and daughter cannot see Blasetti and his entourage as they view the screen test, but they are privy to the men's explosions of derisive laughter. In constantly cross-cutting between Maria's image onscreen, the mother in the projection booth, and the men below, Visconti enacts Maddalena's burgeoning awareness that her gaze is by no means the whole story. Now Maddalena must confront the fact that by forcing her daughter to audition for the part, she has exposed the child to a visual regime of the most degrading and exploitative sort. The disparity between the mother's perspective and that of Blasetti's men shocks Maddalena out of her narcissistic investment in her daughter, forcing her to see that Maria is not an extension of her own fond imaginings but is an object, in the world, open to the most humiliating of visual appropriations.

It is here that the cinema employs its medium-specific properties to the greatest advantage, for by projecting the image of Maria onscreen and submitting that image to such public abuse, the technology externalizes Maddalena's inner process of psychological projection and forces her to confront its moral consequences. This may be considered a form of Dantesque *contrappasso,* a literalization of the metaphor on which her psychology had been so disastrously based. In this way, the cinematic apparatus enables Maddalena to get beyond the impasse of the mirror phase, to acknowledge her error in identifying her idealized self-image in the looking glass with that of her daughter onscreen. Proof of her conversion is her insistence to Blasetti that his men cease ridiculing Maria because "è una ragazzina come tutte le altre" (she's a girl like all the others), a statement that vindicates her daughter's right *not* to be extraordinary, *not* to have to live out her mother's dreams of celebrity. With this announcement, Maddalena reveals her acceptance of the child as other, *come tutte le altre,* and thereby signals her passage, beyond the looking glass, to the other side, or to put it more appropriately, to the side of the *other,* where reflection gives way to relation and daughters can become autonomous selves.

Cinema, for Visconti, is thus profoundly double in nature—at once elixir and true cure, exploiter of public inclinations to glamour, romance, and escape and exposer of its own basis in illusionism and greed. By utilizing its structures of fascination to reflect on its dubious means, the elixir of cinema offers a homeopathic approach to cure—one in which Magnani's divismo plays a crucial role. For it is the illusory nature of her public persona, her mythic continuity between private and professional selves, that gives her onscreen presence its authenticity and power. In acting the part of Maddalena, Magnani puts her own divistic myth of unity to the service of a character who must learn to do the opposite—to dissociate and differentiate herself from her ideal mirror image and from the daughter onto whom she has displaced her dreams of unattainable stardom.

To further complicate matters, when Maddalena looks into the mirror and conjures up her ideal self, at the meta-performative level, Magnani is looking into the mirror of the film and seeing the image of Maddalena, the authentic woman of the people, the basis of her own mythic continuity between professionalism and *istinto popolare* (popular instinct), between *essere attrice* and *essere donna*. But Maddalena's experience in *Bellissima* serves to critique the myth of Magnani by revealing the danger of arrested development at the mirror phase, the risk of identifying with the idealized mirror image rather than misrecognizing it and thus failing to progress to relations with others as full-fledged, autonomous subjects. Thus Maddalena deconstructs Magnani, just as the cinematic apparatus calls into question its own indigenous structures of fascination, offering itself up as both elixir and cure.

If *Bellissima* is "one of the first and most knowledgeable acts of death of the neorealist utopia,"[43] as Lino Miccichè has argued, we can see this death as a cathartic one, a necessary prerequisite to the rebirth of a cinema of national reference. In order to herald this renewal, *Bellissima* had to exorcise the demons of melodrama at the level of story, of corruption and bad faith at the level of industrial practice, and of narcissistic self-involvement at the level of the meta-performance by allegorizing the deleterious effects of all of the above on a mother/daughter relationship. In so doing, however, Visconti revealed the considerable power of the cinematic apparatus to serve as an instrument of cognitive and moral transformation, preparing the way for the medium to reclaim its former status as "the bearer and interpreter of the national-popular consciousness."[44]

italy by displacement

Bernardo Bertolucci's *The Last Emperor*

POWERLESS IN PEKING

When Bernardo Bertolucci won nine Academy Awards for *The Last Emperor* in 1988, it was hailed as a victory for Italy. "I felt like the captain of the national soccer squad," the filmmaker exclaimed when he first heard about the nominations.[1] In the same vein, *Espresso* reporter Giovanni Buttafava wrote, "It was Bernardo Bertolucci who pulled off the World Cup for the first time and [earned] the pride of the national team that returns home victorious with a lot of goals."[2] The desire to Italianize this triumph, however, runs entirely counter to the international conditions of the film's making. Based on the memoirs of Aisin-Gioro Pu Yi, the last ruler of the Ching dynasty, coscripted by Englishman Mark Peploe, shot for the most part on location in China, using primarily English-speaking actors of Oriental or Eurasian descent, and produced by Englishman Jeremy Thomas, who presold shares to an international clientele of distributors, *The Last Emperor* is anything but the film made by, for, and about Italians that would warrant such an outpouring of national pride. Obviously, if we are to make the argument for the Italianness of *The Last Emperor,* it must rest on grounds far removed from industrial, baseline definitions and must honor the kinds of ideological and generic considerations that the writer and film critic Alberto Moravia so aptly raised with respect to Bertolucci's achievement.

"The experience that probably most helped Bertolucci in his film on China and on Pu Yi," observed Moravia, "is that of having participated sentimentally and culturally in Italian political events. Without this participation, there would have been neither the renunciation of novelized history nor the renunciation of the psychological parable of the protagonist."[3] Because Moravia's comment reads as a distillation of the entire argument for the Italianness of Bertolucci's *Last Emperor,* I will make constant use of it throughout this chapter to explore the link between the film's ideological roots in postwar Italian politics and the generic form that it will take as a cinematic historical novel in the grand style of Luchino Visconti.

But the most obvious implication of Moravia's statement is that *The Last Emperor* is more about Italy than China—a paradox that Edward Said explains in his study of orientalism as a fixture of the Western literary imagination.[4] The Orient, for Said, is less a referent than a sign, a signifier of the Other against which the West defines itself. And though Bertolucci explicitly denies that *The Last Emperor* is about Italy (when asked by *Film Comment,* "Why China?" Bertolucci answered, "Because it's not Italy. . . . The Italian present doesn't need—or doesn't want— to be represented onscreen at the moment, at least not by me"),[5] it is impossible to exempt the film from the mirroring function that the East has always performed for the literary West. Orient as reflecting surface, Orient as screen for the projection of an edifying self-image, or, to use a motif from *The Last Emperor,* Orient as a diaphanous veil through which the West can be viewed imperfectly, but perhaps more suggestively—these are the uses to which China is put in Bertolucci's film.[6]

The Italy that Bertolucci finds there is no literal-minded analogue to be sought in the corridors of the Forbidden City or in the wilds of Manchuria but in a vision of history propounded by Antonio Gramsci, refined by Georg Lukács, and made cinematic by Luchino Visconti. Like Gramsci and Visconti, Bertolucci is interested in failed revolutions, in progressive movements whose ideals are appropriated by the system as a way of defusing their threat to the status quo. Gramsci called this preemptive process *trasformismo.*[7] His analysis of the Risorgimento as *"conquista regia e non movimento popolare"* ("royal conquest and not popular movement")[8] became the basis for Visconti's indictment of the newborn Italian state in *Senso* (1954) and *The Leopard* (1963)—a judgment that was given a double focus by its allusion to the postwar trasformismo of the Resistance campaign for internal social change.[9] Bertolucci's own political coming of age coincided with yet another revolutionary disappointment when the events of 1968 ("China had become a projection of our confused utopias," Bertolucci explained to Donald Ranvaud)[10] failed to produce a valid agenda for reform. What emerges from such a historical perspective is a mistrust for all state apparatuses, even for those born from revolutions, where power becomes institutionalized and government seeks only its own conservation.

Those who read *The Last Emperor* as a celebration of Chinese Communist rule, as a Maoist apologia, or as a revolutionary romance misconstrue Bertolucci's critical perspective. "No one can accuse me of Communist propaganda," he exclaims in response to an article in *La Repubblica* that found the film sympathetic to the Chinese Communist regime.[11] Instead, the People's Republic of China is presented as just one more cycle of the historical wheel of fortune, itself internally unstable and subject to violent change from within.[12] If the humane, exemplary governor of the prison of Fushun were allowed to prevail in the world of the film, then perhaps there would be support for the pro-Maoist argument. But when he is made a victim of the Cultural Revolution, humiliated and ridiculed by the Red Guard, we are shown the fanaticism and excesses to which the Maoist regime, like any other ideologically extremist state, is subject. When the drill team of teenage girls performs an inane song-and-dance routine as regimented and humorless as any traditional formation of the bannermen inside the walls of the prerevolutionary Forbidden City, we realize that the new state has manipulated and dehumanized the masses as surely as did the old, and with far less tasteful rituals of subordination.

Nor is Pu Yi's structural relation to the Maoist regime so different from that of his earlier political incarnations. Just as Pu Yi was useful to those who profited from prolonging the imperial charade within the Forbidden City after China had become a republic, and just as he was useful to the Japanese in establishing a surrogate government in Manchuria under the guise of preserving the Ching dynasty, so is Pu Yi useful to the Communist regime as the model convert, the perfect "remolded man" (fig. 8).[13] Though Bertolucci nowhere mentions Pu Yi's two-volume autobiography, significantly entitled *From Emperor to Citizen* and ghostwritten by Communist propagandist Li Wenda, he does make explicit Pu Yi's exploitable status in an important exchange with the prison governor on the eve of his release. "You saved my life to make me a puppet in your own play," observes Pu Yi. "You saved me because I am useful to you." In his allusion to puppetry and theatrical performance, Pu Yi reveals the continuity in his political role by re-

FIGURE 8 | Arrested and sent for Communist "reeducation" in the aftermath of World War II, the once-exalted emperor of the Ching dynasty (John Lone, second row, center) becomes prisoner no. 981. Courtesy of the Museum of Modern Art/Film Stills

turning us to the Forbidden City, whose spaces were visually treated as stages and whose functions were referred to as theater. Far from making linear progress toward an ever-more-enlightened utopian state, history simply traces a series of cycles, governed by varying degrees of political self-interest, exploitation, and greed.

Pu Yi's exchange with the prison governor argues against a pro-Communist reading of the film in still more important ways. Despite the inexplicable critical consensus that Pu Yi undergoes a genuine "Pauline conversion"[14] to revolutionary ideals, his awareness of his usefulness to the regime suggests that he is once more playacting, reciting the part that others expect of him, in order to earn his freedom. That this self-conscious enactment of Marxist dictates in no way affects his essential self is proved in the film's final moments, when Pu Yi produces proof of his imperial identity for an incredulous little boy ("Prove it," the child had insisted) by reaching behind the throne to retrieve the cricket container he had put there as the three-year-old ruler of China. The cricket, still alive, hidden away in the Hall of Supreme Harmony, is emblematic of Pu Yi—unaltered by all the years in the various cages, gilded and otherwise, that had held him until now.[15] When his brother had uttered the same challenge to his imperial identity in childhood ("Prove it"), Pu Yi's response at the age of ten had been far different: he had ordered one of his eunuchs to drink a container of green ink, suggesting that power itself, absolute and arbitrary, was what defined his royal status. Though it is historical circumstances that determined the difference between the ten-year-old's behavioral proof of his imperial identity and that of the old man near death, the film argues for the concept of an irreducible self, formed, I shall suggest later on, by the Freudian drama of the child's early years.

Had Bertolucci wanted to stage a total transformation in the character of Pu Yi, the biographical record would have offered ample material for the personality overhaul required by such Communist "remolding." According to the historical record, the last emperor was sadistic ("flogging eunuchs was part of my daily routine," he writes in the autobiography),[16] prey to temper tantrums, physically inadequate to the task of engendering an heir, and a buffoon. It is significant that Bertolucci chose not to include such scenes as the gratuitous whipping of eunuchs, the childlike outbursts of rage, or the clownish moment in the Tokyo railroad station when the solemnity of Pu Yi's first handshake with Hirohito was marred by the Chinese emperor's fumbling attempts to remove his tight-fitting gloves. Such scenes would not only make for lively cinema but would establish the temperamental depths from which Pu Yi was saved by ten years in Communist prison. Bertolucci's Pu Yi, instead, lacks the rampant sadism and equivocal sexuality of his historical counterpart and, except for the interlude in Tientsin (when Pu Yi, as a degenerate playboy, croons a la Bing Crosby) is no buffoon. Whereas the historical Pu Yi initiates reforms only at the behest of his tutor Reginald Johnston, Bertolucci's emperor is a spontaneous promoter of progress, cutting off his Manchu braid as a sign of his break with tradition, ordering an inventory of court valuables to detect in-house theft, and banishing the eunuchs from the realm they had come to dominate—all on his own initiative. The fact that such reformatory zeal puts him at risk seems to energize Bertolucci's Pu Yi and distract him from his perennial wish to escape for the Oxford of Johnston's gentleman's mythology. That Bertolucci's Pu Yi acts with a measure of dignity throughout his life, and shows preconversion flashes of the very courage that will enable him to stand up for the maligned prison governor before the Red Guard, suggests that his Communist reeducation was not so great a transformation after all.

The final argument against a doctrinaire Marxist reading of the film is Bertolucci's style, which revels in the cinematic possibilities of life before the revolution. By structuring most of the film as a series of flashbacks whose narrative-present is Pu Yi's journey to and confinement in Fushun prison, Bertolucci maximizes the opportunities for stylistically invidious comparisons between "then" and "now." The first such flashback sets the contrastive visual terms for all such juxtapositions. As the suicidal Pu Yi loses consciousness in the bathroom of the provincial railroad station on the journey to Fushun prison, the governor's cry to "open the door" takes him back to the day forty-eight years before when royal soldiers summoned him to the Forbidden City. The cold, barren, pallid realist style of Pu Yi's narrative-present gives way to a richly colored, highly emotional, dynamic, dreamlike mode accompanied by all the trappings of grand spectacle cinema. This flashback reflects a doubly filtered vision—an adult's memory of a child's fantasy-laden perception—and just as it takes Pu Yi back to his own personal, myth-enshrouded past, so, too, does it take Bertolucci back to the origins of Italian cinema in the great costume films of the silent era. Pu Yi's journey in memory thus gives Bertolucci the occasion to indulge his extravagant aestheticism and to acknowledge its cinematic roots in the exotic, orientalist tradition (*La vergine di Babilonia,* Luigi Maggi, 1910; *Marc Antonio e Cleopatra,* Enrico Guazzoni, 1913; etc.) of the early Italian film industry.

The Manchukuo sequences permit Bertolucci another kind of stylistic indulgence in which a play of shadows conveys the dark, sinister forces of Japanese influence on Pu Yi.[17] In fact, this entire segment of *The Last Emperor* constitutes its own melodramatic subfilm, self-contained and separate in style, as well as in mood, from its surrounding cinematic context. Though criticized for being cartoonish in its Mata Hari–type protagonist (Eastern Jewel), its drug-addicted and soon-to-be demented victim (the empress), its insidious predatory villains (especially the Japanese film magnate Amakasu), and its cast of obsequious Chinese supporters, such caricaturized treatment is justified by the flashback structure of the film, which locates these perceptions in the con-

FIGURE 9 | With the three-year-old Pu Yi (Richard Vu) presiding over all the pageantry of the Forbidden City, Bertolucci indulges his aesthetic delight in life before the revolution. Courtesy of the Museum of Modern Art/Film Stills Archive.

sciousness of Pu Yi, anxious to abdicate all personal responsibility for his Japanese collaboration.[18]

Within the narrative-present of the story, filmed in socialist-realist style, Bertolucci can justify his forays into grand spectacle and film noir melodrama by attributing these modes of vision to Pu Yi's backward-looking perspective. But it is clear that Bertolucci's aesthetic judgment is all on the side of prerevolutionary China, be it the voluptuary decadence of the Forbidden City or the sinister elegance of Manchukuo (fig. 9). In his stylistic preference for an old order that he morally condemns, Bertolucci is very much the heir of Luchino Visconti, whose film production from 1954 on exhibited a tension between poetics and politics, between aristocratic aestheticism and progressive social commentary. By choosing periods of historical transition—the Risorgimento, the fin de siècle world of Western Europe, the end of the Ching dynasty—and by focusing on what is coming to a conclusion rather than what is beginning, Bertolucci and Visconti are able to have it both ways, indulging their aesthetic delight in life before the revolution while denouncing it on moral and political grounds.[19] Thus it comes as no surprise that Bertolucci made *The Last Emperor* rather than *The First Chairman,* just as Visconti's Risorgimento films are about the extinction of the aristocratic leopards and lions rather than the rise of the jackals and the hyenas of the newly empowered bourgeoisie.

The Last Emperor is thus anything but the unequivocal endorsement of the Chinese Communist regime that critics have taken it to be. But this is not to deny the film the more generalized Marxist perspective that is the Gramscian legacy to the intellectual Left. When Gramsci theorized that radical change would be better served by the creation of a progressive social consciousness in the masses through cultural rather than through violent revolutionary means, he was enjoining the intelligentsia to abandon its customary political aloofness and to lead in the forging of a true national-popular Italian identity.[20] Georg Lukács, whose literary theory held great sway over the Italian cultural proponents of the Left, defined the critical realist perspective appropriate to writers who would heed the Gramscian injunction to politically committed art. Such writing must make explicit the dynamics of the historical process through the actions of what Lukács called "typical characters"; that is, characters whose "innermost being is determined by objective forces at work in society . . . the determining factors of a particular historical phase are found in them in concentrated form."[21] Nor are these characters unaware of what makes them typical, for their authors endow them with a special consciousness, informed by the "necessary anachronism" that enables them "to express feelings and thoughts about real historical relationships in a much clearer way than the actual men and women of the time could."[22] In choosing the proper subjects for historical novels exhibiting a true critical-realist perspective, the writer should not privilege what Lukács called "world-historical" characters, those heroic figures, such as generals and kings, who make history, but should focus instead on "maintaining" characters, those who experience history without affecting its course.[23]

In the light of Gramsci's imperative to politically committed art and Lukács's influential theory of the historical novel, we are ready to return to Moravia's opening statement about the Italianness of Bertolucci's film. "Without this participation [in Italian political events] there would have been neither the renunciation of novelized history nor the renunciation of the psychological parable of the protagonist."

If by "novelized history" he means the opposite of "historical novel," then Moravia's linkage of Italian political culture to the genre of Bertolucci's film begins to reveal its logic. Whereas the historical novel represents the actions of "maintaining characters" who are typical in the Lukácsian sense that they embody the salient conflicts of their age, novelized history would feature "world-historical" figures, the heroes or forgers of our collective destiny, in texts that would employ the techniques of fiction to domesticate and personalize them. While the historical novel presses its story into the service of historical understanding, novelized history subordinates world occurrences to the needs of the story by privatizing the public domain. Whereas the historical novel offers a critical-realist perspective on its events, novelized history reduces its subject matter to the level of entertainment.

By resisting the temptation to film a novelized history, Bertolucci introduces the first of the many ironies that will typify his approach to his protagonist. Aisin-Gioro Pu Yi, twelfth emperor of the Ching dynasty, should, by all accounts, be a world-historical figure, the embodiment of divine will on earth, the heroic forger of lives, an active agent of destiny. His a priori status, linked with the grandiose apparatus of the spectacle film, leads us to expect an effectual hero motivated by clear-cut moral imperatives, strutting about on a stage of epic proportions. Instead, we get the quintessential maintaining character, a man of ambiguous morality who becomes a pawn of history, powerless to affect its course, confined to a tiny, domestic stage. "It is not Pu Yi's presence in the history of his time," writes Robert Zaller, "but his exclusion from it that constitutes the real premise of the film."[24] This irony resides at the core of Bertolucci's *The Last Emperor,* and failure to perceive it will result in the kind of interpretive error made by Pauline Kael when she takes the generic indicators at face value and expects the sort of heroics that the Hollywood spectacle film so predictably provides. But Kael is insensitive to the broad Marxist thrust of Bertolucci's argument—that there can be no world-historical characters in a society determined by material forces that exceed individual human efforts to intervene.[25] By choosing a character whose world-historical credentials are what qualify him to become history's quintessential pawn, Bertolucci offers a powerful object lesson in historical determinism.

Because Pu Yi fails to act in a decisive, world-historical way, he is subject to stereotypically feminine portrayal by Bertolucci's camera. The filmmaker strategically reverses the gender alignments of mainstream cinema, investing Pu Yi with conventionally "feminine" visual values. In Laura Mulvey's terms,[26] the emperor is represented as the bearer of meaning, not its maker, as the centered object of the viewer's gaze, and not its agent (a power paradoxically reserved for women—the imperial consorts to be precise—within the confines of the Forbidden City). While he occupies the ceremonial position of emperor, Pu Yi is often shot frontally in a centered composition that makes of him a visual icon, in apparent accordance with his divinely ordained authority, but also, ironically, in keeping with the tradition of the cinematically fetishized woman. The royal seal that he affixes to documents, and that becomes such an important part of the film's iconography, reveals the feminizing irony of one who, though he should be a maker of meaning, instead must bear it.

Since the royal seal provides the backdrop for most of the opening credits, we are alerted to its symbolic importance and are aware of its recurrence and variants throughout the film. Twice, others wield a seal for Pu Yi—once when the three-year-old emperor is forced to preside over an interminable signing ceremony, and again, near the end, when he is released from a Communist prison by the application of a seal, now of the People's Republic of China. During the two occasions when he wields the royal seal independently, invisible powers force his hand. As puppet emperor of Manchukuo, his first signatory act gives him the illusion of autonomy that literally seals his puppet's fate. The second signing is of a document authored by others, countermanding his own willed choice for foreign minister. What we realize is that the seal, which should demonstrate the way in which world-historical characters put their authoritative impress on the inchoate matter of history, has reverse relevance to Pu Yi. Like the stereotypical woman who must bear others' meaning, Pu Yi is the material on which the powerful put their stamp, be it the empress-dowager in her dynastic zeal, the Japanese colonialists in their imperial aspirations, or the Chinese Communists in their campaign for mental reformation.

We would be remiss, however, to leave out the psychoanalytic element that is so important an influence on all Bertolucci's work, as the filmmaker himself is fond of pointing out. "I've always studied my films in a psychoanalytic key," said Bertolucci in 1988. "I have been in analysis for fifteen years—I am one of those cases that Freud would call interminable analyses. Every time that I made a film, however, I suspended [the therapy] because the cinematographic setting for me is a substitute for the analytic one."[27] Critics have been quick to accept this invitation to see Bertolucci's China as a screen for the projection of the filmmaker's life-long aesthetic and psychoanalytic struggles for selfhood.[28] However, the idea that the filmmaker simply trades the couch for the director's chair is a temptation against which Bertolucci himself has warned. "Whoever has the patience to examine with attention my films will find that there is, in truth, a refusal to slide into textbook psychoanalysis."[29] In fact, what keeps Bertolucci this side of facile psychologism is his rooting in Italian political culture, according to Moravia's above-mentioned argument that "without this participation, there would have been neither the renunciation of novelized history nor the renunciation of the psychological parable of the protagonist." It would be easy to attribute Pu Yi's passivity, ineffectuality, cowardice, and indecision to his emotionally straitened past, making the film a psychological case study removed from its historical coordinates. And indeed the film offers ample material for such a reading in the womb-like, hermetically sealed world of the Forbidden City, filmed in warm reds and yellows, dominated by powerful feminized forces (consorts and eunuchs), and by the ever-available breast of his wet nurse, Mrs. Wang. In the virtual absence of male authority figures for his early years, the emperor is unable to make the oedipal break from his primal narcissistic attachment to the mother that will enable him to assume a full-fledged adult male identity.

But Bertolucci refuses to let psychology exhaust his explanation for Pu Yi's plight.[30] Robert Kolker argues that, in all his films, Bertolucci politicizes Oedipus by seeing the passage from maternal to paternal identification as one determined by exterior, historical forces.[31] It was Lacan's perception that the father's rupture of the pre-oedipal bond between self and mother propels the child into a symbolic order characterized by the law of culture, of language, of phallocentric power.[32] Althusser went on to describe this passage as the process by which each individual becomes subject to the dominant ideology. "The Oedipal complex," Althusser claims, "is the dramatic structure, the 'theatrical machine' imposed by the Law of Culture on every involuntary, conscripted candidate to humanity."[33] Thus Althusser, via Lacan, is able to make the ahistorical Freudian paradigm for individual psychological development into an explanation for human social formation. Like Althusser, Bertolucci insists on the political determinants of the oedipal drama—a drama that, in Pu Yi, is never successfully resolved. What occurs, instead, is a series of *apparent* oedipal ruptures that, however, far from placing Pu Yi in a position to identify with paternal authority so that he can some day wield it, relegates him to yet another womb-like environment of pre-oedipal stagnation.[34] In an ironic reversal of the Lacanian-Althusserian explanation for the way in which a child's oedipal passage is really a passage into history, here it is history (a constellation of power interests) that conspires continually to thwart Pu Yi's oedipal progress.

The first of his pseudo-oedipal breaks comes at age three, when, in the opening flashback of the film, the child is wrenched from his biological mother and taken to the Forbidden City.[35] The official command to "open the door" on this uterine world of warm reds suggests the birth into history that subsequent events will so vehemently deny Pu Yi. Seven years later, the child is brutally torn away from his mother surrogate, the bounteous wet nurse, Mrs. Wang, when the dowager-consorts suddenly banish the woman from court. It is significant that Bertolucci juxtaposes this important oedipal event with Pu Yi's entrance into historical awareness when he learns that his empire does not exceed the walls of the Forbidden City—that since 1911 China has been a republic. It is Pu Chieh, the emperor's brother, who brings this unwelcome piece of news—a revelation that prompts Pu Yi to climb to the roof of the Imperial Palace to see with his own eyes the reality of the events unfolding beyond his walls. Bertolucci's editorial decision to fuse these two events that are not joined by the historical record suggests his strategic intention to wed Freudian and political considerations in explaining Pu Yi's psychology.

But this rupture of the maternal bond, with its simultaneous passage into historical consciousness, is not the oedipal break it promises to be. As Pu Yi runs to catch up with the palanquin carrying Mrs. Wang, he is powerless to "open the door"—to assert his will to leave the protected confines of the Forbidden City. Nor is the tutor Johnston, who dominates the next series of flashbacks, a paternal surrogate adequate to the task of empowering Pu Yi. When Johnston instructs him that gentlemen always mean what they say, Pu Yi gives voice to a frustration that equates power with language, leadership with the authority to signify. "I'm not a gentleman," observes Pu Yi. "I'm not allowed to say what I mean. They're always telling me what to say." If we were to eliminate the class bias from this statement, substituting *man* for *gentleman,* we would arrive at the Lacanian notion of the oedipal passage into the order of self-authorizing language.

Had Bertolucci wanted to explore Johnston's ambiguous role as paternal surrogate, he could have turned to the historical record, which offers abundant evidence of the British tutor's equivocal influence on his impressionable charge. On the one hand, Johnston was behind Pu Yi's attempts to reform the governance of the Forbidden City. On the other hand, he discouraged Pu Yi from escaping to England before his marriage (at age sixteen), and it seems that he pushed his protégé into the arms of the Japanese after the 1924 expulsion from the Forbidden City. (Had Johnston intervened more forcefully with his countrymen, Pu Yi could have received sanctuary in the British, rather than the Japanese, legation.) The historical Johnston was thus a problematic father indeed, encouraging Pu Yi's best reformist impulses while keeping him beholden to infantilizing influences (Forbidden City dowager rule) and future exploitation (Japanese imperialist maneuvers).

A final, pseudo-oedipal break is precipitated by the death of Pu Yi's biological mother. The expectation that this ultimate severing of the mother/child bond will bring oedipal release is suggested by its convergence with another of the film's important themes: that of impaired vision and its correction by the spectacles that will become Pu Yi's facial trademark for the rest of his life. By juxtaposing his mother's death with Pu Yi's acquisition of glasses (after a hard-fought battle against palace tradition waged and won by Johnston), Bertolucci suggests the passage into a higher understanding that might lead to adult self-determination. But two events sabotage the process. Informed of his mother's death, Pu Yi experiences an inexpressible grief that propels him to the gate of the Forbidden City. When the guards defy his command to "open the door," he vents his rage on the little mouse he had kept hidden away in a secret pocket. Throwing it against the locked gate with all his might, Pu Yi is really destroying the autonomous self represented by the mouse—his only truly private possession and token of the impulse to psychic independence.[36] In the destruction of the mouse, a kind of suicide by proxy, Pu Yi surrenders all hope of ever "opening the door" to the adult world of power, history, and psychological autonomy.[37]

Another index of the failure of oedipal development is the initial use to which Pu Yi's glasses are put. The emperor is first allowed to wear the spectacles not to open his mind through the reading of books, nor to view Peking from the rooftop of the Imperial Palace, but to choose a bride from the photos of candidates prescreened by the dowager-consorts. As Pu Yi looks from the photos to the live faces of the surrounding ladies-in-waiting, the suggestion of a spontaneous sexual awakening is belied by the highly contrived conditions of its arousal. The engagement is timed to distract the emperor from his fantasy of escape to England, and the bride-to-be, several years older than Pu Yi, is clearly to serve as an extension of the dowager-consorts' hold over Pu Yi's private life. The marriage is thus seen as a way of containing Pu Yi's restlessness and of prolonging his sojourn in the womb-like world of the Forbidden City.

Thirteen years later, in Manchukuo, the command to "open the door" will be met by the same refusal it had encountered on so many previous occasions. This time Pu Yi tries in vain to prevent the transportation of his wife to an asylum after the Japanese have engineered the murder of her newborn bastard child. In this third failed attempt at escape, we realize that Pu Yi is doomed to live a life of pseudo-oedipal breaks in which the exit of maternal figures heralds not progress toward adult self-determination but confinement to yet another psychologically infantilizing and politically exploitative regime.

It is time to make one final return to Moravia and consider his thoughts on the twin temptations that Bertolucci's film so scrupulously avoids: those of novelized history and of facile psychologism. To indulge in either would be to "close the door" on the significance of Pu Yi's remarkable story and the history to which it bears witness. American detractors of the film, like Kael and Simon, have instead fallen for the interpretive traps built into Bertolucci's project. Misled by the spectacular style of the film to expect epic action and effectual heroes, or seduced by the film's Freudian theme into expecting entry into Pu Yi's inner-most psyche, these critics have failed to see *The Last Emperor* for what it is—an aesthetically smitten but ideologically vigilant critique of power abuses in various political guises. Far from exempting Chinese Communism from his indictment of political power establishments, Bertolucci shows how the Maoist regime, too, partakes of this univer-sal instrumentalizing tendency. Thus by filming an object lesson on the abuses of power, by refusing the easy solutions of novelized history, psy-chologism, or Communist apologetics, Bertolucci shows that he has learned the bitter truth of Pu Yi: his film will transcend the facile generic and ideological affiliations that lend to reductivist uses. "The cinema rebels from total instrumentalization, from being used as a mimeograph machine," Bertolucci had said regarding the pressure to make militant political films in the late 1960s.[38] But the same could be said of his refusal to honor the conventions of the commercial cinema in its prescriptions for the kind of heroic action and audience identifi-cation that should follow from the use of a spectacular style. Neither the Communist regime nor the one in Hollywood can claim *The Last Emperor* as its Pu Yi, to be used as a pawn of its own ideological or com-mercial agendas.

Though never explicitly mentioned in Moravia's formulation, the authority behind the novelist's appraisal of Bertolucci's film is surely Gramsci, who charged the intellectual Left with the creation of a na-tional-popular culture that would preclude any comfortable with-drawals into romanticized hero worship or psychological case studies and insist, instead, that history be held up to critical-realist scrutiny. It is Bertolucci's beautifully filmed response to the Gramscian impera-tive that requires us to locate the work in a national cinema context. Indeed, without recourse to the Italian progressive intellectual tradition that extends from Gramsci through Visconti to Bertolucci, we would have a far poorer understanding of the filmmaker's commitment to "open the door" to the world beyond the Forbidden City of easy cin-ematic spectacle.

Mediterraneo and the "Minimal Utopias"

of Gabriele Salvatores

Gabriele Salvatores' *Mediterraneo* (1991) marked the completion of the
"exodus trilogy" that began in 1989 with *Marrakech Express* and continued in 1990 with *Turné*.[1] Introduced by a quote from Henri Laborit,
"In times such as these, fleeing is the only way to remain alive and continue to dream," and ending with Salvatores' dedication of the film "to
those who are on their way to escape," *Mediterraneo* aligns itself with the
time-honored tradition of cinematic flight from the here and now.
What adds complexity and moral seriousness to this escapist impulse,
however, is Salvatores' particular choice of a temporal and geographic
"elsewhere" onto which he displaces his yearnings for an idealized national self. By setting *Mediterraneo* on a tiny island in the Greek archipelago during World War II, Salvatores stages a series of historic, cinematic, and cultural encounters that are rich with implications for a
critique of the contemporary Italy from which his film ostensibly takes
flight. The various histories invoked in *Mediterraneo*—and they range
from classical antiquity to the Risorgimento to the revolution of 1968,
in addition to the more obvious World War II chronicle of the story's
literal level—all mingle and collide to form the matrix of Italian national identity in the 1990s. Buried in *Mediterraneo* is also a history of
postwar Italian cinema, with allusions to neorealism and *commedia al-
l'italiana* that comment on the progress of the medium up until the time
of the film's release.

Judging from its opening frames, *Mediterraneo* could be just another
military action-film set in the European theater of World War II. As the
credits begin to roll against the background of a cloudless sky and a
tranquil sea, the prow of an Italian warship in perfect profile enters

screen left like a blade that neatly cuts across the horizon. A montage of shots, parading the ship's cargo of guns, smokestacks, and crew gives the impression that this is a well-equipped, smoothly run military vessel ready to face its next challenge. But the voice-over commentary of the senior officer, Lieutenant Montini, immediately suggests otherwise. Instead of the dangerous mission in the strategically important location that we expect of a military action film, Montini identifies their destination as Minghisti, "an island lost in the Aegean Sea. The smallest, the most remote. . . . Strategic importance: zero."[2] The troops, far from the superbly trained, battle-hungry heroes of the generic tradition, are the dregs of the Albanian campaign—a ragtag group of bunglers, leftovers of "lost battles" and "dismantled regiments . . . having survived by chance" (45). Two of the men (the brothers Libero and Felice Munaron) have had no maritime experience and are dreadfully seasick; another (Strazzabosco) will not abandon his pet mule; a third (Noventa) is a repeated deserter, desperate to join his pregnant wife at home. The landing on the beachhead, fraught with danger in the conventional war film, is almost totally uneventful in *Mediterraneo,* resulting only in a mistaken shoot-out whose sole casualty is a chicken and a later volley of gunfire, also mistaken, that takes the life of Strazzabosco's cherished mule.

In terms of visual style, the film makes use of several anxiety-producing techniques that dissipate once the benign nature of the island is revealed. As the soldiers first patrol the streets of the abandoned port town, a handheld camera moves in their midst, as if it were one of them, prey to the fear of sudden ambush by hidden enemy forces (fig. 10). This mobile and subjective camera, which will become such an important part of Spielberg's technique in *Saving Private Ryan,* disappears entirely once the soldiers abandon their military roles in the film's second half. Another device for visually rendering the Italians' anxiety about their mission is the gaze of surveillance cast upon them at various moments early in the film. This camera, which hides behind rocks and tries to spy on the soldiers from its position of concealment, withholds the identity of its source so that we, as spectators, are aligned with a point of view internal to the story but that is nonetheless unknown to us. Such cognitive uncertainty instills in the viewer the soldiers' own sense of angst as they seek to navigate within an alien, seemingly hostile terrain. When we eventually learn that the "owners" of the gaze of

FIGURE 10 | The rag-tag soldiers of Lt. Montini's squadron patrol the abandoned streets of a remote Greek island in *Mediterraneo*. Courtesy of Penta Film.

surveillance are children and a shepherd girl, the gap between our initial paranoia and our subsequent relief becomes a measure of the distance between the conventional military action film and Salvatores' parodic rewriting of it. In fact, once the soldiers walk through a wall of sheets hanging out to dry and enter a bustling piazza that they thought to be deserted, Salvatores' film leaves behind any vestiges of wartime paranoia and enters definitively into the realm of commedia all'italiana.[3] Significantly, the sheets that mark the dividing line between the illusion of emptiness and the reality of bustling village life are reminiscent of the curtains separating audience from stage. The theatrical metaphor thus invoked has double reference—both to the histrionic way in which the Greeks and Italians will henceforth perform their cultural identities for each other and to the commedia all'italiana tradition with which *Mediterraneo* is so closely aligned.

It could indeed be argued that *Mediterraneo* celebrates its own decline from the conventions of the military action film. Such deviation from generic precedent is paralleled, within the film, by the characters' own relaxation of military discipline. Throughout *Mediterraneo*, the response to Sergeant Lorusso's attempts to assert his authority meet with the dismissive *"ma va a cagare"* (go take a crap). Passwords are routinely forgotten, guard duty is given up for the pleasures of hashish, and the Italian flag proudly set on the island's ancient fortress gradually turns to tatters. Most indicative of their lapse of discipline is the appearance of the soldiers themselves. The Munaron brothers lose no time in stripping down to their underwear, while the others are more gradual in shedding their uniforms. Farina and Montini place white cloths under their hats to resemble members of the Foreign Legion fending off the desert sun, Lorusso, Colasanti, and Strazzabosco don the island garb of gray vests and ballooning trousers as they learn to dance, and all the men turn a deep brown as they play soccer, bare-chested on the scorching beach. So total is their sartorial and physical assimilation into the island populace that when the native male inhabitants return from the war, the Italians look more Greek than their homecoming rivals (fig. 11).

Like the character Lance in *Apocalypse Now,* whose drug-induced adaptability leads him to divest himself of all military trappings and take on the face paint and jungle garb of the Cambodian tribesmen, the Italians "go native" with an ease that belies the myth of cultural superiority on which wars are based. An even more shocking measure of the Italians' regression during their stay on the island is the appearance of the British naval officers who will escort them across the sea toward the end of the film. Pale-skinned, dressed in immaculate white, with pristine knee socks and perfectly pressed summer uniforms, the officers seem to hail from another planet. The fact that the British and Italians are now allies does little to counteract the impression that the marooned men are being taken into custody by an authority that is hostile to their own best interests.

Another index of decline from the norms of the action film is the radio, both instrument and symbol of their link with the outside world. Destroyed by Strazzabosco in retaliation for the accidental shooting of his beloved pet, the radio becomes victim of a mule driver's passion. This incident presents, in embryonic form, everything that will happen in *Mediterraneo,* as the war of twentieth-century Western powers, technologically equipped, gives way to the atavistic impulses lying just below the surface of the modern world. Significantly, the damaged radio is not discarded but is simply set aside. Electronically disabled, the device makes itself useful as a chicken roost and repository for chicken

FIGURE 11 | Dressed in native garb, the Italian soldiers soon become indistinguishable from the local population of the island in *Mediterraneo*. Courtesy of Penta Film.

droppings. Similarly, Colasanti, the platoon's former radio operator, has found a new role as company cook, satisfying the men's primary appetite for nourishment rather than their secondary hunger for military intelligence.

Perhaps the most important measure of slippage from the conventions of wartime engagement is the change undergone by Lorusso. Of all the members of the platoon, the sergeant had been the most devoted to the warrior ideal. Unlike the other soldiers, who were either drafted (Montini, the Munaron brothers, Strazzabosco, Farina) or ready to desert at the slightest excuse (Noventa), Lorusso was a career man whose experiences in Africa and Spain read as a minihistory of Fascist military adventurism in the 1930s. Like Manganiello in *The Conformist* (1970), Lorusso is ready to flaunt his previous service to buttress his authority among the troops, but unlike Bertolucci's career military man, Salvatores' conjures up past experiences to absolutely no effect. "I remember in Africa . . . a group of soldiers decides to sleep in the [native] huts. . . . The next day all we found were their bones" (51). Obviously, Mussolini's colonialist campaigns have done little to prepare Lorusso for the generous welcome that the island populace would soon extend to this Italian occupying force.

Not surprisingly, it is Lorusso who gives voice to the frustration of being excluded from the war effort when the radio is destroyed. "Don't you understand that now we're isolated, cut off? How will we manage now? With smoke signals, like the Indians?" (62). In his allusion to Native Americans, Lorusso offers a displaced version of what will happen to his own platoon as it adapts to the conditions of a pretechnological world. Similarly, the enforced idleness of the island retreat elicits numerous protestations of restlessness on Lorusso's part. "This isn't what I call war. . . . We're sitting around all day scratching our balls, while our men are busting their butts in Russia. . . . Colasanti, would you rather be here or in the midst of battle?" (74). It is significant, and perhaps prophetic of Lorusso's eventual withdrawal from activism, that his fantasy of military glory focuses not on the scene of combat but on that of its euphoric aftermath: "Women, vodka, caviar. . . . Christ, I should have asked to be stationed in Russia" (74). What Lorusso will eventually learn is that by a simple substitution of ouzo and olives for vodka and caviar, the wish-fulfillment fantasy of the spoils of war can be had without going to war at all.

The turning point for Lorusso is the consciousness-altering encounter with the Turkish sailor Aziz. Within the space of one evening, Lorusso shifts from a position of military interventionism to one of noncompliance. Assuming that anyone hailing from beyond the island must be the bearer of world-historical information, Lorusso assaults Aziz with enthusiastic importunings. "And the war? . . . Hitler, Mussolini! The English! War!" (90). Worse than Aziz's ignorance is his indifference—an indifference that spurs Lorusso's next access of military zeal. He suggests that the troops confiscate Aziz's boat and sail for Rhodes, Crete, and beyond to join the front lines. "Here we are, isolated for I don't know how long, in a godforsaken place, and we know nothing of what is going on. We're Italians after all, right? We're soldiers. What are we doing here?" (90). For Lorusso, national identity is tantamount to Fascist military action on the stage of the European theater.

Three years on the island, however, have a significant impact on Lorusso's allegiances. When an Italian aviator lands on the beach to refuel his plane and the marooned soldiers learn of Italy's armistice with the Allies, Lorusso's enthusiasm takes a very different turn. Now there is a fresh call to arms, the call to *rifare l'Italia* (remake Italy) in the wake of the Allied Liberation, and it is this that captures Lorusso's fancy and allows him imaginatively to rechannel all his activist energies in the service of national renewal. "Is it right that we stay here, outside of the world, while down there everything is changing? The country is to be remade . . . beginning from scratch!" (115–16). Lorusso's indiscriminate desire for agency—his willingness to heed the call to national revival, be it through Fascist or progressive ideological means—makes his final disengagement from history that much more momentous. "Things weren't so great in Italy," he explains, at the end of the film, to Montini of his decision to leave Italy forever. "They didn't let us change anything. So I said, 'You won. But at least you won't succeed in considering us your accomplices.'"[4]

With the exception of Lorusso's outbursts, only one other character mentions Fascism, and he does so jokingly, in passing.[5] The film's reticence on the subject has led critics to label *Mediterraneo* antiideological, as a flight from the sociopolitical tensions that characterized postwar Italian culture through the 1970s.[6] Such a reading, however, overlooks Salvatores' quest for alternative bases of Italian patriotism—

a quest that reaches beyond Fascism to other possible precedents for the establishment of a national-popular identity. Of course, the most obvious place to look for such an alternative is the Risorgimento, conjured up in the very name of the Italian warship bound for Greece in the film's opening frames—the *Garibaldi*. The allusion to the general who embodied the Risorgimento's revolutionary ideals sets up a heroic history of democratic origins as the implied alternative to the Fascist mythology of imperial conquest on which Mussolini founded his regime. The Risorgimento is again invoked in the code words that will identify squad members to each other as they stand sentinel in the night. The slogan *Savoia o morte* (Savoy or death) serves as their password, and *Regina Margherita* as the required reply. Again, we see that nineteenth-century unification history has become the privileged vehicle for Italians to announce their status as compatriots—not *Giovinezza, Folgore,* or other such Fascist coinages.

But Risorgimento hagiography is hardly immune to the demystifying operations of *Mediterraneo.* The heroic voyage of the One Thousand in 1860 finds no counterpart in the ill-fated expedition of the warship *Garibaldi* in 1941. The members of Montini's squad, far from resembling the high-minded visionaries of Garibaldi's brigade, are motivated by the sole desire to "save their skin" (48). All that remains of the ship after the British attack on it is the life preserver bearing the name *Garibaldi,* now signifier of a double absence. Not only does the ship that it names no longer exist, neither does the comparison with its victorious Risorgimento precedent. The passwords that made of the Risorgimento a shibboleth for Italian self-identification suffer a similar process of demystification. Lorusso takes an embarrassingly long time to remember the formula *Savoia o morte,* and the rest of the troops go through a list of several options (two of them of Fascist provenance) before stumbling upon the name of the Savoy queen in response.

But perhaps the most devastating blow to Risorgimento hagiography occurs near the end of the film, as Strazzabosco prepares to leave the island with his new donkey, appositely named Garibaldi. With this allusion, the film's Risorgimento subtext comes full circle: the ill-fated Italian warship that brought the soldiers and their technologically driven war to the island is replaced by this ancient and docile beast of burden. The journey of Italian history, Salvatores is telling us, is not the heroic voyage of revolutionary progress embodied by the One Thousand, nor the maritime mission of imperial conquest resurrected by Mussolini, but the slow trek of a donkey along the bucolic paths of the primordial Mediterranean basin.

In the film's progression of Garibaldis, the patriotic love poem scribbled on the walls of the soldiers' first barracks gains new parodic significance. "Italy, by day I think of you, by night I dream of you" (65), writes the anonymous *graffitatore,* invoking the venerable literary tradition of the idealized nation-state as the unattainable object of desire. Personified as the virtuous queen or the wholesome peasant who has fallen from her former position of innocence and prestige, Italy has long been figured as an absence, as a sign of lost perfection in the poetic tradition extending from Dante to Petrarch to Machiavelli and Leopardi.[7] Given Strazzabosco's love for his first mule, his grief at her slaying, and his displacement of this passion onto the new animal, Garibaldi, Salvatores parodies the love-longing traditionally associated with the personified body politic of Italian literary tradition.

In their vain quest for national self-definition—one that finds fulfillment neither in Lorusso's Fascist militancy nor in the return to a Risorgimento myth of *patria*—the soldiers learn to reach beyond *Italianità* to embrace a corporate identity that is inclusive and originary, transcending spatial and temporal bounds. The slogan "Italians, Greeks, one face, one race" becomes the film's ideological refrain, uttered strategically throughout *Mediterraneo* to dissolve the geopolitical distinctions between occupiers and occupied, military and civilian, male dominators and female subjects, foreigners and natives, mainlanders and islanders. First voiced by the local priest in welcoming the Italians into the island community, the slogan is repeated, with a slight variation ("Turks" replaces "Greeks"), by the hashish-dispensing sailor who strips the soldiers of all their belongings, including their weapons. Despite the ulterior motives for the Turk's profession of brotherhood, the results of the theft are effectively to demilitarize the soldiers, and hence to ease their assimilation into island life.

It is Lieutenant Montini, in dialogue with his protégé Farina, who first formulates this pan-Mediterranean identity. "Everything was born here," the classically educated lieutenant tells the young man. "Everything that we are descends from here. Even you, in your chromosomes, in your blood, descend from this sea, from this land" (69-70).[8] The Mediterranean is thus figured as a biological inheritance, a kind of genetic imprinting that the soldiers are invited to decode in the recognition of a common ethnic source. With Salvatores' rejection of nationalism and his proposal of a pan-Mediterranean model for corporate identity, the film ushers in a number of alternative myths of origin. Enzo Monteleone, the scriptwriter of the film, is eloquent in this regard: "When was that emotion born that led me to write *Mediterraneo?* I would say at school, when I read fragments of Greek lyrics, and again during a very long summer spent on the Greek islands: rocks cracked by the sun, blue sea, wind that confounds thought, *retzina* and *souvlaki, karpouzi* and *parakalò,* ancient legends" (7).

Filtered through the Italian collective imagination, a twofold image of Greece emerges: that of the high-school textbook and that of the tourist brochure. It is the character of Montini who brings together both of these facets in the film. A classics teacher before the war, steeped in Greek antiquity but never affluent enough to take the vacation that would enable him to visit the sites of his studies, Montini experiences the immediate sensuous delights of the island paradise, while mindful of its cultural history. "Here, more than 2,500 years ago, before Rome, before everything, the most beautiful civilization in the world was born. There were poets, warriors, artists, divinities" (69), he rhapsodizes. It is Montini's relationship with Farina that doubles and externalizes the process of cultural connoisseurship that Monteleone describes as the inspiration for the film. Farina plays the naive but willing pupil to Montini's *professore,* eagerly receiving and assimilating his mentor's knowledge of the ancient Greek lyric tradition. It is Farina, then, who carries this literary leitmotif throughout the film as he reads translations from the Greek poets in the night, quotes lines of poetry to Vassilissa, the prostitute of whom he is enamored, and obviously incorporates the wisdom of the ancients into his own concept of redemptive love for the fallen woman.

Other characters in the film, though not so erudite as the Montini-Farini team but nonetheless products of a popular culture tinged with respect for the classics, are also alive to the antiquity of the place. The two Munaron brothers, who finally learn to swim, become convinced that their aquatically adept shepherdess is a mermaid (101). Strazzabosco, who has made a pair of wings out of chicken feathers, likes to ride around the island interior astride his mule like a homemade Pegasus and Bellerophon (97). In an attempt to fill the ample leisure of their island sojourn and boost group morale, Lorusso organizes a series of Olympic games (67).[9] Most indicative of the Italian popular attitude toward antiquity is Lorusso's reaction when he learns that homosexual inclinations did not keep Alexander the Great from being a formidable warrior. "Yes, OK, but you're talking about the ancient Greeks, from decades and decades ago" (66). Like homophobia itself, which betrays considerable fear of what is all-too-close an impulse, antiquity is perceived by Lorusso to be both impossibly remote yet only a few years away.

Mediterraneo's focus on historical linkages, which both acknowledge and transcend periodization, has important consequences for the generational concerns of the 1990s. Salvatores, like Moretti, has been labeled a spokesman for the collective experience of post-1968 disillusionment and the resulting withdrawal from the sphere of political action. By returning to the subject of World War II, however, the film builds a bridge between the 1990s generation and its predecessor, between the fathers who were shattered by their military ordeal and the sons who, mutatis mutandis, endured the disappointments of the '68 revolution. As Monteleone put it, *Mediterraneo* was written to "weld the generation of our fathers with mine in a story of travel and displacement, of illusions and frustrations, of love and friendship" (8); or in the words of Roberto Silvestri, "*Mediterraneo* is the first film that relates the dreams of our fathers' generation with those of the '68ers."[10]

This generational impulse may indeed be responsible for some of the film's egregious anachronisms—anachronisms that lead the men to speak and act in distinctly familiar "postwar" ways. The squadron seems to handle the hashish pipe with an expertise that belies their status as novitiates in the culture of drugs. Strazzabosco admonishes Noventa to live for the moment in a language strongly redolent of the '70s and '80s New Age. "Are you still thinking about home? You have to be more Zen. . . . More detachment . . . and at the same time, more abandonment to the present. . . . Detachment and abandonment . . . follow the rhythms of your breathing" (91).[11] In a passage much noted by critics, Lorusso cites Mao when he tries to persuade Farina to come out of hiding and return with his cohort to Italy. "Great confusion under the sky. The situation is excellent" (119).[12]

Mediterraneo's generational focus is not without film-historical implications. In returning to World War II, the privileged subject matter of neorealism, *Mediterraneo* foregrounds its relationship to its cinematic fathers. *Paisan,* the canonical treatment of the interactions between a civilian populace and an invading army, immediately comes to mind. In fact, most of the encounters between American liberation troops and native Italians that make up the six episodes of *Paisan* are parodically rewritten in *Mediterraneo.* Thus, Carmela's generosity toward Joe from Jersey in the lookout tower on the Sicilian coast of *Paisan* is spoofed by the shepherd girl's ministrations to the needs of the Munaron brothers serving as lookouts on the island of Mighisti. The sleeping black MP whose boots are stolen by the scugnizzo Pasquale in the Neapolitan episode of *Paisan* finds his counterpart in Farina, who is tickled by a group of children as he takes a nap. The failure of GI Fred to redeem the prostitute Francesca in *Paisan's* Roman episode is corrected by Farina's deliverance of Vassilissa from her sexually fallen state. Lieutenant Montini's camaraderie with the Greek Orthodox priest recalls the bond forged between the U.S. army chaplain Martin and the leader of the Franciscan monastery of *Paisan.* Finally, the OSS-partisan withdrawal from the Po Valley under the conquering Germans is paralleled by the withdrawal of the Italians from Mighisti escorted by the victorious British naval officers. Though the similarities between *Paisan* and *Mediterraneo* may be purely coincidental, owing to their dependence on the commonplaces of invasion narratives, the parodic relationship of the latter film to the former one reveals the distance between 1946 and the 1990s, between a testimonial view of history and a comically recycled one.

Mediterraneo cites not only *Paisan* but a series of subsequent films that seek to reconfront World War II and its neorealist representations. Manuela Gieri includes Scola's *We All Loved Each Other So Much* (1974) and Monicelli's *The Great War* (1959) along with *Paisan* in the list of films that mediated Salvatores' vision of the war.[13] To this genealogy, I would add the Taviani brothers' *Night of the Shooting Stars* (1982), which frames its narration as a fairy tale and portrays the Liberation as the fulfillment of individual as well as collective wish-fulfillment fantasies.[14] *Mediterraneo,* in fact, contains its own night of the shooting stars, for it is a meteorite shower that prompts Lorusso to voice the collective desire to "remake the country" (116);[15] meanwhile, Colasanti reveals a far more personal and transgressive wish—to make love to Lorusso. In another hilariously parodic moment, Strazzabosco's star-crossed love of mules is requited by the sound of braying and the apparition of "a magnificent white donkey. The animal seems to be awaiting only him" (80). All the elements of the scene—the moonlit night, the empty piazza, the beckoning voice—play on the audience's conventional expectations of romance. For the homesick Strazzabosco, bereft of his only link to the life he led as a mule driver before the war, the appearance of this creature is indeed a dream come true.

Noventa, even more homesick than Strazzabosco, desires nothing other than a lift back to Italy. Desperate to reach his pregnant wife, Noventa is the only member of the squad unable (because unwilling) to assimilate to island life. Pacing the deck of the *Garibaldi* at the start of the film, Noventa is described in voice-over as having tried and failed innumerable times to desert the front. What happens to him in *Mediterraneo* will simply be an extension of this futile and open-ended series of attempts at escape. Like a cartoon character, he pops up wherever a mode of transportation presents itself. Whether it be the boat of Aziz or the plane of the Italian aviator, Noventa's attempts to stow away are always discovered and thwarted. But as magically as the "magnificent white donkey" materialized out of nowhere to fulfill Strazzabosco's fondest desires, so a rowboat arbitrarily appears out of a grotto to take Noventa home.

The Munaron brothers Libero and Felice find their paradise early in the film. Delighted to be stationed on a rocky peak overlooking the harbor, the mountaineer brothers feel so at home that they request permanent assignment to this outpost. To add to the pleasures of their idyllic retreat, a beautiful and willing shepherd girl soon joins their company, happy to distribute her sexual favors equally between the siblings. In the Munaron brothers' subplot, the film reminds us that the pastoral genre indeed originated in Greece and is perfectly suited to Salvatores' argument for the existence of a pan-Mediterranean identity.

In aesthetic terms, the most consequential wish-fulfillment fantasy is that of Lieutenant Montini. Immediately established as the film's focalizer by virtue of the voice-over narration, Montini becomes the squadron's designated reader and writer of history. His knowledge of languages enables him to translate (and sometimes censor) the messages that greet them on the island: a graffiti inscription ominously announcing *Ellàs iné ò tàfos ton Itàllon* (Greece is the tomb of the Italians) (49) and an English-language radio broadcast boasting of the British incursions into the area. Montini is not only the interpreter of the texts that the squadron encounters but also the producer of his own text in the form of a military diary whose daily entries maintain the pretense of discipline and purpose. It is Lorusso who finally exposes the futility of such a chronicle in the total absence of "signifieds" to which a military diary should refer. "What are you writing . . . if nothing is happening?" (66).

By midfilm, Montini gives up the activity of writing altogether, and with it the implied notions of linear time, progress, and eventfulness that historical chronicle is supposed to record. Instead he becomes a painter, a creator of fixed images that remove their referents from the flow of time and freeze them in the still and solemn spaces of eternity. Montini's conversion from writing to painting is nowhere more evident than in his phantasmagoric encounter with Homer, who is supposedly buried on the island of Mighisti. In a scene unfortunately cut from the final version of the film, Montini sets off on a pilgrimage to find the tomb of the bard, but he underestimates the length of the journey and the blistering heat of the sun. Felled by dehydration, the lieutenant hallucinates a meeting with the poet. This Homer takes on the stern lineaments of high-school textbook illustrations and poses a riddle so trivial ("the ones that you find, you throw away, the ones that you don't find, you take with you") that the answer ("lice") momentarily eludes him (96).

Though Homer is edited from the film's final cut, he is reinstated in a line of dialogue that highlights Montini's conversion from written to visual means of representation. Montini, enthusiastic about portraiture, chooses to paint an old man because of his resemblance to Homer. In the screenplay's corresponding scene, Greece emerges as the fulfillment of the painter's search for chromatic perfection. "Someone wrote 'somewhere between Calabria and Turkey, true blue begins,'" observes Montini. "I believe that place is here" (81). Greece thus becomes the painter's Shangri La, the dream-come-true of the Mediterranean artist in search of the perfect palette.

It is significant that Montini is asked to restore the frescoes in the local church, and he does so by grafting likenesses of Lorusso, Strazzabosco, Noventa, and the Munaron brothers onto the bodies of the saints and angels of the ruined paintings. Adapting the soldiers' contemporary faces to the hieratic Byzantine style of the Greek orthodox icons, Montini endows his portraits with an otherworldly dignity and fixity that rescues them from the contingencies of time. When Montini returns to the island in the 1990s, at the end of the film, his first stop is the village church to behold the frescoes he had painted almost fifty years earlier. The frescoes take the place of a flashback, and they make of these memories a sacred history, both at the level of event and at the level of cinematic representation.

The meta-cinematic implications of this scene are not far to seek. What the frescoes are for Montini, neorealism is to the contemporary viewing public. Neorealist films provide the images by which World War II will be remembered and, like the portraits of Montini's men, consigned to the realm of eternity. Neorealism itself has become a sacred icon, lifted above the flow of history whose progress it was supposed to redeem. To counteract this embalming of neorealism, this relegation of it to the archives, Salvatores has launched his own military operation in *Mediterraneo*—not of search-and-destroy but of identify-and-demystify through playful and affectionate revival. No genre is better suited for this operation than the commedia all'italiana, whose familiarity to Italian audiences, whose penchant for social critique, and whose ultimate faith in community, according to Northrop Frye's canonical definition of comedy,[16] makes it the ideal vehicle for Salvatores' attempt to rewrite World War II history for the 1990s.

Of all the characters' wish-fulfillment fantasies, it is Farina's that has the most consequences for the film as a whole. Without roots in Italy ("Are you married, Farina?" asks Montini. "No." "Are you engaged?" "No." "Does someone await you at home?" "I am nobody's son") (69), Farina is a tabula rasa, an identikit waiting to be filled in. It is Farina who is most receptive to the high cultural influences of Greek civilization as they speak to him through the snippets of ancient lyrics that shape his concept of romantic love. It is Farina who does not leave the island and who draws back, like a magnet, Lorusso and Montini at the end of the film. Most importantly, it is Farina who enacts with Vassilissa a drama of mutual redemption, as she vindicates his masculinity and he, in turn, rescues her from a life of sexual commerce. In allegorical terms, the fallen body politic personified by Vassilissa is saved by the virtues of loyalty, purity, and idealism incarnated in Farina.

This conventional narrative structure, with its metaphoric implications for the nation-state to which it refers, has been seen elsewhere in postwar Italian cinema, most notably in Scola's *We All Loved Each Other So Much.* There, Luciana's fallen body, sequentially loved and left by men representing various facets of the Italian geopolitical spectrum, was rescued by marriage to the Communist activist Antonio, signifying Italy's collective redemption under the aegis of the Left.[17] Vassilissa's deliverance through marriage occurs, instead, in a world outside history, in a utopia understood in the etymological sense of *ou* (no) *topos* (place). The body politic can be redeemed only in the imagination, Salvatores is telling us—outside history, beyond national boundaries, in a utopian space somewhere in the Mediterranean of the mind.

Significantly, one of the titles considered for Salvatores' film was *Lasciamoci perdere,*[18] which brings into play the literal meaning (Let's let ourselves get lost) as well as the idiomatic one (Leave us alone). The pun offers a double perspective on the impetus to flight—to escape societal constraints (to be left alone) through physical displacement (to be geographically lost). What the film's actual title does, instead, is to shift attention from the negativity of the escapist drive to its "photographic positive" in the utopian dream. *Mediterraneo,* then, is not about absence or rejection so much as about utopian reinvention, the projection of an idealized body politic onto the screen of a primal, transnational collective identity. In etymological terms, it is the *middleness* of the *terrain* conjured up in the title *Mediterraneo* that suggests this universalizing intent.

Accordingly, the film abounds in small, utopian moments, the *"utopie minime, ma decorose"* (minimal, but decorous, utopias) that pervade Salvatores' entire filmography.[19] There is the soccer game on the beach, the nonproprietary sharing of the same lust object, the dance with the native populace. It would be no exaggeration to argue that the protagonist of *Mediterraneo* is the collectivity, and that its thematic appeal is to the values of friendship, collaboration, teamwork, the *impegno di gruppo* (group commitment) so woefully lacking in the decade of the 1980s. "In a fragmented society that elevates egoism and social climbing to the highest level," writes Riccardo Monni, "*Marrakech Express, Turné,* and *Mediterraneo* teach the importance of the team, the value of roles."[20]

Salvatores' communitarian message is doubled and tripled in *Mediterraneo* by the conditions of production and reception that make of it a *mise-en-abyme,* a reenactment in the film's making, its diegesis, and its reception, of the collective ideal it espouses. From the very start of his career, Salvatores has worked with the same stable of actors and crew, "for reasons of security, of clan, of family, of tribe."[21] This collaboration, built up over a period of five years and four films, became intensified under the specific material conditions of shooting *Mediterraneo*—conditions that paralleled those of the experience being represented within the story itself. "In effect, what Salvatores has foregrounded is the group experience alone," writes Lorenzo Pellizzari, "where the reality of the set (working for weeks in remote and unknown localities, living out interpersonal tensions, confronting some environmental discomforts) cannot but favor, if not 'reality,' at least a certain verisimilitude of the fiction."[22]

The collaborative ideals put into practice in the making of *Mediterraneo* and enshrined in its narration find their ultimate meaning in the link that Salvatores seeks to forge with the viewing public. Conceived in a contemporary context of profound disillusionment, the film proposes a vision with which a 1990s audience could easily identify. Riccardo Monni's analysis of the film's success speaks to this connection. "Perhaps inadvertently, they gave the Oscar to friendship. Or perhaps to that way of being together . . . that belongs to the private lives of Gabriele Salvatores, Diego Abatantuono, Giuseppe Cederna, etc. But it is the same recipe for survival as that of thousands and thousands of nostalgic one-time thirty-year-olds. Having many things in common with the spectators is one of the causes of the success of Salvatores' cinema, at least in Italy."[23]

What better antidote to the fragmentation and solipsism of contemporary Italian life than to set up a specular relationship between the tight-knit community onscreen and the viewing public, to trigger mechanisms of identification so powerful that the spectators will internalize the utopian wish? In this way, *Mediterraneo* does not so much parody as promote the communicative impulse of *Paisan,* whose breakthrough moments of understanding between Americans and Italians, blacks and whites, men and women, adults and children offered brief intimations of a better world. By recasting *Paisan*'s narrative in a comedic vein, *Mediterraneo* puts genre to the service of this utopian creed. If classic comic structure involves "an act of communion with the audience" and aspires "to include as many people as possible in its final society," as in to Northrop Frye's formulation,[24] then Salvatores' rewriting of *Paisan* in commedia all'italiana terms is a way of building Rossellini's message into the generic structure of the 1990s film. Salvatores' *utopie* may be *minime,* but they nonetheless serve to keep alive the dream of an "Italy to remake" that history has been so reluctant to fulfill.

5

From Salazar's Lisbon to Mussolini's Rome by Way of France in Roberto Faenza's *Pereira Declares*

"We live in an epoch where everything is present, contemporary, consumed in real time," wrote Roberto Faenza in the introduction to the screenplay of *Pereira Declares*. "We've lost the dimension of turning back. Of rethinking, or reelaborating. The cinema, instead, has this great capacity: it displaces the past into the present, it gives [the past] a second life, far from contingency and current events."[1] Faenza's comment is rich with implications for an analysis of his 1995 rendering of Antonio Tabucchi's eponymous novel, for it links the temporal displacement of the story's meaning with the doctrine of resurrection that preoccupies Pereira. "I believe in the soul and in its resurrection . . . but not in that of the flesh" (22), Pereira insists in his various encounters with the priest Don Antonio, the Jewish refugee Inge Delgado, and the political activist Monteiro Rossi. The protagonist's obsession with rebirth into eternal life, in spirit if not in body, then, has as its counterpart the filmmaker's commitment to represent history, to give it a new life in a medium whose power critically to revive the past serves to challenge the superficiality of our televisual age. "I like the idea of having realized a film so remote from current events and yet so close to our time," wrote Faenza. "In the epoch in which the dominance of television enmeshes us in a world apparently real and instead ever more virtual, the reemergence of the past can serve to rediscover the sense of the present" (16).

Not only does *Pereira Declares* ask us to update its concerns, it also invites a significant geographic shift within the story's own historical period, from Portugal to Italy, from Salazar's Lisbon to Mussolini's Rome. Italy is directly invoked a number of times in the story: Manuel, the informative waiter of the Café Orquídea, confides to Pereira and Dr. Cardoso that Mussolini has sent submarines to support Franco; Pereira tells his friend Professor Silva that, in Germany and Italy, fanatics want to foment war; and Monteiro Rossi, the agent of Pereira's own political conversion, is half Italian. The young man's genealogy serves both to temper the otherwise categorically Fascist image of Italy that emerges from the story and to motivate the scene that reveals the close cultural kinship between Portugal and the land of Rossi's fathers. I speak of the Salazarist celebration where Monteiro Rossi sings "O sole mio" to a non-Italian, but nonetheless enthusiastic, group of listeners. To the novel's somewhat perfunctory account of Monteiro Rossi's performance, Faenza's film adds a telling detail. The young man begins the song well but flounders when several lines in. While he struggles to recover his composure, the audience comes to his rescue, joining in chorus to supply the missing words in a way that reveals their prior knowledge of the song and their possession of a popular lore that binds southern Europe into a cultural whole.

More important than these direct references to Italy are the implied parallels between Portuguese and Italian nationalism. These latent correspondences make *Pereira Declares* an extended metaphor—a conceit whose literal level points constantly beyond itself to a geographic referent twenty-two degrees of longitude to the east. The critique of Salazarist authoritarianism thus becomes a critique of Italian Fascism by implication, so that the entire strategy of *Pereira Declares* may be seen as one of indictment or condemnation by allusion.

The process of interpretive displacement by which both novel and film achieve their full political meaning is set in motion by Pereira himself within the confines of his story. As editor of the cultural page of the newspaper *Lisboa,* Pereira has chosen to translate a series of French authors whose views enable him, obliquely, to register his own opposition to the regime. Balzac's narrative *Honorine* focuses on the need for repentance—a need that Pereira, as spokesman for an intellectual class whose detachment from politics amounted to tacit consent to the status quo, himself feels. More damaging, though still indirect, is the critique implied by Pereira's choice to translate and publish Alphonse Daudet's "La dernière classe." This nineteenth-century story of French patriotism at the end of the Franco-Prussian War is read as an outcry

against the twentieth-century German aspiration to European dominance. "But as I recall," says Dr. Cardoso in reaction to Pereira's translation plans, "it ends with a hymn to France against Germany. . . . I'm
not at all sure that today, here at home, this story will be appreciated"
(78). In the temporal and spatial markers, "today, here at home," Cardoso makes explicit the interpretive leap from 1871 to 1938, from Al-
sace to Portugal, that will trigger the mechanisms of censorship.

What Cardoso's fears reveal is the way in which all signifiers in an
authoritarian state must be read in relation to a single, politically
charged signified. The slogan that concludes the propaganda film *Revolução,* "Everything for the nation, nothing against the nation" (94), may
be read as the interpretive key to all authoritarian sign systems. Censorship, then, may be construed as a monomaniacal and paranoid form
of exegesis that considers all narratives as political allegories, to be read
in strict either/or fashion, for or against the wielders of power. No story
can be seen as innocent of political reference—all narratives are suspect
until proven "patriotically correct." Tabucchi's (and Faenza's) strategy
of condemnation by allusion, of displaced indictment, whereby Salazar's
Portugal becomes a conceit for Mussolini's Italy, may be seen as a parallel practice of allegorical interpretation, but one that undoes the effect
of authoritarian censorship and restores the subversive force of Pereira's
own journalistic activities.

If I am right in assuming that Italy is the true referent of *Pereira Declares,* then the brunt of Tabucchi's and Faenza's critique is the Italian
intellectuals' refusal of political engagement in keeping with Croce's
claims for the neutrality of culture. *Pereira Declares* chronicles the protagonist's own gradual rejection of Croce's distinction between the cultural and the political in performing his duties as editor for the *Lisboa.*
In the context of his own thirty-year career as a reporter who has been
promoted to the editorship of the cultural page, Pereira believes that he
has now reached a level of pure literary activity that transcends the un-
couth world of "the news." Furthermore, Pereira's belief that the *Lisboa* is "a free and independent newspaper" (78) reinforces his illusion of
disinterested intellectual pursuit. The actual physical separation of his
office from the rest of the newspaper—though it means consignment
to shabby quarters with woefully inadequate ventilation—is yet further
proof that this is an outpost of intellectual serenity and detachment

from the messiness of the news. What Pereira learns, instead, when his translation of Daudet incurs the wrath of his boss, is that the cultural cannot be divorced from the political, and that the intellectual's pretense of neutrality is really a form of denial of, if not outright capitulation to, the status quo.

Pereira's friend Silva, professor of literature at the University of Coimbra, removes any shred of dignity or credibility from the intellectual's position of political detachment. A hedonist ("at our age, if one has a modicum of intelligence, he would do well to enjoy life" [48]), cynic ("it's enough not to take things seriously" [49]), and coward ("I'd flunk him anyway," he says, a propos a student who condemns D'Annunzio as a warmonger and succeeds in proving his argument [50]), it is Silva who gives explicit formulation to the intellectual's withdrawal from a position of ideological engagement. "Why should we give a damn about D'Annunzio or politics? Enjoy life!" (50). Although at an early stage of his own political awakening, Pereira is so disturbed by his friend's cynicism that he hastens to leave his vacation retreat and return to the scene of political struggle.

Just as French literature had supplied Pereira with the means for his critique-by-displacement, so will France supply models for his own new-found role as a politically committed intellectual. The twin examples of François Mauriac, who sides with the Basques against Franco, and Georges Bernanos, who denounces the Vatican for its failure to condemn Spanish repression, provide powerful precedents for Pereira's own forging of an activist intellectual identity. Culture thus is seen as causal, as the decisive factor in Pereira's conversion to political engagement, for it is his very inclination toward French literature that leads him to Daudet and Balzac as vehicles for his own indirect attack on the regime, and then to Mauriac and Bernanos as models for open and direct opposition.

Pereira's newly politicized view of his role as an intellectual owes as much to Italy as to France, however. It is to Antonio Gramsci that Tabucchi and Faenza obviously owe a considerable debt in their thinking about the relationship between culture and power. Gramsci's notion of the organic intellectual, one who bridges the gap between the cultural elite of a given society and the popular masses, becomes central to all postwar Italian leftist theorizing on art. Very much related to the role of the organic intellectual is the concept of the national-popular—a cultural category that emerged out of Gramsci's study of nineteenth-century French literature and the *feuilleton* tradition.[2] France, then, becomes the mediating term between Pereira and Gramsci, between a journalistic practice of political engagement and its theoretical justification.

In its effort to reconcile the dichotomy between the cultural and the political, *Pereira Declares* focuses on a series of other, closely related binary oppositions. Pereira's anxiety about resurrection—his reluctance to have his unwieldy body encumber his soul in the afterlife—brings into play the dualities of spirit and flesh, consciousness and matter. As an alternative to the Christian/moral formulation of the mind/body split, Dr. Cardoso offers a scientific, neo-Freudian approach. When Pereira objects to being questioned about his dream life, Cardoso explains, "Your psyche is related to your body" (72). The burdensomeness of Pereira's mortal coil, weighted down by his advanced years and excess kilos, along with his solitude and morbid attachment to the memory of his deceased wife, leads him to obsessive thoughts of death, both his own and those of his intellectual cohorts, who exist for him simply as potential obituaries to be published in the *Lisboa*. Culture, for the prepoliticized Pereira, can exist only in the realm of the already said— it is by definition posthumous and embalmed, incapable of intervening in the current course of events. When Don Antonio mentions the activist example of Mauriac, Pereira's way of showing his admiration for the French writer is to consign him to the pantheon of the illustrious dead. "Mauriac, what a great man! I must ask Monteiro Rossi to prepare his obituary!" "But why do you want to write his obituary?" objects Don Antonio. "Let him live! We need him!" (96).

Monteiro Rossi embodies the other pole of the story's dualities: young, slender, infatuated with the energetic Marta and passionately committed to life, he is the antithesis of the ponderous Pereira. In one of the story's powerful ironies, it is Pereira who gives Monteiro Rossi rebirth by publishing the young man's obituary as a call to arms and a celebration of the values for which he lived. More importantly, Monteiro Rossi enables Pereira to reclaim his own youth—the youth he had lost when he chose to wed a serious, sickly girl and embarked with her on a life of quiet detachment. In Monteiro Rossi, who sings and whose

hair falls in his eyes as Pereira's once did, the protagonist finds an adoptive son and an image of his earlier self. In the young man's girlfriend,
Marta, who inspires a vocation for action, Pereira sees the road *not* taken
when he chose a wife who required, instead, withdrawal. In the film's
final scenes, Pereira is able to escape to a new life in France—site of the
freethinking culture that enabled him to register his opposition to the
regime—thanks to Monteiro Rossi. The young man had left several
false French passports in Pereira's safekeeping, and in one of them the
protagonist finds enough of a photographic likeness to be able to claim
it as his own. In the film version, Pereira's drive to fulfill Monteiro
Rossi's destiny is emphasized by his use of the young man's travel bag
to carry away the few items of clothing needed for his own escape to
freedom.

Given the novel's preoccupation with binary oppositions and rebirth
into new life, we would expect its cinematic rendering self-consciously
to announce the passage from written text to audio-visual spectacle.[3]
What emerges, instead, is a somewhat conservative, balanced approach
to adaptation that clings to the literariness of the source through the
extensive use of voice-over narration but enlists a number of medium-
specific devices for rendering the novel's themes of authoritarian surveillance, excessive attachment to the past, and the politicization of culture. Even in his use of the highly literary technique of voice-over
narration, Faenza makes a subtle but significant departure from his textual source. In so doing, the filmmaker gives his own, idiosyncratic answer to the most pressing issue confronting the reader of Tabucchi's
novel: the identity of its narrative voice.

Tabucchi foregrounds the problem in the very title of the novel,
Sostiene Pereira: Una testimonanza (*Pereira Declares: A Testimony*), which
privileges the protagonist's act of recounting and elevates that telling to
the level of historic witness. Like Primo Levi's narration in *Se questo è
un uomo* (translated into English as *Survival in Auschwitz*), which presents itself as testimony and invests its readers with the responsibility
to judge, Tabucchi conjures up a judicial setting in which issues of right
and wrong, of resistance and injustice, will be laid out "as in a deposi-
tion."[4] The text thus becomes a bearing of witness and a denunciation,
a legal brief against the Salazarist dictatorship, which asks us to render
a verdict based on the evidence presented in this claim. Indeed, one of

the most striking elements in Tabucchi's prose is the recurrence of the phrase *sostiene Pereira* with a regularity and insistence that obsessively returns us to the scene of speaking. We are constantly reminded that Pereira is in the presence of the writer as he writes, and that the speaker's presence is guarantee of the truth of the events to which he bears witness. The process of testifying—of assertion by Pereira, of reception, and transcription by the listener—is privileged throughout this text in a way that tells us, from the start, that the protagonist survived, that he feels compelled to speak, and that he has found his interlocutor, the "addressable other" who will give public form to private chronicle.[5]

But Tabucchi places his readers in the uneasy position of not knowing the elements crucial to completing this communicative circuit. We do not know from where or to whom the testimony is being given. Anxiety pervades our reading—the anxiety that Pereira's account is the transcription of a police interrogation, that he speaks under duress in some undisclosed location after being caught in his attempted flight from Portugal. Tabucchi's narrative does not, however, preclude other, more benign scenarios. Pereira could be safe in France, having carried out the escape made possible by Monteiro Rossi. The scene of speaking may be soon after the events, or many years later, once the war and the Salazar years have run their course. The interlocutor could actually be a character in the story, such as Don Antonio, Marta, or Dr. Cardoso, who would have a stake in the outcome and whose narrative would be conditioned by that distinctly personal agenda.

These interpretive questions, which linger unresolved throughout the course of the narration, receive a possible answer only in retrospect, thanks to an explanatory note published by Tabucchi in *Il gazzettino* in September 1994, a year after the completion of the novel, and included in the November 1994 edition of the text. In this postscript, Tabucchi attributes the inspiration for his writing to an unnamed journalist, active in Portugal during the '40s and '50s, who had published a ferocious attack, in the guise of a jest, against Salazar and had been forced into exile in Paris. There the Italian writer had met him briefly in the late '60s, only to encounter him again as his body lay in state in a hospital chapel in the post-Salazarist Lisbon of August 1992. Tabucchi gives an explicitly Pirandellian twist to the inspiration for his novel when he describes a series of nocturnal visits of a certain "*personaggio* in search of an author" (Tabucchi, 211), a vague semblance of a character who gradually takes on the definite lineaments and concrete identity of Pereira. "The confessions of Pereira, together with the imagination of him who writes, did the rest" (Tabucchi, 213), explains the author, revealing the identity of the text's interlocutor to be the novelist himself. In the light of this explanatory note, we realize that the book's title and its constant refrain, its insistence on the scene of speaking, is a return to the creative act that brings Pereira into being as a character. With every repetition of the declarative phrase (and they are legion), Tabucchi retraces and reenacts the inspirational process that the historical prototype of Pereira made possible, and that in turn brought him to life in the pages of this text. What is foregrounded, then, in Tabucchi's prose, studded with the words *sostiene Pereira,* is a two-tiered process by which history encounters the literary imagination, which in turn produces the text of witness.

The film acknowledges the importance of the novel's intrusive narrator in its extensive use of the voice-over technique. The narrator's voice intervenes eleven times throughout the course of the film, with great frequency at the beginning (four times within two and a half minutes), diminishing as the plot itself gains momentum, then concluding with a voice-over commentary to complete the frame and bring us back to the imagined scene of dictation that prompted the novel's writing. Out of fidelity to the text, and in keeping with the film's eponymous title, each voice-over intervention begins with the formulaic and by now talismanic *sostiene Pereira.* At a certain point in the story, however, the filmmaker chooses to depart from the source text in what one reviewer snidely called the "first and only 'active' choice of Faenza."[6] Where Tabucchi opts to maintain the anonymity and mystery of the narrator's identity, Faenza instead attributes the voice-over to one of the characters in the story: Dr. Cardoso.[7]

Such a choice has profound consequences, both narratological and ideological, for an interpretation of the film. This is no longer the disembodied voice of an unseen and unquestioned authority hovering above the story from some height of Olympian detachment, but an immanent, grounded presence who speaks from an *after* that is an organic extension of the story's beginning and middle. Dr. Cardoso, who has himself preceded Pereira into exile and shown the protagonist the road

FIGURE 12 | Daniel Auteuil and Marcello Mastroianni prepare for a scene at the Café Orquídea in which Dr. Cardoso announces to Pereira that he is going into exile in France. Courtesy of Jean Vigo Italia.

to escape, is both the knower and the example of how to survive a dictatorship with dignity and moral courage (fig. 12). More importantly, he is a physician whose holistic approach to Pereira's health includes philosophical and psychological as well as medical counsel. The story's focus on Pereira's corporeality, his unwieldy bulk, his heat prostration, his shortness of breath, his fondness for herbal omelettes and sugar-saturated lemonade, invite us to identify his physical condition with that of the body politic of his country—aging, withdrawn, immobilized beneath the weight of dictatorship.[8] Cardoso's affinity for French free-thinkers and specifically the theory of radical psychological change advocated by the school of *médicins-philosophes* has important implications for the ailing Portuguese body politic personified by Pereira. If the psyche is a confederation of souls controlled by a dominant ego, according to the French theory propounded by Cardoso, "in case there emerges a stronger ego, it will depose the weaker one and take its place" (76). Implicit in Cardoso's prescription for psychic change is the metaphor of a political coup that links Pereira's personal malaise to his country's subjugation to tyranny.

This political model for psychic health has special relevance to Faenza's use of voice-over in *Pereira Declares*. Neither in the structure of the psyche nor in the structure of the narrative is Cardoso/Faenza advocating an anarchic mix of elements. A dominant ego must preside over the confederation of souls just as a unified narrative perspective must govern the representation of Pereira's story. By identifying that dominant ego with Cardoso, Faenza is choosing to ally his own authorial stance with the progressive, culturally enlightened cosmopolitanism of the doctor appointed to care, metaphorically, for the health of the national body politic.

Of particular interest is Faenza's choice to defer the concrete identification of the voice-over until midway into the film. This means that the kind of narrative authority we attribute to the *voce narrante* undergoes a radical shift—a shift best analyzed in terms of the taxonomies established by recent French film theory.[9] Gilles Deleuze distinguishes between two kinds of voice-over: relative and near, on the one hand; absolute and elsewhere, on the other. The first kind refers to elements that are natural extensions of the onscreen composition and could eventually become part of it. "This first relation," writes Deleuze, "is that of a given set with a larger set that extends or encompasses it, but which is of the same nature." The second kind points beyond the events on the screen to a higher order of cognition characterized by absolute knowledge and a totalizing perspective. Such a voice emanates from a being who does not interact with the story's characters but instead "evokes, comments, knows" and is "endowed with an omnipotence or a strong power over the sequence of images."[10]

At first the voice-over of *Pereira Declares* speaks with just this kind of absolute authority. Its tone is "cutting and at times also ironic" (21), and its superimposition over footage of Pereira as he goes about his daily routine conveys the effect of condescension from unreachable heights. Once this voice is embodied in Dr. Cardoso, it comes to have an immanent, localizable source that shares the same cognitive ground as the other characters in the story, with the added advantage of hindsight. No longer coming from "a source excluded in a radical way in that it belongs to another order of reality," in Casetti's and di Chio's terms,[11] the voice-over reveals itself to be of Pereira's world, even if it speaks from a temporal-after and a spatial-elsewhere. Furthermore, the fact that Cardoso's thought is grounded in a humanistic philosophy whose tenets are specifically laid out for us to accept or reject (the congregation of souls; the rotation of the dominant ego) makes this voice democratic in its invitation to our enlightened consent to its governing principles.

Just as ideologically fraught as the voice-over is another medium-specific addition that Faenza makes to his adaptation of Tabucchi's novel. Soon after Pereira returns to Lisbon from his stay in the cardiac clinic, Marta takes him to a movie house, where they watch a Salazarist propaganda film entitled *A Revolução*.[12] In the two minutes of screen time devoted to the projection of this film-within-the-film, Faenza presents what amounts to a photographic negative of his own movie. Telling the story of a certain Antonio, head of a subversive organization, who has a change of heart and embraces the nationalist cause, *A Revolução* sytematically mirrors and reverses the structure of *Pereira Declares*. In the propaganda film, Antonio is led by his fiancée, Teresa, to undergo a political conversion and support the nationalist regime, just as Pereira is led by Marta (through her spokesman, Monteiro Rossi) to abandon his apathy and join the anti-Fascist struggle. Antonio's eyes are opened to the marvels of Salazarist social policy, just as Pereira's are opened to the cruel consequences of dictatorship.

By embedding within *Pereira Declares* a pro-Salazarist documentary that inverts the ideological thrust of the outer story, Faenza not only parodies the manipulative techniques of propaganda but also tacitly admits the mechanisms of persuasion that structure his own cinematic enterprise. Most obvious is the shared technique of voice-over narration that takes to authoritarian extremes in *A Revolução* the more subtle uses to which it is put in *Pereira Declares*.

Antonio and Teresa never speak in *A Revolução*—they simply move in obedience to the voice-over commentary that belongs unequivocally to Deleuze's category of the absolute and the elsewhere. At the same time, the voice coerces the audience into agreement with it, punctuating the commentary with first-person-plural adjectives and pronouns ("our government, our president" [93]) and soliciting viewer ratification for the wonders displayed onscreen: "Behold how the children are raised. . . . Behold how our boys and girls grow . . . what can we say about our elderly. . . . What can we say about our houses. . . .

What can we say about our youngsters?" (93). In the paratactic listing of Salazarist achievements—social services from cradle to grave, universal housing and full-employment opportunities—the film makes its argument by the sheer power of accumulation. All of the visual evidence is choral in nature, involving assembly lines of babies, files of running children, fully manned construction sites, and finally, crowds of admirers standing before the presidential palace. The image of a healthy, active, productive collectivity ultimately persuades Antonio of the error of his belief that "everything is going wrong in the country" (93), and the social body welcomes the repentant subversive into its midst. The final voice-over appeal, in the first-person imperative, asks the audience to participate in the onscreen image of mass concord by joining in the recitation of a patriotic slogan. "Repeat after me," the narrator insists.

On the surface, the voice-over of the propaganda film is diametrically opposed to that of the surrounding film. It is constant, coercive, and convinced, leaving no room for its characters to speak or for its audience to reflect on the relationship between what is heard and what is seen. The verbs are all in the present tense, and the voice is unequivocally celebratory, identifying itself with the images of health and plenitude that it proclaims. The narrative voice of the outer film, by contrast, is intermittent, sardonic, and remote, asserting a temporal distance from the events narrated and the experiential distance of the story told by proxy. But despite the radical difference between the use of voice-over in inner and outer films, the technique nonetheless foregrounds the way in which the narrator structures his account and therefore determines the audience response. Though the voice of the propaganda film is authoritarian while that of *Pereira Declares* is affectionately paternalistic, both assert their power to organize the narrative from above. Whether that *above* is, in Deleuze's terms, absolute or relative, elsewhere or near, "its manifestation always represents a strong interference."[13] What emerges, then, is Faenza's acknowledgement of the frankly political nature of culture—the impossibility (and undesirability) of apolitical art, and the active embrace of its ideological mission.

Another link between the two films, the inner and the outer, is their common inclusion of an internalized figure of the observer whose "eyes must be opened." At one point, early in the propaganda film, Antonio is busy taking aim through the viewfinder of the rifle he is planning to use to assassinate Salazar. Soon those eyes are saddened by the news that his mother has died of a broken heart as a result of her son's subversive activities. But Teresa, his "sweet fiancée," undertakes "a work of redemption, opening his eyes to the reality of the country" (93). For the duration of the propaganda film, Antonio is shown in various positions of watching: from above as he observes the babies being expertly processed in a neonatal clinic; again from above as he marvels at a construction site; and from below as he salutes the Portuguese flag. By the end of the inner film, the repentant revolutionary ceases watching and begins to walk decisively as the voice-over announces that "Antonio now knows what he must do" (94).

Pereira's gaze in the outer film undergoes a similar evolution, to opposite ideological effect. The character's obtrusive eye glasses, so essential a part of the iconography of the intellectual, immediately mark him as a viewer, a passive observer of the spectacle of life. In an opening montage of shots, including Pereira's commute to work on a trolley car, the protagonist's eyes are drawn away from his reading to behold an episode of police brutality in the city's streets. This movement of the eyes from inside to outside, from written page to directly observed experience, from culture to politics, anticipates the evolution of the entire film and links that evolution specifically to the faculty of vision. At regular intervals throughout the film, Pereira looks out of his apartment window to survey activities in the military barracks in the adjacent lot. Those activities escalate during the course of the story, culminating in the arrival of a group of very young boys, "almost children," who are being regimented by a shouting officer. They, too, shout savagely, making the scene still more disquieting" (123). With Monteiro Rossi lying dead in his bedroom and the spectacle of militarized youth in the barracks outside, Pereira realizes in what direction his country is moving and vows to intervene to change that course. The gaze of the detached intellectual of the film's opening scenes has been converted into the gaze of the activist intellectual, ready to use the power of the press to take a stand against tyranny.

Pereira's look of burgeoning awareness develops in opposition to another kind of watching—that which the regime directs against him. The gaze of surveillance is embodied by the intrusive and ever-present janitor Celeste, and it is her constant vigilance that first evokes signs of Pereira's displeasure with the regime. Like the mustached Signora Cecilia of Scola's *A Special Day* (1977), who dramatized the way in which Fascist control had infiltrated the domestic space of 1930s Roman life, Celeste personalizes the workings of Salazarist oppression within the private sphere. "Signora Celeste, you are being paid to do your job and instead you always stick your nose into other people's business" (40), Pereira complains. When the lady reminds him that her husband is with the police, Pereira retorts, "I know only too well, and it is precisely this that I don't like" (40). Pereira's awareness of Salazarist surveillance makes his own increasingly enlightened gaze a kind of meta-watching, a consciousness of being watched that sharpens his own critical perspective on the regime. An alternative response to surveillance, a response of fear and withdrawal, is exemplified several times in the film when the camera cuts to a window from which an anonymous elderly man or woman looks onto the street and just as suddenly disappears behind closed shutters.

The link between physical vision and cognitive enlightenment is made explicit throughout *Pereira Declares* in a number of verbal references to "open eyes." In the propaganda film previously mentioned, Teresa labors to save her fiancé from a life of subversion by displaying the glories of the Salazar administration, "opening his eyes to the reality of the country" (93). Toward the end of *Pereira Declares,* as evidence of the escalating militarization of the regime multiplies, the police injunction "eyes wide open: subversives can be found everywhere" (107) is especially irritating to the protagonist. "And he did not like the thing at all" (107), the voice-over narrator informs us. These appeals to patriotic alertness, to vigilant support of a regime whose very power is predicated on the blind obedience of its subjects, serves as the negative version of the process that Pereira himself undergoes as he awakens to injustice and the need for political response.

Pereira's own understanding of the "eyes open" slogan evolves dramatically during the course of the story. Several times, in dialogue with Monteiro Rossi, Pereira admonishes the young man to temper his militancy with a healthy dose of circumspection. "But you have to find a balance," Pereira insists. "With your heart, yes, but with your eyes always open!" (39). A similar formulation accompanies Pereira's subsequent warning to Monteiro Rossi that his love for Marta is leading him into dangerous political waters. "But remember what I told you . . . eyes always open!" (61). In both instances, Pereira equates visual alertness with vigilance—the faculty of circumspection needed to restrain the perilous excesses of passion.

The recurrence of the "eyes open" formula in the final voice-over passage reveals the immense progress that Pereira has made toward the *presa di coscienza* (consciousness raising) that leads to true cognitive and moral enlightenment. Having succeeded in publishing the article denouncing Monteiro Rossi's death at the hands of the secret police, Pereira makes his way to the train station, whence he will flee to France, against the background of the newsboy who shouts the headlines, "Young journalist barbarously assassinated" (134). Elated by the proof of his success in exposing the atrocity to public view, Pereira walks toward freedom in triumph. "Pereira," concludes the voice-over narrator, "declares that while he walked away amidst the crowd, he had the sensation that his age no longer weighed on him, as if he had reverted to being an agile and slim boy with a great desire to live. And then he thought back to the beach of Granja and to a frail girl who had given him the best years of her life. And to remember all this, he wanted to have a dream. A very beautiful dream, with open eyes" (134).

No longer a sign of fear and circumspection, the "open eyes" formula now marks the triumphant blend of passion and reason made possible by Pereira's decision to act. The "very beautiful dream" is the idyll of Pereira's youth—the time when he, like Monteiro Rossi, had an unruly forelock, a bevy of female admirers, and a future of limitless possibilities for personal and professional happiness. Pereira's choice to marry a sickly, ethereal girl and the consequent withdrawal into a childless and detached existence proves in the end to be eminently reversible. In dreaming this dream, Pereira both revives his past and takes it in the alternative direction that Monteiro Rossi's activist and vitalist example inspires. The "open eyes" of the dream signals Pereira's free and enlightened choice to do so, his decision to abandon the fear and caution that necessitated the earlier "open eyes" of vigilance and to embrace the freedom to revive his own youthful idealism through committed action.

Pereira's struggle to reconcile past and present, nostalgia and activism, is given specific expression in the shrine that he erects to the

FIGURE 13 | Pereira's deceased wife has remained a living presence for the widower, who has set up a shrine in her memory and constantly speaks to her portrait. Courtesy of Jean Vigo Italia.

memory of his dead wife. In her portrait, photographed in medium-range shot, we can discern the lineaments of an attractive middle-aged woman whose mouth is composed in a sardonic half smile. Next to the portrait is an antiquated gramophone that plays a sentimental song obviously popular in Pereira's youth and that probably served as the musical accompaniment to the couple's courtship. Dressed in his house coat, padding around his apartment and chatting with his wife's portrait to the background of this song, Pereira evidently organizes his home life around this shrine (fig. 13). The image of the wife, frozen in her ambiguous smile, and the sound of this music makes a spectacle of this past and binds him to it in an endless circle of remembrance and loss.

The grandeur of Pereira's achievement in the story is not so much that he abandons his past, with all its cultural and sentimental accretions, as that he reconciles it with a progressive move into the present. Dr. Cardoso urges Pereira to stop talking to the portrait of his wife and to resolve his problems in the context of the living, but Pereira refuses to give up this longstanding habit. In a visually striking scene, whose split composition reflects the protagonist's internal dilemma, caught between past and present, stasis and change, Pereira speaks to his wife's image about Cardoso's advice to him. "He says I must stop visiting the past. I agree with the congregation of souls, and the new dominant ego . . . but with you, I will continue to talk!" (106). The mise-en-scène of this monologue is divided in half, with Pereira to the right, on the sun-lit terrace overlooking the church of Santa Lucia, and the shrine to his wife to the left, in the dark interior of the apartment.

Not until the final frames of the film is Pereira able to maintain his vow to continue discoursing with his wife. Significantly, this last exchange with her concerns his plan to escape Portugal for a new life of freedom in exile. "I'll explain it to you later" (133), he promises as he prepares to shave his mustache so that he will resemble the photo in his false French passport. "Silly, you thought I would leave you alone" (134), he remarks, as he returns one last time to pack her picture in his travel case. If Pereira's discourse with his dead wife signals his link with the past, these last several lines suggest his will to update that past and to bring it into line with a progressive present. As the camera moves in for a close-up of the photo, the ambiguous expression of the wife's face has settled into an unequivocal smile. Her image gives its blessing to Pereira's new life.

This climactic blend of past and present, of nostalgia and action, was musically anticipated in midfilm by the intricate counterpoint of two themes. Just before Monteiro Rossi brings his cousin Bruno to meet their benefactor, Pereira sits near the portrait of his wife, listening to the song he associates with their youthful romance. But now another melody intervenes—Ennio Morricone's urgent, staccato theme of suspense. This enters into dialogue with the romantic melody and gives musical expression to Pereira's internal struggle.

Though the visual technique of the gaze and the musical language of the soundtrack provide powerful, medium-specific measures of Pereira's conversion, perhaps the most eloquent cinematic manifestation of the protagonist's progress is that of film acting itself. The critical consensus on *Pereira Declares* is that its strength lies in Mastroianni's magisterial performance of the old man, shaken from emotional paralysis and intellectual detachment into committed political action.[14] In an interview published in the preface to the screenplay, Mastroianni establishes the link between Pereira's embrace of a new identity within the film and the actor's approach to his craft.

> And so I said to myself: look at this Pereira, with all his predictability, with his days organized around omelettes, French classics to translate for his newspaper, dialogues with his dead wife's photograph. He is one who at a certain point has the courage radically to change his own life. And then I thought: Marcello, how far you are from the dignity of Pereira. You're more than seventy years old and you continue to be an actor because you don't know how to do anything else. (11)

Though apparently self-deprecating, Mastroianni's comment has the effect of taking us back over a brilliant and varied acting career, studded with impersonations of such committed characters as Professor Sinigaglia, of Monicelli's *The Organizer* (*I compagni,* 1963), Fulvio Imbriani, of the Tavianis's *Allonsanfan* (1974), Gabriele, of Scola's *A Special Day* (1977), and Rosario Spallone, of Wertmuller's *Blood Feud* (*Fatto di sangue,* 1978). Beneath the self-deprecatory surface of this remark, in fact, Mastroianni reveals the source of his power as a performer. The art of becoming another, of bodying forth a charismatic new identity is, of course, what lies at the heart of conversion. And the ability to enact that new self in a convincing way before an audience gives that performance the potential to transform the public through its example.

Within the story itself, there are several instances of radical identity changes, of personal overhauls that serve to protect political subversives from official scrutiny, on the one hand, or to create a flamboyant public image on the other. In the latter category is Gabriele D'Annunzio, whose assumption of a pseudonym is part of an overall strategy of glamorous self-invention. Pereira invokes D'Annunzio as a way of testing Monteiro Rossi's knowledge of European letters, slyly asking him to compose an obituary for the Italian writer "Rapagnetta" (D'Annunzio's real surname). Identity changes serve the opposite function— to hide suspect individuals from persecution—in the case of Marta, who assumes the name of Lise Delauney, cuts her lush hair, loses a considerable amount of weight, and dons obtrusive glasses to obliterate all traces of her earlier self. Pereira will follow suit, shaving his mustache and assuming the French identity (named François Baudin, in the novel) of the fake passport. This passport becomes the last in the series of French texts that have scripted his presa di coscienza and his eventual escape from tyranny.

In Pereira's preoccupation with resurrection and his regular visits to the priest Don Antonio, the story makes Christian conversion an analogy for the political and moral transfiguration that the protagonist undergoes. The death of the old man and the birth of the new, in Pauline terms, offers a precedent for the way in which Pereira has been redeemed within the secular realm. The two forms of redemption, spiritual and political, converge powerfully in the figure of Don Antonio, whose full and passionate adherence to Christian dogma does not preclude a lively sympathy for the anti-Fascist cause.

Mastroianni's ability to enter into the person of Pereira as that character himself comes into possession of a new and better self underlines the way in which acting serves as a model for conversion. This entering-into-character is made explicit in the film's opening sequence when, on the trolley car, the camera, in medium close-up, focuses on Mastroianni's face as the actor deliberately composes his features into those of the self-absorbed newspaper editor. On the meta-performative level, our awareness that we are watching Mastroianni take on the role of Pereira in the twilight of his acting career (he would appear in only two films after *Pereira Declares*) makes that character's presa di coscienza the fulfillment of a filmography that has spanned the entire arc of Italian postwar history. And if Portugal is Italy by displacement, then Pereira/Mastroianni is proof that an aging and aloof national culture can be vitally renewed, indeed reborn, through the cinema of commitment.

family as political allegory

Francesco Rosi's *Three Brothers*

AFTER THE DIASPORA

Toward the middle of Francesco Rosi's *Three Brothers,* Raffaele, a judge, leafs through a photo album of slain corpses, including those of the presumed perpetrator and the victims of the kind of terrorist attacks to which he, too, could be subject were he to agree to preside over a trial of left-wing extremists. As he falls asleep, the photographs modulate into a nightmare about his own assassination at terrorist hands. This sequence reads like a self-quotation: it could be a clip from a number of Rosi's earlier films—from his very first, *La sfida* (1958), whose protagonist is gunned down at the conclusion, or *Salvatore Giuliano* (1961), which begins and ends with blood-soaked corpses, or *Cadaveri eccellenti* (1975), whose title speaks for itself. Raffaele's dream serves as a microhistory of Rosi's film career up to *Christ Stopped at Eboli* (1979)—a career dedicated to *cine-inchieste,* cinematic investigations, into cases involving power relationships between charismatic individuals, corporations, criminal organizations, and the state. Rosi labeled this approach a second phase of neorealism,[1] replacing the immediate postwar cinema of objective witness with a new "critical realism of overt ideological intentions,"[2] and thus anticipating the *cinema politico* of Costa-Gavras and Elio Petri of the late '60s and '70s. Though never a documentary filmmaker, Rosi nonetheless sought to expose the operations of a categorical, partisan truth beneath the surface of events. To that end, he employed a nonlinear, investigative style whose editorial violence would reveal the inner relationships and hidden complicities underlying the official version of the facts.

But the terrorist sequence in *Three Brothers* departs from its cinematic precedents in several crucial ways, and as such it signals the new | 115 direction that Rosi's 1980s production would take. Had he made *Three Brothers* in the mid-1970s, while still bound to the monolithic ideological truths of his cine-inchiesta days, the film would have been dedicated entirely to the terrorist question and would have more properly been entitled *The First Son,* or *The Only Son.* But by 1981 Rosi seems to have come around to a more subtle and nuanced approach to "the case of Italy."[3] "The problem of terrorism? It's a problem that would require an entire film, and it's not that I haven't thought about it. . . . But I have always backed away because I found myself confronted with problems of knowledge: if I had not even fathomed the logic of terrorism, its human and political reality, how could I help the public?"[4]

Daunted by the magnitude of the "problems of knowledge" posed by terrorism, and aware that to understand its logic one must live its "human and political reality," Rosi chooses to inscribe the phenomenon in the experience of one of his characters, thus refusing to endow his representation of the issue with the presumed objectivity of a third-person perspective or to arrogate the authority of an omniscient one. In so doing, Rosi acknowledges the limits of a purely abstract, cerebral approach to the problem and defers to the superior power of personal witness. In addition, Rosi's decision to make his film only in part about terrorism might reflect a conscious, antiterrorist strategy—that is, not to give the phenomenon center stage, not to single it out as the privileged symptom of the diseased body politic of the 1970s, and therefore to deny it the full-court press that only serves to promote terrorist objectives. By making terrorism one of three manifestations of social disorder (the other two are embodied by the younger brothers Rocco and Nicola) Rosi seeks to demystify and delimit his subject matter rather than surrender to terrorism's tyrannical hold over national attention at the time of the film's release.

Another measure of Rosi's shift from the ideological filmmaking of his cinema-politico days is the decision to employ multiple centers of consciousness in his film, and with them to entertain a plurality of perspectives on "the case of Italy," rather than insisting on one totalizing approach. "The three brothers are parts of myself," Rosi explains. "I don't identify with one rather than another."[5] As the brothers discuss, argue, and dream, Rosi's reluctance to take sides makes his film a virtual symposium of views on the plight of contemporary Italy, prompting such approving reactions as Pauline Kael's: "Earlier, full of theory, Rosi imposed his vision; now, he searches it out—he goes deeper down into himself, and much further into his subject."[6]

Most indicative of Rosi's evolution beyond the cinema politico is the fact that the terrorist attack is embedded in a dream. It is highly subjective and personalized, leaving behind the realm of documentary (albeit highly manipulated) factuality for the inner recesses of human consciousness. Already, in his previous film *Christ Stopped at Eboli,* such a movement had been foretold, when Carlo Levi's subjective experience of the peasant world had been translated into the film's own language of long takes, sweeping panoramic shots of the landscape, slow pacing, and an emotional musical score. But in that earlier film, Rosi had scrupulously respected Levi's personal privacy, never entering into the interior spaces that the writer's own text had so jealously guarded. Dreams, fantasies, and memories are never explored in *Christ Stopped at Eboli,* whereas *Three Brothers* depends heavily on such psychic incursions to reveal the inner lives of characters whose reticence, in some cases, borders on the solipsistic. To dramatize this move into subjectivity, the film begins in the mind of one of the brothers, Rocco, who dreams about a junkyard teeming with rats and awakes to find that the "rats" are the boys in his reformatory who have been routinely escaping and pillaging all night. By anticipating and interpreting the bad news that he is about to learn from the police, Rocco's subjectivity is privileged in the film, inviting us into his nightmarish foreknowledge and providing us with metaphoric terms for thinking about the plight of contemporary urban "scavengers," as he will call them later on while leafing through a UNICEF report on disadvantaged children.

Piero Piccioni's soundtrack is extremely important to the development of the characters' inner lives. By introducing Rocco's nightmare with the sound of the dreamer's heartbeat, Piccioni immediately locates us *within* the human organism, suggesting the primacy of internal experience over its external causes. Rocco's heartbeat then modulates into the sounds of string tremolos, miming the swells of emotion brought on by the dream itself. Heartbeats will be heard once again in the film during Raffaele's assassination nightmare, while the string tremolos will continue throughout *Three Brothers,* to link the film's emotionalism to a unitary familial source.[7]

A second character to be introduced through a subjective experience is Donato, the aged father of the family. Walking down a country road, he comes upon a rabbit, and an elderly woman (we presume it to be his wife) urges him to capture it. "I wanted to cook it for tomorrow," she explains, "but it escaped. It was afraid of dying." When Donato seizes the animal and hands it to the woman, she lets it go, walks away, and disappears, rematerializing behind him against the background of their farmhouse. All this remains quite cryptic until the next scene, when Donato telegraphs his sons with the news that their mother has died, and we realize, retroactively, that the hallucination had been a poetic reenactment of her death.

By making us privy to the subjective experience before the information that would give it factual meaning, Rosi privileges the private, interior world of signs over their objective referents and implicates us imaginatively in Donato's loss. So compressed is the poetic language of this daydream that it distills an entire lifetime of domestic routine—of hunting, meal planning, cooking, and general nurturing—into one simple exchange between husband and wife. While the rats of Rocco's dream were bearers of all the negativity of contemporary urban life, Donato's rabbit is the repository of his wife's posthumous consolations. In releasing the animal, Caterina tells her husband all he needs to know about her death: it may have been a capture, but it was also a liberation. Later in the film, this insight is affirmed by Raffaele's ancient wet-nurse, Filomena, who reports that she, too, had dreamt of the dead Caterina and had found her "well and content."

By endowing the subjective sequences with both cognitive and moral authority, Rosi opens up his film to multileveled poetic interpretation. Whereas metaphor governs the relationship between dream images and their referents (Rocco's juvenile delinquents are rats; the dead Caterina is a rabbit), it is allegory that determines the signifying mode of the narrative as a whole. Thus the Giuranna family as a disintegrating corporate unit allegorizes the plight of the Italian body politic in the postwar era. From their origin in the Murgie region of Apulia, the three sons migrate to Rome, Naples, and Turin, respectively, in a reenactment of Italy's demographic shifts from agrarian to urban centers, from south to north. True to the universalizing thrust of allegory, the family's geographic origin is never named—it remains the generic town of southern Italy, whose populace is predominantly composed of card-playing old men. The one visible young woman in the town, Rosaria, is married to a guest worker in Germany who returns home twice a year. When Raffaele encounters an old schoolfriend in the town bar, this lone specimen of non-geriatric manhood is apologetic about not having migrated elsewhere. Like the emblematic Tara of Bertolucci's *Spider Stratagem* (1970), an entire generation is absent from this Pugliese town—and by extension from rural Italy itself—whose population will not be replenished once the elderly have died off. Thus the funeral of Caterina serves to allegorize the death of the rural Italian past and offers the occasion for the brothers, representatives of the new social order, to take stock of a national identity now cut off from its source.

Like so many Italian films of the postwar era, *Three Brothers* found its most sympathetic audiences abroad.[8] The problem with the domestic reception seemed to reside in the film's allegorical structure, which provoked a Crocean resistance to Rosi's didacticism as *non poesia*—as uninspired, sterile, and programmatic. Foreign audiences, on the other hand, seemed willing to accept the film's pedagogy as an integral part of its visionary mode. Since the allegorical method in modern fiction will succeed only when the literal level is sufficient unto itself—expressive in its own autonomous terms—detractors of *Three Brothers* were obviously not engaged enough at the narrative level to move beyond it in search of ulterior meanings. Hence such critics' resentment of a significance that they perceived to be imposed from above; as Francesco Bolzoni put it, "It seems that here, as in his remote beginnings, Rosi first sought an interesting sociological datum and subsequently constructed an appearance of character around it."[9]

Admirers of the film, on the other hand, such as Pauline Kael, defend it in suggestive terms: "Even though the structure is schematic," she argues, "the film moves on waves of feeling."[10] I think, therefore, that the viewer's disposition to accept or reject Rosi's allegorical superstructure is established in the first few moments of *Three Brothers*, in the subjective sequences of Rocco's nightmare and Donato's daydream—sequences that either succeed or fail in carrying us on those "waves of feeling" so necessary to our engagement in the film's literal level. Thus Rosi's privileging of subjectivity is the necessary precondition for his allegorical mode, whose failure, for Italian audiences, may be attributed either to its low threshold of tolerance for terrorist treatments or its Crocean impulse to dismiss allegory as non poesia.

Once we have accepted the allegorical justification for the film's structure, a series of schematic correspondences emerge. The three brothers each personify a facet of the modern Italian condition: they embody the cities to which they have emigrated and they experience midlife crises of a personal or professional sort. In terms of narrative symmetries, each brother enacts his characteristic relationship to the town of origin, and each has a dream or wish-fulfillment fantasy that reveals his hidden self. The allegorical schematicism extends even to the brothers' modes of return to their birthplace: Raffaele, the family celebrity, arrives by airplane and taxi; autoworker Nicola comes, appropriately enough, by car; and Rocco, a semimonastic reform-school teacher, walks in on foot. If Francesco Bolzoni is right in arguing that "the cinema of Rosi is located in the novel of character" and that his characters are *personaggi-funzione* (character functions) who guide viewers through the vicissitudes of recent Italian history, then it behooves us to attend carefully to Rosi's portraits of his family members.[11]

Raffaele, the firstborn, is the most successful of the brothers in professional terms. Donato's obvious pride in his distinguished son emerges in a scene at the post office, when he instructs the clerk to send a telegram to "Raffaele Giuranna, judge," and repeats this appellation, with obvious pleasure at the conjunction of name and title. Based in Rome, Raffaele embodies the professional power establishment: the various spaces with which he is associated (a car in rush-hour traffic, the office he shares with a flunky, his austere but elegant apartment, the corridors of the courthouse) define life in the center of things—in the geographic midpoint of Italy, of class structure, of family, of the judicial system.

But Raffaele's is a center that will not hold: his son is having an affair with an older woman and is absent from home when most needed; his own marital relations are sorely tried by the terrorist threat; and the stability of the government he supports is precarious at best, given the impact of leftist extremism on all social institutions. Rosi, who did not presume to fathom the logic of terrorism, experiences through Raffaele "its human and political reality" by showing its concrete effect on an individual life. Raffaele carries a gun, receives death threats, can maintain no fixed schedule, must always try to blend into a crowd, takes vacations separate from his wife and son, and cannot bring his family to his mother's funeral. In the paranoid dream discussed earlier, a photograph album of terrorist victims modulates into a nightmare of his own assassination, culminating in the flash of the police camera documenting his own bloodstained corpse. The image of his body will now enter the chain of signifiers that constitute the book of terror, to be read by the next prospective judge of a politically sensitive trial.

Though an embodiment of the power establishment, Raffaele is not uncritical of it. As such, he may be said to occupy the center-left of the political spectrum (*pertiniano,* according to the critic Valerio Caprara),[12] advocating constructive, gradualist reform from within the system. In a remembered or imagined dialogue with a judicial colleague prior to his paranoid dream, Raffaele argues that punishment alone is insufficient to resolve the problem of terrorism—that government must address its root cause by deterring youths from political lawlessness through a program of preventive action.

Will Raffaele agree to preside over the trial? Though the film begs the question, and one critic argues categorically that he will refuse,[13] Rosi drops a series of cogent hints to the contrary. "Imagine if someone like you wouldn't accept," snaps Raffaele's wife during a phone conversation in the wake of a death threat sent to their home. Immediately after hanging up, Raffaele engages in a spontaneous seminar in the local bar on the subject of bearing witness against political crimes. "Terror defines itself," Raffaele claims. "It substitutes persuasion with fear. Society can't be founded on fear. The only answer is faith, or all is lost." Events soon undermine Raffaele's institutional confidence, however. In the same bar, late that night when younger brother Nicola goes in for cigarettes, a television newscast reveals what happens to witnesses who turn state's evidence, like the one about to testify at a murder trial who was gunned down on his way to court.

But Raffaele's faith in the system resists such empirical proofs to the contrary. Very early in the film, a fellow magistrate explains why he had resigned from the terrorist case that has now been assigned to Raffaele. "I would have risked my life if I thought I could change something," his predecessor admits. Were the above sentence to be rewritten in the light of Raffaele's faith in the system, the conditional and subjunctive verbs of the contrary-to-fact construction would be replaced by indicative verbs expressing simple causality: "I will risk my life because I think I can change something." By linking willingness to undergo personal sacrifice with a belief in the perfectibility of institutions, Rosi makes Raffaele's choice a foregone conclusion. However, in the paranoid nightmare and in the telephone booth, where Raffaele can barely hold himself up for fear as he receives the news about the death threat, we see the enormous price that the judge must pay for his faith. The dream and the anxiety attacks are measures of what Raffaele must fight in himself, indexes of the internal resistance against which he must struggle to maintain his idealistic resolve.

If the family as a corporate unit functions as a microcosm of the body politic as a whole, then we would expect the Giurannas to express the conflict between radicalism and the power establishment that plagued Italy throughout the 1970s. Though no terrorist, Nicola is the next best thing—a militant unionist who does not shrink from the use of violence to redress the abuses of the capitalist system. Hence the strategy of physically beating department heads joins the repertory of labor's more benign tactics—those of protest marches, strikes, picket lines, and absenteeism—to promote the quest for worker justice. In terms of official party allegiances, Nicola would belong to the militant wing of the PCI (Partito comunista italiano) or to the more radical PDUP (Partito democratico di unità proletaria), a post-1968 organization advocating radical social change that, while not overtly supporting terrorism, did not condemn the use of violence for revolutionary ends.

Predictably, Nicola engages in constant polemics with Raffaele—the embodiment of the status quo within the family unit. As the oldest and youngest siblings, respectively, Raffaele and Nicola are twenty years apart, so that the former would have come of age during the retrenchment of the 1950s, while the latter would have matured in a post-1968 climate of antibourgeois revolt. This means that the Raffaele/Nicola conflict verges on the generational, resembling nothing so much as a traditional father/son struggle for dominance. It also means that while Raffaele would have migrated to Rome in an era of relative openness that would have given him access to a university education and good professional advancement, Nicola would have arrived in Turin during the massive onslaught of southern migrants to the industrial north. Rosi thus goes to some pains to show how the difference in their perspectives is historically and economically conditioned. Like the pitiful, disoriented protagonist of Ettore Scola's *Trevico-Torino, viaggio nel Fiatnam* (1973), cited by Nicola as the cinematic prototype of his own experience, this young Pugliese transplant found himself alienated, ghettoized, and exploited in the inhospitable north. Against such cultural and economic violence, Nicola felt that he had no other recourse than that of militant syndicalism.

Yet in his polemics with Raffaele, the younger brother insists on maintaining a distinction between the violence sponsored by the unions and that practiced by the Red Brigades. "Demonstrations, strikes, and pickets are separated by an abyss from terrorism," Nicola claims. "There are protest marches and protest marches," Raffaele quibbles. "It is called self-defense when protesters carry P-38s and Molotov cocktails. How many kids began terrorist careers this way?" While Nicola argues that there is a qualitative difference between union militancy and terrorism, Raffaele holds that it is merely a question of degree. Once violence enters into the equation, distinctions become arbitrary, and thrashings escalate into killings with appalling ease.

For all Nicola's political ranting and raving, however, his fantasy life reveals preoccupations of a far different sort. It is his marital situation that obsesses Nicola when he is not busy arguing with Raffaele (though the sexual and the political in the film are by no means separable orders of experience). Through his troubled marriage to a Turinese woman, Nicola encounters in his erotic life the regional divisions and tensions that beset the Italian body politic as a whole. "She's a typical northerner," he complains to Raffaele. "We even argued over pasta— with tomato sauce, as I say, or with butter, according to the signora." Nicola's use of regional stereotypes, however, is far more insidious and morally suspect than this petty charge of culinary incompatibility would suggest. "She had a fling," he confesses. "I'm from the south. I can't stand to be two-timed." When Raffaele counters with reminders of Nicola's own sexual truancy—"I'm sure she's stood a lot. I know you"—we realize that the outraged husband is using his regional identity as an alibi. The double standard, it seems, is Nicola's birthright as a southern Italian male.

Thanks to the virtuoso cinematography of Pasqualino De Santis, the best expression of the north/south dichotomy is the visual form it takes in Nicola's daydream of reconciliation with his estranged wife, Giovanna. Though the institutional gloom of the Neapolitan sequence and the rush-hour chaos of those in Rome stand in sharp contrast to the pastoral setting of Apulia, the Turinese sequence seems to occur on another planet.[14] As Nicola lies on his boyhood bed in the house where the brothers grew up and his mind travels north to Turin, he imagines himself in a surreal space—an ultramodern arcade leading to Giovanna's apartment building. As if in a De Chirico painting, Nicola traverses this dreamscape, whose architectural masses cast geometric shadows in shades of greens and grays. With oneiric arbitrariness, a young girl rollerskates in a zigzag pattern before the advancing figure of the dreamer. In terms of lighting, color, resolution of image, and mise-en-scène, nothing could be further from Rosi's visualization of Nicola's homeland, characterized by "the bitter and arid white of a certain south," according to Gian Luigi Rondi. "A white that, with neat lines and precise dry contours, sets itself against black; whether in the extreme close-up of the faces or in the dilated vastness of the establishing shots."[15]

The surreal entrance to Giovanna's apartment building does little to prepare us for the fluorescent brightness and sterile anonymity of her kitchen, where she and Nicola tentatively reconnect after a six-month period of separation. Shot frontally, this rectilinear space tells the whole story. This is *Giovanna's* jurisdiction, and Nicola, having merely entered it, implicitly accepts her terms for being there. Though his movements are aggressive and proprietary, especially when he unceremoniously raids the refrigerator or helps himself to her wine, she is clearly in control. Only when the camera slowly closes in on him as he discusses his feelings about emigration does Nicola temporarily command his place within the mise-en-scène. And since his newfound insights will be the basis for a reconciliation with Giovanna, as well as the construction of a new, nonregional identity, it behooves us to consider Nicola's revelations to her in some detail.

"How was it at home?" Giovanna asks. "Beautiful," he answers, "but also a disaster. For the first time, I discovered a new thing. More painful than the death of a mother. Sorrow for a mother is something that you carry with you for the rest of your life. I discovered that my hometown was no longer a part of me, nor I of it. You know what the true trauma of the emigrant is? He lacks the ground under his feet. He returns to the town looking for happiness and he doesn't find it. Then he returns to the 'city,' to Germany or America, and he feels homesick." Unable to revert to his culture of origin because he has experienced too much, and unable to assimilate into the new social milieu, the emigrant is doomed to live betwixt and between, never at home, always drifting in search of an impossible rootedness. In the face of this dilemma, the emigrant has two choices: to rail against his lot, venting his anger in futile gestures of violence or self-destruction; or to create a compromise space in which he assumes responsibility for the pain of exile and seeks a revised definition of self.

Having confided in Giovanna, Nicola is now offered the possibility of such a space—not in the harshly lit, rectilinear kitchen but in the blue-tinged, heavily curtained bedroom down the hall. Even the camera work changes accordingly, from the static takes or subdued movements of the kitchen scene to the smooth, 180-degree pan that follows Nicola as he circles the bed and undresses in ever-less-tentative acceptance of Giovanna's invitation to spend the night. Even the dialogue shifts register, from the direct, referential comments of the kitchen scene to the oblique, elliptical language of mutual desire. "How hot it is in this room," she begins. "It's the walls," Nicola responds, "at night they radiate the heat they retained from the day." "You wanted a southern exposure," she rejoins.[16] "You're right, I wanted us to get some sun." Nicola's attempt to create a compromise space by incorporating southern elements into a northern setting, understood now in the light of his discovery that he can never return home, suggests a therapeutic approach to the emigrant's plight.

Is the imagined lovemaking only a temporary solution or does it signal Nicola's permanent willingness to forego the double standard that he considered a kind of regional inheritance? Though one critic argues for the transience of this marital truce,[17] the film hints at the possibility of a more lasting resolution to the couple's domestic problems. Nicola daydreams of returning to his wife after having renounced the opportunity for a sexual encounter with Rosaria, the childhood sweetheart who had married another man while Nicola was serving in the military. It takes little to reignite Nicola's passion for her—a few sultry glances are enough to send him prowling around Rosaria's house like the lovesick cat who is patrolling her neighborhood that night. After a passionate embrace, however, the couple decide not to make love: Rosaria refuses to defile her husband's bed, and Nicola does not insist. The reasons for his uncharacteristic restraint are significant, suggesting that his sexually self-serving definition of southern Italian manhood has undergone a radical change. Rather than avenge himself on the love rival who had succeeded in wooing her away from him in the past, Nicola chooses to identify with Rosaria's absent husband, himself an emigrant in the north. Nicola's restraint also reflects an awareness that he cannot simply take up where he left off with his fiancée of so many years ago—that he has undergone irreversible changes as an emigrant whose "hometown no longer enters in [him], nor [he] in it." In Nicola's case, it is entirely appropriate that this truth be played out in sexual terms.

When Nicola and Raffaele engage in their endless polemics on the night before the funeral, it is Rocco who finally puts a stop to the proceedings by insisting that his brothers shift to more private, personal concerns (fig. 14). "Let's talk about us," he implores, "your families, your kids." Rocco, who has neither a wife nor kids of his own, remains the most enigmatic of the brothers, and though he is the only character to have two dreams, they do little to reveal his inner self. This could be explained by the fact that Rocco is indeed selfless, lacking the monadic, ego economy that defines identity in its more conventional sense. As director of a Neapolitan reform school, Rocco is altruistically committed to the cause of rehabilitating youthful offenders before they are beyond reclamation. Accordingly, both his dreams relate directly to his sense of social mission. The first dream, about a rat-infested cityscape, provided Rocco with the metaphor for the disadvantaged children of the world, turned scavengers through desperation and neglect. "We must sacrifice, for humanity. Not just family, our own people. It means changing man's heart. We have to be gentler toward mankind, nature. If not, these rats will do us in, here and everywhere." This apocalyptic scenario is only reinforced by Rocco's description of an incident involving subproletarian encampments outside Naples where lawlessness had invited massive police mobilization. "They intervened with tanks,

FIGURE 14 | On the eve of their mother's funeral, Nicola (Michele Placido), center, Raffaele (Philippe Noiret), right, and Rocco (Vittorio Mezzogiorno), left, argue together but mourn and dream separately in the bedroom they shared as young boys. Courtesy of the Museum of Modern Art/Film Stills Archive.

teargas. A war." Rocco's second dream therefore involves another kind of assault on social misery: a one-man clean-up campaign to rid young people of the syringes, rifles, and easy money that turn their lives into the human debris of contemporary urban existence.

If the other brothers' dreams parody a given cinematic genre—the cinema politico of Raffaele's terrorist nightmare or the "adult" melodrama of Nicola's revery—then Rocco's dream may be said to derive from musical comedy (or MTV before the fact). Set to the music of Pino Daniele's Neapolitan pop song "Je so' pazzo," the dream action involves clean-up squads of kids against stylized theatrical backdrops of New York City, Moscow, and Naples. Rocco experiences a virtual apotheosis at the end of the song as he climbs a mountain of swept-up debris and raises his arms in triumph with a painted Vesuvius arising in the background, on the painted shores of the Bay of Naples. The brazen artifice of Rocco's dream, in contrast to the more realistic modes of his brothers' imaginings, makes explicit its status as pure wish-fulfillment fantasy and only heightens our sense of his inadequacy in the face of such incurable social ills.

When Rocco intervenes in his brothers' ideological debate, he does so both because he is by nature a peacemaker and because he harbors a congenital distrust for political solutions. For Rocco, slogans, programs, party platforms, and elected officials are not the key to social justice. As far as he is concerned, the answer lies in a deeply personal notion of *caritas* that involves "changing the human heart," and as such it associates Rocco's code of ethics with a Christian humanist, or even Franciscan, approach to right action in the world. It should therefore come as no surprise that Rocco's involvement with the town be confined to the parish church. No sooner does he arrive at the house and pay his respects to the dead than Rocco visits the local sanctuary, where the priest has been awaiting him. "I knew you'd come," Don Vincenzo remarks, as if Rocco's advent were somehow foreordained, a necessary element in the providential scheme of things.

Of all the brothers, Rocco is the one most closely bound to the world of his parents. He is the only sibling to experience a flashback of his mother as a young woman and he is inextricably linked with his father through a casting strategy according to which the same actor (Vittorio Mezzogiorno) plays both Rocco and the young Donato. Arriving at the family farm on foot, along the same path that Donato had walked down after fantasizing the meeting with his dead wife, Rocco stops and seems to connect with the landscape in a way that his siblings' automated arrivals necessarily precluded. The casting choice also suggests that, of the three brothers, Rocco remains closest to the utopian values of the land, and in so doing Rosi naturalizes this character's Christian-humanist approach to social injustice.

No study of *Three Brothers* would be complete without consideration of the literary source for Rosi's inspiration. Though the filmmaker goes to great pains to minimize his debt to the textual model, Rosi's screenplay, written in collaboration with Tonino Guerra,[18] owes a great deal to Andrei Platonov's 1936 short story "The Third Son." "The tale of Platonov, which is very short," Rosi explains, "served as a starting point—the death of the mother, the telegram, the brothers who arrive (in the tale they are six, and here three), and the relationship that is born between the old man and the child. We also took the weeping of the child when she realizes that her grandmother is dead. All the rest was invented by us."[19]

Although Platonov's seven-page story could provide only the barest of skeletons for Rosi's screenplay, the filmmaker is unfair to reduce his debt to mere elements of plot. What Rosi fails to acknowledge in the above quote is the way in which Platonov's text authorized not only the narrative structure of the film but, more importantly, its allegorical mode. If Rosi's great achievement in *Three Brothers* is to link familial chronicle to social history, to construct, in the family microcosm, a compelling reflection of events on the national level, then Platonov's "Third Son" offers the richest of literary precedents. "An old woman died in a provincial town," the story begins, and with the death of this shriveled up, biologically exhausted body, Platonov considers the radical changes that take place in the familial body, as a corporate entity, and in the body politic of postrevolutionary Russia as a whole. Through a series of focalizers—the old husband, the country priest, and the third son—Platonov delivers a powerful social commentary whose subtleties and ironic reversals merit close scrutiny if we are to fathom the workings of Rosi's own allegorical mode.

The opening passages of the story are centered in the consciousness of the old man, whose sense of loss permeates all his perceptions, creating a natural and social environment in synchrony with his grief. When an aged female telegraph operator performs with shocking ineptitude, the old man projects onto her his own psychic disarray. "It seemed to him that the elderly woman had a broken heart, too, and a troubled soul that would never be quieted—perhaps she was a widow or a wrongfully deserted wife."[20] Nature, too, reflects his loss: as he waits for his sons by his wife's cold body, a "solitary gray bird" hops about its cage, flakes of "wet, tired snow" fall outside, and the sun shines "cold as a star" (65). If the pathetic fallacy conjures up a natural world in harmony with inner psychic experience, then such a device has special appropriateness to the organic coherence of rural life.

With the arrival of the sons, however, this natural cohesion is shattered; even the prose style suddenly shifts to express the disruptive effects of their advent. From the long, flowing, paratactic sentences describing the old man's experiences, the style abruptly changes to one of short, straightforward statements of fact. "The eldest son arrived by aeroplane the very next day" (65). Technology intervenes, and we soon learn that all six of the sons have done extremely well in the various lines of work that define the new, postrevolutionary state. The oldest is department foreman of an airplane factory; two sons, both sailors, have achieved the rank of captain; another is an actor in Moscow; yet another is a physicist (and a Communist); and the youngest is a student of agronomy. Such accomplishments in the fields of industry, transportation, science, agriculture, and the arts justify the old man's obvious pride in his "powerful sons"—a pride that eclipses his widower's grief. "Their father was not crying any more. He had wept his full alone and was now glancing at his half-dozen powerful sons with concealed emotion and a delight that was quite out of place in the circumstances" (66). As mobile, productive, cosmopolitan, and technologically evolved individuals, the brothers exemplify the glorified self-image of the modern Soviet state. In addition to the proud father, another character responds to these "six powerful men" in a way that suggests how their generational significance is ideologically fraught. Of all people, it is the country priest who views them as "representatives of the new world which he secretly admired but could not enter. On his own, he used to dream of performing some sort of heroic feat to break his way into the glorious future with the new generation" (68). Platonov reserves his most withering satire for this priest, whose aspirations to heroism combine elements of deus ex machina with the latest aviation technology. In this spirit, "he had even applied to the local aerodrome asking to be taken up to the highest point in a plane and dropped by parachute without an oxygen mask, but they had not replied" (68).

"The Third Son," then, involves two temporalities: that of traditional, agrarian, natural time—the time of birth, death, and seasonal cycles—and that of progressive, linear, historical time—that of irreversibility and change. Corresponding to these temporalities are two conceptions of space—those of continuity and of rupture—as signified, respectively, by the two bedrooms of the story. Together in the room with the coffin is the marriage bed, occupied now by the old man and his granddaughter. This room is illuminated by the glow of moonlight reflected by the falling snow outside, as befits a space of generational continuity and natural process. Next door, in a room electrically lit, the six brothers are housed as they had been in childhood, but their talk is of metal propellers and of voyages to foreign ports. They wrestle, laugh, and boast, in keeping with a need to perform their adult identities for one another. The inappropriateness of such behavior does not seem to bother the old man, so smitten is he by his powerful offspring that he would never dare to question their conduct. But one of the sons—the third one, the son of the title—is clearly distraught, and it is he who shames his siblings into a decorous, appropriate silence. Crossing the boundary from the sons' bedroom to the room with the coffin, the third brother stands over the corpse for a moment and then faints from emotion. It is his example of unbridled grief that frees his brothers to mourn, at last. "One by one they slipped off to other parts of the house, through the yard and the night that surrounded the place where they had spent their childhood, and wept" (72).

There could be no more poignant proof of the disintegration of the family unit than the separateness of this fraternal grieving, and Rosi puts Platonov's insight to powerful cinematic uses in his film's corresponding scene. When Rocco wakes up from his dream and goes into the kitchen to make coffee, he looks out of the window to see his siblings mourning in the courtyard below. Photographing the two brothers from behind Rocco's shoulders, the camera reveals Nicola, in long shot, sobbing against the back wall, and Raffaele, huddled apart from him, also mourning in solitude. The spectacle of his brothers' grief triggers Rocco's own outpouring of sorrow—sorrow as much for the emotional distance figured in this mise-en-scène as for the death of their mother.

In the Platonov story, the writer goes to some lengths to express the sons' perception of loss and its implications for a cultural history of the postrevolutionary age. The third brother experiences most acutely what all the siblings had mourned when they first beheld the corpse of their mother: "The lost happiness of love which had welled continuously and undemandingly in their mother's heart and had always found them, even across thousands of miles. They had felt it constantly, instinctively, and this awareness had given them added strength and courage to go about their lives" (66). Read etymologically, this mother is the mater-matrix—the principle of the land, rural life, the humus in which their identities are rooted, the basis of all their subsequent accomplishments in life. If, in diachronic terms, the mother allegorizes the agrarian Russian past, then Platonov's argument is that the successes of the present regime are predicated on the strengths of this ancestral culture. It is of the utmost significance, then, that the son most stricken by the death of the mother is the physicist (who is also, importantly, the only Communist Party member of the family), and as such the most "evolved" of them all. Yet it is he who suffers most intensely from the loss of the matrix and who is most aware of the need for connection to a source. Though we are excluded from his sorrowing—we do not overhear the words with which he silences his brothers, nor do we enter a mind about to lose consciousness before the object of its grief—the third son's reaction becomes normative. Neither the father, blinded by paternal pride, nor the priest, prey to ideological mystification, can offer reliable judgments on the postrevolutionary age, and as such they serve as foils for Platonov's own judgment, implied in the mute and anguished mourning of the third son.

Motivated by a similar impulse to condemn the rise of industrial, urban culture at the expense of its rural matrix, Rosi fully appropriates Platonov's allegory. The three brothers "belong to a generation that has in some way failed," remarks Rosi, "and for this there is the grandfather and little girl to close the circle, to give sense to the film."[21] By invoking the metaphor of the circle, Rosi affirms the temporal continuity that governs the natural world and anticipates the image of the wedding ring that heralds the film's Edenic theme. For Donato's memories of marriage merge with a vision of the agrarian past as earthly paradise— a blessed site of innocence and wholeness. To heighten our sense that this is a privileged space, Donato's flashback occurs immediately after the film's most violent moment—that of Raffaele's imagined assassination at terrorist hands.

At the center of Donato's garden of memory reside a man and a woman—Adam and Eve before the Fall. Though one critic faulted this sequence for its sentimentality, such a reaction fails to acknowledge that this is indeed a flashback, embedded in the idealizing consciousness of the newly bereaved.[22] Shot in slow motion, through the diaphanous cloth of the bridal veil, the opening frames of this reminiscence explicitly announce its soft-focus take on memory. Once the pace increases to normal speed, the camera moves to medium distance to re-

FIGURE 15 | Caterina (Simonetta Stefanelli) and the young Donato (Vittorio Mezzogiorno) search the sand for the lost wedding ring whose recovery allows them to consecrate their marriage a second time in *Three Brothers*. Courtesy of the Museum of Modern Art/Film Stills Archive.

veal a country wedding party, about to be rained out. Though the proverbial "wet bride, lucky bride" may be trite, it is indeed predictive of the long course of happy marriage that awaits the newlyweds. After a brief glimpse at the couple's honeymoon journey in a horse and buggy, the flashback reaches its culmination in a scene of surpassing lyricism. Lingering on the beach, Donato tends to the horse while Caterina amuses herself by burying her feet in the sand and sifting great handfuls of it through her fingers. At a certain point she realizes that her wedding ring is gone. "Donato, aggio perduto la fede" (I lost my wedding band), she announces in dialect. "We won't go until we find it," he reassures her, and he manages to retrieve the ring after cleverly resorting to the help of a sieve (fig. 15). When Donato puts the band back on her finger and kisses her, we realize that this is the true wedding—Adam and Eve alone in the garden. Without mediations, in an untainted, natural setting, the newlyweds reconsecrate their marriage in their own private state of grace. Against this ideal of marital bliss, all other relationships in the film are measured and found wanting: Raffaele's strained marriage, threatened from without, and Nicola's troubled one, destabilized from within.

Read as political allegory, this lapse has important implications for the course of postwar Italian history, suggesting that contemporary Italy has indeed fallen away from the Eden of its provincial, agrarian past. There is another moment in the film, also associated with the mother, that serves to mark the specific historical coordinates of Italy's fall from a prior state of perfection. I am referring here to the film's first flash-back, embedded in Rocco's memory as a way of linking this particular son to his parents' utopian context. As Rocco beholds the image of his dead mother, to the accompaniment of the *nenia* (the dirge of the neighborhood women), the scene dissolves into a close-up of his child's face amidst the sounds of shelling and prayer. Called to his young mother's side, Rocco peeks out from her protective embrace to see the rosary dangling before him, amidst his family members and neighbors who have sought refuge from the advancing front. At a certain point, the artillery sounds give way to the joyous pealing of bells, and the camera pans the townscape, bespattered with pro-Fascist graffiti: *Duce, Vincere, Vinceremo.* Now a lone tank approaches as the little community emerges from hiding. A camouflaged army vehicle, like a strange alien creature, crests the hill, broadcasting the sounds of American jazz from its depths: "I can't give you anything but love, baby." Nothing could be more incongruous than the apparition of this hi-tech equipment spouting an incomprehensible musical language on a primeval Italian landscape. And to compound the indecipherability of the event, Donato and his neighbors interpret this as an enemy assault, raising their hands in surrender. When a living human being jumps out of this machine, kisses the ground, introduces himself in English, surname first, as Galatti, Salvatore, and then switches into Italian to announce "Pure io sono italiano, paisano" (I too am Italian, countryman), the reversal of expectations could not be more complete. In an appropriate end to this scene of incongruities, the soldier than embraces every civilian in sight.

By synthesizing a series of oppositions—Italian versus American, agrarian versus technological, enemy versus ally, this scene invests the Liberation with the highest utopian significance. It is no accident that the liberator in this episode is an Italian American named Salvatore, himself a synthesis of the old and the new, returned to his homeland to redeem it from the sins of its past. As Salvatore hugs the young Caterina, their composite image fades into the present-tense scene of mourning, accompanied by the dirge of the neighborhood women. By framing this reminiscence with prayer—the prayer for the dead, in the here and now, and the rosary on the eve of the Liberation—Rosi associates Caterina's youthful maternal role with the promise of national-popular rebirth and her death with the disappointment of that hope.

As the moment of highest political idealism, when the military victory against Fascism meant that the new Italy could pursue its agenda for domestic self-renewal, the Liberation also had important consequences for the cinema. In such films as those of Rossellini's war trilogy—*Open City* (1945), *Paisan* (1946), and *Germany, Year Zero* (1948)—the experience of World War II gave rise to the cinematic form of neorealism in order to express the revolutionary power of its subject matter. Rosi has made no secret of his enthusiasm for neorealism as a form of political action—itself an outgrowth of the domestic agenda of the Resistance. "We were all desirous and aware of participating in the reconstruction of the country, and we thought that with the cinema we could do something. This, in fact, occurred, because those films, all told, accomplished a great deal. This is neorealism, for me, as a fact of life."[23] It should come as no surprise, then, that the canonical neorealist treatment of the Liberation—that of Rossellini's *Paisan*—should be explicitly invoked in this flashback, where the mutual misunderstandings that plagued encounters between Italians and American GIs in the earlier film would undergo "a neat reversal" in Rosi's decision to make the Liberators Italian Americans.[24] Thus, by alluding to the Liberation in his film's first flashback, Rosi is invoking both the political idealism of this historical moment and its privileged mode of cinematic expression. The Liberation and neorealism, then, serve as twin indicators of contemporary Italy's fall from grace.

But paradise is not utterly lost. In Nicola's daughter Marta, child of the urban north, the dead Caterina seems to be reborn, closing the circle to which Rosi had alluded in his commentary on the current generation. A series of details suggests that Marta is indeed the reincarnation of her grandmother: she sleeps in Caterina's old bed, receives her grandmother's earrings as an inheritance, is juxtaposed with the elderly woman's image in the family photograph collection, and buries herself in the grain just as the new bride had done on the beach in Donato's honeymoon reminiscence. In one scene, a mystical bond between grandmother and granddaughter is established as Marta views the corpse from a secret window high above the place of mourning. From this hidden vantage point, Marta appropriates an omniscient view suggestive of Caterina's own perspective from beyond the grave.

Most important to her role in establishing continuity is Marta's acquisition of Donato's rural wisdom. Without an alarm clock, Marta wonders, how does her grandfather know when to get up in the morning? "Peasants regulate themselves by the stars and the animals," Donato explains. "The rooster crows two times, first at 1 A.M. and then at 4. Old folks get up at the second crowing. Children wait for the donkey to bray at 7. Three stars line up at dawn, called the dipper. The morning star precedes them by half an hour." "If I stay with you," the child observes, "I'll learn all these things. In Turin, there are neither donkeys nor roosters." "But there are the stars" her grandfather reassures her. What Marta learns from Donato, and what she will take back with her to Turin, is the cosmic connectedness of things, the bond between the heavens and the earth, between the natural world and the world of men. As the repository of her grandfather's wisdom, Marta represents genealogical continuity, reversing the effects of the family diaspora and the antitraditionalism of her father's generation. Such continuity is perhaps best expressed in the image of the egg that Marta offers to her grandfather after the funeral cortege makes its way offscreen.

If *Three Brothers* is about mothers as signifiers of origins, it is important to note that the film's only child, Marta, is literally motherless. Giovanna is off in Turin, and there is no maternal surrogate within the reconstituted family in the south. Yet we do not sense that Marta is in any way bereft or incomplete. In connecting with her culture of origin, she is gaining the metaphorical mother that Nicola regretted losing as emigrant—"lacking the ground under his feet," as he told Giovanna in his daydream of reconciliation. Marta's discovery of her matrix is rendered in specifically cinematic terms in one of the film's most lyrical moments. Sent off by Nicola to play in the barn, Marta leads our gaze through a labyrinth of miscellaneous farm implements that De

Santis's camera work succeeds in endowing with the magic of child-hood curiosity. In one long, fluid take, the camera precedes her into the barn, cranes up and down again, shooting her behind the very carriage that the newlyweds had taken on their honeymoon (another connection with the young Caterina), then follows her as she moves left to examine an array of cowbells suspended on the wall, then circles her and cranes up as, at the end of the take, she moves through the archway into an inner chamber. Now Marta begins to ascend to successive levels of the barn, stopping to play with the chickens housed on the next story and then climbing to the uppermost floor, the granary, where she disrobes and buries herself in the grain as if she had finally found her true element.

In one of the film's most significant departures from the Platonov story, the old man and his granddaughter do not follow the coffin to the grave site but remain behind to give their own meaning to Caterina's demise. Where Platonov's mystified old man was less grief-stricken than "proud and content that he, too, would be buried by these six strong men, and just as finely" (72), Rosi's widower transforms his loss into a poetic reaffirmation of his marriage vows. Back in the room where her corpse had lain, Donato finds Caterina's wedding band and places it on his own finger. This is, of course, the second time he has found the ring, and it recalls that Edenic moment when bride and groom had reconsecrated their marriage on the beach. With this farewell gesture, Donato reweds Caterina, now in the presence of Marta, who will "close the circle," to use Rosi's own metaphor for generational continuity. Nor is this ring devoid of political significance, for the Italian term for a wedding band is *fede*, recalling Raffaele's plea for a society based on faith and hope, not violence and fear.

If marriage serves as a microcosm of the ideal society—the synthesis of opposites figured in the Liberation scene—then the analogy between the wedding band and the social bond is easily drawn. In the image of the circle, Rosi is issuing a plea that Italy keep faith with the ideals of its rural past and that it seek to recover the matrix, if not in the historical order, at least in memory and art. When Marta returns to Turin, she may not be able to see the stars in the industrial night sky, but she will at least know that they are there.

7

The Alternative Family of
Ricky Tognazzi's *La scorta*

When Ricky Tognazzi announced that "cinema has the responsibility of intervening in reality,"[1] he was aligning himself with a venerable tradition of postwar Italian filmmaking, from neorealism, which conceived of itself as a vehicle for the reconstruction of Italian national identity, to the cinema politico of the late 1960s and 1970s, which offered a critique of the contemporary institutions of power. This tradition served as "an invitation to react, to use the tools that a democratic state makes available to isolate the well-known forces of social disintegration and to try to free ourselves from them before it's too late."[2] Just as neorealism emerged in the wake of the Resistance and translated into cinematic terms that movement's hopes for social renewal, so did cinema politico follow on the heels of 1968 and give expression to the revolutionary ferment of those years. In its relentless exposé of corruption, abuse of power, and collusion between official institutions and criminal forces, the angry, denunciatory nature of this later cinema was predicated on a confidence in the medium's cognitive and moral powers to move the public to outrage and reform. It would be disingenuous, however, for Tognazzi, filming in 1993, to claim the same revolutionary faith that could motivate the cinema-politico filmmakers to launch their appeal to viewer activism in the post-1968 era.[3] What Tognazzi's identification with his cinema-politico predecessors reveals, instead, is a self-consciousness that invites us to analyze his relationship to the genre he so deliberately updates, to take the measure of the distance between 1975 and 1993, and to ponder the significance of the attempt to revive the genre in the last decade of the millennium.[4]

138 | In technical terms, Tognazzi's debt to his predecessors is unequivo-

cal. The choice of Ennio Morricone, whose tense, jerky soundtracks have become the musical hallmark of cinema politico, announces Tognazzi's participation in the continuity of the genre. The highly mobile camera, the abrupt cuts, the frequent recourse to close-ups, the fast-paced editing—all these call attention to the presence of the cinematic apparatus and hark back to the stylized technique inaugurated by Costa-Gavras in *Z* (1969) and refined by Italian cinema-politico directors Elio Petri, Damiano Damiani, Giuseppe Ferrara, and Francesco Rosi. Despite the technical virtuosity of this cinema, however, its visual quality is austere, essential—indeed, antipicturesque. Architecture is invariably functional/modern, office interiors are washed out and flat, lighting is undistinguished. Even when landscapes are breathtakingly lush or dramatic, the cinema-politico camera cannot linger on them, for the anxious soundtrack pushes us on to confront the possible threat lurking around the next curve of the road or behind the next promontory on the horizon.

Several other antecedents join that of cinema politico to give *La scorta* its generic identity. In one of the film's defining sequences, the magistrate De Francesco is taken to his office in a ride across town at breakneck speed, with blaring sirens, screeching breaks, nervous musical score, and camera work that cranes up to dizzying aerial heights. A throwback to the thriller, whose high-velocity chase scene, perfected in *The French Connection,* has become a fixture of the genre, this sequence also evokes, if somewhat ironically, a stock motif of the indigenous Sicilian film. I speak of the traditional procession through the streets of the town to celebrate important religious occasions, with special emphasis on local saints. The speeding-car trip, which begins at De Francesco's doorstep and leads to a modern office building whose internal geometry has a distinctly futuristic cast, mimics and reverses the slow march of the archaic and unchanging religious procession through the city streets. A set piece of so many Sicilian films, from Pietro Germi's *Divorce Italian Style* (1961) and *Seduced and Abandoned* (1964) to Franco Zeffirelli's *Cavalleria rusticana* (1982), and transplanted to Hell's Kitchen in Francis Ford Coppola's *Godfather Part II* (1974), the procession had offered public cover for the enactment of private passions. The high-speed ride to the office parodies this Sicilian trademark movement through town, making the public element of this spectacle the very source of its danger. In the siren-screeching race across Trapani, De Francesco's high-profile identity is simultaneously announced and protected from the dangers of external exposure. In this modernized, paranoid version of the traditional religious procession, Tognazzi reveals both the cultural and generic provenance of his *cinema politico alla siciliana.*

Like his cinema-politico predecessors, whose stylization distinguished their work from unmediated documentary reportage, Tognazzi, too, locates his film between the poles of external reference and aesthetic autonomy. "If, on the one hand, *La scorta* wants to render homage to the victims of Mafia crime," writes Giona Nazzaro, "on the other, [the film] wants to strive to be an autonomous cinematographic product, with its own aesthetic rules and motivations."[5] It is this dual ambition that has confounded reviewers of the film, denying them the comfort of standard critical categories and interpretive labels. "For a film such as this," Maurizio Regosa asks, "should we use social, political, and moral criteria, or rather, specifically cinematographic ones?"[6]

To complicate the documentary pole of Tognazzi's undertaking, critics note that *La scorta* has double reference—both to the true-life experiences of Judge Francesco Taurisano and his bodyguards in Trapani[7] and to the assassinations of anti-Mafia judges Giovanni Falcone and Paolo Borsellino in 1992.[8] Though the story of Taurisano is the one that is directly represented on the screen, it is the murders of Falcone and Borsellino that determine the atmosphere of social trauma that underlies this film. Indeed, we would not be misled in identifying the Falcone/Borsellino tragedies as the unspoken signified of *La scorta.* Accordingly, what sets the film's plot in motion is a double assassination powerfully reminiscent of the historical episode. It is the murder of anti-Mafia Judge Rizzo and Marshal Virzì that motivates carabiniere Angelo Mandolesi to return to Trapani as a bodyguard and Judge Michele De Francesco to request a transfer to the Mafia-troubled island from Varese. When the newspaper headlines announce "Trapani: the nth deadly ambush," we realize that the film refers both to an ongoing process of corruption and terror and to the specific murders of Falcone and Borsellino, which had come to stand, by a kind of double antonomasia, for them all.

What distances Tognazzi's film from its cinema-politico predecessors is its refusal to end as it began, its decision *not* to conclude with yet another crime photo of a bloody corpse slumped on the seat of a car or sprawled on the pavement of a street. Rosi's 1975 *Cadaveri eccellenti* ends with such an image, justifying its title and epitomizing the genre that denounced the power elite as implacable executioners of anyone who dared to expose the injustice of the system. Tognazzi's film begins with footage of the murdered Rizzo and Virzì and is later plagued with images of the martyred Frasca and the slain Bonura and Marchetti, but it does not come full circle with the dreaded shots of the slaughtered De Francesco and his entourage that the genre has led us to expect. Their illustrious corpses are not the next to face the flashbulbs of news photographers and to enter the files of the "nth deadly ambush" to strike Trapani—and by extension, Italy—in recent years. Tognazzi's film breaks the cycle, identifying his camera's final gaze not with that of the crime photographer but with that of the magistrate himself, as he leaves the shore on a boat headed for the mainland. De Francesco may have been temporarily defeated, but he is not dead. The film's final shot, from De Francesco's high-angle perspective, is of the four men who have formed a remarkable and unlikely utopia together with him.[9] The gaze of the magistrate, leaving for the mainland but vowing to return to complete his mission, is the gaze of the engagé filmmaker who has attempted to open an established genre to new signifying possibilities.

Another way to think about the distance between 1975 and 1993, between *cinema politico classico* and the *neo–cinema politico* of Tognazzi, is the distance between center and periphery that characterizes the shift in the film's focus. The novelty of *La scorta* resides not in the configuration of its social reality but in the displacement of emphasis from the wielders of power to those who must protect them (fig. 16). This shift gives *La scorta* a peculiar relationship to the cinema-politico genre from which it derives—a relationship that could be described as eccentric in the etymological sense of the term. *La scorta*'s concern for those who literally encircle the judge with their own bodies, whose fates depend on the decisions he makes from his own center of power, means that the genre itself has been displaced, from center to periphery, from agency to reaction. The eccentricity of the film is one more index of the distance separating 1993 from a time two decades earlier when cinema-politico filmmakers could indeed conceive of their project as a concrete intervention in the historical process.

FIGURE 16 | Andrea Corsale (Enrico Lo Verso), left, Angelo Mandolesi (Claudio Amendola), center, and Fabio Muzzi (Ricky Memphis), right, strike poses of protective readiness as they prepare to accompany Judge Michele De Francesco to his office. Courtesy of Istituto Luce.

Yet Tognazzi's eccentricity does not condemn his perspective to hand-wringing defeatism and doom. Though portrayed as victims of a society that does not believe in capital punishment but that condemns the bodyguards of an anti-Mafia judge to certain death, according to Muzzi's bitter assessment, these characters do not wallow in the defeatism that such a perspective could invite. Instead, the film confers upon the members of *la scorta* (the escort) the privilege of moral agency and the dignity of their commitment to a cause. It is these characters, devoid of the entitlements of the judge's bourgeois background (e.g., his predilection for Beethoven) and professional prestige, who rise above the material pressures of their lives (Corsale must support a family and exert "pull" to get decent housing; Frasca must hide his engagement to a local girl; Muzzi is angling for a transfer to a safer post) to join him in his judicial crusade. At the film's turning point, the members of la scorta cease to function as passive victims of circumstance and freely choose to undertake a far more active role in the anti-Mafia investigation than their custodial functions would require. As they progress from the depths of material self-interest to the heights of committed action, this microcosm is Tognazzi's utopian alternative to the angry denunciation of the cinema-politico films of the 1960s and 1970s.

Throughout *La scorta*, Tognazzi makes multileveled use of the metaphor of family to describe the dismantling of corrupt and malevolent social units and the reassembling, or even invention, of new ones. Angelo Mandolesi's motivation for transferring from Rome to Trapani to enter into the service of an anti-Mafia judge is essentially a familial one. Pietro Virzì, the marshal assassinated along with Judge Rizzo, had been a mentor to Mandolesi. "Pietro taught me everything," Angelo tells his mother. "Together with him, I became a man." Though we are not made privy to the details of Mandolesi's family past, we infer that it is a troubled one, involving parental separation and a fatherless childhood. In leaving Rome, where his father resides ("good riddance"), and volunteering for a position in Trapani that will allow him to avenge the death of Virzì, Mandolesi is substituting a surrogate paternal figure for his biological one. This choice, motivated by powerful personal ties as much as by anti-Mafia zeal, anticipates the decision that all the members of the judge's escort will make in preferring their new utopian family, headed by De Francesco, to the old patriarchal structures of favoritism, corruption, and self-interest.

In Mandolesi's case, the theme of a broken biological family is expressed with great cinematic economy in an early sequence in the film. As he arrives home in Trapani, it is clear that this is a woman's space. In a parody of the Annunciation, an aged crone cries out to the unsuspecting and delighted Signora Mandolesi: "It's Angelo." After the mother and son warmly embrace, the camera cuts to the dining-room sideboard, festooned with photographs that give a thumbnail sketch of the family past. Two of the photographs feature a mother and child: to the right is a portrait of a woman and boy grinning frontally for the camera, while at the center is a large photo of a woman holding a baby up in the air. On the other side of this photo, surrounded by a wide border of wood, is a smaller picture of a man in uniform, distanced as much from the mother/son images by its thick ornamental frame as by the remote formality of its military pose.

Another discredited father figure, this time within the patriarchal scheme of the Sicilian magistracy, is Salvatore Caruso, the solicitor-general, whose power to do favors and command obligation earns him

Muzzi's admiring label of *padre eterno*. Caruso indeed exercises his authority to provide for those who show the proper filial respect by offering to expedite Corsale's application for upscale housing in return for the latter's services as a spy. No sooner does Corsale inform him of De Francesco's maneuvers to link the assassinations of Rizzo and Virzì with the Mafia's control of local water supplies than Caruso remarks, "Tell your wife I'm looking into that thing [*quella cosa*]." *Quella cosa,* of course, is the family's rank on the waiting list for better housing, the quid pro quo for Corsale's activities as informer. By referencing Corsale's wife, Caruso privileges the concept of family as the justification for spying and sets himself up as the benevolent father who will see to the domestic needs of his protégé.

Caruso appoints Corsale *capo-scorta* (head bodyguard) because he believes that he can control him through the promise of favors that will enhance the young man's domestic position as *capo-famiglia* (head of family). In his accountability to Caruso, however, Corsale finds himself in direct conflict with Mandolesi, whose own "family" loyalty to Virzì requires his total commitment to the anti–Mafia struggle. Once Corsale switches "fathers" and allies himself with the judicial cause of De Francesco, his roles as head bodyguard and head of family come into direct conflict. Now everything that Corsale does in the name of professional duty puts his biological family at risk. Where the domestic life of the Corsales had previously been merely infiltrated by news of Andrea's new assignment (the youngest son shoots his parents with a toy gun in mid embrace; the oldest son asks if his father's car will explode upon ignition), now that life is literally threatened from without. The most insidious of means, the anonymous phone call, is used to inform Lia that her sons are being observed down to the fine points of their daily attire. "I saw your son Igor at school," says the anonymous voice over the phone. "He looked cute in that red T-shirt. Instead you dressed Mattia in green." Nothing could be more ghoulish than this parody of maternal interest in sartorial detail, revealing an intimate knowledge of Lia's children's lives that implies total power over them. Understandably distraught by these implied threats to her family's security, Lia resents Mandolesi's bachelor status and consequent freedom from the vulnerability to which Corsale subjects his wife and sons. Ultimately, Corsale's duties cause his literal separation from his family when Lia and the boys are sent off to stay with his mother-in-law in the wake of Frasca's violent death.

Even before he was assigned to guard De Francesco, Raffaele Frasca had been obliged to suppress his own sentimental life. Engaged to Milena, a sales clerk in a pastry shop, Raffaele did not want to suffer the fate of a colleague transferred out of Trapani for romancing a local girl. But it is Raffaele's choice to guard De Francesco's daughter, Roberta, even when officially off-duty, that leads to his death by the bomb destined for her. Thus his insistence on membership in the new professional family denies Frasca the familial future promised by his engagement to Milena.

De Francesco is himself literally without family. He has accepted the assignment in Trapani as much to escape the scene of his failed marriage in Varese as to escape the notoriety that he has gained as a judicial troublemaker. So strained is his relationship with his wife that he dare not phone her for cooking advice, and she, in turn, refuses to go up to his apartment after accompanying their daughter to his building in a cab. It is at Roberta's birthday party, celebrated with great exuberance by De Francesco, his bodyguards, Lia, and the three little boys, that we realize how much this group comes to resemble an extended family. In Corsale's three sons, Roberta seems to have found the siblings she never had, and Lia sees in the young girl the longed-for daughter ("Why don't we try for a girl?" she asks Corsale as they watch Roberta blow out her birthday candles).

For the conception of this strange new family, we must look to an earlier scene—one that unfolds in the innermost recesses of the house, in the space usually reserved for maternal occupancy. I speak of the kitchen where De Francesco receives Corsale as he prepares his solitary evening meal. Wearing an apron, brandishing a spatula, De Francesco announces both his appropriation of the female role and his self-consciousness in doing so. Of the women in his life, neither mother nor wife is capable of advising him on the cooking techniques that would rescue his tasteless pasta-with-broccoli. Corsale is able to help by making the distinctly Sicilian suggestion of adding anchovies to De Francesco's bland sauce. This exchange, so unremarkable in substance, is momentous in its breakdown of the social barriers that organize Italian life. First of all, the unannounced visit of a subordinate to his boss

FIGURE 17 | Andrea Corsale (Enrico Lo Verso) confesses to De Francesco that he has been leaking information about the judge's anti-Mafia investigation to his boss in *La scorta*. Courtesy of Istituto Luce.

in the privacy of the latter's home involves a breach of the boundaries between the public and private spheres on which traditional Italian social relations are based. The north/south division, which so often plays itself out in the culinary realm, is successfully bridged in this anchovy-enhanced recipe. And the gender dichotomy, obviously transcended in De Francesco's cooking activities, is further overcome by the exchange of male confidences in the place conventionally reserved for female gossip over coffee and cigarettes.

In this liberated domestic space, purged of stereotypes, Corsale can come clean (fig. 17). He can divest himself of his loyalty to a corrupt system of patronage and pledge himself to a new father—one who will let him live by the passionate intensity that he so admires in Mandolesi, a man driven by "an internal anger" "like a wounded animal." We can trace the origin of the new family—its conception—to Corsale's admission of betrayal and De Francesco's decision to reward this display of honesty by keeping the young man on as head bodyguard. Corsale's conversion, in turn, inspires Mandolesi to rejoin the team that he had abandoned after the two had come to blows in the parking garage below the offices of the judiciary.

By the end, Muzzi, too, is inspired to convert, rejecting the long-coveted transfer to a safer position outside Trapani. In finally announcing his decision to remain in the escort, Muzzi's quip "I don't have the courage to go away" reveals the radical transformation that his own sentiments have undergone during the course of the story. As the only draftee in the group of otherwise professional carabinieri, Muzzi is the least experienced and the most faint-hearted of the group. Among his first words are expressions of disappointment that he did not have the pull to land an easy job. "As long as they don't put us in the escort," he adds. The next scene, Muzzi's training session for la scorta, spells the end of even that hope for salvation—"we'll be blown up to protect a guy who'll die anyway." Once informed that the escort will not have the protection of an armored car, and that only two of the four guards can have bulletproof gear, Muzzi suggests that they "draw straws to see who dies and who gets to wear the vest." As the forthright spokesman for the fear that such an assignment necessarily entails, Muzzi's formulation of his desire to stay in la scorta by the film's end is especially poignant. The very syntax of the phrase *non ho il coraggio di andarmene* (I don't have the courage to go away), with its surprising substitution of the expected infinitive for its opposite, shows the magnitude of the young man's change of heart.

The broken families of De Francesco and Mandolesi and the threatened one of Corsale are not the only foils to the new notion of family that emerges in the film: another relationship between a man of power and his escort is encoded in familial terms. Senator Bonura and his bodyguard Marchetti share bonds that exceed those of a professional nature; not only is Marchetti the recipient of the senator's gifts (he wears an elegant silk tie as a sign of his boss's favor), but his baby boy, to be born in two months, will be godson to Bonura and will bear his first name—Nestor. As the one who will hold the baby in his arms during baptism, the senator will assume the important position of teacher and moral mentor to the child and will thus come to play a theologically sanctioned role of great importance within the Marchetti family structure. Like Rizzo and Virzì, Bonura and Marchetti will share a violent death at the hands of the Mafia, but for reasons that diametrically oppose those that condemned the former pair. Bonura had tried to have it both ways—publicly supporting the judiciary's anti-Mafia crusade while privately colluding with the Mazzaglia family interests. When that private collusion is exposed, Bonura must be silenced, along with his "adoptive" son, Marchetti.

Another malignant social unit that uses the family as its structuring principle is, of course, the Mafia itself. Unlocatable and abstract, with a family head *(capo-famiglia)* never seen in the film, the Mafia family is all the more sinister for its invisibility. In investigating Giuseppe Mazzaglia, Mandolesi learns that the mob boss has no criminal record whatsoever and that his sole appearance in police files is as the victim of car theft. The only avowed mafioso that we meet in the film, Nino Carabba, was originally a member of a rival family and therefore perfectly positioned to do Mazzaglia's dirty work.

Family is used as a term of disparagement by De Francesco to describe the inner workings of the judiciary in its attempt to cover up its own inadequacies and misdeeds. When De Francesco demands an inquiry into the disappearance of some important files and is instead subject himself to trial by inquisition, he snarls, "I don't like this family business." In the end, of course, De Francesco is disowned by the official family of investigative law. The exclusive use of voice-over in the film's semifinal sequence gives cinematic expression to the authority of the system to remove this deeply disruptive element from its midst. Reluctant to acknowledge the letter of dismissal himself, De Francesco asks Corsale to read it aloud as they pack up the office and take their leave. It is therefore Corsale's voice that we hear on the soundtrack reciting the litany of official grievances against the maverick judge. With this acoustic background of relentless indictment, the *cinéma-vérité* camera shows us business as usual in the offices of the magistracy. Uncooperative elements will not be tolerated by the system, which will purge itself by bureaucratic bulletin if not by an assassin's bullet.

As would be expected of a film that rethinks the traditional idea of family, gender is an issue of considerable consequence. There is a great deal of anxiety about the meaning of masculinity among the men of la scorta. De Francesco's defiance of gender boundaries in his donning of an apron is undermined by his obvious ineptitude as a cook. (Could we consider the scorched broccoli a vindication of his manhood?) Virility, and its concomitant attributes of courage and grit, are opposed to sentimentality—little boys should not be cuddled when they are awake or they will become like Muzzi, faint-hearted and soft. When Corsale sends his family away for safety, he asks Lia to kiss the boys for him at night, but only after they are asleep. Rather than engage in an emotional display of remorse and pardon, it is on the shooting range that Corsale and Mandolesi resolve their quarrel, admiring each other's marksmanship and implicitly agreeing to join forces once more.

Early in the film, however, Tognazzi establishes masculinity as a signifier of something beyond the confines of gender. When Mandolesi claims Virzì as his surrogate father, it is because "together with him I became a man." But Virzì's brand of manhood comes to mean a commitment to something over and above the self, a willingness to seek justice against the worst possible odds. Furthermore, manhood means solidarity with another, as evidenced by the Virzì-Rizzo collaboration—a collaboration that leads Virzì to share the fate of the body he chooses to guard. Within the world of the film, manliness is associated with civil virtues of the highest order—a coming-of-age in the renewed and redeemed social family of Italy.

If the kitchen scene in De Francesco's apartment marks the conception of the new family of idealized social relations, then the scene of the meal around Corsale's dining-room table marks its consecration. The ritual of breaking bread together has sacramental force in this episode, harking back to the biblical prototype of the meal of solidarity and self-sacrifice enacted in the ritual of Communion. Though the holy wafer of the Sacrament is replaced by cannoli and the number of disciples is reduced to four, the ritual supper of De Francesco and his men is as solemn and binding as its scriptural antecedent.

The scene begins with a close-up of the last remaining pastries, a sign of Raffaele Frasca's secret engagement to Milena and anticipation of his own mortal sacrifice for his new family of justice seekers. The camera, assuming the role of host, "does the honors," beginning with De Francesco and then circling the table to introduce the remaining guests. The dialogue makes explicit this scene's function in building a new, unconventional family of social relations that will replace a variety of corrupt and dysfunctional familial structures, both literal and metaphoric. As the camera circles the table, Corsale's oldest son asks De Francesco if he has a wife. The boy feels a natural need to locate this attractive and commanding guest in the context of the most meaningful social unit a young child can know. "Yes, I have a wife. And I also have a daughter. Her name is Roberta. She lives with her mother in Varese." When the boy asks "is she afraid of bombs?" he reveals, of course, his failure to comprehend the logistics of broken marriages. But of greater significance is his insight into the way in which public service and private interests collide, just as his own father's duties as head bodyguard and head of family make mutually exclusive claims on his loyalties. This tension reaches the breaking point in the final shot of the scene, where soundtrack and image come into violent conflict. Having sealed their pact of allegiance to De Francesco in his judicial crusade, Mandolesi exults: "If we're united, how much TNT will they have to put under our butts to blow us up?" Against this soundtrack of macho bravado and faith in the efficacy of the new family to defy the old patriarchal structures of intimidation and greed, what we see onscreen is Lia, signifier of the *biological* family, which stands to lose the most in this challenge to a corrupt and dangerous status quo.

Throughout this scene, Tognazzi's camera work and dialogue have maintained an admirable balance between the mechanisms of leadership and collective consent. While the camera regularly returns to De Francesco as the visual fulcrum of the mise-en-scène, it also sets up separate fields of vision, shifting from shot-countershot relations between Mandolesi and Corsale, who sit to one side of the judge, and Muzzi and Frasca, on the other. The editing also permits across-the-table exchanges so that relations between all members of the escort are clearly established.

Once Corsale's wife and children leave the dining room, the stage is cleared for the serious business of the evening to commence. "I've been eating alone too long," the judge begins. "It is a pleasure to find myself among friends." Having centered on De Francesco, the camera now cuts to Frasca, whose smile of genuine delight confirms the truth of the judge's observation. In his next claim, De Francesco makes explicit the metaphoric significance of this *convivio* when he equates "eating alone" with his troubles on the job. "In the public prosecutor's office, things aren't going well." Isolation at the workplace has prompted him to seek this alternative source of support. "I'll continue the investigation of the wells," he announces, "even though Caruso took it from me." "If you're continuing the work of Judge Rizzo," Corsale replies, "we'll continue the work of Marshal Virzì."

Corsale's response makes a series of connections vital to the solidarity of their enterprise. By linking their current crusade to the recent history of the anti-Mafia struggle, Corsale transforms the deaths of Rizzo and Virzì into a life-affirming call-to-arms. In psychological terms, he signals his solidarity with Mandolesi, whose filial bond with Virzì had motivated the deep-seated, personal passion for justice that Corsale so admired and envied. Most importantly, the statement of continuity in *relational* terms—as Virzì was to Rizzo, so we will be to you—vindicates the centrality of the bond between body and guard, between judge and escort, that resides at the heart of Tognazzi's social message. It is this relationship that emerges as the true "hero" of the film, above and beyond the individual instances of heroism with which the story abounds. In formal terms, this *convivio* of committed men returns us to the opening scene of the film, when Virzì's father prepares for the arrival of his son and Rizzo as dinner guests. That meal, of course, is never eaten, for the murder that sets the plot in motion occurs in the street below as the old man prepares the table and puts out the carafe of wine. The dinner-table scene of De Francesco and his men, with all its implications for the forging of an ideal community of commitment, is the continuation of the meal that was so violently interrupted at the start of the film, and the proof that the profoundly antisocial, dystopian act of the assassins could not ultimately prevent this solemn rite of community from taking place.

Just as the pact between De Francesco and Corsale had already been sealed in the earlier scene in the judge's kitchen, the present exchange reaffirms that understanding and establishes it in terms that privilege Mandolesi's role in the triangle. Now the camera crosses the table to Frasca, who responds to Corsale's query, "Raffaele, what will you do?" with a vivid and telling formulation. "Judge, my father left me three things: my intuition, my physical appearance, and a bunch of keys—the keys to my life. It's a question of finding the right lock [*serratura*]. You, in my opinion, are that lock." Frasca's response reads like a miniature fairy tale, complete with challenge to the young prince to win his inheritance, the magic number three, and the riddle to solve. By couching his answer in the language of folklore, handed down literally from father to son, Frasca links his own decision to fight injustice with the traditional values of the land. The image of the *serratura*—an image that must be unlocked in order to apply the father's dictum to the concrete circumstances of his son's life—reveals the cognitive work that Frasca himself must perform at this crucial moment. In interpreting the metaphor, and specifically in identifying its "signified" with De Francesco himself, Frasca has made the personal moral choice that his father's lesson required.

Now the camera moves to Muzzi. "Aren't you going to ask me?" he blurts out. But the men across the table answer for him. Cutting to Mandolesi and Corsale, the latter confirms with, "We know that you're with us." Muzzi does not object, and the camera settles on him, in mute assent. Only later, in the bunker, will he definitively speak for himself in the remarkable announcement of his refusal to accept the long-awaited transfer to a safer place.

The implications of the dinner-table scene do not limit themselves to the four men who vow, each in his own way, to accept the judge's invitation to act. A visual analysis of this scene reveals the camera's inclusion of the film's viewers as fellow guests, as cognitive and moral partners in the pact that this onscreen community has sealed in solidarity with the judge. The unspoken question posed by the camera, in a variant on Corsale's query to Frasca, is "What will *you* do?" If the true hero of *La scorta* is the relational bond between the body and its guards, when that body is committed to the pursuit of an ideal that can renew an ailing and corrupt social family, then the film's mission must be a motivational one. It must seek to instill in its spectators a mimetic desire, a solidarity with the fictional community that the viewers will in turn seek to replicate in the world beyond the screen. "Now, if *La scorta* lives equally its own life," writes Giona Nazzaro, "that is due to the fact that both among the actors and between the film and its spectators it has established a feeling of solidarity."[10] *La scorta* then seeks to mediate and perpetuate the chain of personal bonds that enact, in miniature, the filmmaker's utopian vision. The ordinariness of these men, their characterization through the use of "dialectal sprinklings, according to the dictates of postwar neorealism,"[11] may be understood as a way of inviting viewer identification. The bodyguards' very accessibility, their refusal to adhere to the category of the exceptional, means that *La scorta*'s example can—indeed, should—be reproducible in the lives of its viewers.

When Corsale remarks to Mandolesi, apropos of a convicted criminal undergoing rehabilitation in Caruso's office, "People change," he may be deluded in the corrupt context of the Sicilian judiciary, but he gives voice to Tognazzi's own faith in the mimetic power of *cinema impegnato,* of committed filmmaking. And when De Francesco takes leave of his escort with the promise "I'll do my best to return," it is not hard to discern the filmmaker's own commitment to renew the struggle through cinematic means.

8

The Gaze of Innocence

LOST AND FOUND IN

GIANNI AMELIO'S *STOLEN CHILDREN*

The title and format of *Il ladro di bambini*—which in its English version is titled *Stolen Children*—immediately announce the film's double allegiance to Italian national cinematic tradition.[1] The most obvious recourse is to De Sica's 1948 masterpiece *Bicycle Thief (Ladri di biciclette)* and to the neorealist director's penchant for social criticism through the perspective of childhood innocence in *The Children Are Watching Us (I bambini ci guardano,* 1942) and *Shoeshine (Sciuscià,* 1946).[2] The links to neorealism are so numerous and explicit that critics have seen in Gianni Amelio's film "a sort of 'homecoming' in the sense, too, of a return to the best traditions of our cinema."[3] Amelio himself is quick to acknowledge his debt to neorealism. "When I began to film *Stolen Children,* a film that took for its subject precisely the Italy of Rossellini and De Sica, I said to myself: neorealism is the key, not the neorealism of then, but what neorealism could be today."[4] According to orthodox neorealist practice, the film was shot on location, focusing on the lives of ordinary people speaking an unadorned vernacular, using unobtrusive camera work, an uncontrived story line, improvised directing technique,[5] and, for the most part, nonprofessional actors. In this last regard, Amelio was so intent on finding children devoid of affectation to play the roles of Luciano and Rosetta, the sibling protagonists, that he refused to have casting calls or hold auditions for the parts. Instead he insisted on personally wandering the industrial outskirts of Milan and Turin in search of his child actors. When this strategy yielded no results Amelio traveled south, where he found Giuseppe Ieracitano on the streets of Reggio Calabria and Valentina Scalici in Palermo. They were given the brother and sister leads.[6]

The film's denial of dramatic structure, its refusal to offer a hierarchy of incident, creates a paratactic flow of events that confers significance on even the most trivial details. Amelio's strategy of dedramatization means that the purchase of sandwiches and soft drinks or the trip to the ladies' room will assume the same importance as Luciano's near collapse from asthma or Antonio's capture of the camera thief.[7] In his meticulous attention to the minutiae of everyday experience, Amelio approaches Zavattini's ideal of *pedinamento,* of following a character as she goes to buy a pair of shoes, for example, and showing "all the elements that go to create this adventure, in all their banal dailiness." In so doing, the cinema reveals its special affinity for documentary observation. "No other medium of expression has the cinema's original and innate capacity for showing things that we believe worth showing, as they happen day by day, in what we might call their 'dailiness,' their longest and truest duration."[8] Zavattini's call for a cinema of *vera durata,* where time is not a function of plot but a space for the ripening of character, finds its fulfillment in many of the pauses, silences, and "dead times" of Amelio's film. The result is a cinema at once elliptical and anti-elliptical—discrete in its hinting at the unplumbed emotional depths of its characters, yet exhaustive in its documentation of life's surface.[9]

But Amelio's invocation of *Ladri di biciclette* in his title goes beyond issues of neorealist practice to develop the very essence of its social critique. Of course, there is the bitter irony of substituting children for bicycles as the titular objects of theft in Amelio's 1990s update. In the postwar subsistence world of De Sica's film, the bicycle is the sine qua non of material survival, the entrée into the workplace that will enable Antonio Ricci to provide for his family and restore his sense of self-respect. The supreme value accorded to the object of theft in *Ladri di biciclette* is tragically absent in *Il ladro di bambini.* Unlike Ricci's bicycle, no one wants the children in Amelio's film, and their journey through Italy is considered a kidnapping solely when viewed in kafkaesque terms by the very social system that abandoned the carabiniere and his two charges to their own devices. The only social worth attached to these "stolen goods" is their punitive value against the one person who cared enough to take personal responsibility for their predicament.

De Sica's sweeping indictment of postwar Italian institutions—the church, the law, the bourgeois family, the trade unions—finds its 1990s counterpart in Amelio's survey of institutional failure to alleviate the children's plight. During the interrogation by the commissioner in Noto, Antonio idealistically asserts his belief that the work of a carabiniere *è un lavoro utile* (is a useful job) (97), reflecting his pride in both catching the camera thief and successfully escorting the children "home" to Sicily. When the commissioner refuses to reward this *lavoro utile* and instead reprimands Antonio for operating on his own recognizance, the literal-mindedness of the law and its failure in humanitarian terms become clear. "You should not think," says the commissioner of Antonio's therapeutic activities on the children's behalf. "You must follow orders! The orders are written here, loud and clear" (99). It is in the distance between the letter of the law and Antonio's deep sense of human justice that Amelio locates his film. Within this double view of experience—the noisy, external, callous, morally compromised view, and the quiet, internal, tender, and profoundly humane and innocent one—*Stolen Children* stakes out its fragile utopian vision.

Another link between Amelio's social commentary and De Sica's in *Ladri di biciclette* is what I will call the "multiplying effect" of certain visual techniques used by both directors to universalize the implications of their stories. By this I mean the use of mise-en-scène to make their protagonists exemplary of an entire underclass whose suffering has not, however, served to unite them politically under the aegis of a common cause. In *Ladri di biciclette,* De Sica multiplies Ricci's tragedy by a series of visual essays whose effects verge on the mathematical. From the dizzying tilt shot in the pawnshop that leads the viewer's eye up endless shelves of hocked bedsheets or along rows of pigeonholes at police headquarters with case folders that suggest an infinity of unsolved crimes—De Sica's Rome seems filled with potential victims and perpetrators of theft. At the open market of Piazza Vittorio we see interminable rows of bicycles, probably dismantled and reassembled for quick sale; there are crowds of irritable people waiting at the unemployment office, others lining up for the bus. . . .

Amelio makes similar, though less hyperbolic, use of the multiplying effect by focusing on the homeless and the derelict: Rosetta drinks out of the beer bottle of a street person passed out in a park filled with hucksters and vagrants; Luciano collapses near another human wreck along the flanks of Stazione Termini; a woman in the Roma Ostiense station is shown surrounded by plastic bags that, we can assume, hold all her worldly belongings. The scene in this grim waiting room seems to encapsulate so many other times of boredom and delay throughout the journey—times filled with junk-food meals, fitful naps, and lethargic silences. It is significant that the waiting-room scene is shot in deep focus, forcing the viewer to acknowledge that our protagonists are not alone in their rootlessness, that this is a society in transit, waiting for the next lap in a journey without program or purpose. Throughout *Stolen Children,* Amelio universalizes his story by means of a camera technique that, beginning with a close-up of an individual face, moves out in long, circular dolly shots to encompass the character's surroundings.[10]

As in De Sica's film, the protagonists' plight in *Stolen Children* points beyond itself to a general condition of civic breakdown, and the film's celebrated minimalism, its "aesthetics of subtraction,"[11] may be considered the appropriate signifier of its social signified—the collapse of the very "imaginary of human consortium"[12] that could sustain a rich and full cinematic representation. In allegorical terms, Italy itself has been "orphaned" of its cultural progenitors in recent times, bereft of the moral and social guidance so necessary for its successful *traduzione* from past to future.[13]

In addition to *Ladri di biciclette* and the neorealist movement for which it stands, *Stolen Children* also owes a debt to another powerful Italian cinematic tradition. I speak of the journey film,[14] to which the Italian map so readily lends itself with its peninsular layout along a north-south axis that enables continental Italy as a geographic whole to be experienced linearly in time. In such Italian movies, all the metaphoric layers of the archetypal journey narrative, in which physical movement is paralleled by interior progress of an ideological, spiritual, and psychological sort, have a built-in national referent. Of foundational importance to this genre is *Paisan,* where the military journey of the Allied Liberation forces from Sicily to the Po Valley is also the story of the agonizing attempt to forge a postwar national identity.[15] A journey film that precedes *Paisan* but that artificially resolves the daunting challenges to the achievement of a unified national self is *1860,* Blasetti's 1934 revisitation of the Risorgimento in the service of Fascist historiography. Germi's *Cammino della speranza* (1950) and Tornatore's *Stanno tutti bene* (1997) both use the journey from Sicily to the north to critique a fragmented and indeed fraudulent national idea. Of all the films in the genre, *La strada* (1954) is the one least concerned with national-historical values in its insistence on the primacy of the inner psychological and spiritual progress of its two hapless travelers.

If the above sample is any indication, then the Italian road film can be said to proceed in a decidedly northern direction.[16] Such a trajectory brings into play a series of stereotypical oppositions between south and north—agrarian versus industrial, Mediterranean versus European, traditional versus progressive, poor versus affluent, and so forth—implying that travel from one end to the other recapitulates the forward movement of civilization itself. Though not a journey film in the strict generic sense, Wertmuller's *Seduction of Mimi* (1972) makes use of this cliché by equating the protagonist's transfer from Sicily, where he toils in a rock quarry, to Turin, where he becomes a metalworker, with civilization's progress from the age of stone to iron.

Stolen Children moves against this directional current, beginning in the housing projects of suburban Milan and ending in Gela on the southern coast of Sicily. But Amelio's film implies an earlier journey from south to north, *il cammino della speranza* (the path of hope) of Rosetta and Luciano's parents, who embarked on the archetypal itinerary of Sicilian immigrants looking for a better life in the industrial centers of Milan and Turin. In between the prenarrative journey of the Scavellos and the mother's arrest at the beginning of the film, we can infer a saga of disappointment, alienation, and degradation. It is the generic saga of the displaced southerner, and it involves ghettoization in the sterile and immediately decrepit housing projects of the industrial suburbs, the disintegration of the family unit, and the desperate recourse to trafficking of the most iniquitous sort in the name of survival.[17] All this is telescoped into the very first minutes of the film, told in shorthand that would be intelligible to contemporary Italians and would draw on international audiences' familiarity with such full-blown representations as Visconti's *Rocco and His Brothers* (1960). The squalor of the kitchen, the paint flaking off of the stairwell walls, the dejected, ravaged face of the mother who speaks in a rudimentary Sicilian dialect, the absence of a father—all these tell the familiar story of the shattered dream of immigration.

Despite its abject poverty, however, the Scavello household boasts two television sets, purveyors of the bourgeois image to which the family so desperately aspires and index of the same misplaced priorities that will lead to the investment in Rosetta's orthodontia. Though we see little of the soap opera being shown on the television screen, we are privy to its dialogue, which consists of melodramatic platitudes uttered in an elegant, educated Italian completely alien to the Scavellos' world. Nothing could be farther from the televised lovers' protestations of sincerity than the sordid scene being enacted in the Scavellos' master bedroom, where an eleven-year-old girl views the same soap opera while giving herself sexually to her mother's wealthy friend. Watching the TV show and reciting the protective prayer *angelo custode* (guardian angel), Rosetta seeks doubly to distance herself from the horror of her situation. In fact, religion and television function as a combined opiate throughout *Stolen Children*. We see it in the juxtaposition of the statue of the Virgin Mary and the television set in the lobby of the Catholic institute in Civitavecchia and in the withdrawal of the bored young girl, during the celebration of her first Communion, to a televisual corner of the restaurant in Reggio Calabria.

From the starting point of absolute social breakdown in the arrest of Signora Scavello and the removal of her children, the film undertakes the daunting task of creating an alternative family unit—one relegated to the margins of the social mainstream and as short-lived as it is miraculous. The genius of the film is its chronicling of the gradual and believable process by which the trio comes to forge bonds so powerful that they can withstand the onslaughts of a prying and hostile world. Thus, Rosetta is able to overcome the deep distrust engendered by her mother's ill-usage of her, Luciano is able to break through a silence verging on autism, and Antonio is able to defeat the bewilderment and frustration of this bureaucratic "mission impossible."

The characters' evolution is rendered verisimilar by Amelio's refusal to shy away from its difficulty, and he is eloquent in depicting the depths from which the threesome must struggle to achieve solidarity. Through his mise-en-scène, Amelio marks the nadir of the relationship as the trio makes its way to Stazione Termini in Rome. Against the background of a building in the process of demolition, Luciano begins to fail—he can barely carry his backpack, and his breathing is labored. The threesome passes by a homeless man, hunched over a curb, and after a few more steps Luciano collapses by a fence. It is only now that Antonio learns of Luciano's asthma and of the consequent need to suspend all travels while he rests. This news propels Antonio into a fit of fury—he kicks the fence, then a suitcase, and he, too, slumps down on the curb, mirroring the posture of the vagrant seen moments before. Lingering on this spectacle in a shot of medium length, Amelio's camera paints a ground-zero picture of disconnection and despair, with Luciano and Rosetta arrayed on one axis (but too far apart to imply bonding) and Antonio huddled on another, to the right, his back to the children as if to shut out their existence. Estrangement could find no more eloquent representation. The use of one-point perspective is also a powerful signifier of the difficulty, even futility, of the journey. As the parallel lines of the street seem to converge at an impossibly remote vanishing point, far beyond the flanks of the railroad station, the interminability of the mission is graphically laid out, and the perspective suggests how impervious the urban wasteland is to Antonio's mission. The fact that Luciano cannot breathe at this point speaks volumes about the toxicity of city life.

The journey of *Stolen Children,* with its stops in Civitavecchia, Rome, Reggio Calabria, Ragusa, Noto, and Gela may be seen as a series of failed attempts to recreate the lost family of Milan. The first stop, the Catholic children's home of Civitavecchia, offers all the appearance of a reconstituted family in Christ, with the nuns as the proverbial sisters, the priest as paterfamilias, and the other orphans as instant siblings. Another hopeful sign is that the director is himself Sicilian, hence a displaced person sensitive to these children's increased need for social acceptance in the north. But it is his very identification with the children that leads him to reject them. His awareness of their "difference" as immigrants is what motivates him to turn them away. Amelio's critique of the church, like De Sica's in *Ladri di biciclette,* focuses on the distance between the surface rhetoric of caritas and the actual practice of exclusion. In De Sica's work, Ricci and Bruno are essentially expelled from the church that ministers to the poor, and as a consequence they lose their lead on finding the thief. In Amelio's film, Luciano is blatantly excluded from the pious teachings of the catechism class, which repeats in chorus the nun's dictation while he walks by, in poignant solitude.

"Live life as a gift," the nun intones. "To live day by day, without a plan [is to waste this gift]" (22–23). Of course, a description of life as a formless, aimless trajectory without a plan also describes the plot of *Stolen Children,* as the trio wander from place to place in the impossible search for rootedness. The bitter irony of the nun's dictation is that it is the Catholic institute's refusal to accommodate Luciano and Rosetta in the first place that necessitates the peripatetic nature of this plot. Religious hypocrisy surfaces again in the lyrics of the pupils' hymn sung when the protagonists depart. "It doesn't matter who we are," they sing. "What matters is that we love each other" (28). Needless to say, the rejection of Luciano and Rosetta by the institute gives the lie to all such professions of caritas.

Perhaps the most poignant example of exclusion occurs during a brief encounter within the orphanage walls. Left on his own to wander about its unwelcoming corridors, Luciano climbs the stairs to the infirmary. There, a lone child sings exuberantly to herself. Devoid of hair (perhaps she has been shaved for lice, or perhaps she is suffering from a more dire malady), the little girl is entertaining herself by looking into a mirror, combing her nonexistent tresses, and singing a song whose words recapitulate, in the form of a beast fable, the plight of Rosetta and Luciano in the film as a whole. "Ho visto un pesciolino, piccolino. È tutto raffreddato, inquinato. . . . E tutto . . . che . . . all'ospedale, per i pesci, posto non ce n'è" (I saw a little fish, little, tiny. He's got a cold, and is polluted. And in the hospital, there's no room for fish") (23). The relevance to the two child protagonists of the film, outcasts because of their socially tainted status and out of their element in the hostile north, is painfully obvious. The thematic cluster proposed by the song, in which sickness, pollution, and exclusion form an inextricable whole, will meet its therapeutic counterpart in another scene involving cleansing, health, and reintegration in the film's second half. Obviously drawn toward the sick child, Luciano casts a gaze upon her that is both tender and curious. "Are you male or female?" (24), he asks, meeting her look with an intensity and wonder reminiscent of Gelsomina's visual communion with another sick and solitary child in *La strada.* In both films, the gaze shared between two characters—one a protagonist, the other hitherto unknown and mysteriously ill but also an object of profound recognition—constitutes a breakthrough moment, one that transcends the story line and gives fleeting intimations of a privileged, heightened sphere of interpersonal understanding. In Luciano's case, the link is one of shared marginality, of fluid and uncertain identity. Luciano's confusion about the sex of the hairless girl reflects both his own groping for a masculine identity and the film's overall concern with gender roles and their behavioral consequences.

Another failed attempt to incorporate Luciano and Rosetta into a family takes place in the restaurant run by Antonio's sister in Reggio Calabria. For one thing, Antonio must invent a fictional family for the children to explain why he is escorting them south. To his own sister, Antonio claims that Luciano and Rosetta are the progeny of his commanding officer and that they are traveling home to Sicily after visiting their father in Milan. Ironically, it will be a commanding officer, in Sicily, who will reprimand Antonio precisely because he has escorted these children "home." When Antonio first announces to his sister the fiction of his protégés' family connection, Rosetta takes him to task for lying. Antonio's justification, "commanding officers are important" (57), is rich with implications for the double register on which much of the carabiniere's actions operate. The lie both acknowledges Antonio's need to conceal the truth by means of a socially enhancing subterfuge and expresses his true esteem for the children despite their lowly parentage.

Not only do Rosetta and Luciano acquire a fictitious genealogy in the restaurant scene, they also become visually incorporated into Antonio's extended family. When a group photo is taken of the celebrants at the restaurant, Rosetta and Luciano are naturally included in the throng. Having befriended another girl and donned a dress, Rosetta assimilates enthusiastically into these bourgeois surroundings, while Luciano, more subdued, is nonetheless a willing participant in Antonio's family scenario.

The shattering of the fiction, under the prying eyes of the Signora Papaleo, does not prevent Antonio, Luciano, and Rosetta from constituting their own familial entity later on. Despite Antonio's relative youth, the two French tourists in Sicily assume that he is the children's father, and Luciano displays explicitly filial sentiments in a moving exchange in Noto. Echoing an earlier announcement that he would join his father when he is fifteen years old, Luciano now indicates that it is Antonio he will seek out at that magical age; in Amelio's words, "He recognizes in him the father that he never had."[18] The carabiniere has come to fill the paternal void in Luciano's life, and the boy's love for Antonio takes the distinct form of wishing to emulate the latter in both professional and personal roles. "Would they take me?" he asks Antonio of the carabiniere selection process (86).

Antonio's assumption of a parental role has important implications for the film's concern with gender stereotypes.[19] The definition of maleness arises early in *Stolen Children*, when Luciano's mother, trying to get the clinging boy to leave the premises before Rosetta's client arrives, accuses him of effeminacy.[20] "Aren't you going out to play with your friends?" she coaxes him. "Stai sempre attaccato a mia come 'na femminedda. C'addiventasti, fimmina?" (You're always attached to me, like a little girl. Is that what you've become, a girl?) (3). When Antonio takes on the parental role, he exhibits a marked discomfort with its feminizing repercussions. "What's needed here is a social worker, not me," Antonio says to the colleague whose apartment they use as a resting place after Luciano's asthma attack. "This is a woman's job" (38). In ministering to the needs of the children, Antonio employs a significant combination of stereotypical maternal and paternal strategies. "You know why you're suffering?" Antonio asks Luciano after his collapse. "Because you don't eat anything. You have to eat . . . if not, you'll always be sick! . . . And instead, if you eat, you'll become big and tall and these things won't happen to you any more" (41). This maternal solicitude for the child's health and nutrition is immediately followed by a statement of impeccable masculine logic. "And then, if you run into older kids who mess with you, you know what you do? You'll take care of them. You'll sock them. You'll give them what they deserve" (41).

Antonio exercises his parental role with Rosetta in a far more intricate way. The setting is the ladies' room of the Roma Ostiense station, where Rosetta has gone in defiance of Antonio. When he realizes that she has disobeyed, Antonio confronts Rosetta in the ladies' room against a mirrored backdrop. The rich psychological meaning of mirrors as public projections of the self, as announcements of the split between consciousness and image, and as sources of optical illusions are all brought into play in this scene. In a trompe l'oeil effect, Antonio is shown advancing toward the washbasin, then entering the same space from screen right to reveal that the first image of him was, in fact, a mir-

ror reflection. When he turns around to face the toilet stall, we see Antonio simultaneously in profile and reflected from the back in a doubling that gives obvious expression to his own inner division. Once
Rosetta enters the frame, Antonio withdraws and we watch her reflection as she brushes her teeth and asks the man to admire their
straightness. Her once-flawed smile was corrected at great expense with
orthodontia, she explains. "Now, everyone who sees me—do you know
what they say?" She looks at herself in the mirror and mimics in a
grown-up voice: "'What a beautiful mouth you have!'"(43). Rosetta
here reveals her knowledge of, and complicity in, the process of self-
objectification. In the mirror, she beholds the image that has been sub-
sidized by her mother to increase her marketability. In using the deep-
ened voice of her clients to utter the compliment "What a beautiful
mouth you have!" Rosetta assumes the perspective of those who eye
her with desire, and she signals her willingness to accept their vision
of her.[21] The condition into which she seems to have entered as she
studies her mirror image is trance-like in its power to absent her from
her immediate surroundings and plunge her back into a memory of
coerced and inappropriate eroticism. In this self-induced, hypnotic state,
Rosetta is obviously reactivating the defense mechanism that allowed
her to survive those traumatic encounters.

It is Antonio who breaks this spell, disrupting Rosetta's enchantment
by the mirror and challenging her to reject the image admired by her
pedophiliac clients. "Who says these things to you? Did I say them?"
he fulminates, shaking her out of reverie. Rebuking Rosetta's absent
parent, Antonio then corrects the viewpoint of the panderer-mother
with the moralizing gaze of true maternal solicitude. "If instead of
thinking about such nonsense your mother had thought about your
welfare, you wouldn't be here now"(43). Rosetta, stung to the quick by
this charge, is driven to aggravate the split between the self and the
image in the mirror by exploiting her sexualized persona to blackmail
Antonio. She threatens to accuse him of molesting her and tries to goad
Antonio into violence so that she can report him to his superiors. The
strength of Rosetta's reaction against Antonio's condemnation is, of
course, the measure of its truth, and her last-ditch defense of her sexualized persona precedes her final abandonment of it. In threatening to
implicate Antonio in her squalid scenario and in witnessing his refusal

to play along, Rosetta is able to exorcise these impulses and work toward the formation of a new concept of self.

It is Antonio's gaze that grants Rosetta her second chance—and by extension it is also Amelio's. Just as Antonio's perspective condemns and corrects that of Rosetta's clients, so Amelio's perspective reverses the tabloid exploitation of the story. In fact, the film was inspired by a photograph that Amelio had seen in a newspaper of a nine-year-old girl whose mother had forced her into prostitution.[22] Onscreen, in *Stolen Children,* we see a magazine cover with a photograph of Rosetta (eyes blocked out, the image captioned "She is only eleven years old. Her mother prostituted her. Sordid traffic in sex" [69]). The scene recapitulates the story of the inspiration for the film and offers the starting point for Amelio's dignified exploration of the aftermath.

What the film does, through the character of Antonio, is to desensationalize the story, desexualizing Rosetta by restoring her dignity and giving back the childhood that had been "stolen" from her. But there is a lurid undercurrent, a tendency toward voyeurism, against which Amelio's film must constantly struggle. In conceiving the idea for *Stolen Children,* Amelio obviously had to battle against his own prurient interest in the subject matter—an interest that emerges in his reaction to the photograph of the policeman and the child prostitute that inspired the film. "An atrocious tabloid story," Amelio says of the photo. "The child was shown from the back, as she walked down a street, holding hands with a grown man. . . . It was a photo that contained a strong dose of ambiguity. For a second, one could think that the man was the one to whom her mother had sold her."[23] The image of the policeman hand-in-hand with the child prostitute is replicated in the "chaste ambiguity" of the relationship between Antonio and Rosetta within the film.[24]

The prurient curiosity against which Amelio had to struggle in making *Stolen Children* resurfaces among the characters of the story in the restaurant scene, where Rosetta's tabloid identity is exposed under the scrutiny of Signora Papaleo. This shameless exponent of the new Italy, whose husband has made his fortune in illegal building projects, is eager to condemn the victimization of a hapless eleven-year-old. An avid consumer of the tabloid press, which caters to just such moral self-righteousness as Signora Papaleo's, the woman is immediately suspicious of Rosetta's need for police escort. It is she, then, who sees in Rosetta the real-life counterpart of the eleven-year-old prostitute on the magazine cover. The tabloid image of Rosetta, with eyes blocked out and only the "beautiful mouth" in view, reveals the consequences of the sexualized self-image that Rosetta had asked Antonio to admire in the bathroom mirror. Now that image functions to sell magazines and to allow the Signora Papaleos of Italy to revel in moral as well as economic superiority over the Scavellos and the other denizens of the country's dark underside.

In a very real sense, Rosetta perceives herself to be a prisoner of the magazine image—a hostage to that permanent record of her shame. No matter how much she evolves beyond the moment frozen in the photograph, it will remain in the storehouse of public memory, retrievable by whoever will want to use it against her.[25] Internalized, this image will stand for the inner division with which Rosetta will be plagued as she struggles to come to terms with the trauma of her past. The photo is the bad self, the objectified, commodified, and ultimately ostracized victim of an unnatural mother with whom she was forced to comply. Now, with Antonio's support, a second self is emerging, capable of judging that earlier incarnation, with all the guilt and anger that such a comparison must bring. For Rosetta, the photograph stands for the *knowledge* of her shame—she constantly asks Antonio by whom the image has been seen. "Do the people of the institute know?" she asks Antonio. "Have they seen the magazine? . . . Has my brother seen it?" (74).

Antonio, then, is the counterforce to the tabloid approach, the nonreader of the sensationalized narrative of Rosetta's life. In fact, when the girl begins to open up and recount the story of her sexual abuse, Antonio immediately puts a halt to her confession. "Enough, you don't have to worry any more" (74). Antonio's response can be applied as much to the film's own antivoyeuristic stance as to the character's restraint of any prurient curiosity he might harbor. The carabiniere's rejection of the tabloid narrative amounts to a rewriting of the story from an entirely different perspective. By making Rosetta the object of prurient interest, the press publicly punishes her for what she was forced to do. Antonio's dismissal of the tabloid account derives from the rejection of its moral premise: that Rosetta is somehow guilty of her coerced prostitution, the sociosexual bearer of original sin. "Rosetta hasn't done anything wrong either," Antonio answers, when Luciano proclaims his own innocence of the sordid proceedings. "What business is it of yours? You're just kids" (71).

Since Antonio's gaze becomes normative for Amelio, the film can be seen as an antidote to the exploitative, objectifying, and indeed pandering role that the mass media plays within the world of the story.[26] We have already seen how television soap operas functioned both as wish-fulfillment fantasy and opiate in the first sequence. That message is prolonged throughout the film in the TV screens that seem to lurk in almost every set, from the waiting room of the Catholic children's home to the lobbies and bars of the railroad stations. There are sets in the carabinieri's apartment in Rome and at the festive lunch in Antonio's sister's restaurant; even the T-shirt that Rosetta wears on the second day of the journey is imprinted with the image of a television set, making the TV medium itself the privileged object of representation.

Popular music serves as another major pollutant of modern life. Where television sets are not projecting their ubiquitous messages of consumer consolation, similar fare comes over the radio. Hit songs fill the air in almost every public space within the film, and a conversation about pop singers takes an ugly turn when the carabiniere roommate of Antonio's colleague issues an equivocal invitation to Rosetta to join him in the bathroom. Throughout *Stolen Children,* TV and radio infiltrate not only the lives represented on screen but the very form of their cinematic representation: the classical distinction between background and foreground is flattened into "a single dimension, dotted with pixels of the TV screen or snippets of pop tunes without tempo."[27]

Amelio's film, then, may be seen as a form of expiation, as a way of distancing his use of the medium from the abuses to which other forms of mass entertainment all too easily lend themselves. *Stolen Children* proposes a kind of homeopathic cure in the juxtaposition of two photo images—one, the tabloid magazine cover, the other, a picture of Antonio at the age of six, dressed up as the legendary Zorro; it is presented to Luciano by Antonio's grandmother. This photo, like the one of Rosetta, features a child playing an adult role, the identity concealed. But there the similarities end. The Zorro photo stands, by synecdoche, for the course of a normal childhood, marked by annual festivities at carnival time, with all the elaborate familial activities that such occasions require. We can speculate that the squalid and deprived upbringing endured by Rosetta and Luciano brought no such images of childhood masquerade.[28] Of further relevance is the very legend of Zorro, the rich landowner who becomes a heroic reformer of social injustice and who stands in diametrical opposition to Rosetta herself, the abject victim of social injustice. That the little boy dressed as Zorro will grow up to be a carabiniere, agent of justice and rescuer of victims, makes the commissioner's reprimand of Antonio, in Noto, that much more pointed a commentary on the military's obstruction of its potential action heroes.[29]

It is when Luciano first sees the Zorro photo that the young boy begins to open up to Antonio.[30] The process of identification and emulation begins here, as Luciano sees a possible self in the boyhood image[31]—and sees what that child Zorro has become in the adult Antonio. The photo, which Luciano studies while sitting at an outdoor cafe in Noto, seems to fulfill its legendary promise in that very scene, as Antonio enacts the role of the swashbuckling hero, chasing down the camera thief and delivering him to the authorities. As if it had a kind of talismanic value, Luciano takes out the photo on their last night together now that the journey has reached its destination. Shedding tears as he looks fondly at the image, Luciano reveals his awareness of what he is about to lose. Rosetta, too, has seen the photo. As Luciano and Antonio frolic in the sea, she pulls it out of her brother's backpack. Looking at it, she smiles in recognition of the bond that now links the man and the boy. Exhilarated, she calls out "I'm hungry"—not in the peremptory way in which she had imposed her creature needs in the past but as a joyous proclamation of life. The photo has enabled her to complete her own journey back to childhood innocence. She, too, has been "rescued" by the six-year-old Zorro.

Stolen Children, then, traces the interplay of two gazes: there is the tabloid perspective on the world, promoted by the mass media and targeting the likes of Signora Papaleo, and there is the gaze of Antonio, conferring innocence—a gaze that retrieves the stolen childhoods of Rosetta and Luciano. The two viewpoints have a linguistic counterpart in the wordplay that characterizes a number of exchanges between Antonio and the children. The first instance is profoundly serious: it involves Rosetta's confusion between the physical and moral referents of language. "He always said that I was dirty . . . but it's not true. . . . I always wash myself" (74), she tells Antonio of her encounters with a sexual client. In her refusal to accept this man's attempt psychologically to degrade her, Rosetta reveals her essential innocence—her belief that it is enough to cleanse herself physically in order not to "be dirty." The doubleness of language is also foregrounded in the outdoor restaurant scene in Sicily, when Luciano and Antonio trade jokes that turn on wordplay. One such joke involves a double entendre that reveals Luciano's awareness of a sexual tension between Antonio and two French tourists. "Do you know why the bull always butts his horns against the fence posts? Because he wants to *fare la bua*" (83). This joke brings together the infantile with the risqué in a way that bears poignantly on Luciano's early exposure to adult sexuality. *Fare la bua* is baby talk for "to hurt oneself," but it also means "to mate with the lady bull." Antonio deliberately responds with the most innocent interpretation: "So he wants to hurt himself—is he an idiot?" Luciano, however, lets him in on the "adult" level of meaning. "No . . . he wants to mate with the lady bull, the wife of the bull." Even in revealing his adult knowledge, however, Luciano does so with a certain dignity and decorum. The female animal is identified as the *moglie* of the bull—their sexuality is both monogamous and legal.

The turning point in Luciano's journey, the decisive event that allowed him to bond so powerfully with the carabiniere, was the boy's receipt of the Zorro picture from Antonio's grandmother. As important as the gift itself was the relationship between the old woman and her grandson revealed in their tender embrace by the roadside in front of the restaurant. Luciano is privy to this embrace, and Amelio emphasizes his witness in a shot taken from behind the boy's back when he watches from the rooftop as the two converse below. Though too far away to hear their words, Luciano is obviously aware of their mutual affection, which crosses generational lines, linking contemporary Italy to its ancestral past. The juxtaposition of old and new is made explicit in the mise-en-scène as the grandmother tends a flower garden by the side of the busy thoroughfare.[32] Antonio calls attention to the clash of worlds when he tries to reassure her, "Oh well, there's traffic, but you have your plants, your things . . . your daisies" (61). Most important is the continuity of values signified by the grandmother/grandson relationship: those of hard work and moral integrity. "I live my own life, but at least I'm honest, as you've taught me to be. Mother Mary! [You're] always working!" (61).

The values of honesty, labor, and land, values of a rural, agrarian, preindustrial age, stand in stark contrast to the new Italy exemplified by the restaurant of Antonio's sister. Poorly built and eternally under construction, the ever-expanding restaurant represents an Italy bent on unregulated economic growth at the expense of its core values.[33] Significantly, the sister sees no place in her household for the old grandmother, whose advanced age and retrograde ideas have made her a burden and a liability. "When they get like this," she remarks, off-handedly, "it's better that the Lord take them away" (56). The family lives above the restaurant in unfinished quarters, sacrificing comfort to the need for immediate profits, in a kind of self-imposed exile that the sister compares with the condition of Italy's Third World immigrants. "You see, we're camping out. Like the Albanians. Indeed, worse!" (64).[34] Most disturbing is the corruption that underlies the economic practices of the new southern prosperity. Doctors issue fake certificates of disability so that pensions can be collected; building codes are routinely violated so that construction can progress unimpeded. When Antonio labels these behaviors "criminal" (66), he is accused of betraying the culture that he has left behind. Amelio's point, in adding the character of the grandmother, is that the critique of southern corruption need not come from an exclusively outsider's perspective. Such a critique can emerge from within, from a comparison of the new south with the best traditions of the old.[35]

Despite the troubling encounter with Signora Papaleo, Antonio's reconnection with his grandmother and the retrieval of the childhood photo make possible the film's most ecstatic and important scene—the characters' immersion in the sea on the Sicilian shore before their arrival in Noto.[36] Preceded by the one-point perspective of a road that neutralizes the inhuman urban mise-en-scène in Rome, the composition of this frame suggests that perhaps the ideal vanishing point has been reached. As they stop by the side of this road, and as Antonio goes to get snacks, Rosetta rushes to the beach. There she wades into the water, wets her hair, and seems to commune with the elements. Antonio intuitively grasps her need to do this and grants her the necessary

FIGURE 18 | Antonio (Enrico Lo Verso), in the distant background, and Luciano (Giuseppe Ieracitano), right, respect the need of Rosetta (Valentina Scalici), foreground, to commune with the sea in *Stolen Children.* Courtesy of the Museum of Modern Art/Film Stills Archive.

time and space (fig. 18), fending off Luciano's impatience in the process ("let's leave her alone") (77). This is clearly a baptismal moment for her, one of purification both in the physical and moral sense, of consecration, indeed of ritual rebirth. Luciano, too, finds health in this hiatus as Antonio urges him to breathe deeply and expel all the polluted air from his damaged lungs. "The sea air is good for asthma. Breathe! Take a good deep breath" (78).

In its redemptive function, this scene returns the threesome to a state of Edenic innocence, of perfect balance between the natural and the human, and between humans. The bond that Luciano has developed with Antonio is so complete that the child can admit he cannot swim, that he can entrust his aquatically helpless body to the strong arms of the man (fig. 19). When Antonio hoists Luciano onto his shoulders and they emerge from the water like a huge, exotic sea creature, it is as if some primal life-form were newly evolving out of the ocean floor. All this takes place on a screen devoid of buildings or other signs of con-

FIGURE 19 | *Above:* In an ecstatic moment of connectedness between human and natural, man and boy, Antonio teaches the asthmatic Luciano how to swim. *Below:* Filmmaker Gianni Amelio directs Valentina Scalici on the set of *Stolen Children*. Courtesy of the Museum of Modern Art/Film Stills Archive.

temporary life, stripped of the condominiums and traffic that blight the beginning of the sequence. The lighting and the brilliant colors are all natural, and the music is a haunting mix of bongo drums and flutes that give the scene an aura of primordial mystery. There could be no more perfect antidote to the song of the polluted and unhospitalizable fish, sung by the little girl in the infirmary, than this scene of health restored through immersion in the sea.

Like all Edenic moments, this one is short-lived. The stop at the shore was but a temporary reprieve, a false paradise in the elusive quest for home, origins, and wholeness. The two French tourists who momentarily join the strange new family unit, providing both sexual tension for Antonio and aunt-like affection for the children, lead the utopian band to Noto, itself a utopian project born out of the ruins of the earthquake that leveled the southeastern corner of Sicily in 1693.[37] But Noto, like all of Sicily and Italy, is disintegrating. "Sicily is beautiful," marvels one of the French tourists, "but it is falling into ruins" (95). The magnificent church of Noto cannot be enjoyed by Amelio's camera without the obstructions of scaffolding that frame the vista, fragment the screen, and highlight its crumbling structure. The baroque cityscape, so theatrically conceived, with its dynamic facades ideally placed for viewer delectation, becomes instead the stage for petty theft; this is where the French tourist's camera is stolen. In chronicling the degradation of Noto, Amelio makes a conscious film-historical allusion to an earlier cinematic use of the city as an architectural monument. Antonioni's *L'avventura*, which Amelio explicitly cites as the inspiration for his choice of Noto as a setting for *Stolen Children*,[38] uses the beautiful baroque church as the backdrop for an important dialogue between the protagonist Claudia and Sandro, her architect-lover who has sacrificed his aesthetic ideals to commercial ambition. By setting this exchange in Noto, Antonioni establishes the baroque cityscape as the paragon of architectural idealism from which Sandro has fallen away in his surrender to greed. Amelio, in alluding to Antonioni's idealization of Noto in *L'avventura*, makes film history yet another measure of the decay of the utopian architectural project. It is as if, for Amelio, the corrupt Sandro of Antonioni's 1959 film had come to personify the whole of Italy of the 1990s.

In one of the final cityscapes of the film, as Antonio drives the children to the piazza in Gela where they will await the dawn, Amelio repeats the shot of the endless, desolate street, led by converging sightlines toward a vanishing point offscreen. The futility of the journey is announced in the repetition of this mise-en-scène, which has become the hallmark of urban anomie. In a very real sense, the journey ends where it began, in a hostile city environment that has no place for this miraculous threesome, this "strange family that seems true, possible, new, but that the world and the law cannot accept."[39]

Although it is a sweeping indictment of contemporary Italian life, *Stolen Children* is not a thesis film.[40] It is neither didactic nor shrill, and its denunciation is not imposed from above but emerges from within, from an identification with Antonio's own deepening commitment to the children. In the film's avoidance of any form of voyeuristic interest in its subject matter and its refusal to objectify the children, its focus may be said to be "relational." Such a focus is internal to the film, and it is exemplified by the way in which the three characters view each other. They do so "relationally"; that is, each child watches how Antonio interacts with the other sibling, while the carabiniere, in turn, watches and facilitates the children's interactions with each other, in what Bruno and Roberti call "the intersections of the gaze."[41] These "relational" gazes then condition the behaviors that will shape the subsequent interactions, in turn to be apprehended by the next round of relational gazes, and so on. I have already mentioned Rosetta's benevolent glance at Antonio and her brother in the swimming-lesson scene and her heightened understanding of their relationship in light of the Zorro photograph; Luciano, for his part, seems moved by the spectacle of Antonio's consolation of his sister by the roadside after Signora Papaleo exposes their ruse. Although the brother, slightly jealous, later warns Antonio against his sister's manipulative bouts of weeping, the boy is obviously touched by the man's capacity to comfort her.

In replacing the voyeuristic leer of the tabloid press with the relational gaze of his film, Amelio puts into practice the psychological ideal of intersubjectivity, itself formulated to counteract the objectifications of Freudian thought. In her feminist critique of psychoanalysis, Jessica Benjamin argues for a shift in emphasis from the oedipal phase, which locates identify formation in the processes by which the child (especially the male child) must dissociate from the mother, to the pre-oedipal phase, in which the child's sense of self is forged through communion with her. By giving the pre-oedipal stage priority over its successor, Benjamin privileges the notion of intersubjectivity—the relation of self to others as separate and equal subjects of consciousness—over relations to others as "need-satisfying objects," a concept implicit in the Freudian paradigm.[42]

Amelio's Antonio is doubly remarkable in his ability to overcome both the cultural and psychoanalytic push for men to disown their early mother/child experiences of communion. Because he is not threatened by his own instincts to nurture and care, he can foster the intersubjective bonds that characterize the earliest stages of child development. It is as if he were enabling Rosetta and Luciano to start all over again, to undo a disastrous upbringing in a way that erases not only their extreme deprivation, but even the usual familial pressure toward gender polarization and monadic selfhood. This pushing back of the developmental clock, this atavistic return to an earlier moment of connectedness, might well explain the scene by the sea, where Antonio and Luciano seem to merge into some primeval, composite life-form and Rosetta joins in their celebration of oneness.

But this utopian family unit cannot last, and Antonio's official reprimand will send him far from the children, if not completely out of the carabinieri ranks. Throughout the film, he has presided over the evolution of the sibling relationship, starting at its lowest point in the railroad cafe of Civitavecchia, where a ferocious brawl left Rosetta with a sore eye and Luciano on the verge of an asthma attack. Instead, in the train between Rome and Reggio Calabria, Antonio watched as Rosetta cradled the head of the sleeping Luciano. This was a decisive scene, for it followed directly upon Antonio's condemnation of the mother who had paid for orthodontia rather than thinking of her child's well-being. By cuddling Luciano, Rosetta shows Antonio that she has taken his lesson to heart, conferring on her brother the maternal affection that she had been denied, and tacitly apologizing for her misbehavior after his rebuke in the ladies' room.

The intersubjective gaze proposed by *Il ladro di bambini,* set in binary opposition to the objectifying leer of the mass media, may be seen as Amelio's decisive contribution to the Rossellinian strain of neorealism.

Distinguished by "the moral urgency"[43] of his camera, Rossellini's cinema pursued its ethical-cognitive mission to extract the "truth" (though
a highly partisan one), from the profilmic world. Taking this as his point
of departure, Amelio aims to go beyond "the gaze cast on things, to su-
persede the objective sign and enter into the X ray of thoughts and
emotions."[44] But it is in his intersubjective stance, his insistence on the
mutuality of the gaze of his characters, that Amelio adds a profoundly
new and morally compelling dimension to Rossellini's achievement. "In
Stolen Children," Amelio explains, "I watch the characters for the love of
watching them, and inasmuch as they suggest [material] to me, I could
continue to tell their story for an indefinite period of time."[45]

Antonio's function as facilitator of the intersubjective gaze reaches
its climax in the film's concluding scene, although he himself is absent
from the final shots. Amelio's parting images reveal that the children
have thoroughly internalized and assimilated Antonio's example. It is
dawn, the traditional harbinger of new hope, but here the scene is one
of unspeakable desolation. Surrounding the empty piazza where Antonio's car is parked are groupings of grim apartment projects; traffic is
just beginning to whiz by. Luciano, hunched over on the curb, is filmed
from the back as Rosetta approaches. Over her arm is Luciano's jacket,
which she drapes around his shoulders to protect him from the morning chill. She, too, sits on the curb, though not close enough to form a
cozy unit. After a brief silence, she utters perhaps the only supportive
words the situation will afford. "Maybe at the institute there's a soccer
field. . . . They'll pick you immediately to play" (102). What the children have learned, this finale tells us, is the ability to truly relate—a
virtue personified by Antonio and now internalized in them. "It's as if
[Luciano] had understood," Amelio says of the boy's acceptance of his
sister's maternal gesture, "now that the carabiniere is out of their lives,
that solitude can be alleviated by solidarity."[46]

In this tiny hope, this glimmer of renewal, Amelio aligns his ending
with that of the great neorealists whose scathing social critiques were
not without the leavening of humanistic promise.[47] Rossellini's *Open
City* (1945) ended with the march of the child activists back into Rome,
sobered by the spectacle of Don Pietro's martyrdom and ready to begin
the daunting work of social reconstruction. Bruno retrieved his father's
hat and took the man's hand in a supreme gesture of acceptance and

solidarity at the end of *Bicycle Thief*. The rice workers symbolically forgave Silvana, whose betrayal of the collective was expiated by her suicide at the conclusion of De Santis's *Bitter Rice* (1948). In this spirit, "Rosetta concludes my film with a gesture of affection and infinite, even maternal, solidarity toward her brother," Amelio confirms. "Change may also inhere in this."[48]

postmodernism; or,
the death of cinema?

9

Ginger and Fred

FELLINI AFTER FELLINI

In embryonic form, Federico Fellini's third-to-last film was to have been one episode in a television mini-series starring Giulietta Masina and involving a number of other prominent directors, including Michelangelo Antonini, Carlo Lizzani, and Luigi Magni. When the project fell through, Fellini decided to expand his own proposed contribution into a full-length feature film. Initially drafted to meet the requirements of a one-hour television program, the story of the elderly couple Pippo and Amelia, united after a thirty-year separation to perform on the air, had to undergo a delicate and well-balanced process of amplification.[1] First, the television show-within-the-film, *Ed Ecco a Voi* (in the English version, *We Are Proud to Present*), had to be expanded to hyperbolic proportions to sustain Fellini's commentary on the medium, without, however, allowing it to overwhelm the love story. Second, the elderly tap dancers had to be given enough depth of character and background to bear the weight of a feature-length narration, without resorting to excessive dialogue of an expository nature, such as: "Pippo, remember how we used to imitate Ginger Rogers and Fred Astaire on the vaudeville stages of provincial Italy back in the 1940s?" "Ah yes, Amelia, we were so happy, until I was unfaithful to you, and you left me, and I had a nervous breakdown, and you went to Liguria to marry Enrico and become a bourgeois housewife." The third process of amplification involved establishing an organic relationship between Fellini's wildly satiric treatment of postmodern culture and the sentimental plot, so that their linkage in the film would not seem contrived.[2] It is to this third process that the following analysis is devoted.

The continuity between *Ginger and Fred*'s representation of contemporary media culture and the story of the two elderly vaudevillians reunited for their final pas de deux can best be understood in the
context of Fellini's "hyperfilm"—the unitary, ongoing creative project
that links the artist's biography to his cinematic corpus at a relatively
high level of abstraction and in which the author's life in filmmaking
comes to coincide with the film of his life.[3] The term *hyperfilm* is not
meant to suggest the kind of horizontal movement between related
writings made possible by the technology of *hypertext,* but rather to
suggest the construction of an elevated or heightened film that hovers
above Fellini's works like a Platonic ideal.

This virtual film may be defined as a series of points at which
mythobiography[4] and meta-cinema converge—where the progress of
Fellini's fictionalized life story comes to signify the creative struggles of
the filmmaker at a given stage in his aesthetic itinerary. The most transparent example is *8½,* in which film and hyperfilm come to intersect
in the almost total identification between Guido and his author. In another obvious example, *I vitelloni* uses Moraldo's attempts to outgrow
a belated adolescence to reflect on Fellini's own efforts to liberate himself from the baggage of a cinematic and cultural past. Similarly, *La dolce
vita* dramatizes how Fellini's relocation to Rome occasioned a revolution in his aesthetic vision; and *Casanova*'s aged and decrepit narrator,
speaking in the first person, enables the filmmaker to vent his own anxieties about the decline of a career dedicated to crowd-pleasing spectacles of a transgressive sort. My purpose in this chapter, however, is not
to trace the workings of the hyperfilm throughout Fellini's career, but
rather to posit its existence and to demonstrate its centrality to an interpretation of *Ginger and Fred.* For it is in the hyperfilm that the satire
of postmodern culture and the evolution of the love story will find
their common ground.

One of Fellini's foremost strategies in constructing the hyperfilm is
the recycling of motifs from his own cinematic past to locate the current work in relation to an ongoing autobiographic/meta-cinematic
process. *Ginger and Fred* abounds in such self-reflexive recalls, from the
motorcyclists who swarm around the discotheque Satellit, like the new
barbarians at the end of *Roma,*[5] to the surrealistic beacon that presides
over the night, like the sci-fi tower of *8½.* In the procession of midgets,

FIGURE 20 | Amelia (Giulietta Masina) and Pippo (Marcello Mastroianni) steal a few moments to practice their routine amidst the construction rubble of a studio bathroom in *Ginger and Fred*. Courtesy of the Museum of Modern Art/Film Stills Archive.

eccentrics, super-endowed women, and other grotesques who parade across the stage of *We Are Proud to Present, Ginger and Fred* incorporates an entire history of Fellinian allusions to the circus (found in *La strada; I clowns; Juliet of the Spirits*) and the variety show *(Variety Lights; I vitelloni; Nights of Cabiria; Roma)*. Fellini's beloved world of photo-romance *(The White Sheik)* is invoked in the description of Fred as "overwhelming in his Gypsy-Cossack pot-pourri: acrobatic, languid, tender, and savage" (168). But most indicative of this impulse to conjure up a cinematic past are the filmmaker's choices of Giulietta Masina for the part of Amelia Bonetti (alias Ginger), Marcello Mastroianni for the part of Pippo Botticella (alias Fred), and Franco Fabrizi for the part of the television host Aurelio. When all three appear on the stage of *We Are Proud to Present,* they stand as a living filmography, a tableau vivant, of the author's career.[6]

"This is the fourth film that Giulietta Masina and Marcello Mastroianni have made with me as protagonists, but never together," explains Fellini. "Two filaments of my cinema that thus come together in *Ginger and Fred;* they unite. They tell a single story" (45) (fig. 20).

This impulse to synthesize and coordinate hitherto separate strands of his cinematic past puts *Ginger and Fred* in a privileged relationship to the hyperfilm, so that the collaboration between the two characters in the narrative enables Fellini at once to reflect on his life with Giulietta Masina and to unify the elements of his filmography. Mastroianni's role as the author's onscreen surrogate (established in *La dolce vita, 8½,* and *City of Women*) is reconfirmed in *Ginger and Fred* by a series of hints. His assumption of the stage name Fred (the English nickname for Federico, but also belonging to Astaire) may be a mere coincidence, but the same cannot be said of Mastroianni's donning the trademark Fellinian hat[7] and his personification of "the right to live irresponsibly . . . to flee maturity, understood as renunciation, extinction, surrender" (45).[8] Masina herself has double value as a reference in Fellini's filmography, signifying both the wife/other, "fated projection of wounded innocence" (45), and autobiographical self-reflection as the feminine principle within his own psyche, the Jungian anima so cryptically inscribed in the ASANISIMASA episode of *8½*.[9]

Of the two elderly vaudevillians, Amelia is the privileged partner in a number of ways. It is her personal itinerary that formally delimits the narrative: her arrival at Stazione Termini sets the film in motion and her departure signals its conclusion. Amelia immediately becomes the film's focalizer, mediating our view of the TV world through her astonished, disappointed, or disbelieving eyes. Most importantly, her dual status as Fellinian self-projection and feminine *other* enables her to play out, on several levels, the author's own drama of creation in *Ginger and Fred*. Fellini's ambivalence toward television is repeatedly enacted by Amelia, who admits to an irresistible fascination for the medium when asked by a journalist why she accepted the invitation to appear on *We Are Proud to Present,* but who is scandalized by the tacky and unprofessional preparations for the show. "It's disgusting, a madhouse, an equestrian circus, midgets, transvestites" (179) she complains to her daughter on the telephone the night before the performance. Not surprisingly, the very terms used by Amelia to denounce the television megashow have been applied repeatedly to Fellini's cinema itself, variously described as the *circo felliniano,* the "Fellinian caravan of midgets, admirals, transvestites, impersonators, violinists, intellectuals, imbeciles, angelic bandits," the usual "Fellini circus and freak show," and so on.[10]

Amelia's resistance to appearing on television may be read, on another level, as Giulietta Masina's resistance to appearing in a Fellini
film—a reaction to which both husband and wife have borne witness
on a number of occasions. "At a certain point," explains Fellini, "Giulietta, as always happens when she makes a film with me, begins to resist" (110).[11] Despite the considerable tensions it generates on the set,
such resistance can prove to be productive. "I often accept Giulietta's
objections," Fellini admits, "because I must take heed that certain of her
rebellions, certain of her resistances, also serve to improve the character, to make it more human, given that they come from the psychology
of the actress who interprets it" (111).[12]

At its most obvious, *Ginger and Fred* portrays the struggle between
the cinematic past and the televisual present as a battle between good
and bad, between innocence and decadence, between memory and
oblivion. Fellini plays out this duality in Amelia's hotel room as he juxtaposes the television monitor with the mirror on her closet door. Casting a look of distinct disapproval at her reflection, Amelia proceeds to
smooth back her skin and to conjure up her old performing self: the
"Ginger" of her days with "Fred." With this gesture, Masina's face becomes a living archaeology, a palimpsest of performances written over
earlier ones whose traces nonetheless show through to give her presence onscreen a thickness and a layered quality that reaches back in
time. The broad, clownish visage, illuminated to make its surface screen-
like in such films as *La strada* and *Nights of Cabiria,* becomes a text for
Fellini, a repository of filmographic memory.[13] What obliterates the past
of cinema, what erases the historicity of Masina's face, is the series of
images flitting across the television monitor reflected in the mirror,
where each impression cancels out its predecessor in a kind of moving
vacuum, denying any cumulative meaning or narrative progress. In
schematic terms, horizontal movement through the image chain precludes the vertical movement through memory: television montage denies the palimpsest of film. To make explicit the way in which television denies the workings of time, Fellini concludes Amelia's channel
hopping with a demonstration of facial calisthenics led by an elderly
German gym teacher who insists that "old age exists no longer," as she
screws her wrinkled features into a variety of senile contortions.[14]

Space as well as time is obliterated by Fellini's television, which pokes fun at its "global village" pretensions by showing that the medium works less to open out local minds to worldwide information channels than to reduce the world to the level of a provincial sideshow. The many impersonators who populate the cast of *We Are Proud to Present* and who, ideally, should display the international and transhistorical dimensions of video culture, from Gandhi to Verdi to Queen Elizabeth to Pope Pius XII, really dramatize the shrinkage of perceptual horizons to the familiar confines of one's own backyard.[15] Thus we have Ronald Reagan hailing from Grottaferrata, Clark Gable and Marcello Pruss speaking impeccable Sicilian, and Woody Allen complaining about a room without a loo.

Television culture works not only to provincialize but to reduce all its personalities to the same cognitive level, so that everyone emerges as a prodigy or a star, evoking the same brand of prurient curiosity as do the subjects of *Gente, People* magazine, and Ripley's *Believe It or Not.* Thus no analysis of the social determinants of crime is accorded to a kidnap victim whose importance resides solely in that he commanded the highest ransom in recent history. A parliamentarian's hunger strike to legislate an end to hunting and fishing is presented as a mere PR tactic. The mafioso Don, responsible for nefarious crimes, is greeted as a star—"in his own way, he's a divo, too" (201)—who obliges his fans by composing a song for the show. The transformation of all television personalities into what I will call "celebrity bites" brings with it an obvious moral leveling: mafioso boss = war hero = saintly friar. No matter how culturally or morally disparate these individuals are, they occupy equivalent positions in the procession of personalities who will command absolute public attention during the two minutes of screen time allotted to each of them. This makes Fellini's television a quintessentially escapist medium, dominated by sports, quiz shows, thrillers, music videos, and age-denying calisthenics, while serious social problems are either ignored or given the most perfunctory consideration.[16] The network pays lip service to the need for responsible reportage in the show *On the Margins of the Metropolis,* featuring two token paupers, but the broadcast itself is relegated to the margins of *Ginger and Fred.* All we learn of it is the studio president's pious approval—*è doveroso, è doveroso* (it's our duty)—when informed of the public interest show by his lackeys. Fellini's television also collapses the hierarchy of culture by exploiting Dante to sell watches and by equating Proust, Kafka, and Verdi with the likes of Andrea Celentano, Marty Feldman, and Kojak.[17]

Of course, Fellini saves his most scathing critique for commercials and their considerable power to disrupt. "The arrogance, the aggression, the massacre of advertisements inserted in a film! It is violence done to a human creature: [the TV commercial] strikes it, wounds it, mugs it. A film, an artistic creation in which everything is calculated to have that certain breathing pattern, rhythm, cadence, musicality, subjected to a brutal external intervention, hammered out, this strikes me as indeed criminal" (75). In *Ginger and Fred,* the violence done to programming by such intrusions is not only aesthetic but thematic, where the most infelicitous juxtapositions subvert the emotional impact of television drama. Thus the gory image of a crime victim, shot in the head, precedes an ad for risotto, and the plea of the emaciated parliamentarian on a hunger strike is followed by a commercial featuring giant rigatoni. Even more disturbing is the placement of a polenta ad, accompanied by the jingle "What more do you want from life?" after the interview with the former clergyman who gave up the priesthood for love.

This hyperbolic and grotesque vision of television is historically as well as personally motivated on Fellini's part. *Ginger and Fred* bears witness to a precise cultural circumstance: the radical change in Italian television that took place in the 1980s when the state monopoly of broadcasting gave way to an unbridled freedom of private-channel offerings at the initiative of media magnate Silvio Berlusconi. More than any other country in Europe, Italy went on a kind of televisual binge, an orgy of indiscriminate consumption provided by a medium subject to no apparent regulation.[18] As a consequence, the policy of limiting advertisements to a few discrete intervals between programs (the celebrated "Carosello" from 9 to 9:20 P.M. comes to mind) was replaced by one of total license to commercial interruption.

Fellini's parody in *Ginger and Fred* goes beyond the mere surface proliferation of ads in the wake of Berlusconi's deregulation to include the deep structural mechanisms by which these messages generate desire. In so doing, Fellini targets advertising strategies that use sex to sell their products, be they bath soap, sausage, or flavored panties. The eroticism of these commercials enables Fellini not only to exploit the phallic imagery of the products he uses (mostly gastronomical, with a high density of delicatessen) but also to construct a paradigm of desire that depends entirely on mediation. The fact that the model of desire within the commercial—often a gorgeous woman salivating over a Lombardoni sausage—displays an attraction to the product entirely inappropriate to the object itself suggests that advertising works on René Girard's principle of triangulation.[19] What we as subjects really want, in Girardian terms, is to have or to become the model of desire. This means that our attraction to the ostensible object is really an alibi, a deflected and displaced version of the transgressive wish, in the case of Fellini's ads, to identify with the sex bomb on the screen or to possess her. The commercial's underlying message is that if we buy the Lombardoni product we will be magically transformed into either the phallic object of the kind of sexual desire that the model displays or that we will become the model, thus arousing those desires in others.

It follows, by the same Girardian logic, that the apex of all desire is *to be on television*—to perform as the model of desire, to stand as the paragon of perfection that advertisements promise us we will become, once we accept their incentives to consume. For Girard, the attainment of the object itself will be fraught with disappointment, failing, as indeed it must, to transform us into the handsomer, stronger, richer creatures of the advertising slogans. Thus, the medium's power is based on creating a need that only it can satisfy—the consumer's hidden dream of "modeling" on television. In so doing, television keeps its viewers bound in a system of displaced consumerism whose built-in dynamics of disappointment propel them to ever higher levels of spending and ever more thorough enslavement to mediation.

It is in this hermetically sealed system of televisual signification that Fellini's satire reaches philosophical seriousness. The notion of an external referent, lying outside the play of signifiers and guaranteeing the gold standard of semiotic currency, is replaced by the infinite specularity of signs reflecting other signs—in Baudrillard's words, "a simulacrum never again exchanging for what is real, but exchanging in itself, in an uninterrupted circuit without reference or circumference."[20] Accordingly, there is nothing arbitrary about Fellini's decision to construct the set of the megashow entirely of mirrors and to clothe the host in a mosaic of reflective surfaces (fig. 21). This makes the space of television spectacle, like architecture itself in Jameson's interpretation, par-

FIGURE 21 | In a scene that satirizes the self-mirroring world of video communication, Aurelio (Franco Fabrizi), the host of a TV special, takes his place on set. Courtesy of the Museum of Modern Art/Film Stills Archive.

take of a "privileged aesthetic language" in which "the distorting and fragmenting reflections of one enormous glass surface to the other can be taken as paradigmatic of the central role of process and reproduction in postmodernist culture."[21] Fellini dramatizes the way in which the television medium feeds on itself in the crowds of journalists hovering about the studio cafeteria in search of the inside stories behind *We Are Proud to Present*. Hungry for a scoop, these journalists accord the megashow the importance of a primary news source on par with a military coup, a legislative crisis, a natural disaster, or a major crime. Indeed, on the level of narrative structure, Fellini exemplifies the self-containment of video spectacle by tightly restricting the temporal and spatial coordinates of his film: the time frame is limited to the twenty-four-hour period required by the logistics of rehearsal and broadcast; the settings consist of the series of closed spaces (train station, minivan, hotel, bus, cafeteria, dressing room, broadcast studio, train station again) needed to usher the performers through the television process.

Fellini's impersonators offer further proof of television's aspirations to recreate the world as self-enclosed simulacrum. When Amelia first encounters the two impersonators of Lucio Dalla—exclaiming, "You're identical!"—it is unclear whether she is marveling at their resemblance to the real-life celebrity or to each other in a mirroring relation that privileges the lateral contiguity of signs and ignores the referent entirely.[22] "T.V. makes fun of itself," Fellini comments, "with these imitators who imitate characters from politics or entertainment, then with other imitators who imitate the imitators in a kind of play of mirrors, an infinite specularity that gives a sort of demented vertigo and distances ever more the authentic, the original. Everything is at second hand, everything is reflected, alludes, in this saga of approximation" (96). Even gender is simulated in Fellini's media culture when the transvestite Evelina Pollini emerges as the undisputed star of the show and her mystical calling to alleviate the sexual needs of prison inmates participates in the ersatz religiosity of the entire Christmas special.

But Fellini's attitude toward television is far more ambivalent than this surface condemnation would suggest. He had himself made two television films—*A Director's Notebook* (1969), for NBC, and the documentary *I clowns* (1970), as well as several commercials, shot in the 1980s. As Mario Giusti observes, "It is not by chance that Fellini arrives at *Ginger and Fred* full of sausages and giant rigatoni after his two celebrated spots for Campari and La Barilla, and that many of his own collaborators on the film are also very active in commercials."[23]

Needless to say, in Fellini's television as shown in *Ginger and Fred,* the glimpses of rock concerts, thrillers, commercials, and announcements of forthcoming programs that flicker across the monitors located in virtually every set in the film are not drawn from real Italian broadcasts. Entirely of the author's invention, they fall under the general rubric of *fegatelli,* snippets of film that Fellini always shoots before and after the making of the movie proper and that he may or may not incorporate into the final cut.[24] It soon becomes clear that these snippets serve as far more than parodies of their television counterparts, emerging instead as highly distilled, densely packed nuggets of Fellinian creativity. Unconnected to narrative context, unbound to any overarching structure, the video clips provide occasions for unfettered imaginative play, allowing the filmmaker to indulge his love of hyperbole, gags, excess, and exuberant flashes of originality. The fegatelli permit him to retrace his own aesthetic itinerary, to regress to the level of his apprenticeship in the humor magazines of the late 1930s and early 1940s and to merge the adolescent sexual imaginary with the gastronomic wish-fulfillment fantasies of an advanced consumer age. When arranged in close succession, as in the channel-hopping scene in which Amelia flips from a thriller to a risotto commercial to a music video to a demonstration of facial calisthenics, the fegatelli reveal Fellini's preference for loosely episodic narrative structures and his propensity to insert gratuitous images according to personal whim.

The presence of at least one television monitor in each set of the film also provides the carnivalesque clutter and frenzy that is so integral a part of Fellini's aesthetic, dividing the visual field into two planes, each vying for the viewer's attention. Much like the celebrated Insula Felicles sequence in *Satyricon,* in which Encolpio and Gitone walk past a series of openings affording glimpses of prurient scenes and invitations to partake of their pleasures, the monitors in *Ginger and Fred* offer windows onto another order of experience. The television window gives onto a world where "you, too, will be handsomer, stronger, richer if you use ——," according to the generic ad slogan flashing across the train station in Rome. The glimpses of a heightened reality in *Satyricon* and *Ginger and Fred* may be seen as degraded versions of the mysterious "beyond" that beckons so many of Fellini's protagonists throughout his filmography. The transcendent place to which Gelsomina is mystically connected in *La strada,* to which Giulietta has paranormal contact through seances and hallucinations in *Juliet of the Spirits,* to which Ivo can communicate when he hears voices from a well and talks to the moon in *La voce della luna,* Fellini's final film—such a place is equated, in *Ginger and Fred,* with the privileged existence promised by postmodern enticements to consume.

A number of critics have argued that Fellini does not represent television in *Ginger and Fred* so much as reinvent or transfigure the medium,[25] taking what lends itself to his own aesthetic needs and exaggerating those elements to the point where satire and self-parody intersect. It is here that another casting choice, that of Franco Fabrizi to play the role of Aurelio, the television host, reveals its logic: the actor's previous performances as senior *vitellone* (overgrown adolescent) Fausto and bumbling *bidonista* (con man) Roberto serve to implicate Fellini's filmography in this critique of television spectacle.[26] This grown-up bidonista/vitellone, with his facile smile that disappears as soon as the camera switches off, his bonhomie that gives way to cowardice during the power failure, and his glib chatter that degenerates into expletives, is the "true star of the show" (20), the center around which the Centro Spaziale Televisivo revolves. But Aurelio is more than just a divo; he is also an auteur, capable of imposing his own vision on the viewing public through mass-media technology. He is like quiz-show host Mike Bongiorno, who, according to Fellini, is the paragon of the television auteur in his power to propose "over and over again, with his little shape, so distorted and delirious an image of our own country, or perhaps of the human condition."[27] And it is precisely in his role as auteur of television, "this grand deposit, this mastodontic ark brim full, regurgitating, overflowing, with all the materials of which spectacle has always been nourished" (44), that Fellini cannot help but find in Aurelio a vulgarized alter ego. In identifying with the television host, Fellini thus acknowledges his own participation in postmodern cultural practices and admits that any critique that he levels at the medium will ultimately redound to himself.

There is another way in which Fellini complicates his position in the film-versus-television dichotomy. Not only does his hidden complicity with television call into question any absolute allegiance to older forms of entertainment over new, postmodern ones, but so, too, does the cinema's own failure to live up to an implied standard of authenticity. Like television, cinema, for Fellini, is a medium of simulation, offering a transfigured image of the world, at many removes from any "objective reality," just as *Ginger and Fred*'s protagonists are themselves impersonators whose stage identities derive from the highly constructed mythic personas of two American film stars. In fact, the dance sequence at the center of *We Are Proud to Present*—the moment that has been cited as the film's only instance of authenticity, when television artifice melts away and genuine emotions shine through[28]—is itself highly derivative, standing at a considerable distance from anything that we could call an originary experience. Pippo and Amelia's 1985 dance on television reenacts their routine of thirty years before, which in turn reflects the filmed performance of Astaire and Rogers in the 1930s, which in turn records the original on-location dance, and so on.[29] The distinction between television and the cinema on the grounds of authenticity is therefore less one of kind than of degree. Fellini's sympathies for the cinema may be obvious, but he cannot bring himself to celebrate the medium in absolute moral terms as the apotheosis of the genuine and the true, just as he cannot bring himself fully to condemn television for its failure to signify. If anything, he locates the two media on a continuum of positions that extend from referentiality to simulation. On such a scale, the cinema comes closer to the referential pole, without ever coinciding with it, while television moves ever further toward self-signification.

Fellini does not come to an acceptance of the "fallen" status of all spectacle without a struggle, however, and that struggle is played out with great poignance in *Ginger and Fred*. It is Pippo who gives voice to the filmmaker's longing for the referent, to his nostalgia for an art form that can signify. "Tap dancing is not only a dance," he tells an interviewer before the show. "It is something more. . . . It was the Morse code of the black slaves. A kind of wireless telegraph. . . . In the cotton plantations . . . the black slaves could not talk among themselves, because if they spoke instead of working, the overseer whipped their skin off . . . so what does the black slave do? He communicates with the comrade of his plight in this way [Mastroianni makes hand gestures to demonstrate the footwork of the dance]. . . . Watch out, there's the guard. . . . I have a knife. . . . They're doing him in. Or rather . . . I love you . . . and I, too" (214). In his insistence on a performance that exceeds the level of its signifiers, Pippo lays the groundwork for an art that not only refers beyond itself but that actively intervenes to change its historical referent. Tap dancing began when the Slave Act of 1740 prohibited the use of drums because they could be heard from plantation to plantation and could be employed, so the white slaveholders feared, to incite rebellion. By substituting intricate footwork for the outlawed drumbeats, slaves created a secret language of subversion masked by its surface appearance of entertainment.[30] The relationship between the Morse code of dance and the slaves' real-life oppression is thus a direct and dynamic one. Tap dance is both a response to historical injustice and an appeal to act in a way that will bring about its alleviation.

Pippo's manifesto of an art that refers beyond itself to the real circumstances of the performers' lives has a powerful impact on Amelia, whose reaction suggests a possible happy ending for their romance. "We'd been tip-tapping together for fifteen years and you never told me anything! But look, Pippo, this is something very important, very beautiful. I have goose bumps" (215). It had not occurred to Amelia until now that Pippo could have been proclaiming his love to her all those years through dance. His declaration also hints at the way in which the upcoming television performance could serve to rekindle their relationship, especially when read in light of the Hollywood film on which the dance sequence is modeled. Mark Sandrich's *Follow the Fleet* (1936), starring Fred Astaire and Ginger Rogers, offers a powerful precedent for the way in which spectacle can modify the sentimental circumstances of the performers' lives. The Hollywood musical tells the story of two dancing partners, reunited after a separation of several years, who put on a benefit show and thus succeed in reconciling several pairs of lovers. By making the spectacle itself the agent of plot resolution, *Follow the Fleet* explicitly formulates Fred Astaire's own insistence that dance be an organic part of the narrative, advancing and promoting it in significant ways. In 1973 he wrote, "I think the audience always slumps—even more in movies than on stage—when they hear an obvious dance cue, and both the picture and the dance seem to lose some of their continuity. Each dance ought to spring somehow out of character or situation, otherwise, it is simply a vaudeville act."[31] Hence it is the very mounting of the spectacle at the end of *Follow the Fleet* that rectifies all the film's narrative predicaments. In the aftermath of the show-within-the-film, Sherry Martin (played by Ginger Rogers) is convinced by the triumph of their professional reunion that her partnership with Bake Baker (played by Fred Astaire) should be continued offstage. The climactic routine "Let's Face the Music and Dance" is itself a performance within a performance within a performance, with the inner dance surrounded by a pantomimed narrative that the choreography addresses and resolves. In this frame story, an elegant gambler who has just squandered his fortune meets a desperate society lady about to leap to her death, and, rather than self-destruct, the two decide to "face the music and dance." Thus *Follow the Fleet* is composed of several layers of embedded spectacles, each of which remedies the interpersonal dilemmas of the surrounding narrative in a triumphant affirmation of art's power to intervene in life. Will Amelia and Pippo, like their exemplars Bake and Sherry, decide to renew their personal and professional collaboration as a result of their broadcast triumph? "It would have been better if you were married. . . . It works better" (169), the assistant director of the television show remarks upon learning that Amelia and Pippo had never wed. "The public always likes love stories. Companions in art and in life" (169).

In two scenes near the end of *Ginger and Fred,* the protagonists seem on the verge of the kind of breakthrough that would indeed make them "companions in art and in life." A power failure takes place at the very start of the televised dance, transporting the two performers back in time to the blackouts of the 1940s and clearing the air of all the light waves, sound bites, and emissions that clutter the postmodern world. Here, in this oasis of calm, Amelia and Pippo can share an unguarded moment of intimacy. Freed from all their defense mechanisms and the need to project their public personas, Amelia and Pippo withdraw into a secret space of authenticity deep within the self, "as in dreams, far from everything," says Pippo. "A place that you don't know where it is, how you arrived." The darkened stage allows the couple to become characters in a hypothetical Golden Age Hollywood romance. Two possible minifilms emerge—one ending in tragedy as the couple dies in a terrorist attack—"they broke up thirty years ago and are reunited to die together," fantasizes Pippo—and the other concluding happily as they run off together to start a new life in love. But electric power is restored on set to thwart these romantic scenarios.

The blackout sequence provides a moment of stylistic repose in a film otherwise governed by the audiovisual techniques of television.[32] During this welcome interlude, the crowded surface of the screen gives way to a space of true depth, whose various planes are no longer defined by the organizing presence of a video monitor competing with the narrative action of the foreground but by the genuinely engaging intimacy of the couple that silences and stills everything around them. With the return of power on the set, the audiovisual values of television are restored, and Pippo and Amelia must go on with the dance, foregoing the temptation to escape that the momentary darkness had held out to them.

A second near breakthrough occurs in the railroad station, where the partners bid each other farewell after the show. Only now does Amelia learn that Pippo's wife has left him and that he is free of emotional attachments. But before she can react to this news, two young people who had seen the couple on television insist on getting autographs at the moment when the mutual feelings raised during the blackout scene could have been explored.[33] Pippo, who cannot come right out and say, "Amelia, I need you," must resort to the code language of their show. "Amelia! . . . Vuuuuuuuu." With this sound effect, he recalls the framing narrative of their own climactic dance routine in which Ginger, about to depart forever on an ocean liner, runs down the gangway into her lover's arms, vowing never to leave him. For Pippo, this reevocation is a plea for renewal, an appeal to make life imitate spectacle, to "follow the fleet" of their Hollywood paragons in becoming once more "companions in art and life." Amelia pretends to run back to him with open arms, but for her it is all a charade. Pippo's inability to say "Amelia, I need you" reenacts the communicative failure of their entire relationship, and she is unwilling, or unable, to read his gesture as an encoded plea for love.[34] There will be no carryover from stage to life in Amelia's case, where the boundaries between the inner spectacle of the dance and the outer narrative of the sentiments are fixed and inviolate. Unseduced by their performance, she will not play Ginger to Pippo's Fred but will go back to her hometown on the Italian Riviera to be the widow of the staid Enrico, with whom it was all *molto diverso.*

Fellini could have ended his film right there, just as he could have ended it after the dance sequence or after the backstage denouement. But the film survives the departure of its protagonists. After the camera bids Amelia farewell on the receding train and withdraws from Pippo in the bar, Fellini chooses to linger on the antenna salesman who boasts Rome's receptivity to sixty-six channels, finally settling on a television monitor featuring a commercial for Scolamangi, the pasta that makes you lose weight. With these final frames, the film comes full circle, bringing us back to where we began with Amelia's arrival at the train station in Rome. But in so doing, Fellini transforms that setting, a traditional site of cinematic romance, into a quintessentially postmodern media space of antennae sales and television advertisements.[35] In contemporary video culture, romance is reduced to gastronomic lust, story to sound bites, and life-altering spectacle to video clips.

The question of causality remains deliberately ambiguous in *Ginger and Fred*. Did the failure of the television reunion to bring about an offstage happy ending spring from the emotionally flawed relationship of the couple itself? Or is postmodernism at fault for thwarting the progress of an old-fashioned Hollywood romance? In other words, is the obstructed love story a mere allegorical expression of the antihuman workings of contemporary media culture? Or does the sentimental plot have its own logic—one that finds analogies on the level of culture critique but is not exhausted by it? Recourse to the hyperfilm would suggest the second conclusion, wherein *Ginger and Fred* allows the author to advance both his own fictionalized life story and his aesthetic investigation without subordinating one to the other. In the moral principles embodied by Giulietta Masina and Marcello Mastroianni throughout Fellini's career—those of "wounded and triumphant innocence" (45), on the one hand, and of "the right to live irresponsibly and flee maturity understood as renunciation, extinction, surrender" (45), on the other, the filmmaker projects the eternal dilemma of his mythobiography. It is this human failure, this inability to script a happy ending to the couple's story, that provides Fellini with the occasion to pit older forms of spectacle—those of vaudeville and 1930s Hollywood cinema—against that of postmodern media culture, as a way of dramatizing his own quest for a genuinely communicative and referential art in the age of simulation.

For a brief and utopian moment, that quest meets with success in *Ginger and Fred*. This occurs, of course, in the dance sequence, for it is there that past and present, audience and performers, cinema and television all come together in a moment of imaginative transcendence. Most of all it is Amelia who personifies the transfiguring power of spectacle as she "lets herself be carried away by the sweetness of the music" (264). Here Fellini's camera reveals to us her own process of self-mystification, her own belief that she has become, for the space of this dance, both the legendary Ginger and her own younger self. Like La Saraghina in *8½,* whose grotesqueness was tempered by her sheer joy in being transformed into the graceful creature of her dreams, Amelia is at once pathetic and sublime. She is both the aged relic who makes a fool of herself for public consumption and the heroic trouper who believes in the transformatory power of spectacle.[36] It is at this point that the rivalry between television and film aesthetics gives way to a unified vision in which the video and movie cameras merge in joint celebration of a spectacle that transcends its technological means.

Unlike its exemplar in *Follow the Fleet,* this visionary moment is a finite one that will have no repercussions in the world beyond the stage.[37] Art's power of renewal does not survive the limits of the performance, and the dance spectacle is helpless to alter the course of two lives consigned to loneliness. But this does not signal Fellini's surrender to the insignificance of spectacle and to the consequent triumph of postmodern simulation over an art that aspires to something beyond the mere proliferation of signs. Unable to attain the truth at the end of the signifying chain, but unwilling to renounce the quest for it, Fellini's cinema takes the only position that it can—an oppositional one—to record its own struggle for authenticity in the face of great personal and cultural odds. In the final analysis, the place where art and life will converge for Fellini will be in the hyperfilm alone, in the privileged exchange between mythobiography and the filmmaking process that transfigures and redeems it.

10

Giuseppe Tornatore's *Cinema Paradiso* and the Art of Nostalgia

Of the films discussed in this part of the book, Giuseppe Tornatore's *Cinema Paradiso* provides the most compelling example of what Frederic Jameson would call "nostalgic postmodernism."[1] Reevoking the *temps perdu* of an enchanted childhood and adolescence in the Sicilian provinces, *Cinema Paradiso* focuses with particular poignancy, and regret, on the role of the movies in animating the life of the town. Not surprisingly, nostalgia has been at the center of the public response to *Cinema Paradiso,* motivating both the film's fall and its subsequent rise in critical esteem. Initially panned by Italian reviewers as "cinema di papà" that "tugs at the heart strings," *Cinema Paradiso* was shown at Cannes, where it enjoyed "an unexpected success both on the part of the public and the critics who abandoned their sullenness and gave themselves totally over to the workings of nostalgia." With this "return to feeling," Tornatore takes his place at the forefront of the new generation of filmmakers who reject "the aridity of certain estranging results of a few years ago."[2] In analyzing the resounding success of *Cinema Paradiso* with audiences in the United States, Patrick Rumble argues that Tornatore is able to tap into a desire for rootedness, stability, and community that Americans have been forced to repress in the name of social mobility and economic advancement.[3]

Though nostalgic in its relationship to an idealized past and postmodern in its use of pastiche, *Cinema Paradiso* subjects the film medium to a critique that exceeds the bounds of nostalgic postmodernism. In Jameson's understanding of the term, postmodern forays into the past involve not a confrontation with a historical referent but a mimesis of the style by which an earlier era represented itself to itself. "The nostalgia film was never a matter of some old-fashioned 'representation' of historical content, but instead approached the 'past' through stylistic connotation, conveying 'pastness' by the glossy qualities of the image, and 1930s-ness or 1950s-ness by the attributes of fashion" (*Postmodernism*, 19). Such appropriation, or "aesthetic colonization," results in the "waning of historicity" and the consequent failure of the new work of art to acknowledge the underlying material processes that would enable us to experience history "in an active way" (*Postmodernism*, 19, 21).

In *Cinema Paradiso*, Tornatore defies the reductiveness of postmodern citation by embedding earlier film footage in his 1989 work so that "aesthetic colonization" cannot take place. Every time Tornatore splices images of old movies into *Cinema Paradiso* (and the instances are legion), he calls attention to what his film *is not*—that is, he announces the irreconcilable distance between the current work and its cinematic forbears. Indeed, Tornatore constantly plays his film off against the great works of Hollywood's Golden Age, French poetic realism, and Italy's own postwar classics in ways that provide an internal critique of the powers of cinematic fascination. It is this that complicates the film's postmodernist identity and offers an incisive moral as well as aesthetic commentary on the medium's evolution from midcentury to the present.

Unlike the neorealists and their heirs in succeeding decades, Tornatore is less interested in the referential value of the cinematic sign than in its power to shape the public imaginary. *Cinema Paradiso* is a film that makes film reception its privileged object, and it is here that Tornatore offers his distinctive contribution to the contemporary cinema of nostalgia. Though critics faulted Tornatore's citations of film classics as arbitrary and unsystematic,[4] his method can be justified as an accurate mimesis of the way in which cinema was experienced by the provincial public of Giancaldo. Tornatore's random cinematic allusions represent the indiscriminate cinephilia of 1940s and 1950s popular culture, which made of all films, no matter how diverse, one vast invitation to imaginative escape. If Tornatore's inventory of references (*And God Created Woman, Gilda, Little Caesar, I vitelloni, Blue Angel, Bitter Rice, Anna, I pompieri di Viggiù, Casablanca, Stage Coach, Modern Times, Fury, Ulysses, The Lower Depths, Seven Brides for Seven Brothers, Dr. Jekyll and Mr. Hyde, La terra trema, Nel nome della legge, L'oro di Napoli, Catene, Poveri ma belli, Il grido)* and movie stars (John Wayne, James Stewart, Henry Fonda, Gary Cooper, Charlie Chaplin, Buster Keaton, Laurel and Hardy, Totò, Alberto Sordi, Vittorio Gassman, Silvana Mangano, Brigitte Bardot) is unsystematic, so, too, is the audience's response to them, which reduces all cinema to the same level of reception. Thus art films are juxtaposed with commercial fare, Hollywood productions with French and Italian ones, fiction with newsreels, auteur with genre films, comedies with melodramas. Each film alluded to in *Cinema Paradiso* partakes of the transcendental quality of the Hollywood super-spectacle, so that even works set in contemporary Sicily, committed to raising the social consciousness of the viewing public, are banished to the never-never land of cinematic fabulation. As the audience exits from a screening of Visconti's *La terra trema,* for example, Ntoni Valastro's plea for workers' freedom from the bosses is entirely lost on the crowd, which accepts the uncontested authority of Don Vincenzo to control all hiring in Giancaldo. Similarly, at the end of Germi's *Nel nome della legge,* the crowd cheers as the hero defeats the film's mafioso leader in a fairy-tale happy ending that will have no bearing on the audience's consciousness of its own plight.

Cinema, then, stands at the center of Tornatore's sweeping nostalgia for a bygone world in which popular film culture merges with all the objects of his protagonist's elegiac longing for lost perfection: his youth, his historical roots in the Sicilian provinces, his sense of family and community, his unconsummated romance with Elena. The fusion of these elements in Salvatore's memory is beautifully expressed through the continuity of visual and sound devices that lead the protagonist back in memory to Giancaldo. The middle-aged Salvatore, now a successful filmmaker in his own right, has just heard the news that Alfredo is dead, and as he lies awake in his apartment in Rome the sound of wind chimes outside his bedroom window takes him back forty years to the sound of the bell that he, as altar boy, was supposed to ring at appropriate intervals during mass. The ringing of this instrument then gives way to the sound of the censorship bell used by Father Adelfio to signal that Alfredo must edit out love scenes from the films being previewed for his parish cinema. At this point, Tornatore shifts our attention from the scene's auditory to its visual coordinates as Father Adelfio orders Alfredo to adjust the framing mechanism of the projector. Now three gazes converge on the screen—Father Adelfio's censorious, moral gaze, Alfredo's technical one, and Totò's voyeuristic, transgressive peeping from behind the curtains as he watches the un-expurgated footage that the general public of the town will never see. For Totò, this is indeed the primal scene that psychoanalytic critics posit as the basis of all cinematic pleasure. In one shot, taken from Alfredo's perspective, as Father Adelfio performs his role of superego to the town's collective consciousness the screen is partially blocked by the priest's darkened silhouette, expressing in physical terms his power to obstruct full access to the film.

Salvatore's return, in memory, to Giancaldo culminates in a shot that merges the auditory continuity of the bells with the visual focus on framing, establishing the context of this individual reverie within the communal space of the town. Bells provide the transition from Father Adelfio's vigorous signal for censorship to the tolling of the tower chimes that sound the hour and synchronize the lives of all the town's inhabitants. Looking down on the central piazza from the vantage point of the clock tower, Tornatore's camera comes to align itself with the frame that encloses the bells. This device blends the visual and acoustic fields in a unified, establishing shot of the collective stage on which the drama of Salvatore's childhood and adolescence will unfold.

The continuity between the space of the movie house and that of the town's piazza is made explicit in a scene that precedes the destruction by fire of the old Paradiso. I refer to the moment when Alfredo takes pity on the large number of people turned away from the movie house for lack of seats. When he projects the film image onto the facade of a building flanking the piazza, the entire topography of Giancaldo is transformed into the space of a movie house (fig. 22). "This movie house at the center of the town was like a beating heart," Tornatore remarked in an interview with *Cineforum*.[5] If the cinema is a heart, according to the filmmaker's metaphor, then the audience is the body, acting out, somatically, the directives of its most vital organ. In fact, the spectator-body goes through entire life cycles in *Cinema Paradiso,* from the courtship, marriage, and parenting subplot of the couple Angelo and Rosa to the explicit copulation of an anonymous two-some, to the peaceful breast-feeding of a baby despite its mother's

FIGURE 22 | In the scene preceding the fire that will destroy the old Cinema Paradiso, Alfredo (Philippe Noiret) watches with Totò (Salvatore Cascio) as an overflow crowd thrills to the spectacle of outdoor movies. Courtesy of the Museum of Modern Art/Film Stills Archive.

convulsive laughter at a Totò episode, to the death of Don Vincenzo, shot in his seat during the screening of a gangster film.

A companion piece to *Cinema Paradiso,* and one that further explores the bond between cinema and the mass public, is Tornatore's 1995 *Starmaker,* the story of a con artist named Joe Morelli who tours the Sicilian countryside pretending to be a talent scout for the movies. Much of the film is composed of footage from Morelli's bogus screen tests in which he asks aspiring actors to pose "profile right, profile left, profile center" and then to recite a prepared speech that will show them to their best advantage. The resulting performances range from unabashed and ungrammatical family chronicle ("in June of 1926, our parents have birthed [*hanno nato*] another little brother, where they gave the name Calogero") to powerful and moving historical witness ("we'll hang the last king with the guts of the last pope, said Garibaldi to Nino Bixio"). Morelli's camera, signifying the power of the cinema to fulfill their wildest dreams of stardom, brings out in these individuals an idealized self-image, a cherished mythic persona often hidden from those around them.

Far from patronizing these naive and unburnished self-presentations, then, Tornatore's film revels in their authenticity and the occasions they afford for surpassing lyricism and passion. There is the shepherd whose inarticulateness borders on aphasia, but who manages to produce a hymn to nature of true Franciscan beauty; there is the freedom fighter (played by Leopoldo Trieste) who abandons his fifty-year silence to testify (in Spanish) to his moment of revolutionary glory; and there is the woman, ostracized for consorting with Allied liberation soldiers, who vents her anger at her unjust plight. Each screen test implies a complete film of its own, a mini bio-pic lurking beneath the surface, rich with the complexities of a life whose desires and longings must be distilled into the thirty seconds allotted to each auditioner.

What emerges from all these fragments of condensed lives is a composite portrait of Sicily itself in all of its human wealth and variety. And just as the alleged transformatory power of Morelli's camera elicits each individual's mythic persona, so does *Star-maker,* on a collective level, address the mythic status of Sicily in the Italian cinematic imagination— the land of Visconti's *La terra trema* and *The Leopard,* of Sciascia's Mafia novels adapted to the screen, of Germi's Sicilian-based sex comedies, and many more. In *Star-maker,* then, two mythic systems come together—the myth of cinema for Sicilians (which Morelli exploits to his personal advantage within the narrative) and the myth of Sicily for the cinema (which Tornatore, in turn, explores and refines for his own authorial purposes).

In the most breathtaking scene of the film, a three-minute sequence recorded in a single extended shot early in *Star-maker,* Tornatore makes explicit the convergence of these two mythic regimes. To prepare for their screen tests, Morelli distributes to the townspeople of Realzisa lines of dialogue from *Gone with the Wind:* Rhett Butler's lines, on scraps of blue paper, to the men; Scarlett O'Hara's lines, on pink scraps, to the women. Tornatore's choice of *Gone with the Wind* has twofold logic: it is the quintessential Hollywood classic, thoroughly familiar even to the residents of this provincial Sicilian outpost, and it is the quintessential film of the American South, whose Southernness plays into the island's own sense of cultural identity with respect to the Italian mainland. Thus America's film tribute to its myth of the South becomes the filter through which Italy constructs the myth of its own south in a double, cross-cultural mythologizing process. Tornatore's rationale for choosing *Gone with the Wind* becomes obvious as the townspeople rehearse their lines and reveal just how deeply entrenched the film is in their collective imaginary, and how prone they are to distort, interpret, embroider, personalize, and, of course, Sicilianize the story.

Tornatore's film technique in this three-minute extended-shot sequence admirably mirrors the way in which the fascination of the cinema washes over Realzisa in the wake of Morelli's arrival. Tornatore's camera flows seamlessly through the town, taking advantage of its horizontal and vertical contours to climb from level to level, to move in and out of houses and shops, to ascend along the road to arrive at the piazza on its uppermost plateau. All this is accompanied by the music of "Stardust," as if Hollywood itself had provided the soundtrack for the life of this town. In its tour through Realzisa, the camera affords a number of voyeuristic glimpses into the physical preparations for the screen test. A man sits in an ancient tub, his wife pouring the rinse water from a bucket; another man shaves; two women practice their lines with their hair in curlers; an old woman dozes; a freshly pressed suit is lowered on a hanger and delivered by a boy to a man in a barber chair. Everyone from adolescent girls to elderly pensioners to even a group of deaf mutes participates in the preparations, revealing the cinema's power of social bonding and its ability to elicit Sicily's virtuoso performance of the self.

Whereas *Star-maker* conducts its survey of the public's cinemania in the streets, piazzas, homes, and countryside of provincial Sicily, *Cinema Paradiso* is more concerned with what happens within the four walls of the movie house of Giancaldo. In one particularly revealing sequence, Tornatore uses an intricate camera technique to comment on the way in which *Cinema Paradiso* makes spectatorship its privileged object. While filming the local debut of Fellini's *Vitelloni*, Tornatore places his camera behind the movie screen of the Paradiso and shoots the audience head-on, viewed through the filter of the screen's surface. As a result, the images of the film being projected (starring Alberto Sordi) are superimposed on the faces of the viewers in ghostly transparency. "Here the eye of the lens is the subject of the film-object," observes Marcello Walter Bruno. "It's not the spectators who watch the film, but the film that watches the spectators." By reversing the subject/object relations of the film-within-the-film, Tornatore, by extension, makes us, in the viewing audience, the object of his own film's gaze. "The game of specularity is perfect and the collective gaze in the camera activates that absolute countershot that makes of the real movie house the extension of the one represented. The film envelops its own spectators in the darkness of a movie house that is pure representation."[6]

Since the internal audience is as much object as it is subject of the cinematic spectacle, Tornatore shows how this group *performs* its responses to the entertainment on screen. They cheer at the outcome of Germi's Mafia film, they weep noisily at the melodramatic *Catene* (one man actually recites the lines before they issue from the lips of the actors onscreen), they laugh uproariously at the antics of Totò, they shrink in horror at the grimaces of Mr. Hyde, they sigh appreciatively at the embrace that was not edited out of *Anna*, and the young male viewers masturbate at the sight of Brigitte Bardot's derriere. This is interactive cinema in its most primitive state.

To further emphasize the dialogic relationship between what happens on and off the screen in the movie house of Giancaldo, the old films shown at the Paradiso often reflect wittily and ironically on the surrounding action. The movie whose outdoor projection causes the blaze that destroys the theater and blinds Alfredo is entitled *The Firemen of Viggiù,* and the precise moment when the film ignites coincides with the onscreen "shooting" of the comedian Totò. In *I vitelloni,* Alberto Sordi mocks some street workers, who soon get their revenge on their tormenter, just as, during the showing of the film in Giancaldo, the elitist who routinely spits down on the rabble from his more expensive seat in the Paradiso's balcony gets a pizza thrown in his face. In the longer version of *Cinema Paradiso,* Totò's belief that Elena has left him is paralleled onscreen by the grief of Aldo, the protagonist of Antonioni's *Il grido,* when he is jilted by Irma. In perhaps the most sophisticated instance of on- and offscreen specularity, the narrative structure of *Anna,* involving a nun looking back on a life of sin, mirrors and reverses the transformation of the movie house itself from the heavily censored parish cinema of Father Adelfio to the venue of the more liberated entertainments of Don Ciccio.

In mourning the loss of the grand cinema and its dynamic relationship with the viewing public, Tornatore is doing something much more than wallowing in nostalgia for its own sake. The very process of representing the connection between the old movies and their audiences serves to recreate that connection in us. We, too, go through the gamut of responses, from hilarity to anxiety, to grief, to identification, to incomprehension, to ironic distancing, to enchantment—both in direct reaction to Totò's story and vicariously through the inner spectators as they in turn react to the films of an earlier time. Thus the very mode of representing the paradise lost of cinematic enchantment enables Tornatore to recreate that paradise in us, so that we become, for the space of the film, the resurrection of this ideal audience, honorary citizens of Giancaldo.

Were this all there is to Tornatore's film, we would be right to apply Jameson's disparaging label of nostalgic postmodernism to *Cinema Paradiso*. The film is entirely focused on itself as mass medium, it removes the signifiers of the past from any critical-realist historical context, and it bespeaks the breakdown of the hierarchy of culture. But to advance such a reading would be to ignore the moral critique of cinematic fascination that grows out of the film's engagement with Italian literature and the history of ideas. From this perspective, Tornatore's position on film spectacle becomes far more ambiguous and complex, endowing his work with an ethical dimension that removes it from the facile realm of postmodern nostalgia.

In the context of biblical and Renaissance epic traditions, paradise is anything but an unproblematic space of Edenic innocence and wholeness—it is also the locus of the Fall, site of man's guilty embrace of forbidden knowledge. The earthly paradises of Ariosto's *Orlando furioso* and Tasso's *Gerusalemme liberata* are dangerous illusions, deceptive simulacra of the perfect peace and plenitude that crusading knights thought they would find in the arms of their lady loves. Finally, *Cinema Paradiso* would be unintelligible, I believe, if considered apart from an analysis of the myth of romantic love on which so much Western literature, from the *Roman de la Rose* to *Madame Bovary,* is based.

Theological readings of Tornatore's title are unavoidable, given the film's insistence on the continuity between the spaces of church and cinema. The Cinema Paradiso is a parish movie theater, located next to the sanctuary, presided over by a statue of the Virgin Mary and patrolled by Father Adelfio. The logic of this juxtaposition of sacred and profane goes beyond mere antithesis, however. What is revealed, instead, is a deep structural identity between Mass and mass medium, between liturgical drama and filmic spectacle, both of which hold out the promise of communal participation in transcendence. If the church service is an enactment of Christ's sacrifice, and Communion enables each believer to partake in its offer of redemption, then the cinema provides its secular equivalent in the myths of heroism and romance made available to viewers through narcissistic identification. *Paradiso,* therefore, implies the state of grace, be it spiritual or imaginative, that church and cinema award to their respective devotees.

The Italian title of Tornatore's film is *Nuovo cinema paradiso,* referring to the movie theater's second incarnation after the fire that destroys the building and leaves Alfredo blind. At its most obvious, the remodeled movie house represents a "new testament" in the life of the town, liberated from the restrictive morality of the old parish cinema, free to witness the overt sexuality allowed under Don Ciccio's secular proprietorship. The film's new testament also refers to a new age in Salvatore's life, and for Tornatore demands a marked difference in cinematographic technique. Because the old Cinema Paradiso presided over Salvatore's boyhood, the subject matter invited a quick-paced, anecdotal, gag-filled style. The new movie house, however, is the staging ground for Salvatore's young manhood, whose decisive dramas are sentimental, and for Tornatore that requires a slower, more measured use of camera and less-obtrusive editing procedures.[7]

But the ostensible division between old and new cinematic paradises is a false one, masking their true identity as places of desire, of wish-fulfillment fantasies based on the glamour, romance, heroism, and exoticism so woefully lacking in everyday life. A small-time racketeer becomes Little Caesar; a two-bit prostitute can imagine herself as Brigitte Bardot; and Totò's missing father will return, like Clark Gable, to carry his mother up the stairs. It is here that Tornatore's critique of cinematic pleasure comes in—a critique that centers around the problematic figure of the projectionist, Alfredo, and that demands recourse to the uncut version of the film (originally 157 minutes, reduced to 121 minutes for theatrical distribution after its screening at Cannes).

In the film's abridged form, Alfredo is a completely benign figure: friend, protector, teacher, model—in short, the paternal stand-in, filling the void left by the death of Salvatore's biological father, who never returned from the Russian front (fig. 23). Not even in the abridged version does Tornatore limit Alfredo's role as projectionist to the physical confines of the Paradiso, however. Projection is also the psychological mechanism that underlies Alfredo's relationship to Salvatore, who becomes the object of the older man's movie-induced desires for glamour, escape, and romance. Throughout his tutelage of Salvatore, Alfredo displaces onto the young boy all of the frustrated ambition and discontent with his own lot that years of consuming Hollywood wish-fulfillment fantasies have bred in him. "Some day you will have other, more important things to do,"[8] Alfredo assures the boy, who is, at least for the moment, absolutely thrilled to be entrusted with the responsibility of projecting films at the Paradiso. As a young adult, newly returned from military service, Salvatore is told that he must leave Giancaldo behind if he is to amount to anything in this world. "Go away! This is a malignant land!" (119). Alfredo tells him on a seashore littered with the old rusty anchors of the ships that had docked there for too long. "Go back to Rome. You're young, the world is yours. And I'm old. I don't want to hear you talk any more, I want to hear you talked about" (120). When Salvatore bitterly asks, "Who said this? Gary Cooper, James Stewart, Henry Fonda?" (120), he expresses his awareness that Alfredo's worldview has always been mediated by cinematic models, and that he, in fulfilling the old man's frustrated ambitions, is expected to join this galaxy of stars.

Judging from its results, Alfredo's intervention in Salvatore's life seems all for the best: the young man's exile from paradise was the necessary precondition of his art, the separation that would allow him to return, many years later, and recreate his lost world through film. "You need to go away for a long time, for many, many years, to find your people again, the land where you were born" (119), Alfredo had advised. Like *8½*, then, *Cinema Paradiso* is a film about the process of liberation that the director had to undergo in order to make the film we just saw. Like Fellini's metafilm, *Cinema Paradiso* circles back on itself, ending at that point in the director-character's own personal development when the making of his autobiographical work could finally begin.

But the Alfredo of Tornatore's unabridged film is a far more problematic figure. In the original version, Salvatore's return to Giancaldo

FIGURE 23 | The small but spunky Totò poses with the towering Alfredo, his mentor, friend, confidant, surrogate father, and, eventually, scriptwriter of his life. Courtesy of the Museum of Modern Art/Film Stills Archive.

culminates in his reunion with Elena after a hiatus of thirty years. We learn that she has married Boccia (the class dimwit, who has since become a politician, the satiric implications of which are not far to seek). Elena has had two children by Boccia. The woman's most momentous revelation, however, concerns Alfredo's role in ending her romance with Salvatore on that fateful day when she failed to arrive on the five o'clock bus. What we learn in this interview is that Elena actually had kept the appointment but had arrived late, finding Alfredo in the projection booth instead of Salvatore, who had rushed off to seek her. When Salvatore returned to the Paradiso, Alfredo denied that Elena had come. With this lie, the projectionist puts an end to the romance and forcibly rewrites the script of Salvatore's life, making it conform to his grandiose plans for the young man's career in the cinema. It is Elena herself who justifies Alfredo's coercive tactics, thereby voicing her own endorsement of the "sublimation theory" of artistic creativity and her consequent status as Salvatore's muse. "If you had chosen to stay with me," Elena tells him, "you wouldn't have made your films. And that would have been a pity! Because they are so beautiful. I've seen them all" (153–54).

Even if Tornatore himself subscribes to this logic—with all its self-congratulatory implications for his own filmmaking, as suggested by the autobiographical references throughout *Cinema Paradiso*—his condemnation of Alfredo's strategy is nonetheless quite real. By playing God and writing the screenplay of Salvatore's life, no matter how benign his motives, the projectionist denied his protégé any exercise of free will, usurping his liberty to choose love over fame, domestic happiness over artistic achievement. The middle-aged Salvatore makes no secret of his moral outrage at Alfredo's intervention. "I would never have imagined that all should end because of the man who had been a father to me. A madman!" (153). Salvatore's condemnation of Alfredo's interference in his love life has important implications for our judgment of the role of cinema itself in the formation of film viewers' collective psychology. When Salvatore cries out, "Cursed Alfredo! He even enchanted you!" (151), the use of the term *enchanted* is strategic, conjuring up the incantatory powers of the very cinema that Alfredo so fatefully embodied.

It is in this presumption to define true love that Alfredo exercises his most pernicious influence on the young couple, and by extension that Hollywood exerts its most insidious power over the popular mind. In a dialogue that ostensibly devalues the myth of transcendent passion, Alfredo implies that this is really the only show in town. "My child," he tells Elena, "fire always becomes ashes. Even the greatest love ends sooner or later. And afterwards, there come other loves, so many. Instead, Totò has only one future" (150). In Alfredo's terms, the battle between fame and love can have a single legitimate outcome, if love is interpreted to mean exclusively the grand passion that is enshrined in the classic Hollywood cinema but unsustainable in real life. By privileging this definition of love, Alfredo aligns himself with an entire literary tradition of erotic mystification, of obstacle-seeking passions such as those that Denis de Rougemont ascribes to Tristan and Isolde and to their literary offspring in *Love in the Western World*. Now Alfredo's strategy reveals its logic: by truncating the young couple's romance, by blocking its natural progress toward marriage and domesticity, Alfredo keeps their love at the level of mystification—that is, of cinema.

It is here that Alfredo's parable of the soldier and the princess becomes relevant. Salvatore finally realizes that the lover leaves off his quest on the ninety-ninth day without reaching the hundredth in order to protect himself from disappointment. "Yes, just one more night and the princess would have been his. But she might not have kept her promise. And that would have been terrible. He would have died. So instead, at least for ninety-nine nights, he lived in the illusion that she was there waiting for him" (119). Though Salvatore fears the disappointment that the princess would not maintain her promise, disappointment in Alfredo's terms would mean something else—the inevitable letdown consequent to the *fulfillment* of the grand passion, the demystification of idealized desire in the face of domestic routine. By keeping Salvatore on *this side* of disappointment, Alfredo sustains him in the illusion of the unattainable, perfect love. And this, we are to believe, will become the driving force behind Salvatore's entire adult life, motivating both his unsuccessful quest to replace Elena in his affections and his compensatory successes as an auteur. "Even though the years passed, in all the women I met, I sought only you. . . . Then, maybe, I learned to live with your absence. I've been lucky, it's true, but something was always missing" (153). In his grudging way, Salvatore, too, gives credence to the "sublimation theory" of artistic creation.

Near the end of the film's unabridged version, the middle-aged Elena and Salvatore do finally consummate their love. It is a 1980s update of the passionate kiss that ended so many film romances of an earlier, less erotically explicit time. But their embrace nevertheless marks an end: this grand passion, like those of its Hollywood exemplars, will not have to undergo the disappointments of the day-after. It is Elena who gives voice to the need for closure *now,* while the passion remains at its height—while it remains cinematic. "Now that it has happened," Elena remarks, "I don't think there could be a better finale" (158)— the term *finale* seeming to have been chosen deliberately to suggest the end of a spectacle, not a life experience.

At last we are prepared to interpret the film's own grand finale in the montage of kisses rescued from the Paradiso's cutting-room floor, spliced together by a blind Alfredo and given to Salvatore as a posthumous gift. One possible reading of this gift could be that Alfredo is hereby restoring to Salvatore what he had edited out of the young man's life. But a more likely reading is that Alfredo is splicing Salvatore's own climactic love scene with Elena into this montage of grand cinematic passions—that, thanks to the projectionist, Salvatore's romance will remain at the level of cinema, one more element in the great signifying chain of romantic transcendence. And we realize, retrospectively, that the greatest seducer of them all has been Alfredo himself, victim and purveyor of Hollywood's seductions, unwilling to countenance the many other forms that love can take after the grand passion has subsided.

"You, maybe, don't believe me, but I will become the male lead in your life" (81), the young Salvatore, fledgling super-8 filmmaker, had said to the image of Elena projected onto his bedroom wall. In the end, Salvatore becomes just that—a romantic hero, condemned to live life *as cinema,* a projection of desires that can find fulfillment only in the illusory paradise of the silver screen.

From Conscience to Hyperconsciousness in
Maurizio Nichetti's *The Icicle Thief*

Were Italian cinema to be compared with a collective psyche in which certain films or directors would assume specific mental functions with respect to the whole, then *Bicycle Thief* would certainly be its conscience, or in Freudian terms, its superego. Ettore Scola made this the explicit theme of his original subject for *We All Loved Each Other So Much* (1974), which was to have concentrated on the character of Nicola,

> a provincial professor who, after having participated in the
> Resistance, was impressed by *Bicycle Thief* during a screening at
> the cine-club of his town. He abandoned his work, his family,
> and came to Rome to try to meet De Sica. The film was to be
> exclusively the story of a long trailing after [De Sica] that lasted
> thirty years. The character followed De Sica and became for
> him . . . a veritable obsession. De Sica constantly encountered
> him and the man confronted him with moral problems,
> problems of conscience. De Sica, as we know, produced
> alternatively great works and rather mediocre ones in which he
> lent himself out as an actor. There was, then, this "Jiminy
> cricket," this conscience that followed him, reprimanded him,
> persecuted him, and the film ended with the same phrase as the
> one that has remained in the definitive version: "We believed
> we'd changed the world and instead the world changed us."[1]

Though the film's final screenplay evolved beyond its exclusive focus on Nicola to include three interwoven plots that together track the course of postwar Italy from the Resistance to the mid-1970s, the original subject speaks eloquently of the place that *Bicycle Thief* occupies in the collective psyche of the Italian cinema. Like Nicola, whose obsession with the film causes him to stalk De Sica and implicitly reproach the director for his lapses into commercialism, *Bicycle Thief* serves as a kind of cinematic conscience, an Edenic moment of perfect innocence and wholeness against which all subsequent filmmaking is seen to have fallen away. When Bruno takes his father's hand at the end of *Bicycle Thief* in a sublime gesture of acceptance and love, it might have signaled the "despair over a paradise lost"[2] on the narrative level, but it created a cinematic Eden, a Golden Age of neorealist filmmaking, according to Nicola's remarks at the end of the screening of *Bicycle Thief* in his home town of Nocera Inferiore.[3]

The Nicola of Scola's original screenplay, this walking, talking ghost of cinema-past who haunts the latter-day De Sica and, we can assume, all of Italian post-neorealist filmmakers with the measure of their failure, translates into narrative terms what I will call the "*Bicycle Thief* topos." Gianni Amelio invokes it when he entitles his 1992 film *Il ladro di bambini* (distributed in the English-speaking world as *Stolen Children*) in an explicit recall to the "ethical mandate of the earlier work."[4] For perhaps the most incisive formulation of the topos, however, we must leave Italy and adopt the perspective of a Hollywood outsider, Robert Altman, who makes strategic reference to the neorealist work in *The Player* (1992).[5] Not by coincidence, it is at a screening of *Bicycle Thief* that the unscrupulous producer Griffin Mill (played by Tim Robbins) is able to track down David Kahane, the screenwriter full of righteous anger at the Hollywood establishment, in the sequence preceding his murder. De Sica's work stands, by synecdoche, for all the values that the screenwriter finds so woefully lacking in the corrupt, mercenary, and vacuous world of American filmmaking, whose formula for success, according to Griffin Mill, includes "suspense, laughter, violence, hope, heart, nudity, sex, happy endings—mainly happy endings." The producer's focus on closure, on the kinds of endings prerequisite to Hollywood success, explains, of course, Altman's own obsession with endings at the metatextual level—how will his *own* film end? How will the film developing within the film end? and so on. When listening to Mill's catalog of successful plot elements, it is his emphasis on happy endings that prompts his girlfriend's question, "But what about reality?" just as it is the ending of *Bicycle Thief* that is anthologized in both *The Player* and *We All Loved Each Other So Much*.

Endings, then, are the points at which films choose whether or not to engage the "real" world, whether or not to link their viewers' imaginative investment in the story they just experienced with the need for accountability in the public sphere. Neorealism makes this choice in its very open-endedness, in its refusal to bring closure, in its rejection of the climactic rescue, the definitive jail sentence, or the cathartic death that would neatly package the film as a formed and finite entity that would not otherwise impinge on its viewers' lives or attention span. In renouncing closure, neorealism forfeits the interpretive possibilities that Frank Kermode attributes to the ending as the privileged point that retrospectively gives meaning and coherence to the entire work.[6] By foregoing this hermeneutic advantage, the neorealists destabilized their narratives, consigning them to an indeterminacy that promoted their goal of active viewer collaboration in the interpretive process.[7]

The admonitory function of *Bicycle Thief*—its power to haunt the present and measure its slippage from some absolute standard of integrity and social commitment—receives its most sustained and complex treatment in Maurizio Nichetti's 1989 *The Icicle Thief*, whose very title in both Italian and English announces its investment in the earlier work (I discuss the titles later in this chapter). Nichetti's postmodern perspective, however, adds considerable irony to his treatment of *Bicycle Thief*, softening and complicating his critique of contemporary media culture while at the same time poking fun at the pretensions of the latter-day neorealist filmmaker-within-the-film. This intricate strategy is made possible by *The Icicle Thief*'s three-tiered narrative structure, which includes (1) an inner film (also entitled *The Icicle Thief*, which I will henceforth simply call the "inner film") to be aired on television (fig. 24); (2) events in the television studio involving the frustrated filmmaker, named and played by Nichetti himself (henceforth, "the auteur"); and (3) an evening in the life of the typical viewing family consisting of a father, mother, and 2.8 children.

Because Nichetti opted not to include actual footage from De Sica's original but chose instead to make his own version of the neorealist work, the auteur's film exists as a mere potentiality—a virtual movie

FIGURE 24 | Antonio Piermattei (Maurizio Nichetti) and Bruno (Federico Rizzo) pose with a bicycle in one of the publicity stills that cover the walls of the TV studio in *The Icicle Thief.* Courtesy of the Museum of Modern Art/Film Stills Archive.

rendered unstable by its own indigenous defects as well as by its televisual mutilation. For one thing, the inner film is a pastiche of platitudes drawn not only from *Bicycle Thief* but from Rossellini's *Open City* (1945), De Sica's *Umberto D* (1952), Fellini's *Nights of Cabiria* (1957), and even the biographical record of Rossellini's affair with Ingrid Bergman, making *The Icicle Thief* a neorealist potpourri, a filmographic trivia game, an exercise in "name that allusion." By borrowing indiscriminately from a number of neorealist sources, Nichetti underscores the contradictions and inconsistencies within the movement that have made neorealism such a problematic and controversial critical label. This is not the place to rehearse those debates, but it will suffice here to say that when the Rossellini of *The War Trilogy* can be seen to have more in common with Fascist documentarists than with Visconti or De Sica, who in turn resemble, respectively, less each other than their predecessors in French poetic realism and white-telephone comedies, then to invoke them is to reactivate the very instability inherent in the postwar movement itself. And Nichetti does so with a vengeance, incorporating a series of random and chaotic neorealist allusions throughout his film: Don Pietro of *Open City* and his tutelage of Marcello are paralleled in the character of Don Italo and his mentorship of Bruno; Agostino's aromatic cooking in Don Pietro's rectory is recalled in the Piermatteis' diet based almost exclusively on cabbage; Umberto D of De Sica's eponymous film is reincarnated in the dignified old man who lives in the Piermattei tenement and is seen descending the common stairwell; the hymn heard throughout the Santuario dell'Divino Amore scene in *Nights of Cabiria* is echoed in the one sung in Don Italo's church. Nichetti even makes allusions to the ancestry of neorealism. For example, the scenes of Antonio's apprenticeship at the glass factory hark back to the general documentary antecedents of the movement— in particular, to Walter Ruttmann's 1933 film *Acciaio*. The proto- neorealist film *Ossessione* is recalled in Nichetti's episode on a riverbank after the presumed drowning of Maria—analogous in *Ossessione* to the police interrogation at the site of Bragana's murder.[8] Finally, in a refer- ence to the biographical incident that led Rossellini away from neore- alist filmmaking toward a cinema of greater interiority and depth, Nichetti includes a quote from Ingrid Bergman's "fan letter" to the di- rector in the wake of *Open City* and *Paisan*. As tall, Aryan Heidi pins the diminutive Nichetti character to the wall upon learning who he is, she gushes, "I always wanted to meet an Italian director. I love your movies. The black-and-white is great. I'd like to work with you in Italy, but the only thing I can say is '*ti amo*.'"

Obviously, the references to *Bicycle Thief* dominate all others in *The Icicle Thief*, but they are as arbitrary as they are superficial, revealing no profound critical engagement with the precursor text. In a totally gra- tuitous scene, complete with poster hangers, street sweepers, and a thief with a German cap, a bicycle is indeed stolen, but it is not Antonio's and it has no relation to the themes of economic necessity or to un- derclass self-victimization that distinguished De Sica's original. Anto- nio orders an omelet sandwich for his first day at work, but it is not replicated in the smaller omelet given to Bruno in the poignant father- son lunch-pocketing scene of *Bicycle Thief*. Bruno works at a gas pump and prepares the family dinner of cabbage, revealing that he, like his neo- realist counterpart, occupies the only adult role in the household. But this is a part that Bruno happily surrenders the minute he is exposed to the kiddy paradise of commercial television. Like De Sica's Bruno, Nichetti's polishes the pedal of his father's bike, but not to point out the tiny dent that prefigures the far greater tragedy of the vehicle's disappearance in the original film. Both Antonio Ricci and the auteur in *The Icicle Thief* are met with police indifference to the theft of personal property—"look for it yourself. You've made your report, *va bene così*," they are told, as they search for the stolen goods: Ricci for the bicycle; the auteur for the chandelier. But the stakes for the latter-day neorealist director within the film are merely aesthetic ones, while Ricci faces economic and social defeat of a far more devastating sort.

Ironically, Nichetti makes one of his most incisive allusions to *Bicycle Thief* in a scene that ostensibly has nothing to do with the neorealist precursor. I refer here to the moment when Antonio rescues Heidi and dries her off, removing her surface color in a technical tour-de-force that took Nichetti three months to complete.[9] The film-historical viewer cannot help but recall Ricci as his hands pass over the contours of Rita Hayworth in the attempt to smooth out the wrinkles, bubbles, and blemishes of the badly affixed poster for *Gilda*. Both scenes mark decisive turning points at which things go terribly awry, as if contact with these disproportionately large foreign female bodies were enough to spell disaster. For at this point, Antonio Ricci loses his bike, and Maurizio Nichetti loses his plot.

This undigested, pastiche quality is not the only explanation for *The Icicle Thief*'s instability, however. For one thing, Nichetti has recklessly relocated the story from the Roman streets of De Sica's original to the high-tech airwaves over Milan—a shift linguistically revealed by the change in the protagonist's name from Antonio *Ricci* to the decidedly Lombard Antonio *Piermattei*. This uprooting has far more to it than onomastics, however, just as Rome and Milan are far more than mere geographic indicators: they are cultural signs, synecdochal markers for the deep conflicts that divide the Italian map between the modernized, affluent, industrial, European north and the traditional, poor, bureaucratic-agrarian, Mediterranean south. To relocate this story from Rome to Milan is thus to recodify all its cultural designators and to stretch to the straining point the distance between neorealist model and contemporary revisitation.

Another explanation for *The Icicle Thief*'s instability may be found in Nichetti's misunderstanding of neorealist genre requirements. A litany of disasters comprises the film's original plot. Antonio is to be paralyzed when run over by a truck on his way home, forcing Maria, his wife, into prostitution to support the family and the children to be consigned to an orphanage. In this catastrophic chain reaction of events, the narrative fails to link its protagonists to a concrete social environment that would condition their fate. It also fails to offer even the glimmer of hope for renewal that animates such films as *Open City, Bicycle Thief,* and *La terra trema.* Nichetti's film thus falls into the category of what French critics called "Roman miserablism,"[10] by which they meant films that appropriated the outer trappings of neorealism—indigent characters, slummy settings, tragic plots—without acknowledging the deeply progressive vision that underlies the genre's indictment of social ills. Taking miserablism as my point of departure, I would argue that *The Icicle Thief* would not be a return to neorealism at all, but a revival of one of its two degraded offshoots—the second offshoot being "rosy realism," which borrows the external apparatus of the neorealists but adds a guilt-alleviating happy ending: "Poor yes, but with a smile and a song."

From the very start of *The Icicle Thief,* Nichetti leaves no doubt as to his "miserablist" take on the past. Whereas Ricci learns that he has been offered a position as a poster hanger in the opening scene of *Bicycle Thief,* Piermattei at the beginning of *The Icicle Thief* learns that he is first on the rejection list. Condemned to the unremitting dreariness of their miserablist film, Nichetti's characters are naturally driven to rebel. Bruno refuses to go to the orphanage and Maria is ecstatic in consumer heaven, unwilling to return to her neorealist tenement until the director coaxes her back with promises of unlimited access to material goods. As shopping cart after shopping cart of cornflakes, spaghetti, champagne, and tennis rackets are crowded into the narrow confines of the Piermattei kitchen at the film's conclusion, Maria and Antonio exchange a passionate embrace of "consumer arousal."[11] This ending meets with the appreciative tears of the television-viewing wife, who obviously misses such attentions from her husband.

Nichetti's misunderstanding of neorealist plot structure results in an equally flawed conception of character. Unlike the long-suffering but relatively undeveloped wife of *Bicycle Thief,* Nichetti's Maria has aspirations that totally disqualify her from neorealist narrative: she wants to sing and dance on stage and be a middle-class homemaker, and she would never dream of giving up her trousseau sheets as De Sica's hero-ine had done without a second thought. As out-of-place as she is in a neorealist context, however, Maria makes the perfect heroine for rosy realism. Her petty-bourgeois ambitions are summed up in the image of the chandelier that she invokes in rapt anticipation of the paycheck that Antonio will finally bring home. "Now we can afford a chandelier like the one I once saw at a movie theater. It was so beautiful. It had eight lightbulbs, glass flowers, and leaves, all shimmering. When it was turned on, it lit up the walls. I always dreamed of a chandelier. Even in bomb shelters, during the war, I thought—when the war is over, I'd have a beautiful house with a big room and a chandelier like the one in the movies." This elaborately worked out image of a light fixture, each facet of which acts like a miniprojector capable of bending and scattering its beams to create a multicolored illusion of plenitude on the sur-rounding walls, is a perfect metaphor for the cinema. Significantly, Maria links the chandelier to her own dreams for social improvement—dreams that undeniably redound to their source in Hollywood-induced fantasies of glamour and wealth. Antonio's theft of the chandelier on his first day of work at the Lux factory indicates his desire instantly to fulfill Maria's consumer longings, to be the economic hero who alle-viates her hardships with one magic gesture of appropriation. For the brief time in which he ecstatically carries the chandelier on his bicy-cle, it is as if he were in possession of pure cinema, shareholder in its "factory of dreams." But Antonio's moment of grace is short-lived: once he sets down his bike to rescue the drowning Heidi, intruder from the world of commercial TV, the chandelier disappears, and with it the myth of pure cinema slips irretrievably beyond his grasp.[12]

Maria's chandelier dialogue with Antonio is designed to recall an-other conversation between a man and a woman using a wartime set-ting to project onto a future of happiness that will justify all of the mis-ery and suffering of the recent past. This is the exchange between Pina and Francesco in the stairwell on the eve of their wedding in *Open City;* they are discussing the seemingly interminable war:

FRANCESCO: And everybody thought it'd be over soon and that we'd only get to see it in the movies. But . . .

PINA: When'll it end? Sometimes I just can't go on. This winter seems like it'll never end.

FRANCESCO: It'll end, Pina, it'll end, and spring will come back and it'll be more beautiful than ever, because we'll be free. We have to believe it, we have to want it! . . . Because we're in the right, the right's on our side. Understand, Pina?

PINA: Yes, Francesco.

FRANCESCO: We're fighting for something that has to be, that can't help coming! Maybe the way is hard, it may take a long time, but we'll get there, and we'll see a better world! And our kids'll see it! Marcello and—him, the baby that's coming.[13]

The postwar futures conjured up by Maria's materialist reverie in *The Icicle Thief* and Francesco's profession of partisan faith in *Open City* could not be more different—one personal, domestic, and consumer-oriented, the other selfless, collective, and politically utopian. In her petty bourgeois desires and aspirations, Maria resembles far more the character played by Anna Magnani in Visconti's *Bellissima*—the ambitious, star-crazed Maddalena Cecconi—than Magnani's martyred heroine of *Open City.* When the inevitable commercials interrupt Maria's forward-looking fantasies with images of soapsuds and aperitifs, they provide appropriate fulfillment for the strictly consumerist terms in which her utopia is conceived.[14]

If Maria's fantasies of affluence and glamour are cinematically inspired, it is fitting that her son's be prompted by the consumerist incentives of the newer medium. Even before the electrical blackout that plunges Heidi into the waters of the inner film and irreparably destabilizes its plot, consumerist influences had infiltrated the Piermattei world. After an ad for the candy bar Big-Big, the inner film resumes with the Piermattei family enjoying a dinner of boiled potatoes. Looking straight out of the television set into the viewing family's living room, Bruno seems to fixate on the well-fed son as the latter consumes his evening helping of Big-Big. For a while, Bruno synchronizes his chewing with that of the child viewer on the other side of the TV screen before turning to his mother and asking her to buy him the product. When neither parent demonstrates brand-name recognition, Bruno proceeds to sing an advertising jingle and do a silly dance that indicates some form of toxic exposure to the commercial that had aired just minutes before.

In calling attention to the unbridgeable gap between the postwar subsistence economy of the 1948 Piermatteis and the postmodern prosperity of the viewing family, Nichetti is alluding to a central episode in *Bicycle Thief*.[15] In De Sica's film, the unattainability of middle-class affluence is made palpable in the restaurant scene, where an invisible barrier seems to separate the Riccis from the adjacent table of bourgeois patrons. The delight of father and son at the prospect of a well-earned lunch dissipates in the face of their socioeconomic reality—a reality made only too explicit in comparison with the prosperous family at the next table, consuming seemingly unlimited quantities of food and drink. The distance between adjacent tables is really a class abyss of unbridgeable proportions. It is Nichetti's genius to express that distance in media terms, where the "glass ceiling" that virtually surrounds the protagonists of *Bicycle Thief* becomes the cathode tube of the postmodern film.

Bruno's receptivity to the Big-Big message is only a minor intimation of what is to come, however: commercials will wreak havoc on the integrity of the inner film, changing not only its narrative structure but its generic identity in momentous ways. When Heidi enters the Piermattei household after the power failure, causing a distraught Maria to "commit suicide" to the world of the inner film, Nichetti's script evolves from neorealist melodrama to murder mystery. On the riverbank where Maria was last seen, hypotheses abound: Don Italo, the parish priest, speculates that Antonio was involved in the black market and probably tried to push Maria into prostitution, murdering her because she refused to comply. Antonio's subsequent eagerness to get back to the apartment, where the scantily clad Heidi awaits him, moves the story line in the direction of sexually explicit scenarios. By the time it reaches closure, this unstable and infinitely elastic plot has traversed a remarkable generic spectrum, from miserablist beginnings to murder mystery and soft-core pornography and then to its rosy-realist conclusion.

These multiple metamorphoses are prefigured and encapsulated in Nichetti's very title (the English translation, while wittily recalling *Bi-*

cycle Thief, does not do justice to its generic journey). In the Italian title *Ladri di saponette* (lit. *Thieves of Soap Bars*), Nichetti marks the terminal points of the title wording's itinerary, beginning with neorealist homage and ending with the bourgeois wish-fulfillment fantasy of detergent commercials. But the synthetic leap of the title also says something about viewer reception of films broadcast on television. "A person who watches TV for a few hours and goes to bed," Nichetti observes, "doesn't remember if a face is from a film, a commercial, or the news."[16] To blend in his title elements from the inner film and from the soap commercials that punctuate it is to proclaim from the very start Nichetti's awareness that, in viewers' minds, his televised work will be perceived as pastiche. Though the viewer-father confidently announces his knowledge of the distinction between the perceptual codes proper to cinema and to TV ads ("if it's in color it's a commercial, if it's in black and white it's a film"), Nichetti's work systematically undermines such cognitive certainties by showing that the boundaries between the two are much more porous than the viewer's statement would suggest.

In subjecting the inner film to such wild and destabilizing interferences, Nichetti is taking to absurd extremes the anxieties that plague directors who show their films on television— "because a movie on TV *becomes* TV," he explains, "a different form of attention, with commercials interrupting."[17] The fear that the film's reception will be tainted by commercial interruptions is taken to hyperbolic lengths when its very plot is derailed by advertisements and its generic identity modified beyond recognition. To reinforce his point, Nichetti devises a sexual conceit for video assaults on his film's integrity, taking his cue from his characters' own confusion of amorous and consumerist drives. When Maria supposes that her husband has been unfaithful to her, the betrayed wife constructs an allegory for what is happening across media: the inner film is having an affair with a commercial. Adultery on the level of story has become adulteration on the level of form: Antonio's violation of his marriage vows parallels neorealism's breach of generic decorum. The resultant mixture of 1940s cinema and 1980s advertising images is a wanton commingling of electronic signals, a transgressive crossing of boundaries, a miscegenation of frequencies and codes. And the scandal inscribed in the inner film when Maria disappears to neorealism and is presumed murdered is really the formal scandal of hitherto separate media that consort in promiscuous union in the airwaves of Milan.

How does the family of middle-class spectators react to this scandal? With great equanimity and calm. The father, a connoisseur of female nudity, is titillated, but not unnerved, to see Heidi in the neorealist tenement. The pregnant mother, who is constantly distracted by household demands from without and fetal movements from within, is totally satisfied by the rosy-realist turn of events. The son Francesco, who has been busily constructing out of Lego blocks Saint Basil's Cathedral in the Kremlin as he consumes his ration of Big-Big, has fallen asleep. But the most up-to-date viewing habits are exhibited by the youngest family member, Anna, who channel surfs. In her restless switching from program to program, Anna is the quintessential postmodern viewer, just as television becomes the quintessential medium of pastiche. Channel surfing *is* her show: with the power vested in Anna by the remote control, the child creates her own entertainment, editing the flow of images, determining their rhythm and shape.[18] Like her brother, who builds a giant structure out of tiny blocks,[19] Anna constructs her reality out of the little bits and pieces of programming that succeed each other on screen as her thumbs tap restlessly on the little control panel in her hands. Unlike the mother, who in the time between dinner and bed wants to immerse herself in one sustained melodrama (preferably the Washington, D.C., soap opera *Capitol*), Anna reads television transversally, cutting across all the offerings at a given moment. In Anna's show, meaning inheres in this oceanic flux of images, in their kaleidoscopic change, in the horizontal relationships of random juxtaposition determined by her fingers and thumbs and the whim of broadcast frequencies. With her consciousness full of TV bites—paratactically ordered fragments of television programming— Anna is Italy's future, as is her unborn sibling, whose fetal movements are already attuned to his mother's viewing habits ("he always kicks when I sit down to watch a show").[20]

In the distance separating the viewing family of *The Icicle Thief* and the subsistence family of *Bicycle Thief,* Nichetti concentrates the force of his film's social satire. The defining activity of the comfortable Milanese viewers of 1989 is to watch television while consuming its advertising products, whereas the Piermatteis of 1948 struggle to stay alive on a diet of potatoes and cabbage. The gap represented by this forty-year postwar history amounts to the difference between a Third World and a First World economy, between a society dedicated to the production and consumption of primary goods and services and one dedicated to creating and satisfying a secondary appetite for images.[21] In tracing the evolution of the typical Italian family from 1948 to 1989, Nichetti may well have had in mind another film at the midpoint of that itinerary—Ermanno Olmi's *Il posto* (1963), made in the throes of Il Boom. In that film, the protagonist, Domenico Cantoni, could be seen as the 1960s update of Bruno Ricci, competing for a job in a huge, unnamed corporation—the generic emblem and instrument of Italy's postwar economic rebirth. If Nichetti is indeed following such a genealogy, then Massimo, the spectator-father of *The Icicle Thief,* could be seen as the middle-aged version of Domenico, now the plump paterfamilias, securely ensconced in the company hierarchy. By periodically revisiting Bruno Ricci, in his various reincarnations as he progresses from the threadbare child of 1948 to the upwardly mobile young man of 1960 to the successful patriarch of 1989, Italian filmmakers can take the socioeconomic pulse of Italy as it evolves from postwar subsistence to postboom sateity.

Nichetti's comparison between the neorealist and contemporary families goes beyond the obvious material differences to consider their cognitive and metaphysical implications. Whereas the Riccis/Piermatteis directly confront social experience, emerging into the streets, churches, and public halls of the city to seek a means of survival, the viewing family sits complacently in the living room, exposed to only telemediated events.[22] For this family of spectators, there is no primary experience—they exist only to react to a representation of the way another family reacts to primary experience in an earlier and simpler time. As such, the 1989 family lives in a world of simulation, preferring images to their real-life referents, experiencing events at several removes from their occurrence, perceiving reality only in ways that can be encoded, transmitted, and received along the airwaves of a technologically advanced civilization.

A semiotic leveling takes place in the viewing family's world, where mass-media images assume the importance of life-defining events. When Carlina, the spectator-mother, asks, "Is that Splash ad still around?

It's been eight years. Yes, we weren't married yet and I lived with Angela and Luisa,"[23] she is equating the longevity of a commercial to the
calendar of her intimate personal journey—from nubile independence
through engagement, marriage and two and one-half pregnancies. The
Splash commercial has come to bear the weight of a bildungsroman, a
coming-of-age text that enables Carlina retrospectively to relive the
formative years of her biography—a biography that finds its fulfillment
in marriage. The interests of Massimo, her husband, are very different:
for him, TV commercials trigger a bachelor train of thought. His focus
on the seminudity of advertising models and his indifference to the burgeoning body of his wife reveal the split between erotic fantasy and
marital reality that the mass media so lucratively exploit. But in both
cases, what Nichetti is illustrating is the telemediated quality of postmodern family life—the way in which perceptions and interactions are
determined by the workings of television. As such, Nichetti's postmodern viewer may be said to suffer from a case of *hyporeality*—a kind
of experiential undernourishment that no amount of candy bars and
aperitifs can replenish.[24]

Lobbying against the reduction of all experience to the level of televisual pastiche is the internalized figure of the director, who struggles
in vain to preserve the integrity of his film against commercial onslaughts. In the opening minutes of the film, the Nichetti character remains silent as he is dragged through the corridors of a studio by the
loquacious Clara, becoming the brunt of a number of sight gags such
as slipping on paint and tearing his clothes to shreds so that he has to
be sewn together and lacquered into place on camera (all this is a
throwback to Nichetti's previous career as a director and actor of comedies with a heavy emphasis on mime) (fig. 25).[25] Then Nichetti's first
words after breaking his silence show that he has emerged quite suddenly from the chrysalis of comedy to become a fully formed and self-
protective auteur: "I wanted to watch it," Nichetti says of his film as it
is being broadcast on the air. "Don't worry," Clara reassures him. "Now
there's just ads." "That's what I wanted to monitor!" is Nichetti's anxious response. "This isn't my film. Tell them the real story of my film,"
he begs critic Fava, who then proceeds automatically to rattle off the
plot of Ernst Lubitsch's *Heaven Can Wait,* the next movie on his list to
introduce. Throughout the television studio sequence of *The Icicle Thief,*

FIGURE 25 | The clownish image of the Nichetti character within the film harks back to the actor/director's past experience in the comedic genre. Courtesy of the Museum of Modern Art/Film Stills Archive.

Fava stands as the embodiment of the snobbery and excesses of an international auteurist approach to the medium, where to drop names, plot summaries, and critical clichés is enough to be considered an expert in the field.[26]

Though the film critic ostensibly snubs Nichetti, setting up an opposition between the former's auteurist arrogance and the latter's status as lowly comedian, the young director himself comes to act more and more the auteur as he progressively loses control of his film. In his eagerness to reassert his authority, Nichetti behaves in rude and peremptory ways, evicting a Japanese family, complete with luggage and children, from a taxi he grabs for himself, exploiting a cyclist to transport him to the Lux factory at breakneck speed, and unceremoniously entering into the world of his characters, attempting to coerce their respect for him based on his possession of privileged knowledge—knowledge they ignore. "Who are you? I've never seen you before," says Don Italo to Nichetti as he erupts into the sacristy. "I instead know you very well," retorts Nichetti—who, however, must still depend upon the priest to tell him Antonio's address. "Next time I'll do a close-up of the street name so I won't have to ask anything of anyone. OK?" This combina-

tion of arrogance toward his characters and dependence on them becomes more acute when the auteur confronts Bruno and the baby
Paolo in the Piermattei apartment. "I know you as if you were my own
sons. I know this house with my eyes closed." Yet Nichetti is powerless to convince Bruno to adhere to his script, which would consign
the child to an orphanage. "Send your sister," the boy shouts back in
defiance as he leads Nichetti on a chase from the neorealist streets of
the inner film to the traffic-choked intersection of a contemporary
aperitif commercial. In this variant on the conventional cinematic chase
scene, it is appropriate that the obstacles be cocktail tables, bathtubs, and
washing machines, for these are the luxury items that lead the neorealist
characters themselves off course, that cause them to abandon their miserablist script for the more consumer-friendly agenda of contemporary
television.

Bruno's defiance of his author's denouement has twofold significance. On the one hand, it suggests a deep and demystified reading of
Bicycle Thief, whose characters, devoid of class-consciousness, would
have been delighted to enjoy the prosperity of the bourgeois family at
the adjacent table in the restaurant. In noticing the glass wall that separates them from the diners who can afford a meal of many courses,
champagne, and all the amenities, Antonio and Bruno are not moved
to reflect on social injustice or to imagine possible programs of economic reform. They are simply motivated to reembark on their quest
for the bicycle and for the financial security it promises to bring them.
The Riccis are hardly revolutionaries, and their social environment
offers them no access to an ideology that would translate their frustration into corrective political action. They are simply aspirants to a
middle-class comfort that is as beyond their reach as the space of the
1989 viewers' living room is to the Piermatteis. But once the studio
blackout enables them to undergo economic time travel and experience the consumer paradise of commercial TV, then the latent desires
of the Riccis can become the manifest desires of the Piermatteis. Heidi,
whose tall body is out of all proportion to the neorealist mise-en-scène,
is really the Big-Big of the postwar Italian collective dreams,[27] the personification of the abundance and glamour of an advanced consumer
economy to which they all aspire, with varying degrees of openness.

The neorealist characters' apostasy from the established script has

importance for the literary history of *The Icicle Thief,* linking it to an entire Pirandellian tradition of frame-breaking behaviors—of characters
who defy the authority of writers and directors in order to act in accordance with their own inner desires for self-expression.[28] Like the
family in *Six Characters in Search of an Author,* whose narrative Pirandello rejects in the preface to the play but who go on to impose their
tragic story on a director seeking to rehearse another script, Nichetti's
characters assert their free will and wage a battle against authorial omnipotence that reaches nearly theological proportions. In a Pirandellian
move to blur the distinctions between the inner world of the fiction
and the outer world of the playwright and his public, Nichetti the auteur races back in time and crosses the boundaries into his own film
in a vain attempt to get his story back on track. But despite his illusion of privilege and power over the world of his creation, Nichetti becomes yet one more character in a film he can no longer control. His
status as victim is made explicit by the doubling effect of Nichetti's performing both Antonio's and the auteur's roles, so that when they confront each other in jail they are portrayed as equally helpless, equally
subject to the prison house of uncontrollable circumstance.[29] In fact,
the auteur emerges as finally *less* free than Antonio, who at least can benefit from the solidarity of other family members to obtain release from
jail: Bruno alerts Don Italo to the arrival of the newcomer, who looks
like his father and can conveniently take the rap for Maria's murder.

But rudeness, arrogance, and impracticality are not the most griev-
ous of the auteur's sins. When he explains, "Maria goes into prostitution to feed her sons—it's the most powerful scene in the film," we
realize that the auteur's worst crime, in ideological terms, is his exploitation of his characters for the sake of melodramatic effect. Just as
Antonio had been suspected of pimping for his wife and then killing
her when she failed to go along with him, Nichetti is ready to push
his character into prostitution in a form of auteurist abuse, expecting
to reap artistic profit from her surrender to economic necessity. Antonio's alleged pandering on the narrative level becomes simply a higher
order of pandering on the level of metatext: in both cases, a woman is
forced to sell her body against her will and a man will benefit from
the transaction. Similarly, the auteur's insistence on consigning Bruno
to an orphanage, much against the will of the character who would in-

finitely prefer romping with his peers in a Big-Big ad, amounts to a sophisticated form of child abuse.

By the end of the film, having yielded to his characters' wish for a
rosy-realist conclusion, the auteur is finally humbled. He has given up
the lofty rhetoric of authority, privilege, and control and surrenders to
the forces of postmodern media culture that have brought about the
much-heralded "death of the subject." As a sign of his defeat, the auteur ends up imprisoned within the bounds of the television screen as
surely as the fish are confined by the aquarium strategically placed by
the side of the set. Early in the film, the equivalence of the cathode tube
and the aquarium had been made explicit by the daughter Anna, who
had muted the sound and proceeded to imitate both the mouth movements of the film critic on screen and those of the contiguous fish. Her
mime, however, served to generalize the critique, to suggest that not
only TV's own protagonists but also its viewers were reduced by the
medium to the level of a subhuman, aqueous existence, limited to the
confines of a transparent bowl, subjects and objects of obsessive,
voyeuristic gazes. As the trapped auteur looks out of the television set
into the living room while Carlina and Massimo tidy up before bed,
the shot is taken through a fish-eye lens whose concave edges suggest
that this household is indeed an aquarian space. If Nichetti does not go
so far as to intimate that television keeps its viewers in the fetal condition of Carlina's unborn child (who becomes active only when
Mamma sits down to watch), he does strongly imply the analogy
between a world organized around television viewing and the confined, controlled amniotic environment of the fish bowl. They are both
hyporeal.[30]

But Nichetti's critical attitude toward contemporary media culture
is not as simple as this stifling of the auteur would suggest. By doubling
and ironizing himself as both director of the inner film and implied author of all levels of *The Icicle Thief*, Nichetti assumes the position of
complicitous critique that Linda Hutcheon attributes to all postmodern practice, whereby the artists' stand within contemporary culture de-
prives them of any detached perspective from which to sit in judgment.[31] By making the internalized figure of the artist a caricature
whose exaggerated claims of purity align him with the insufferably pretentious auteurism of the film critic Fava, Nichetti sets up a critical dis-

tance that enables him to establish a more liberated position for himself as postmodern pasticheur. For one thing, Nichetti was himself a director of commercials, and he exhibits his insider's knowledge of the craft with an exuberance that defies any position of unequivocal censure.[32] In addition, by making the original film of *The Icicle Thief* so unremittingly miserablist that we welcome the relief of commercials, Nichetti further tempers our impulse to categorically dismiss television culture.

Like Fellini, who used ads in *Ginger and Fred* as a pretext for his own stylistic fetishes, to indulge his love of gratuitous and discrete flashes of creativity unattached to a surrounding narrative context, Nichetti exploits the commercial breaks for the energizing, carnivalizing power of juxtaposition itself. In the televisual pastiche made possible by a studio blackout, Nichetti has an excuse to invent his own postmodern mélange, to play games with the various recombinant possibilities offered him by this disparate mix of neorealist and commercial conventions, to let the media cross-fertilize, to follow this new electronic *ars combinatoria* wherever it may lead him.[33] As in biology, where hybridization is key to breeding stronger and more adaptive genetic strains, Nichetti experiments with the creation of composite codes and mutant genres, fascinated as much by the processes of metamorphosis and contamination as by their results. In fact, *The Icicle Thief* may be seen as a sustained study of the coming-into-being of a new, postmodern hybrid mode, and of the energizing effects of that transformation.

In his bumbling homage to De Sica's classic, the inner Nichetti takes his place in the succession of filmmakers, from Scola to Amelio to Altman, who have made *Bicycle Thief* the moral standard against which all subsequent cinema is measured and found wanting. What precisely is this nostalgia that the *Bicycle Thief* syndrome represents? "We believed we'd changed the world, and instead the world changed us," Nicola had said in both the original and final versions of *We All Loved Each Other So Much*. In giving voice to his disappointment, Nicola speaks not simply for the failure of his generation to bring about the new Italy envisioned by the Resistance in the wake of Fascism and war. What he specifically regrets is the *cinema's* failure to do so—its failure to become the privileged instrument of social transformation heralded by neorealism. Film as a concrete intervention in the real, as a foundational act, as a building block in the "moral reconstruction of our country"[34]—this is the loss that Nicola mourns.

Cristina Degli-Esposti has argued that Italian cinema's basis in ideology has given way to a basis in "discourse."[35] By this she means that films can no longer engage in direct sociopolitical commentary but can do so indirectly, at a second remove, by reflecting on the nature of the medium rather than on an "extramural" set of signifieds. Degli Esposti's observations on the primacy of discourse coincide with Jim Collins's idea of postmodern *hyperconsciousness:* "a hyperawareness on the part of the text itself of its cultural status, function, and history, as well as of the conditions of its circulation and reception."[36] Tracing the part played by *Bicycle Thief* throughout the history of postwar Italian cinema and exploiting the ambiguity of the Italian word *coscienza,* we may see the film's role as evolving from social conscience to hyperconsciousness, from cinematic engagement with the real to a withdrawal into self-reflexivity and meta-discourse. But because the term *coscienza* blends cognition and morality, I would argue that Nichetti's revisitation of *Bicycle Thief* is not an abdication of neorealism's "ethical mandate"[37] but a reproposal of it.

By recalling *Bicycle Thief* in *The Icicle Thief,* even as he willfully distorts and misunderstands the original, Nichetti reinforces our memory of the neorealist film and vividly brings it back to life. While watching the "neorealoid" film and listening to the plot summary of its multiple catastrophes, we cannot help but think, "No, he's got it all wrong," in a way that heightens our appreciation for the uniqueness and power of the earlier film. By juxtaposing the cinematic conventions of the past with mass-media codes of the present, Nichetti invents a hybrid language that reinvigorates them both and helps us to define our own position in the space of postmodern culture. The pompous Claudio Fava inadvertently gets it just right when he claims that "only through images can filmmakers explain the past and interpret the present"—a formulation that, although it may not prepare us for the messiness of the encounter between neorealism and contemporary television, does hint at that encounter's tremendous powers of cultural renewal.

Postmodern Pastiche, the *Sceneggiata,*

and the View of the Mafia from Below in

Roberta Torre's *To Die for Tano*

"Originality? Everything was created in the first six days," Ermanno
Olmi affirmed at a conference on literature and film held in Florence
in 1997. "Originality, therefore, inheres in our way of looking at things
already seen forever."[1] Though the Mafia may not have been created in
that first week, it has been around long enough to have become one of
the foremost cinematic clichés of our times, inspiring Goffredo Fofi
to coin the term *Mafiologia* to label an entire genre "whose variations
are scarce and whose repetitions are interminable."[2] In subtitling *To Die
for Tano* "the first musical on the Mafia,"[3] Roberta Torre makes explicit
her aspiration to originality in Olmi's terms, insisting on the generic
novelty of her approach and announcing the aesthetics of pastiche that
will characterize her portrayal of Cosa Nostra. Her representation of
the Mafia is thereby "provoked, recontextualized, carried beyond
cliché"[4] in a way that holds up its subject matter to the devastations of
ridicule. "There is nothing that a malicious laugh cannot hurt," writes
Emanuela Martini. "Therefore, not only 'can' one laugh at the Mafia,
one 'must' laugh at it. Maybe it's the only thing to which there is no response."[5] Paradoxically, by reveling in the artifice of musical comedy,
Torre's film promotes and renews the agenda of Italy's most hallowed
realist tradition—that of heightening public understanding of social
problems in order to lead toward intervention. In Fofi's words, "*Tano da
morire* helps us to understand how this culture is rooted and continues
to function; it explains the Mafia to us, in some way, from below. It allows us to understand better in order to be able, if we truly wish, to better intervene."[6]

234

Key to Torre's originality in *To Die for Tano* is precisely this aspiration to explain the Mafia "from below," to adopt a grassroots approach to its representation. For Torre, this does not mean a naive, "objective" attempt to document the real-life history of the murder of Mafia boss Gaetano Guarrasi in 1988 and of his sister Franca on her wedding day in 1990. On the contrary, it means an examination of the way in which chronicle becomes collective memory and collective memory becomes legend. Her film thus abounds in pop-cultural mediations between fact and fiction, foregrounds its own search for novel modes of representation, and unabashedly proclaims the filmmaker's subjectivity as a transplanted Milanese woman fascinated by the myth of the south. "In Palermo I found what I didn't have in Milan," Torre explained in an interview with Luca Mosso. "Stories, faces, bodies. An overflowing humanity that elsewhere seems to me to be a bit exhausted, chilled, boxed in cold, even high-tech, places."[7] Half a century earlier, another Milanese director had testified to his fascination with Sicily, this time in Homeric terms.[8] Though stated in a somewhat less elevated register than Visconti's, Torre, too, sees in Sicily an anthropological throwback— a place of primal passions and creatural abundance, rife with narrative possibilities for an artist coming from the imaginatively "cold" regions of the north. It is no exaggeration to state that Torre builds into her film her reason for moving from Milan to Palermo: the energizing effect of her relocation is evident in the exuberance with which she represents the "stories, faces, bodies . . . [the] overflowing humanity" of her adoptive home.

What Torre finds so stimulating is the very chaos that distinguishes the culture of Palermo from that which she left behind. "I liked, and I still like, to be amidst a disorder that doesn't belong to the place I come from. When I try to stage it, I don't try to give an order to what strikes me as incomprehensible. . . . I don't feel uneasy [about the disorder] and I let myself sink into it."[9] The unbridled creativity of *To Die for Tano* is Torre's testimony to the stimulating effect of the cultural chaos that greeted her in Palermo, pushing the filmmaker to ever zanier and more inspired forms of spectacle.[10] "For me, it was like trying to render visually and aesthetically, in terms of pictorial discourse, this series of stimuli that came to me from being here in Sicily, from the Sicilians, from this type of Sicilian."[11] It is the disorderly "referent" of the film that authorizes Torre's stylistic recourse to pastiche, musically expressed in the duet between Jew's harp and saxophone that provides the film's leit-motif in a hybrid blend of Sicilian folk music and the contemporary forms emanating from jazz. The film is a potpourri of media and modes, including puppet shows, pop-art graphics, disco and rock musicals, television news, and MTV, as well as more standard feature film techniques. It is as if Torre had sought specifically to address Mario Sesti's critique of the Italian cinematic landscape of 1996. According to Sesti's diagnosis, "What is missing is precisely those promiscuous, borderline figures able to move between television, cabaret, avant-garde, and repertory theater and cinema, capable of contaminating the one with the modicum of new that is born from the other."[12] In *To Die for Tano,* Torre displays just that promiscuity and brinksmanship that Sesti calls for, promoting the cross-fertilization of media that will hybridize and renew the language of cinema for a postmodern age.

As a director of actors, Torre had considerable success in transmitting to the nonprofessional cast her own energy of inspiration, which in turn released in them the liberating power of tendentious humor. The opportunity to perform a comedy that enabled them and the audience "to overcome enthusiastically, with laughter, a series of burdens that people carry within"[13] was obviously profoundly emancipating for everyone involved in the production. Torre's unconventional perspective on the Mafia becomes profoundly subversive in its refusal to present the monolithic, usual image of the organization. Her daring to look at it from the slightly oblique angle required by humor challenges the frontality of the official, canonical view of the issue. "My purpose was to call into question the system of values of the Mafia that is usually represented in a univocal way. The interesting thing is that the so-called serious films on the Mafia tend to bring credit to this representation. They never dream of challenging it!"[14]

Torre's vision of Palermo is, in Bakhtian terms, a carnivalized one—one in which the traditional social hierarchy (especially that of the Mafia itself) is turned upside down in a world that celebrates disorder, corporeality, excess, passion, violence, the marginalized, the transgressive.[15] Set in the Vucciria, the famous marketplace of Palermo, the film may be said to represent the stomach of a swollen and grotesque body politic, dedicated solely to the fulfillment of its creatural needs. Most of the characters are overweight, not unlike the individuals who popu-

FIGURE 26 | In the grand finale of the "Rap di Tano," all the customers and vendors of the Vucciria, the famous open market of Palermo, join in singing the praises of the slain Mafia boss. Courtesy of Lucky Red.

late Botero's artistic imagination, brimming with obese divinities and their counterparts on earth. In the film's climactic production number, "Il Rap di Tano," the entire Vucciria joins in song to celebrate the exploits of the slain Mafia boss, amidst all the gastronomic wealth that the market has to offer. A refrain is sung by a John Belushi look-alike who pops up from behind every manner of groceries, and each stanza of the song is intoned by a different food vendor. The lyrics involve a survey of all the delights of the Vucciria: first an octopus salesman exhibits his wares, then the song moves to a produce seller using a banana as her microphone, to the refrain from behind a pile of artichokes, to a baker singing into a baguette, to a man carrying a crate full of vegetables, to a woman amplifying over a fish, to a butcher brandishing his knives among beef carcasses, to a group of women displaying jars of sauces and preserves, to a fruit vendor bebopping with melons, to the refrain from among assorted shish kebabs. The story of Tano is thus visually and musically wedded to the sensuous abundance of the market—a feast of solos and choruses that equates the slain Mafioso's saga with the food source that nourishes the corporate body of Sicilian culture (fig. 26).

FIGURE 27 | The female chorus of the film provides running commentary on the legend of Tano Guarrasi from under the hairdryers of Pina's beauty salon. Courtesy of Lucky Red.

In telling the story of Tano Guarrasi "from below," Torre has many of the characters speak as though they were being interviewed, promoting the fiction that this is an unmediated, grassroots account of events, with all the distortions, contradictions, omissions, and mystifications that such oral histories involve. In preparing the screenplay, Torre interviewed at length Guarrasi's brother-in-law Enzo Caruso, who serves, then, as the narrator of the film (played by nonprofessional Enzo Paglino). The narrator, sitting against a black background lit by bare lightbulbs, speaks directly into the camera throughout the film. His is a unifying voice in a saga that alternates, somewhat randomly, between the sequence of events immediately preceding Tano's assassination in 1988 and the progression leading up to Franca's wedding and murder in 1990.

"This is a true story, or maybe it was," the narrator begins. "It's the story of Tano Guarrasi, man of honor of the Passo Rigano family. Killed in his butcher shop with six pistol shots through his entire body. It is also the story of a great love between him and his sister. It's also the story of a funeral and a wedding. So let's see how it ends up." The narrator, of course, is the spokesman for the collective memory of the community, and as such his account is marked by repetition, hyperbole, dis-

continuity, inconsistency—in sum, all of the distortions to which popular history is subject.[16] One of the most striking elements of this account is its obsessiveness. After announcing it as the story of a funeral
and a wedding, the narrator returns with periodic regularity to both
events, following no discernible logic whatsoever. Far more linear, instead, are the intrusions of the women in the "chorus," who comment
progressively from under their hairdryers in the beauty parlor as they
prepare for Franca's wedding, to which they are all invited (fig. 27).
Governed by the temporality of shampooing, setting, drying, and
styling, their testimonies culminate in a proclamation of communal love
for the murdered Mafioso boss as they exit the beauty salon, into the
Vucciria where the "Rap di Tano" is staged.

Though these women often quarrel among themselves, they always
arrive at a consensus that becomes normative in the choral mode of
Greek tragedy. The first gossip session in the beauty parlor begins au-
thoritatively. "I can't get over it," announces one of the women. "Two
years after the death of Tano Guarrasi, Franca Guarrasi is about to get
married. I can't deal with everything that's happening. . . . Now we've
all been invited and we're all going." To this assertion the other women
nod their assent and vocally intone "Sì, sì"—a gesture of unanimity that
will be reflected later by the group of senior Mafiosi men when they
agree to the snuffing out of a rival's life. It should be stated from the
outset that the collective female voice is in perfect accord with the
Mafia ethos, that the chorus is composed of self-proclaimed *donne
d'onore* who admire Tano's displays of power, condone the hairdresser's
murder of her husband, and loathe the *pentiti* (stool pigeons) as *spioni*
(spies) worthy of extermination. Such is their adherence to the indigenous honor code that even the mother of two men executed by
the Mafia for turning state's evidence vigorously denounces her sons as
traitors. This woman's hair turns into Medusa-like serpents as she disowns her sons in Euripidean or Shakespearean terms, claiming, in a dis-
avowal of reproductivity reminiscent of Lady Macbeth or in an impulse
to infanticide worthy of Medea, that she never gave birth to such vile
creatures but only dreamt them.[17]

In a later beauty-parlor sequence, the women force a confession
from their hairdresser, Pina, by threatening her with a blow-dryer and
a heat lamp. These are the weapons of women, and they join in the ar-

senal of props that implausibly crowd the beauty parlor with symbols of "housewifeliness." There is a table with multicolored espresso cups and saucers, a colander with raw beans ready for stringing, and an ironing board to which Pina returns after confessing in a torch song to the murder of her husband. Convinced by her ballad of abuse and revenge, the women form a chorus line, kicking in unison from under their hair dryers and singing "You're right" in feminine solidarity. Once their hairdos are complete, the women utter the decisive verdict on Tano—"he was a hunk"—that leads to the climactic "Rap di Tano." In its final incarnation, this collective female presence is metamorphosed into a group of vixens: these are Furies who claw, growl, and hiss as Tano and Franca embrace in the hereafter.

That the brilliance and exuberance of this choral performance won the collective prize for best supporting actress in Venice in 1997 is perhaps the best testimony to the powerful bond that a woman director was able to establish with her female cast. Of the "feminine presence that overflows in the film," Torre states, "it's a world to explore whose doors are opened to me each time. With the men, I encounter diffidence, but with the women, I find no type of resistance."[18] The motor force of the film might indeed be said to inhere in the relationship established between Torre and her collective female protagonist—a relationship that is foregrounded throughout *To Die for Tano*. In addition, therefore, to the energy of liberation that Torre was able to release in all her actors by engaging them in a Mafia spoof, the filmmaker was able to strike chords that resonated specifically with the female members of the cast. The opportunity to caricaturize their feminine condition, to gain a distinctive voice with its own authoritative slant on events, to metamorphose into powerful, mythic versions of themselves (the Medusa, Lady Macbeth, Medea, the Furies), and to celebrate the props of their domesticity (the ironing boards, espresso cups, colanders), was obviously profoundly stimulating and emancipating for Torre's female performers.

In addition to the women's chorus, a number of other characters offer popular testimonies to the legendary status of Tano, including all those who crowd around his freshly slain body in the butcher shop. The camera work here cleverly mimics what the dead Tano would himself see were he miraculously reendowed with consciousness (which will in fact happen at the end of the film). Shooting from the corpse's perspective, Torre shows from below faces surrounding the body and engaging in histrionic displays of grief. In the case of the four sisters, the narrator tells us of their secret relief that their sexual warden is gone and that now they are free to marry. In other scenes scattered throughout the film, Torre uses the theatrical device of spotlighting the face of a character whose inner thoughts are then spoken confidentially to the audience, unheard by the other characters on screen. Thus we learn of Maurizio Scanna's grief at the death of his godfather, his source of pocket money for cigarettes and clothes, and Salvo lo Cicero's regret at losing a fellow bon vivant.

But the richest source of testimonials to Tano's memory is the recurrent scene of the wake, which Torre inserts at regular intervals throughout the film. Against a black background, Torre divides her screen in half, placing, to the right, the bier surrounded by candles and neon crosses and, to the left, a series of "talking heads" conversing about the dead man. It is here that the four sisters voice their resentment of their brother's surveillance, calling life with Tano *un inferno,* from which his death will bring them deliverance. The contradictions in popular memory surface in another wake scene in which Tano is pronounced at once "bad [because] he was frightening" and "not domineering, [it's just that] he made himself respected."

Another way in which Torre aligns her film with the mythology surrounding the slain Mafia boss is by representing the dreams and omens that form the apparatus of popular hagiography. Torre's informant in preparing the film, Enzo Caruso, begins his biography of Guarrasi with a degraded version of the kind of augury that accompanies the birth of legendary heroes. "It was the fourth of February, 1934 . . . his mother was playing the numbers and at the moment of his birth, a neighbor who was betting on the same numbers leaned over the balcony and yelled, 'Jack pot!' And the midwife shouted from her balcony, 'It's a boy!' In short, a lucky start . . . and so begins this story."[19] Although not included in Torre's film, this omen suggests the theme of destiny that will surface in *To Die for Tano* through dreams, signs, and premonitions. Two such signs occur during Franca's wedding festivities—the ominous falling of her bridal veil to the dance floor and the uncanny appearance of her brother's funeral procession (from 1988) as she and her bridegroom emerge from the church in 1990. "We all saw the funeral," explains the narrator. "A torment, a persecution. We went to the party anyway and ate and drank and made merry." By insisting on the *collective* witness to this apparition, the narrator reveals the link in the popular mind between funeral and wedding, between brother and sister, between Mafia violence and sexual oppression, between the mob rivalry that kills men and the familial overprotectiveness that subjugates women.

Another set of omens belongs solely to the consciousness of Franca. These omens occur during the film's two flashbacks, involving Franca's childhood memories enigmatically linked to the events in the narrative present. The first flashback is triggered by the spectacle of Tano's bloodied corpse. As Franca looks up from the body, her face is spotlighted, then it fades behind a cartoonish panel of a swirling bull's eye, against a musical background of female voices, chanting weirdly, signaling the transition into a distant past. The flashback is a silent minifilm, shot in black and white on grainy stock with a musical accompaniment of a single piano, as might have been heard in the movie houses of an earlier time. In this minifilm, the child Franca is witness to her brother's refusal to return home on schedule, his subsequent beating by an irate father, and her brother's nightmare that causes him to squawk like a chicken and awaken the entire family. The dream supplies the punch line to an extended joke that hinges on a culture-specific pun. Within the dream, Tano is portrayed as a rooster among a flock of dancing chickens, prefiguring the way in which his culture's obsession with *gallismo* (the hypermasculinity associated with the *gallo*, or rooster) will be his undoing. If the effect of the flashback is to prime the audience for a narrative of predestination, those expectations for tragedy are immediately undercut by the comic silliness of the dream.

The same can be said for the second flashback, which occurs during Franca's fainting spell at her wedding feast. The swirling bull's-eye design reappears and ushers her back in time, and her recollection—again shot in black and white and devoid of dialogue—now is of a little girl in bed who is awakened by the spectacle of a grotesquely deformed moon, sculpted in clay and dangling from a string. This ceramic moon, shown against a haunting musical accompaniment of wood blocks, is an object of wonder and fascination for the girl; it then fades into obliv-

ion as a mocking voice intones, "You will not marry"—and the flashback ends with the adult Franca regaining consciousness as the wedding feast resumes. Like the earlier flashback, the memory promises to
offer an interpretive key to a tragic destiny that the film then undermines through comic irreverence.

Parody and pastiche thus emerge as the dominant modes of *To Die
for Tano* in an omnivorous appropriation of styles that provide the film
with its surface look as well as its ideological substance. In her recourse
to captions that provide the exact coordinates of place, date, and time
(down to the minute), Torre spoofs the thriller's pretensions to scientific precision in its investigatory procedures. When such captions are
applied to the beauty-parlor gossip sessions (Vucciria, 21 settembre 1990
ore 11:20) as well as to Tano's murder (Vucciria, 20 ottobre 1988 ore
22:01), the film calls into question any semblance of documentary seriousness to which such generic markers may otherwise point.[20] Eyewitness news reportage also comes under parodic scrutiny. The film
shows the bumbling attempts of Massimo Pullara (played by himself)
to cover the Guarrasi case. Filmed in black and white and employing
the imagistic poverty of eyewitness video, Pullara is shown with microphone in hand and the official seal of TV Trinacria in the lower left-
hand corner of the screen. Constantly undermined in his attempt at authoritative journalistic coverage, the reporter comes up against the
culture's code of *omertà* (reticence before the law). When he tries to interview bystanders, they deny not only knowledge of the case but that
anything happened at all. "Nothing happened, we know nothing," say
Tano Lipari and Salvo Lo Cicero after the public massacre of Franca
Guarrasi at the wedding party before the eyes of hundreds of witnesses.
Like the cartoon character who pops up for more abuse no matter how
many times he is knocked down, or like Bergson's mechanical man
who automatically repeats behaviors that bring on disaster, Pullara per-
sists in exposing himself to the stonewalling, manhandling, and brow-
beating of his informants—and all on live-action TV.

In his final appearance on screen, Pullara offers a rational, crimino-
logically plausible explanation for Franca's murder: it was, he says, either "revenge, a settling of accounts" or a bungled attack intended for
one of the wedding guests, Tano Lipari, who had close ties to a certain
Cirincione, one of the odious stool pigeons. The reporter's logic, of

course, ignores the rich, folkloristic link between funeral and wedding that turns the squalid Mafia feud into a grandiose saga of jealousy and love. "As far as I'm concerned," says the narrator, commenting on Pullara's hypotheses, "it's none of the above. Tanino came to take his sister." As if to confirm this popular explanation for Franca's death, Torre represents the siblings, both dressed in white but bloodied by gunfire, embracing in joyous reunion and dancing the twist together against the black background of eternity.

There are also other mass-media objects of Torre's parody in addition to the thriller genre and television news. MTV, with its fast cutting, its arbitrary imagery, and its reveling in artifice, is alluded to throughout *To Die for Tano,* especially in the "Rap" that serves as the boss's musical apotheosis. *West Side Story,* with its finger-snapping choreography and painted cityscapes, provides the model for the display of Tano's macho power; *Godfather II,* with its funereal opening, is echoed in the procession that introduces (and weaves throughout) Torre's film; *Saturday Night Fever* is spoofed in Tano's Mafia initiation scene; and Sinatra-esque crooning and cabaret culture in general provide the atmosphere for meetings of Cosa Nostra. In this plethora of media and pop-cultural influences, Torre is not only creating an aesthetic of pastiche but commenting on the breakdown between media representations of the Mafia and their referents, on the way in which lived experience comes to imitate its mass-media caricatures; as Emanuele Martini put it, "How can one distinguish between the babbling *ad arte* of the godfather, Marlon Brando, and the improbable Italian of Riina?"[21] The stylization of mass-media representations thus comes both to mirror and to encourage the stylization of the culture to which it refers.

But perhaps the most important pop-cultural model for Torre's film is the *sceneggiata*—melodrama set to music that originated in Naples and came to dominate pop culture in the Italian south (as well as New York). Torre's choice of the Neapolitan songwriter Nino D'Angelo to compose the music for her film is based on precisely this logic. "The Neapolitan song is a language common to the entire South. I believe that the origins are very ancient; lost in tradition. . . . My choice to use the Neapolitan sceneggiata is not a bizarre invention but a very precise choice; those people cannot help but sing in Neapolitan. The sceneggiata is part of their culture."[22]

As the organizing principle of *To Die for Tano,* the Neapolitan musical melodrama offers an ideal venue for Torre's attempt to offer a pop-
ulist view of the Mafia. By adopting the sceneggiata format, Torre aligns
her film with grassroots traditions of storytelling. This is the way that
the culture represents itself to itself; it is the filter through which information is processed and chronicled, and that, in turn, conditions the behaviors of the makers of chronicle. It is in the context of southern Italian culture that Torre can call the musical a form of realism.[23]

A similar link between lived experience of the Mafia and the
Neapolitan sceneggiata is established in *Godfather II* (1974) when a
friend takes Vito Corleone to a performance in the theater catering to
the Italian immigrant population of Hell's Kitchen. It is in this theater
that Vito first beholds the local boss Don Fanucci, who, significantly,
stands up in the audience and blocks the spectators' view of the action
on stage. Asked to identify this formidable figure, Vito's friend replies
Mano nira (The Black Hand), with all the legendary baggage that such
an appellation implies. When Vito and his friend go backstage to admire the beauteous star of the show, they find her captive of Don
Fanucci, who threatens to scar her lovely face should her father refuse
to pay his monetary tribute to the boss. The continuity between what
happens on stage and behind the scenes in this episode of *Godfather II*
establishes not only the melodramatic tenor of lived experience but also
the susceptibility of the southern Italian immigrant populace to subjugation by the likes of Don Fanucci precisely because he fits into a
ready-made slot within the collective imaginary.

The sceneggiata plays an important part in Ettore Scola's *Maccheroni*
(1985), whose Neapolitan protagonist, Jasiello (played by Marcello Mastroianni), is both actor and writer of popular melodramas for his local
theater. But Jasiello is also the writer of the script of life: he creates the
persona of action hero for his American friend, Robert (played by Jack
Lemmon), and this script becomes the blueprint for Robert's subsequent feats of anti-Mafia heroism. In the sceneggiata's generic, melodramatic concern with the forces of absolute good and evil and in the
intense rapport between spectators and onstage action we could perhaps even trace this tradition back to the *teatro dei pupi* and the performances of the *chansons de geste* that so engrossed the audience, for
example, in the Neapolitan episode of *Paisan.*

But it is in the astuteness of her staging of the sceneggiata that Torre performs the most delicate part of her representation "from below." "This slice of popular culture has sometimes been recuperated as trash, but never recognized for its value. There has never been a link between this culture and official culture. I try to find a middle ground: I don't pretend to be considered one of them, but at the same time, I don't want to give up getting to know them, entering in that world."[24] It is through the musical component of the sceneggiata that Torre is able to avoid the trap of condescension, of viewing this world from the superior distance of the amused and sophisticated bystander. Instead, through the catchy tunes of Nino D'Angelo and the enthusiastic performances of these nonprofessional singers and dancers, Torre takes us inside the mechanisms of mystification and self-delusion that enable Tano to see himself as a superstar, Anna to see herself as a twentieth-century Juliet, the Mafia to see itself as an agreeable men's club, the beauty-parlor gossips to see themselves as a tragic chorus, and the entire community to see itself as the disciples of a modern-day martyr hero. Through musical performance, Torre shows the transformation of these characters, from the grotesque, swollen figures that they objectively are to the glamorous, mythic creatures of their fondest imaginings.

It is the same delicate operation that Fellini performs in *8½* to represent the overweight, garish, and disheveled prostitute Saraghina as magically transformed by the rhumba into the lithe, glamorous young creature of her dreams. Similarly, *Ginger and Fred* uses the transformative power of dance to take the audience along with the aged Amelia and Pippo as they imaginatively recapture the youth and romance of their prime for the duration of their television performance. In a more recent, non-Fellinian example of musical self-transfiguration, the rap singer Er Piotta uses "ironia and auto-ironia" to play the role of the pudgy, insecure, and objectively ludicrous aspirant to disco stardom in the music video *Supercafone,* while taking us inside the mind of the young man and showing us how he can believe in his apotheosis through song. In all these cases, the music endows these singers and dancers with subjecthood, enabling us to see their performing bodies as projections of some cherished inner self. For this to happen, such performances must have the power to evoke in us our own personal experiences of rapture, prompting us to reconnect with the memory of musically inspired self-transformation. It is this mechanism, then, that saves Torre's sceneggiata from being a mere exercise in cultural tourism, enabling us to participate vicariously in the characters' own process of self-idealization through performance.

With the exception of the "Rap," shot on location in the Vucciria, *To Die for Tano* was filmed entirely in studios; it revels in an antinaturalism that verges on abstraction. In visual terms, Torre's film oscillates between the neon brightness and super-saturated colors of the beauty-parlor scenes and the mysterious black scenography of the wake. In a transitional device located at regular intervals throughout the film, one or more sets of bulging eyes emerge from the black background and modulate into the surfaces of ceramic skulls that jiggle and jostle each other in a postmodern danse macabre. At once folkloristic and exotic, these puppets suggest a culture of death that is "Mexican, Third World" in its ability to "turn death into spectacle."[25] Torre's carnivalization of death is foretold in the very title of the film, whose play on words announces the connection between the amorous and the mortuary that the narrator reaffirms in calling the film "the story of a funeral and a wedding." Punning on the phrase *t'amo da morire* (I love you to death), with its hyperbolic equation of romantic intensity and self-destruction, the title links popular culture's love/death nexus with Mafia violence in that they both spring from a collective fascination with the annihilating extremes of experience.[26] Gaetano Guarrasi, the quintessential mob boss, is a *being for death*—his very identity is predicated on a constant flirtation with mortality. "I knew it, I knew he would end up like this," muses one of his colleagues in a sentiment echoed, with variations, by any number of others in his coterie.

Compared to Gregory Peck by his admirers in the female chorus, Tano—and by extension the Mafia as a whole—become products of the Sicilian genius for self-staging. The opening funeral procession, with its brass band and its wailing women brandishing what seem to be white pom-poms, is the first example of the kind of performativity that will dilate and expand to engulf the whole of Torre's representation. In fact, the film's first song-and-dance routine, which presents a portrait of Tano in all his sexual jealousy and physical violence, ends with the closing of curtains and the applause of an unknown inner audience. Later, Tano's welcome into the Mafia is represented as a sleazy night-club routine in which the initiate must appear onstage, do some bumps and grinds, and listen to the sentimental crooning of the old Mafia boss Don Paliddu Billizza, to the tearful appreciation of his new cohort. In subsequent gatherings, the mob activities remain at the level of night-club entertainments, and mafiosi celebrate their identity in a chorus line, wearing party hats, blowing noisemakers, and declaring, to the musical accompaniment of a disco band, *Sim la Mafia* (We are the Mafia). This then leads to an elaborate production number with an all-male cast of dancers who rub noses and strike poses, while Tano does his John Travolta impersonation. So omnivorous is the appetite for spectacle that it can even accommodate an anti-Mafia poem into its evening's entertainment. When Stella Marina is invited onto the night-club stage to recite her verse-lament against mob violence, it, too, is applauded as part of the theatrical apparatus that the Cosa Nostra has set in motion, and that testifies to its inexorable hold on Sicilian life.

At the same time, the film does not shy away from the homicidal operations on which Mafia power is built. Tano's gunning down of his rivals in the first production number may be patently undercut by the conventions of musical comedy, and his own assassination may be so stylized as to be unbelievable, but the truth of Mafia bloodshed is captured in a shocking sequence of sight-and-sound incongruities. In introducing three "senior" mafiosi, the narrator portrays them as innocuous, if eccentric, old men. On screen, instead, we see glimpses of their activities: a victim, tied and bound, is probably dead; another has his brains blown out; a briefcase filled with money is lovingly opened and displayed.

Religion is an important part of the cultural magma that gives rise to Tano's hagiography. The wake, festooned with neon crosses, is reminiscent of the Catholic kitsch of Baz Luhrmann's *Romeo + Juliet,* whose excess of religious ornamentation, including overwrought shrines, cruciform tattoos, holy jewelry, and even Mariologically emblazoned gun handles, made Christianity into a surface covering for a polytheistic Caribbean culture. The same pagan energy seems to underlie the Catholicism of Torre's film, with its occult dream symbols and auguries, and especially in the Manichean struggle between angel and devil suspended above the wake scene toward the end of the film. Serving as yet another way for Torre to assume a grassroots view of Sicilian culture, Roman Catholic kitsch represents the form that religion must take in order for it to be consumable within an eclectic and commercialized popular context.

It is this form of Christianity, then, that offers Torre her alibi for the film's final refusal to judge, morally, the world she has chosen to represent in *To Die for Tano*. Against a background of crosses, Tano returns from the dead to offer the following plea: "And now, do me a favor. Don't ask me too much if I'm in Heaven or Hell." In Tano's concluding words, it is not hard to read the position of the filmmaker, at once fascinated and horrified by her subject matter, but absolutely unwilling to pass judgment on it "from above."[27]

the return of the referent

Filming the Text of Witness

FRANCESCO ROSI'S *THE TRUCE*

In his decision to film Primo Levi's *La tregua* (published in English under the title *The Reawakening*), Francesco Rosi faced a doubly formidable challenge. Not only was he adapting a text of indisputable literary merit and thus risking all the invidious comparisons that such projects routinely invite, but he was adapting a work that testifies to the "slaughter . . . that will be remembered as the central fact, the stain, of this century."[1] Because *La tregua* is a text of witness, it exhibits a special, almost biblical referentiality, so that any adaptation seen to deviate from the letter could elicit charges of heresy. The testimonial authority of Levi's memoir means that even the inevitable modifications required by the audio-visual format will be seen as suspect, greeted as violations of the sacrosanct relationship between the language of witness and its referent. Filming the text of witness thus poses, in its most acute form, the general problem attendant upon any adaptation of a work of literature to the screen.[2] All of the standard objections to the process raised by "fidelity critics"—those who hold that the film has a solemn responsibility to illustrate the text faithfully—will be inevitably intensified by the moral and historical truth claims inherent in first-person accounts of the Shoah.

On the other hand, such intolerance to the interpretive freedom of the filmmaker works against the driving force of Holocaust testimony, which is to keep the story alive through constant elaboration, adaptation, and retelling in terms that will engage new generations of listeners. The text of witness is thus an ongoing, open-ended narrative that resists definitive formulations and rejects closure. "What the testimony does not offer," writes Shoshana Felman, "is a completed statement, a totalizable account of those events. In the testimony, language is in process and in trial, it does not possess itself as a conclusion, as the constatation of a verdict or the self-transparency of knowledge."[3]

Levi's own literary production offers eloquent proof of the need constantly to rewrite the text of witness. After his most straightforward rendering of his experiences in *Se questo è un uomo* (1947) (translated as *Survival at Auschwitz*) and *La tregua* (1963), Levi sees fit to "reprocess" the story by chemical means in *Il sistema periodico* (1975) *(The Periodic Table)* and then to revisit it at a still higher level of abstraction in the thematically organized essays of *I sommersi e i salvati* (1986) *(The Drowned and the Saved)*. Not only does Levi feel compelled to rewrite and rethink his story at various temporal removes from the events, he denies that there could ever be an originary Holocaust writing, a truly referential account of what happened at Auschwitz. "At the distance of many years, we can affirm today that the story of the camps has been written almost exclusively by those who, like myself, did not scrape the bottom. Those who did so did not return, or their capacity for observation was paralyzed by suffering or by incomprehension."[4] Hence the need to bear witness at one remove; "We, touched by luck, have tried with greater or lesser knowledge to recount not only our destiny, but also that of the others, the drowned, as it were; but it was a discourse 'by proxy,' the story of things seen close-up, but not experienced directly."[5] In his refusal to claim a privileged relationship between his writings and the Holocaust referent, along with his own compulsion constantly to reinvent the text of witness, Levi invites others to take up the challenge—to interpret, elaborate, adapt, and in so doing to keep the testimony alive.

But there is another way in which Rosi's adaptation fulfills the testimonial imperative of Levi's writing. Integral to the retelling, according to psychoanalyst Dori Laub, is the presence of a listener, an "addressable other" who enables the victim to contain the enormity of trauma, which has "no beginning, no ending, no before, no during, and no after."

> This absence of categories that define it lends [the trauma] . . .
> a timelessness and a ubiquity that puts it outside the range of
> associatively linked experiences, outside the range of

comprehension, of recounting and of mastery. . . . To undo this entrapment . . . a therapeutic process—a process of constructing a narrative, of reconstructing a history and essentially, *of re-externalizing the event*—has to be set in motion. This re-externalization of the event can occur and take effect only when one can articulate and *transmit* the story, literally transfer it to another outside oneself and then take it back again inside.[6]

Testimony, then, cannot occur in the absence of an addressable other, an "authentic listener" willing to take on the cognitive and moral responsibility of receiving the narrative. This is what I will call "the covenant of witness," an agreement on the part of the listener to accept the full burden of knowledge, and to quote Levi in the prefatory poem of *Se questo è un uomo,* "meditate that this has happened." Of the two recurrent nightmares that haunted Levi's sleep, the one most frequently recalled involves the terror of not finding listeners willing to enter the covenant of witness, of returning home and telling the story to a group of family and friends who remain indifferent, distracted, and finally withdraw from his presence. "I had dreamed something of the sort, we all had dreamed, in the nights of Auschwitz, of talking and not being heard, of finding freedom and of remaining alone."[7]

By retelling the story with the creative latitude justified by Levi's own refusal of absolute authority and by adapting the story to a mass medium that will exponentially increase the audience of "addressable others," Rosi becomes an "enabler" of witness as his film takes its place in the ongoing process of testimony.[8] In what I consider to be the enunciative center of the film, Rosi conflates two episodes from the book to make explicit the moral impulse behind his adaptation of Levi's text. Rosi brings together the scene in the market of Cracow, where Primo learns to sell shirts under the flamboyant mentorship of the Greek, with that in the train station of Trzebinia, where a group of onlookers marvel at the protagonist's Auschwitz attire. In the memoir, the presence of a kind and cultured lawyer in the crowd who could speak French and German convinced Levi that he had finally found the interlocutor he had sought so long—"the messenger, the spokesman of the civilian world" (60) who would enable him to put into ordered, narrative terms the inchoate experience of Auschwitz—in other words, the listener who would allow him to bear witness. "I had an avalanche of urgent things to tell the civilian world, things about me, but about everyone, of blood, of things that should have shaken every conscience to its foundations ... of Auschwitz nearby, and yet, it seemed unknown to all, of the mega-death from which I alone had escaped, everything" (60). As the lawyer translates his outpouring of testimony into Polish for the benefit of the crowd, Primo soon realizes that his account has been censured, that "Italian political prisoner" has been substituted for "Italian Jew" as the explanation for his internment at Auschwitz. When Primo questions the lawyer about his mistranslation, the response "C'est mieux pour vous. La guerre n'est pas finie" (61) offers chilling proof of the difficulty he will face in finding and engaging the sympathies of an "addressable other." Though a matter of mere coincidence, the identity of Levi's mistranslator as a lawyer is laden with irony. Not only has Levi's advocate failed to win his client a fair public hearing, he has subverted the metaphoric system on which all Holocaust testimony is based—that of a court of law whose judges "are you," according to the author's charge to his readers in the appendix to the 1976 edition of *Se questo è un uomo.*[9] The textual passage ends with the dispersion of the crowd, which has somehow understood the substance of Primo's quarrel with the lawyer and refuses to receive the testimony.

Because the corresponding scene in the film is accompanied by an extremely obtrusive cinematic device—one that calls attention to the presence of the filmmaker and to his particular take on events—we may see this as a signatory moment where Rosi makes explicit his acceptance of the imperative to witness. When Primo asks the lawyer, "Why didn't you tell them I am a Jew?" the patronizing French answer of the text is not forthcoming. Instead, the camera cranes up high enough to afford an aerial view of the scene as the crowd withdraws from Primo. In foregrounding the technology of the medium at the moment when the lawyer ceases his activity as translator, Rosi announces his own role as a translator of Levi's memoir, as mediator between the written word and the language of audio-visual spectacle. The lawyer, of course, is the foil for Rosi, who will in turn correct the character's deliberate misrepresentation of the chronicle with a bold, frontal assault on the truth. Accordingly, John Turturro's Primo Levi is far more aggressive in this scene than his textual counterpart, openly confronting the Polish crowd with the evidence of Holocaust history. "At Auschwitz, not far from here, there was a camp full of innocent people—men, women, mothers, children, burned in crematoria, in ovens."

Rosi builds into this scene his awareness not only of the filmmaker's role as translator of the written text but also of the unconsumability of his message. By conflating the episode of the marketplace with this scene of the need for translation, Rosi acknowledges his film's status as consumer object in search of a mass audience. When Primo holds up the Greek's white shirt for sale but is unable to peddle it because of his own striped jacket with its ominous number and yellow star, Rosi both announces the "discomfort" of his message and challenges his audience not to withdraw from it, not to become the crowd within the marketplace that disperses at the mere mention of Auschwitz. At this point, Rosi is consciously invoking us as the audience that history denied Levi in *La tregua*—as the audience that accepts the burden of moral accountability, that will not turn away from the uncomfortable truth of Auschwitz.

In convening us as the audience of witness, Rosi inscribes his own awareness of the challenge facing the director to invent a film language adequate to the task. One of Rosi's most effective strategies is to make explicit through a series of performative moments the power of spectacle to bring about social transformation. A complex and moving example occurs in the scene in the Russian variety show staged in celebration of the Allied victory in Europe. Halfway into the entertainment, a Soviet officer performs an imitation of Fred Astaire, using a Cossack sword in place of the gentleman's cane and making a number of Bolshoi adjustments to the American dancer's choreography. With the introduction of the Hollywood musical into the language of this scene comes the invitation to a collective wish-fulfillment fantasy that exceeds national borders and ideological divides. The Fred Astaire–Ginger Rogers collaboration becomes a universal signifier of glamour and romance, enabling the Holocaust survivors to identify so powerfully with their Hollywood exemplars that they can imaginatively overcome their wretchedness and be swept up in the magic of myth. Exchanging shy looks of desire, the men and women in the audience do as the lyrics suggest, slowly beginning to dance "cheek to cheek," oblivious to the distance separating their threadbare, emaciated selves from the luxury and elegance of the Hollywood icons. While unapologetically showing us these characters for what they are—broken by-products of the Nazi industry of death—Rosi also invites us to enter into their own process of self-transformation, to experience, from within the myth, its powers of imaginative escape. What more poignant proof of triumph over the bestiality of the camps than to be able to feel the first stirrings of sexual desire through the elegant and civilized filter of Hollywood romance?[10]

If the text of witness is brought into being by means of its verbal appeal to an addressable other, then the film of witness must find a medium-specific equivalent to that address. Rosi achieves this by establishing a regime of gazes mediated by the character of Primo within the film that he then turns back on us at the conclusion. In fact, the director attributed his decision to cast John Turturro in the lead role to the actor's "way of interiorizing experiences and reexternalizing them through delicacy, humor, but also the great firmness with which Primo Levi expresses his ideas. Turturro has the possibility of an innocent eye that really struck me."[11] It is through the act of looking that Rosi translates the first-person narrative of Levi's memoir into cinematic terms, making Primo's gaze the conduit of information through which the Holocaust and its aftermath are registered and conveyed to us.[12]

Rosi's decision to have the actor John Turturro wear glasses privileges Primo's function as focalizer, as visual mediator between the events of the Liberation and our perceptions of them (fig. 28). Like the written text, the film is bracketed by acts of seeing, of raising the eyes up from the bondage of a ground-level existence to begin the "return to life,"[13] as coscriptwriter Stefano Rulli was to describe the story. When the Russian soldiers arrive to liberate the camp, Primo lifts his eyes in a gesture that will signal the start of the journey from Auschwitz to Turin—an itinerary at once geographic, ideological, personal, and cinematic. From the exchange of intense gazes between Daniele, who chooses to burn his Auschwitz jacket, and Primo, who decides to retain his and "remember," Rosi establishes his protagonist as a kind of visual scribe, as an observer whose act of seeing is also a writing of history. As the film progresses, that gaze will register a variety of responses to the journey, ranging from bewildered disbelief when the Italian officer at Cracow denies him and the Greek entrance to the barracks, to the astonishment of his eyes within the dream of Auschwitz, to de-

FIGURE 28 | It is through the act of looking that the protagonist (John Turturro) becomes a visual scribe who translates into the language of cinema Primo Levi's first-person text of witness. Courtesy of Francesco Rosi.

sire for Galina, to shock at the spectacle of German prisoners in their turn reduced to hard labor and starvation.

Though usually the "owner" of *lo sguardo,* and often a participant in a dialogic exchange of gazes, in two important scenes Primo becomes the object of visual spectacle. The task of communicating with a family of exotic Russian peasants in order to obtain a roasting chicken for the Italian refugees falls to Primo, who linguistically is the most evolved member of the group. Having exhausted his stock of Indo-European poultry synonyms, however, Primo is reduced to performing a most undignified pantomime, making him the source of the peasant family's delight and prompting the daughter to furnish him with the longed-for referent—a plump and savory *kuritza.* Primo's spectacle is thus doubly successful, disarming the audience members by his willingness to play the fool and predisposing them to reward him for their comic pleasure in his charade.

By the end of the film, Primo becomes the object of a far more serious and momentous gaze—that of a German officer in the train station at Munich. "We had arrived in German territory, there where it all began," Primo informs us in voice-over. "We felt as if we had enormous things to say to every single German, and every German should have something to say to us." As the train stands motionless in the station, Rosi's camera cuts from window to window, each one filled with survivors, all in mute observation of the German prisoners, who refuse to return their gaze as they work repairing the tracks. Against a backdrop of Allied banners, lit sporadically by the flaring sparks of soldering irons, this is indeed a spectacle—one that ironically reverses the heroic documentaries of German industrial strength and military splendor propagated by the Third Reich. When Primo steps forward and succeeds in making eye contact with one of the prisoners, this man kneels down at the sight of the Auschwitz jacket with its embroidered Star of David and bows his head in contrition. It is important to note that the ending of this scene signals both a departure from the narrative of Levi's text and an acknowledgment of his subsequent reflections on the subject.

> No one looked us in the eyes, no one accepted the challenge: they were deaf, blind, and mute, locked in their ruins as in a fortress of willed ignorance, still strong, still capable of hatred and disdain, still prisoners of the ancient knot of pride and guilt. I surprised myself in seeking among them, among that anonymous crowd of sealed faces, other faces, well defined, many linked by a name, of those who could not *not* have known, not have remembered, not have answered; of those who had commanded and obeyed, killed, degraded, corrupted. A vain and foolish attempt because not they, but others, the few just ones, would have answered in their place. (251)

In the one German prisoner who does not withhold his gaze but bows down before a survivor of the Shoah, Rosi has chosen to dramatize a minority stance, that of "the few just ones." In the penitent kneeling of the German prisoner, Rosi makes a specific allusion to West German Chancellor Willy Brandt's famous act of reverence before the Warsaw ghetto monument in 1970.[14] By making Primo the object of the gaze of remorse in Munich, Rosi reverses the terms of the earlier episode in the Cracow marketplace, where the spectacle of the Star of David had prompted a mass withdrawal from him. Though the contrite soldier is only one in a group of otherwise unrepentant Nazis, his willingness to take moral responsibility for Holocaust history indicates Rosi's guarded hope that his film will find its audience of "just ones" and awaken the slumbering consciences of the rest.

It is therefore appropriate that *The Truce* ends with the visual sealing of the covenant of witness between Rosi and the spectators of his film. To do so, the director has Primo recite in voice-over two excerpts from the prefatory poem to *Se questo è un uomo*:

Voi che vivete sicuri
Nelle vostre tiepide case,
Voi che trovate tornando a sera
Il cibo caldo e visi amici:
    Considerate se questo è un uomo
    Che lavora nel fango
    Che non conosce pace
    Che lotta per mezzo pane
    Che muore per un sí o per un no.
    . . . .
Meditate che questo è stato.[15]

You who live secure
    In your warm houses,
You who find warm food
And friendly faces
Returning home each evening:
    Consider if this is a man
    Who works in the mud
    Who knows no peace
    Who struggles for half a piece of bread
    Who dies for a yes or a no.
    . . . .
Meditate that this has happened.

In the second-person-plural imperative of the poem, Levi convenes his readers as the community of witness. He wrenches them out of their complacency by attacking the material foundations of civilized life—a secure domestic space, regular meals, familial solidarity—and compels them to confront what is left of the human condition when all its vital supports are removed. In the commands *considerate* and *meditate,* Levi exhorts his readers to travel the distance separating the world of *tiepide case* and convivial dinners from the mud-infested quarters and starvation rations of Auschwitz and to accept the moral demands that such an imaginative journey imposes.

This direct address to the reader in Levi's poem finds its cinematic equivalent in the protagonist's gaze directly into the camera at the end of Rosi's *The Truce*—a transgressive technique that shatters the fourth wall of theatrical illusion and makes us the object of the filmmaker's gaze, just as Levi's direct address shatters the walls of his readers' "warm houses" and forces them out into the cold and muddy spaces of history. By looking us straight in the eye, Rosi's protagonist dispels the comfortable fiction that we are invisible spectators of a scene that would be happening anyway, forcing us to accept that this reconstruction is being staged *for our sake.* In Rosi's words, such a restaging is "an operation indispensable to renewing the necessity of not forgetting, in times like these in which the risk of a general denial of the Holocaust and of the traumas imposed on Europe by Fascism and Nazism seems ever more threatening."[16]

By concluding his film with excerpts from the poem that marks the threshold of Levi's first concentration camp chronicle, Rosi makes his work an adaptation not only of *La tregua* but a retroactive commentary on all of Levi's Holocaust writings. In so doing, Rosi indicates that the end of Levi's journey from Auschwitz is no end at all, but a circle that revolves ceaselessly around the central and all-encompassing horror of the camps. With this ending to the film, which takes us to the beginning of the protagonist's ordeal of bearing witness through writing, Rosi demonstrates his profound sensitivity to the meaning of Levi's title. Whether construed literally as "cease-fire" or figuratively as "respite" or "truce," *La tregua* proclaims its ephemerality, its transience as the pause between hostilities. One of the many meanings that Levi attributes to his title is, in fact, the military one: "It was the great truce: because the other hard season that was to follow had not yet started, nor had the ominous name of the Cold War yet been pronounced" (66).

But in a more immediate and private sense, *La tregua* was a time spent betwixt and between stable orders, a time of fluidity, experimentation, and freedom from personal constraints. "The months just now traversed, though hard, of wandering at the margins of civilization, appeared to us now as a truce, a parenthesis of unlimited openness, a providential but unrepeatable gift of destiny" (253).[17]

Implicit in this title is an invitation to historicize, to interpret the *tregua* as a period that is over and that is retroactively defined by what brought it to an end. For Levi, writing in 1961–62, with full knowledge of how difficult reentry would be and how painful the task of bearing witness, the period of "wandering at the margins of civilization" was a privileged time, as was the Russians' enjoyment of "that happy moment of their history" (211) before the onset of the Cold War. For Rosi, filming *The Truce* thirty-five years after the writing of the book, the idea of a utopian season that has drawn to an end dilates and expands to include Italy's entire journey from World War II to the present.

In bringing his film up to date, Rosi gives prominence to the theme of *italianità,* of the need to define, or even to invent, an Italian national identity in the wake of Fascism and war. This impulse recurs throughout *The Truce,* beginning with Primo's cry to Daniele, "See you in Italy," when they are separated in the opening scenes of the film (fig. 29). Such an exhortation makes Italy the goal of the journey in far more than a geographic sense. Italy as the place of reunion, as the promised land where the diaspora of the Holocaust will come to an end and Levi's ordeal of exile will be over, where the progressive loss of everything that defined him as a man—family, community, national identity, and cultural heritage—will be reversed. Throughout the journey, Primo is constantly seeking out compatriots, not only for practical reasons of communication but to reconstruct his own identity as an Italian and to experience, in miniature, the homeland that he so longs to reclaim. "Does anyone speak Italian?" is the first thing he says after being hauled onto a truck and leaving behind one of the precious shoes bestowed upon him by Mordo Nahum, the Greek. "I'm Italian," he announces each time he arrives at a new encampment, as if this label alone will win for him the longed-for rootedness so lacking in the fluid and anarchic world of post-Nazi Europe. "You're not Italian!" exclaims the good German woman who opposed Hitler and was exiled to Katow-

FIGURE 29 | In an intensely emotional moment later in *The Truce,* Primo and Daniele (Stefano Dionisi) reunite. Courtesy of Francesco Rosi.

ice for her temerity. "Italians have black hair and passionate eyes. Your eyes have no passion. You must be Croatian!" "We are very much Italian," Primo responds, "but we come from a place where people forget passion, family, country, culture. All." Though the German woman's

FIGURE 30 | In this group of compatriots—from left to right, Unverdorben, Col. Rovi, Daniele, Cesare, D'Agata, and Ferrari—Primo has found a microcosm of the homeland he so longs to reclaim. Courtesy of Francesco Rosi.

concept of italianità is confined to the level of amorous cliché, Primo expands her definition to include passions of a familial, political, and cultural sort. Auschwitz thus represents the ground zero of passion, understood as the ability to transcend the self, to struggle for a cause other than individual survival. To be fully Italian, to have passionate eyes, means to rededicate one's life to those ideals—of family, community, political struggle—that Auschwitz had systematically sought to destroy.

Primo finally does manage to find a simulacrum of Italy in the motley crew of compatriots who become his fellow travelers through the countryside of Eastern Europe (fig. 30). Though their social and regional variety may seem contrived—there is Daniele, the sole survivor of the ghetto of Venice, Ferrari, a pickpocket from Milan, Cesare, the mattress maker from Rome, and D'Agata, the Sicilian crazed by food and sex—this group's identity comes right out of the pages of Levi's memoir.[18] In the lulls-in-travel scenes, where each member of the band tells his story, and in their collective adventures en route the film lapses into a picaresque mode whose fragmentary structure is appropriate to the discontinuities and contradictions of the Italian national identity it comes to signify.

From the perspective of 1996, looking back on a time of fullness and hope, Rosi focuses with special nostalgia on the relationship of the intellectual Left with the myth of the Soviet Union—a relationship that is seen to be central to the Italian dream of postwar cultural renewal. Levi, too, elevates Russia to mythic status, but in terms that are far more anthropological than political. The subject of constant invidious comparison with German authoritarian rule, the Russians are seen as benignly anarchic and truly heroic (66–67). In keeping with the classicizing view of Levi's literary perspective on this post-Holocaust odyssey, Russia is constantly seen as epic, indeed Homeric, in its primordial grandeur (102). As the memoir proceeds and the odyssey is beset with bureaucratic obstacles, Levi grows more and more disenchanted with the Russian regime, with its arbitrariness and its administrative ineptitude (223). In Rosi's film, however, the disappointment that Levi overtly shows toward the Soviets is banished to the margins. It is projected onto an awareness of a future beyond the events represented on screen, but one that provides the perspective from which Rosi looks back with nostalgia on what Levi called "that happy moment of their history" (211) and on what it signified for the Italian Left. The most powerful vehicle of that myth is the recurrent image of the locomotive, which is often shot in low angle as it races across the screen to drive the narrative literally to its destination. What gives this image a power verging on the iconic is the imprint of the bright red star at the center of the huge, black mass of the engine, whose contours are blurred by the steam of its forward progress.[19] It would be no exaggeration to call this image the logo of the film, especially considering that the publisher Einaudi placed it on the cover of the 1997 edition of the book.

But it is in the scene of the Russian victory performance that Rosi expresses the yearning of the Italian Left for the myth of Soviet redemption. At its most obvious, the scene represents the Russian collectivity as irresistibly attractive, with the jolly Marja Fjodorovna and the benign Dr. Dancenko in the front row of the army personnel who sing their song of victory—a song that impresses upon us the specifically Soviet responsibility for defeating the Nazi scourge. But when Galina comes on the stage, dressed as a traditional Russian maiden, singing a popular ballad, she becomes a personification allegory for her homeland, the idealized embodiment of Soviet national identity.

Primo's infatuation with her thus comes to take its place in a long-standing literary and cinematic tradition whereby the desires aroused by the individual body erotic can be applied metaphorically to matters of state.[20]

The object of Rosi's nostalgia, then, is Italy's love affair with the myth of the Soviet Union—an affair doomed to disaster when the reality of the regime revealed itself in the decades-long vicissitudes that led to its final collapse in 1991. Yet Rosi mourns the grandeur of the vision sustained by the myth—a vision of epic dimensions that dared to dream of a better world. In *The Truce,* the possibility of a new postwar order is built into the choral dimension of the film, whose vast numbers of extras give visual expression to a Europe in the throes of communal rebirth.[21] In its insistence on the mass scale of the experience, then, the film is as much about Europe's quest for identity as it is about one man's personal ordeal. The interplay between collective and individual experience finds musical expression in the counterpoint between Primo's motif, entrusted largely to a solo flute, and the choral theme, which is large and orchestral in range.[22]

If the grandeur of the political vision sustained by the Soviet myth is the object of Rosi's nostalgia, so, too, is the cinematic style that was its vehicle of diffusion. Carlo Dansi, for example, sees *The Truce* as Rosi's homage "to past years when Italy had the courage of enterprise,"[23] while the film's composer, Luis Bacalov, comments that "this is a film like ones that are no longer made in Italy. And few were made to begin with."[24] In terms of cinema history, then, the *tregua*—the privileged season that has come to an end—is certainly that of Rosi's master, Visconti, but also of Rossellini, De Santis, and De Sica, of Bertolucci before he abandoned Italy, of the Tavianis. The truce is the season of committed cinema, when the industry was epic in purpose, if not always in scale; when filmmaking was seen as an intervention in the life of the country; when motion pictures mattered. In turning to the Holocaust as its privileged subject and in memorializing Italy's foremost survivor of this "central fact, the stain" of twentieth-century European history, Rosi is bringing together the best tradition of his country's committed art with the most solemn act that a historical reconstruction can perform—that of bearing witness. It is up to us, then, to become the "addressable others."

14

The Seriousness of Humor in
Roberto Benigni's *Life Is Beautiful*

"It is precisely the uneasiness manifested by those who have theorized on the Comic," wrote Umberto Eco in 1968, "that inclines us to think that the Comic must be somehow connected with uneasiness."[1] Comic unease goes far to explain the intense mixture of enthusiasm and discomfort that greeted the release of *Life Is Beautiful*.[2] Eco's comment is especially helpful in defending the function of comedic devices within the story as a critique of Fascism and in defending the challenge that *Life Is Beautiful* poses to the history of Holocaust representations on the screen. Eco's pronouncement grows out of his interpretation of Pirandello's essay "L'umorismo" (On Humor) and it is the latter that will serve as the basis of my own study of Roberto Benigni's Holocaust comedy. For Pirandello, humor is far more than a triggering device for laughter: it is a philosophical category, a form of cognition that juxtaposes our conventional perceptions with *il sentimento del contrario* (the sentiment of the contrary)[3] in ways that disrupt and destabilize our established responses to experience. *L'umorismo*, then, is a profoundly subversive force, challenging us to question received wisdom both on the level of ideology and aesthetic convention and prompting the "liberating laughter" that Benigni hopes to inspire in his audience.[4]

It is in this broad, Pirandellian sense that I wish to consider Benigni's humor in *Life Is Beautiful*, and to defend it against the "Holocaust fundamentalism" of its detractors—those who insist that historical accuracy be the principal criterion for judging representations of the Shoah.[5] In using the term *fundamentalism* I am deliberately and strategically implying that for such critics the factual record stands as a sacred textual source that gives the Holocaust the status of a religious absolute any deviation from which amounts to heresy. "We tell them [individual Holocaust stories] to each other in the evening," Primo Levi wrote in *Survival at Auschwitz,* "and they take place in Norway, Italy, Algeria, the Ukraine, and are simple and incomprehensible, like the stories in the Bible. But are they not themselves stories of a new Bible?"[6] As Levi fully realized, and as Holocaust fundamentalists would do well to acknowledge, this new scripture, this historical text of witness to a truth that defies human understanding, like its biblical prototype, invites a multileveled approach to interpretation. To limit Holocaust art to the letter of the historical record, to require a rigid adherence to factual detail, is to permit only documentary accounts into the repertory of acceptable genres for Shoah representation.[7] Indeed, were such fundamentalism to be taken to its logical conclusion, not even the documentary form, with its subjective criteria for the selection of material and its implicit or explicit explanatory impulse, could meet the standards for absolute, univocal truth that fundamentalism requires.

In contrast to a monolithic approach to Holocaust representation, I would like to invoke the notion of testimony, of bearing witness—a notion that, while affirming the truth value of the historic referent, encourages a multiplicity of narrative means. If the purpose of Holocaust witness is dynamic transmission—the passing on of the testimony in a way that invests its receivers with the moral obligation to convey their knowledge to others—then the narrative must remain open to constant elaboration, adaptation, and rearticulation in ways that will recommend it to new generations of listeners.[8] To insist on a documentary approach to the representation of the Holocaust is to consign it to the archives, to embalm and distance it in a way that will deprive the history of its urgent moral claim to our attention.

The very framing of *Life Is Beautiful* may be seen to align Benigni's film with the tradition of Holocaust testimony. "This is a simple story, and yet it's not easy to tell," the voice-over narrator, who we later learn is the grown-up Giosuè, begins. "As in a fable, there is pain, and, as in a fable, it is full of marvels and happiness."[9] With this mixture of personal witness and fairy tale, of documentary reference and the fantastic, far from "a preemptive, prophylactic move to insulate his film from strong charges of falsifying history," as Stuart Liebman claims,[10] Benigni incorporates *Life Is Beautiful* into the history of Italian films that look

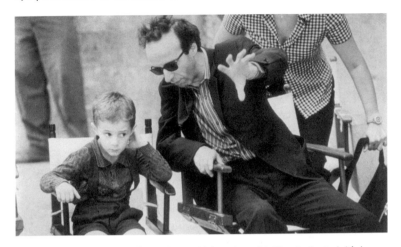

FIGURE 31 | Roberto Benigni (who plays Guido) confers with Giorgio Cantarini (who plays Giosuè) on the set of *Life Is Beautiful*. Courtesy of the Museum of Modern Art/Film Stills Archive.

back to World War II, the privileged subject matter of neorealism, but acknowledges the changes that time, memory, and the evolution of the medium inevitably bring. At the end of the film, the voice-over narration concludes: "This is the sacrifice that my father made. This was his gift for me." In framing his film as the childhood reminiscence of an adult speaker, Benigni aligns *Life Is Beautiful* with the Taviani brothers' *Night of the Shooting Stars* (1982), whose narrator is a grown woman recounting an episode of her youth during the Allied Liberation of Tuscany.[11] Just as Cecilia in the Tavianis' film claims that her story is true, though not all the details of her account are accurate, the adult Giosuè acknowledges the fairy-tale quality of his biographical account. And like the receiver of the narrative in *Night of the Shooting Stars,* who is revealed to be a sleeping baby in the film's last frame, the implied listener of *Life Is Beautiful* is Giosuè's child, the new generation of Holocaust witness to whom Guido's gift will be given (fig. 31).[12]

Visually, the opening frame sequence is as vague and mystifying as the voice-over narration: a fog-enshrouded figure holding a child nearly emerges into view before receding into the vaporous background of the set. The memory of this enigmatic opening lingers at the edges of our consciousness until late in the second half of the film, when the scene rematerializes.[13] It is the aftermath of the Nazi dinner party to which Giosuè has been disastrously invited. As the father carries his sleeping son back to their barracks in the night and fog, what appears to be a mass grave full of twisted corpses opens behind them. In this brief, wordless scene, Guido is confronted with the ultimate signified of the Holocaust, the referent that all his machinations have sought to mask.[14] The image of the man holding his sleeping child against this phantasmagoric background presents, in germinal form, the entire narrative of the film's second half. Guido's job is to keep Giosuè "asleep" to the horrors that await them in the pit. The mortal stake of Guido's game emerges here, for Giosuè's survival is contingent upon his father's ability to skirt that pit, to keep the child from falling into the despair that would mean surrender to Nazi attempts at dehumanization. We could say that this horrific spectacle is the tear in the fabric of the screen (to use Dudley Andrew's eloquent formulation),[15] the hook that links all of Benigni's comic antics to a deadly serious historic context, the gold standard that underwrites the coinage of his comic invention.

While contributing to the tradition of Holocaust witness, Benigni is also obeying a personal, autobiographical impulse in making *Life Is Beautiful*. "My Dad organized this for me, too, when I was little" (116-17), Guido explains to Giosuè of the "surprise" outing that the Nazis have engineered on the occasion of the child's fifth birthday. The term used, *organizzazione,* is a highly fraught one, referring to the Nazi mania for order and control, which Guido imaginatively transforms into the mechanism for a well-planned vacation. But the comment reaches beyond the referential confines of the story to include the biographical impetus behind Benigni's performance: the filmmaker's own father's recounting of his two-year detention in a Nazi labor camp after the Italian armistice with the Allies in September 1943. "Night and day, fellow prisoners were dying all around him," Benigni explained. "He told us about it, as if to protect me and my sisters, he told it in an almost funny way—saying tragic, painful things but finally his way of telling them was really very particular. Sometimes we laughed at the stories he told."[16] In the light of this personal anecdote, the voice-over conclusion to the film gains new resonance. When the adult Giosuè recounts to his own child the story of Guido's sacrifice, concluding that "this was his gift for me," *Life Is Beautiful* becomes a *mise-en-abyme,* wherein the experience of suffering-turned-into-humor is handed down from elder to younger Benigni, in the authorial prehistory of the film, from Guido to his son in the film's diegesis, and from Giosuè to the next generation of witness in the film's public reception.

Thus to introduce *Life Is Beautiful* with a preview of the scene of horror veiled by fog and skirted by a father carrying his sleeping child is to announce from the very start the film's commitment both to refer and to mask, or perhaps to refer *through* masking, what Morandino Morandini called "a horror that, . . . hidden, is more evident than if it were shown."[17] The bipartite organization of *Life Is Beautiful,* which is really two films in one,[18] may be explained by the structural need to establish this principle of "masked reference." Guido's power to create a fantasy so compelling that it can override the horrors of Auschwitz requires all the energies of the film's first forty-eight minutes to establish. Thus the story begins with a minor example of the triumph of illusion over reality when Guido is mistaken for King Victor Emmanual II as his car careens into a crowd awaiting the monarch and the protagonist's gesture of dismissal is interpreted as the Fascist salute. While his assumption of royal identity is inadvertent in this first instance, it is active and deliberate in the next. When Guido introduces himself as a prince to an astonished child, proclaiming, "Qui tutto è mio, qui principia il principato del principe" (Here, everything is mine; here begins the principality of the prince) (9), verbal invention takes on a life of its own. Guido's act of self-anointment then leads, by a kind of etymological momentum, to the founding of an empire and, of course, the quest for a *principessa.* The speech act itself, obeying the inner laws of lexical progression, becomes performative, bringing into being the imaginary kingdom it conjures up. Dora will indeed fill the role of the *principessa,* and the young nobleman will steal her from the ball on the back of a garishly painted, once-white horse at the end of the film's first half.

The parallels with Fascism are easily drawn, and Benigni specifically sets up Guido's wish-fulfillment fantasy as both a spoof of the ideological pretensions of the regime and ultimately as an antidote to them. Guido's power of imaginative transformation and Fascism's imperial aspirations coincide at the very moment when Guido crowns himself prince. "We'll call this place Addis Ababa. Away with the cows, bring on the camels. Away with the chickens, bring on the ostriches" (9). Guido's impulse to turn domestic barnyard animals into an Ethiopian bestiary reveals the elements of exoticism and romance on which Italy's dream of an African empire was built. Indeed, Mussolini's rhetorical strategy in conjuring up this imperial myth is revealed to be simply a more official version of Guido's own language of abracadabra. But the most scathing critique of Fascism's expansionist agenda comes during the engagement party of Dora and Rodolfo at the Grand Hotel. The festivities culminate in a lavish procession in which "four Africans . . . in folkloristic costume carry down the stairs on their shoulders a baldachin with an immense Ethiopian cake on top" (95). The pastry, featuring a giant ostrich with a precariously balanced egg in its beak, confers upon Mussolini's imperialist policy the status of a confection, a bonbon to be enjoyed and consumed by the admiring Italian masses. *"This,"* exclaims Guido's uncle "in an ironic tone" as he shows the cake to his nephew, *"is the empire!* The hotel is offering it to our guests" (76).

The hotel, of course, is the Grand Hotel, symbol of 1930s elegance imported from the American screen and appropriated by Fascism as proof of Italy's entry into modernity under Mussolini's enlightened rule.[19] Like the characters in Fellini's *Amarcord* (1974),[20] who consider Fascism to be on a par with all things glamorous and transcendent (the Rex, the Grand Prix, Gary Cooper films, the baron's peacock), the Grand Hotel serves as the locus of elegance and romance, where the engagement party of a Fascist official with his beloved would naturally be held. In Danilo Donati's set design, Benigni presents his critique of Fascism in visual terms. It is significant that the huge ballroom of the hotel is round and windowless, constituting a self-contained, hermetically sealed world cut off from all external influences and distractions. The antiseptic whiteness of the decor is strategic, alluding to the interiors of Hollywood domestic scenes of the 1930s, when white was a signifier of the wealth needed to keep it clean.[21] On the windowless white walls are "realistic portraits of men and women of the upper middle class that seem to be conversing among themselves, drinking champagne or smiling serenely" (75). As the ballroom actually fills up with guests, the specular relationship between the frescoes and the human occupants of the room is all too obvious. In critiquing the style of Fascism, Benigni is critiquing Fascism *as* style, as spectacle, as a form of representation that rejects anything alien to its preferred self-image and that exists, finally, in the realm of simulation. Real people seek to imitate the images of false glamour, imported from America, which Fascism presents to them as if they were looking at their mirror reflections, in a circle of narcissism and inauthenticity that only Guido, with his alternative fantasy world, is able to escape.

Because Guido is a master of fiction making, a skilled artificer of illusion, he can see Fascist signifiers for what they are and can commandeer them for his own purposes. Because he can appropriate the language of officialdom, Guido is able successfully to impersonate the Fascist minister of education who visits Dora's school. He can ask the apposite questions in a technical language that convinces his listeners of the power that such linguistic mastery confers. Bandying about such terms as *didactic circular, curricular schedule,* and *pediatric hygiene,* Guido's speech act, his very utterance of these words, creates a belief in his power to do so. His legitimacy is performative. Later in the film, Guido's gift for official-sounding speech will help him convince his son of the authenticity of the game he has invented. The ease with which Guido appropriates such technical terms as *reserved, classified, registered, disqualified,* and *eliminated* to mask the horrific reality of genocide persuades Giosuè of the truth of his father's claims.

This gift for mimicking the language of officialdom enables Guido to deliver a brilliant spoof of the Fascist discourse on race. In a variation of a scene from Agnieszka Holland's *Europa Europa* (1991) in which the Jewish protagonist is picked as an ideal specimen of Aryan manhood, Guido chooses himself to exemplify Fascism's racist ideals. Standing before one of the many stylized busts of Mussolini that adorn the film, against the inscription DVX (Latin for *Duce*), flanked by the slogan *Libro, moschetto, fascista perfetto* (book, musket, perfect Fascist), Guido proceeds to proclaim his racial superiority, beginning with the outer ear. "Spanish ears are laughable. French cartilage cracks me up. The Russian auricle is disgusting" (51). Bringing into ludicrous juxtaposition two disparate semantic fields—those of primate biology and those of competitive nationalism—Guido deflates Fascism's rhetorical exploitation of both. Guido's body becomes the self-proclaimed Fascist body politic, the perfect anatomical surface on which the worldwide battle for racial supremacy will be fought and won. In his next quip,

Guido makes a foray into racial history. "This is called 'bending of the Aryan leg with circular movement of the Italic foot . . . Etruscan ankle on Roman shin.' In Belgium they're green with envy" (52). This passage, unfortunately cut from the American version of the film, traces an idealized ethnohistory of the Italian stock, moving up Guido's leg from the Etruscan and ancient Roman lower limb to the glorious Aryan kneecap of today.[22]

Guido's ability to appropriate and recast authoritative language for his own purposes is also used to his amorous advantage. In part one, by assigning agency to Dora he is able to summarize, and cleverly rewrite, the script of his pursuit of her up to this point in the film. "I stop under a roof and you fall into my arms from the sky. I fall from my bike and I find myself in your arms. . . . I go to inspect a school and I find myself facing you once more. I stop my car in front of the theater and suddenly you get in and you even appear in my dreams. Could you please leave me in peace? You've really got a crush on me!" (64). In this long catalog of events, paratactically ordered and punctuated by the recurrent first-person pronoun object *mi,* Guido indicates his passive role in this courtship, his status as the victim of Dora's amorous assaults. But in Guido's revised version of the story, although the events of the plot remain the same, they are organized according to a radically different interpretive grid. It is in this difference, in this gap between the official, authoritative reading of signs and the subversive, alternative readings that Guido's power and humor reside. And it is here that Pirandello's notion of *umorismo,* or "sentiment of the contrary that is born from a special activity of reflection" (*L'umorismo,* 137),[23] becomes especially relevant to the workings of Guido's comic ingenuity in the film's second half.

At the heart of Guido's humorist operation is the process of translation, understood both in the technical sense of linguistic shift and in the broader sense of *translatio*—a carrying across.[24] The substitution of one perspective for another, the replacement of the Nazi program of dehumanization and destruction with an alternative program of gamesmanship winnable by all contestants, is a form of translation in this broadest sense. The scene in which the literal and figurative meanings of translation come together occurs early in the second part, when Guido and Giosuè have just been inducted into the camp. Though completely ignorant of the German language, Guido volunteers to translate for the Nazi corporal who will explain the rules of the *lager*. Guido's ignorance of German actually helps him come up with an alternative of his own devising, letting him focus on the pure sound of the language in order to invent benign equivalents in Italian, allowing him to overlook the dire meaning of the Nazi commands so that he can indulge in unfettered verbal play. In fact, all of Guido's subsequent gamesmanship will depend on this blend of formal mimicry and willed ignorance of the horror, this ability to acknowledge the external forms of camp life while denying (and obstructing) their murderous intent.

This long and brilliant scene of "creative mistranslation" adapts, in a comic vein, an episode from Gillo Pontecorvo's *Kapo* (1960) in which a concentration-camp inmate, Thérèse, is required to translate to her fellow prisoners the SS rationale for executing one of their group. In an act of resistance, Thérèse refuses to continue with the translation process, thus rejecting her role as liaison between Nazi law enforcers and their subjects. Because translation is such an integral part of the German apparatus of control, Thérèse's recalcitrance is seen as a serious breach of authority, earning her three months of solitary confinement on one-half rations. After serving her sentence, Thérèse returns to the barracks broken in spirit and body and chooses to end her life on the electrified barbed wire that encloses the camp.

Guido's subversion of the translation process is just such an act of resistance. He simply replaces Thérèse's silence with a creative and constructive mistranslation—one that transforms the Nazi policy of dehumanization into a life-affirming sport. "Pay attention!" barks the German. "I'll only say it once!" Guido's translation: "The game begins . . . whoever's in is in. Whoever's not in is not in." The German admonishes, "You've been brought here in this camp for one single reason." Guido's translation: "Whoever scores one thousand points wins. The winner gets a real army tank" (130). As the translation process proceeds, we see that the ostensible gap between the German and Italian versions is really a gap between diametrically opposed ways of organizing experience. In Guido's translation, the German system of oppression turns into a system of play, the regime of forced obedience becomes one of voluntary adherence, the imposition of arbitrary punishment gives way to the reassurance of familiar behavioral guidelines, and the audience of victims becomes a team of possible winners.

Central to Guido's translation strategy is the reduction of the *universe concentrationnaire* to the confines of the familiar domestic space of childhood. "There are three important rules," growls the German: "(1) don't try to escape the camp; (2) obey all the orders without question; (3) organized attempts at revolt will be punished by hanging. Is that clear?" Guido translates: "In three cases you lose all your points. Those lose who (1) start to cry; (2) want their mommy; (3) are hungry and want a snack. Forget it!" (131). What Guido does is to reduce the Nazi threats against disobedience into the benign parental admonitions against childishness. Though Guido's translation is stern in its denial of maternal refuge and between-meal snacks, it nonetheless creates the impression of household routine that helps make sense of this world to Giosuè and establishes an imaginative continuity with his previous life. And the Nazis are cut down to size by becoming simply "those bad bad guys who yell" (148)—hyperbolic versions of the strict teachers, irritable parents, and grumpy neighbors who temporarily darken the horizons of all normal childhood experience.

In linguistic terms, it is significant that Guido's translation is not simply from German to Italian but from *lagerjargon,* a corrupt subspecies of German arising from the concrete conditions of camp life, into Tuscan. *La toscanità* has been a staple of comic film production throughout the 1990s: "From Nuti of yesterday to the Benignis, Benvenutis, Virzìs, and Pieraccionis of today," observes Claudio Fava, "it is the most curious and curious-making phenomenon of Italian cinema of the 1990s."[25] In *Life Is Beautiful,* the *toscanità* of Benigni's performance adds considerable ideological force to Guido's act of translation—his "carrying over"—from a dehumanizing, pseudomilitarized system of communication into the profoundly human, personal, regionally rooted dialect that lies at the heart of Italy's debates on its linguistic and literary identity. *Toscanità,* then, is rich with implications for the cultural process that transforms the lagerjargon into its polar opposite under the imaginative auspices of Guido.

In this scene of creative mistranslation, Benigni establishes three distinct audiences: that of bewildered prisoners who remain outside any form of understanding; that of Giosuè, who is regaled by the news of the game; and that of the film's spectators, privy to the disparity between original and translation. The interplay between our level of awareness and Giosuè's is what provides the material for the extended joke of the film's second part. But the joke has the seriousness of Pirandello's umorismo and belongs to Freud's category of the tendentious: the use of humor to make a point.[26] It is this multiplying of audiences that rescues *Life Is Beautiful* from the gratuitous and exploitative humor of *The Monster* (1994), the film that immediately precedes it and that shares its use of historical subject matter (the crimes of the serial murderer Pietro Pacciani, *il mostro di Firenze*) but uses this reference for the purposes of entertainment. Because Benigni is performing for the sake of his fictive son's survival within the narrative of *Life Is Beautiful,* that comic virtuosity is subordinated to a higher, historically consecrated goal. And the inclusion of an inner audience, that of the child, enables us to double our own spectator position so that we may at once enjoy the comic performance in our identification with Giosuè while standing at one critical remove and reflecting on the life-sustaining purpose of Guido's exertions. This doubling of audiences makes explicit the Pirandellian operation of "doubling in the act of conception" (142) that lies at the heart of umorismo. While the comic, for Pirandello, resides in the *avvertimento del contrario* (*L'umorismo,* 135), or awareness of disparate perspectives, the humorous resides in the *sentimento del contrario* (ibid.), or the concomitant philosophical reflection on the meaning of that disparity. In Pirandellian terms, the inner audience (Giosuè) laughs at the *avvertimento del contrario,* whereas we laugh at its *sentimento.* And it is this doubling that endows Pirandellian humor with its philosophical and ethical *gravitas* (ibid., 138).

By making Giosuè the inner audience of Guido's performance, Benigni establishes childhood innocence as the standard by which the Holocaust is interpreted and morally judged.[27] Like Bruno Ricci in *Bicycle Thief,* Giosuè becomes the conscience of *Life Is Beautiful,* the morality-conferring witness of his father's plight. In perhaps the most wrenching scene in the film, Guido appeals to Giosuè's inner sense of justice to make him disbelieve the evidence of mass murder that surrounds them.[28] "Giosuè! You fell for it again," Guido exclaims. "And yet I made you out to be a quick, clever little boy. With us . . . with people . . . they make buttons? . . . with Russians they make belts, with the Poles they make suspenders? Buttons and soap" (159). By actually stating what the Nazis did in turning human bodies into utilitarian objects and by using the child's innate sense of rightness as a measure of implausibility, Benigni forces us to perceive the horror anew. We are asked to relinquish our historical knowledge and jadedness as we confront what it means to manufacture buttons, soap bars, belts, and suspenders out of human bodies. Not only does Guido put this ghoulish process into words, he heightens the sense of absurdity by imagining the following minidrama. "Eh, tomorrow I wash my hands with Bartolomeo, button my jacket with Francesco, and comb my hair with Claudio" (159). By naming their fellow inmates in the barracks and then hypothetically turning them into the instruments of the civilized man's *toilette,* Guido gives fullest imaginative life to the horror.[29] In the original screenplay (cut from the Miramax version of the film), Guido's final ploy is to imagine genocidal perversities that even exceed the bounds of Giosuè's report. "It'll get to the point where one day they'll tell you that with us they make lampshades and paperweights" (159). Here Benigni reopens the breach between the inner audience of Giosuè's witness and the outer audience of spectators privy to the historical knowledge that Guido's fantasy of human lampshades and paperweights came to be true. In taking to absurd lengths the Nazi harvest of human bodies, Guido's fanciful logic just barely manages to keep pace with the very history it seeks to deny.

The splitting of the audience into outer and inner, Giosuè and us, has profound ideological, as well as moral, implications. In Freudian terms, jokes form communities by reaffirming the shared values that enable listeners to "get it."[30] Every time we smile at the disparity between Giosuè's mercifully deceived perspective and our fully informed one, we reaffirm our bonds as a community of knowers. That knowledge involves a recognition of the gap between the reality of the camps and Guido's benign interpretation. Every time that Guido must invent a new gimmick to accommodate yet another instance of horror into his game plan, we must retravel the distance between the Nazi original and the "Italian" translation, between atrocity and life-sustaining misinterpretation. We retraverse that distance when Guido construes the crowd of people outside Auschwitz as proof of how popular a vacation spot this is; when he explains the bifurcation of the line into left and right as the dividing up of contestants into teams; when he marvels at how everything is *organizzato;* when he interprets Nazi severity

FIGURE 32 | Upon entering the camp barracks for the first time, Guido must rise to the challenge of convincing Giosuè that this horrific place is merely the setting for an innocuous game. Courtesy of the Museum of Modern Art/Film Stills Archive.

as a measure of the value of the prize; when he displays the tattooed number on his arm as evidence that he is enrolled in the game; when he explains that the back-breaking work of carrying anvils to the blast furnace is for the soldering of the metal body of the tank; and when he concludes that all the children have disappeared because they are simply hiding. Every time we laugh, every time we make the cognitive leap that enables us to "get it," we retrace the distance separating Guido's signifier from the Nazi signified. By "getting it," we are bound in a new community of shared understanding that counteracts the Nazi dystopia and acknowledges the community-building value of Guido's exertions.

Freud's theory of "joke work"—the labor that the jest must perform to overcome the listener's inhibitions against the sexual or aggressive impulses that are released by the tendentious humor—implies that Guido must engage in a parallel practice of "game work." Where the Freudian joke teller must labor against the repression of unconscious forces, Guido is up against the conscious knowledge that Giosuè is receiving from his environment. Guido's task is therefore both emotional and intellectual—he must improvise ever new ways of accommodating the horrific facts to his interpretive grid, and he must convince Giosuè by his own exuberant example of the recreational value of their undertaking. This is where Guido's virtuosity comes in, and where the film becomes "meta-performative" in its commentary on the power of acting to bring into being what it represents. "Guido needs to gear himself up because Giosuè is about to burst out crying" (128), the screenplay indicates, as the two enter the barracks for the first time (fig. 32). This charge of energy needed to fuel Guido's performance is the actor's surge of adrenaline before going on stage to undertake a particularly demanding role. At this point in the film, we see that Guido's heroism is indeed performative, that his strength resides in his ability to enact successfully his self-appointed role as *animatore* (camp counselor, recreation leader) in the most engaging and persuasive of ways.

Guido's game work, however, is not limited to the inner audience of Giosuè. At the metalevel of the film's commentary on itself as a medium, and on Benigni's career in the cinema, *Life Is Beautiful* has considerable "work" to do. In fact, it would be no exaggeration to claim that Benigni builds risk into the very fabric of the film, foregrounding the audacity of his cinematic experiment. To pull off its daring enterprise, to make a comedy about the event "that will be remembered as the central fact, the stain, of this century," in Primo Levi's words,[31] Benigni must overcome a number of obstacles. Not the least of his challenges is that of subsuming and transcending his own comic persona and the genre within which he operates. This ingenious yet naive *personaggio*—over-sexed yet childish, vulgar yet deeply cultured—whose earlier films were constructed around plots designed exclusively to display Benigni's comic talents, now must subordinate that performativity to the demands of the Holocaust referent. To put it another way, when the train pulls into the station at Auschwitz—an image we have already seen in the documentary footage of Lanzmann's *Shoah* (1985), as well as in the fictional context of Spielberg's *Schindler's List* (1991) and Pontecorvo's *Kapo* (1960)—we ask ourselves what will happen this time, given the unexpected comic cargo of this all-too-familiar, tragic conveyance?

In addition to centering on the game work of Guido's character, the film also foregrounds and privileges Benigni's work in converting his comic persona and preferred genre into something quite new and ex-

FIGURE 33 | In *Life Is Beautiful,* the family romance cannot have a happy ending, for the year is 1944, the place is Nazi-occupied Italy, and Guido is Jewish. Courtesy of the Museum of Modern Art/Film Stills Archive.

traordinary in *Life Is Beautiful.* The transformation is highlighted in the deceptively smooth transition between the two parts of the film, when the camera focuses on the greenhouse into which Guido and Dora disappear for their first night of love; immediately thereafter, Giosuè emerges from the same greenhouse, pulling his toy tank. Apparently seamless, this spatially and temporally continuous shot really signals a gap of five years. Underlying the visual continuity of the shot, then, is a series of contradictions. On one level, we infer that the birth and idyllic childhood of Giosuè are the logical extensions of his parents' love story, the continuation of the passion into the family romance. But the happily-ever-after formula of the love story does not apply to this particular "after," for the year is now 1944 and the conventional projections of a future of marital and familial bliss cannot be fulfilled in this historic context (fig. 33). The deceptively smooth transition of the greenhouse shot masks the rupture that takes place behind the scenes with the Nazi occupation and the imminent deportation of the unsuspecting trio. The imagistic association of this greenhouse with the earthly paradise, as Guido had once described it to Ferruccio (32), reveals its true identity as an Edenic space. The deportation is, then, the fall from grace, the expulsion of this fairy-tale family from the garden of love into the gutters of Holocaust history.

Nonetheless, our old generic expectations linger, and the reappearance of Dr. Lessing, a carryover from the film's first half, leads us to think that maybe we have in him an example of the "good Nazi," like Spielberg's Schindler or the one-handed Karl of *Kapo*. In fact, the shared passion for riddles that links Dr. Lessing and Guido in a brotherhood of intellectual gamesmanship suggests a possible plot device for a conventional happy ending. Dr. Lessing could propose to Guido a riddle whose answer would contain the key to escape. Or Dr. Lessing would be so thankful to Guido for solving the most elusive of puzzles that the German would save him out of sheer gratitude. Instead, Dr. Lessing presents an unsolvable riddle, one that keeps him awake at night, while the Mengele-like job of selecting human beings for life or death leaves him unfazed. This plot twist leads nowhere: it is a red herring, intended to disabuse us of any conventional expectations for a comprehensive happy ending. In the case of the riddle, Guido's game work is insufficient, and Nazi behavior remains an insoluble enigma.

The cleft that divides the film in half, just as deportation itself marks the irreversible break between the victim's "before" and "after,"[32] distinguishes the structure of *Life Is Beautiful* from another Italian Holocaust film, Wertmuller's *Seven Beauties* (1976). Wertmuller's film, which also plays on the violent contrast between the prewar life of the protagonist and his current plight in the camp, constantly shifts from present to past as a way of foregrounding the ironic relationship between the protagonist Pasqualino's two conditions. The numerous flashbacks, which recount the glory days of a small-time Neapolitan crook eager to avenge the insult to the family honor caused by his sister's prostitution, are set in opposition to the present in the concentration camp, where Pasqualino prostitutes himself to the female commandant in order to insure his survival.

Benigni's decision, instead, to divide his film into two entirely separate parts heightens the shock value of the deportation and invites comparison with another ground-breaking film portrayal of World War II—Rossellini's *Open City* (1945), whose halfway point marks a shift from domestic romance to historically induced tragedy. The love story of the earlier film, promising to culminate in the marriage of Pina and Francesco, is shattered by her death from Nazi gunfire. With this opening out to the streets of war-torn Rome, the intimate domestic story is forced into history, and cinematic neorealism is born. With *Life Is Beautiful,* a similar rupture takes place in midfilm, when the romantic idyll is replaced by persecution history, and the *commedia all'italiana* gives way to a new, hybrid genre that moves audiences to a powerful, destabilizing mixture of laughter and tears.[33]

That mixture of hilarity and grief is the note on which *Life Is Beautiful* closes. Giosuè's final words to his mother, *abbiamo vinto* (we won), make Benigni's achievement in the film one of considerable generic and philosophical complexity. Superficially, Giosuè's claim is true: the Orefice team has indeed won one thousand points, the promised tank has materialized, mother and son are reunited, and Guido's gamble with Liberation history has paid off. We laugh with delight and relief because the requirements for Pirandellian comedy have been met. Two entirely disparate systems, that of Guido's fantastic game and that of World War II history, have come together in the American tank that rounds the corner to liberate the camp. But the *avvertimento del contrario* gives way to a higher philosophical reflection, its Pirandellian *sentimento,* when we consider the devastating cost of that triumph. Dora and Giosuè cannot know at this point that Guido himself has paid the price of their victory—that his final toy-soldier antics to divert Giosuè have earned him a mortal bullet. Thus the generic happy ending, which would require an all-inclusive "us" in the "we won" formulation of triumph, is not forthcoming.[34] It is in the ironic and reduced scale of this victory and in the reflection on its historic and psychological cost that Benigni locates the profoundly serious and ground-breaking humor of his Holocaust comedy.

Caro Diario and the Cinematic
Body of Nanni Moretti

Francesco Rosi, in a deeply moving and thoughtful response to Clive James's *New Yorker* commemoration of Fellini, mourns the death of the cinema "that . . . has always been the mirror of the collective themes of national life."[1] Developing James's argument that the drive "to get the whole of their country's life"[2] into each film was the mission of postwar Italian filmmakers, Rosi claims that cinema became the privileged vehicle of national-popular rebirth after the humiliation of Fascism and the ravages of war. As such the medium provided a form of activism for a generation impelled by a desire to record the history that was unfolding before its very eyes and to awaken the sleeping consciences of those who preferred not to see.

For Rosi, the waning of this tendency to national cinema is attributable to the loss of a unified self-image—to a social disintegration that has caused Italian filmmakers to lose faith in themselves and in their ability to convey a common vision. Whether this breakdown in the link between film and collective identity is a temporary manifestation of social malaise in the age of Berlusconi or a permanent condition only further to be aggravated by a continuing climate of civic withdrawal, such a development flies in the face of the entire history of Italian cinema. From the first feature work, *La presa di Roma* (1905), whose Risorgimento subject matter coupled the inception of the film industry with the birth of a nation, through neorealism, which made film the agent for the postwar rebirth of a nation, Italian cinema has proclaimed its status as national signifier, as chronicler of the life of the body politic from infancy to advanced middle age. This collective impulse is the premise of Angela Dalle Vacche's book *The Body in the Mirror*, which | 285 claims that film is a social technology wherein "the body on screen serves as the reflection of a fictional, national self." Such a cinema offers its spectators "terms of identification, an image of how they need to see themselves in order to have access to a national identity and imagine their roles in the historical process."[3]

Until the 1993 release of *Caro diario,* the films of Nanni Moretti could be located within this tradition of the social body. From 1976 until 1989, all seven of his feature-length films starred Moretti himself in the role of Michele Apicella, widely perceived to be the emblem and standard bearer of the post-1968 generation. Though Michele is but one of a gallery of eccentrics who populate the casts of Moretti's first two feature films—*Io sono un autarchico* (1976) and *Ecce bombo* (1978)— he emerges as the lead character and the focalizer whose dominance becomes explicit in the next five works. After *Ecce bombo,* the collective is left behind and Michele becomes the sole protagonist, experiencing solitude in a variety of acute forms: as the artistic megalomaniac of *Sogni d'oro* (1981), the psychotic idealist of *Bianca* (1984), the spiritual exile of *La messa è finita* (1985), and the political has-been of *Palombella rossa* (1989).

Despite this increasing isolation, however, the role of Michele Apicella would be forever marked by the conditions of his cinematic birth in the communal world of *Ecce bombo,* the film that, according to Mario Sesti, "came to be considered the most significant example of generational comedy."[4] Conceived as a character in a choral film, giving hyperbolic expression to the look and style of youth culture—taller, thinner, hairier, and even more eccentric than his peers—Michele would henceforth be burdened with the weight of *rappresentatività*—the tenured spokesman of his generation, the *uomo-simbolo* (man-as-symbol) of his age.[5] Indeed, no matter how far Moretti strayed into solipsism and political indifference in the development of Michele's persona, he would insist on his protagonist's social identity by constantly circling back to the pivotal years immediately following the 1968 revolution. "Ten years ago, there was political commitment, too," reminisces the mother of the temperamental filmmaker-protagonist Michele of *Sogni d'oro.* Now, "he gets the newspaper, reads the headlines, and then goes immediately to the entertainment section." In *Palombella rossa,* a glib journalist reminds Michele, the amnesiac leader of the PCI (Partito Comunista Italiano), that "you have a past as revolutionaries and a present as parliament members integrated into the system. Your erstwhile comrades, yes, they betrayed . . . they have become rich and they don't fight for certain ideals as they did before." But it is Andrea, the terrorist of *La messa è finita,* who gives fullest voice to Moretti's generational consciousness. "I was thinking," he says in the confession booth to Don Giulio (another incarnation of Michele, played by Moretti), "that, all told, years ago I was like you . . . and then, little by little, the others brought children into the world, they left, they returned, they found jobs, they changed jobs, they changed religion, political opinion, and only I have stayed where I was."

Moretti's insistent return to that moment of "great desperation and confusion,"[6] when youth culture aspired to make sense of its revolution, confers on Michele Apicella, no matter what role he assumes in the film of the moment, the status of generational signifier. In fact, it would be no overstatement to claim that Andrea's speech charts the entire movement of Moretti's cinema as it radiates out from the post-1968 moment like so many spokes from the hub of a wheel. Each film can be seen as an attempt to trace another of the paths traveled by the *Ecce bombo* collective, and each Michele Apicella may be understood to enact an option listed by Andrea in his account of what happened to "the others": the Michele of *Io sono un autarchico* and *Palombella rossa* is the father of a child; the Michele of *Sogni d'oro* pursues a high-powered career; the Michele (renamed Don Giulio) of *La messa è finita* joins the church; and the Michele of *Palombella rossa* compromises his political ideals. Nor would we be unjustified in seeing another possible Michele in Cesare Botero, the cynical socialist leader played by Moretti in Daniele Lucchetti's *Portaborse* (1991).

So insistent is Moretti's camera on linking Michele's physical presence to his particular cultural milieu that his body becomes a metaphor of the social body from which it emerges—a corporeal sign, a "somagraph," of the *Ecce bombo* world.[7] Thus, as the filmography progresses and we watch that body age, the hair shorten, the mustache and beard appear or disappear, we interpret the somagraph as the story of the changes in the body politic—"the petite bourgeoisie in red"[8]—to which it corresponds. This diachronic reading is made explicit in the opening shots of *La messa è finita,* where an astonishingly clean-shaven, short-haired Moretti reminds us, by contrast, of the old persona that has been shed for this film, bringing to the forefront of our awareness the construction of the fictional self-portrait on which his entire cinema is built. With this opening shot, Moretti challenges the public to discover the essential Michele under the clerical garb of his new alias, Don Giulio, to find the continuities between the *Ecce bombo* radical and the spiritually questing priest. The luminous face of Don Giulio becomes a palimpsest whose hairless surface reveals no trace of Michele's scruffy youth but whose intense pursuit of caritas comes to resemble, in Christian terms, the revolutionary's search for utopia. Moretti issues his most striking invitation to consider the continuities between Don Giulio and Michele in the scene where the young priest visits his parents before reporting to his new parish in the suburbs. As he enters his boyhood room, Don Giulio is framed against a photograph of his earlier, hirsute self.[9] Later in the film, Andrea will give the account of his generation that will circle back to this ground-zero moment, making Don Giulio's story one of the spokes of the wheel, one of the many possible turns taken by the participants of the *Ecce bombo* collective. But in this earlier scene, Moretti tells the tale in iconographic shorthand—it is enough to juxtapose these two images, that of the furry-faced revolutionary and that of the clean-shaven priest—to establish the somagraph of his age.

Palombella rossa complicates the diachronic reading of Michele's body by incorporating not simply a still photograph of his earlier self but actual footage from Moretti's first film, the super-8 short *La sconfitta* (1973). This flashback constitutes both a sociocultural and a filmographic return, implicating Moretti's entire cinematic production in the biography of the fictional Michele. "Do you remember? Do you remember? Do you remember?" inquires his friend Fabio Traversa as he prompts the amnesiac protagonist of *Palombella rossa* to recall a forgotten past. By making Michele's biographical flashback into a recall of Moretti's first film, the author gives his protagonist's life story a meta-cinematic dimension. As such, Michele's chronicle becomes not just the personal story of a middle-aged man facing career and family difficulties, and not just the generational saga of the youthful revolutionary who sells out to the center-left system, but also the tale of an alternative film practice that began with the liberated, if limited, medium of super-8 technology and evolved to the highest levels of industrial sophistication.

The contrivance of this imaginary autobiography enables Moretti not only to play out all the possibilities of the *Ecce bombo* moment, to create a generational emblem and a meta-cinematic device for tracking the progress of his art, but also to engage in a certain form of social satire. By organizing his films around a protagonist who both is and is not Moretti, the filmmaker exhibits the same ambivalent relationship to his character that the character, in turn, establishes with his social environment. This pseudo-autobiographical approach enables Moretti to register the kind of "complicitous critique" that Linda Hutcheon has applied to the sphere of postmodern thought,[10] wherein social critics cannot escape the very cultural practices they condemn in others and there is no "outside" from which to stand apart and judge. Within the world of the films, Michele is the agent of such complicitous critique. In *Palombella rossa,* for example, he rails against the use of meaningless jargon and pretentious bombast, while himself delivering the most clichéd of orations. In *La messa è finita,* Don Giulio faults his parishioners for their inability to communicate, but refuses to listen to utterances that meet with his displeasure. Michele's dual position as focalizer of the satiric vision and object of it is replicated on a second level by Moretti the author, whose self-casting as the lead character both implicates him in the film's social criticism and allows him to judge his protagonist from a safe, ironic distance.[11]

Michele also serves an important generic function, enabling Moretti to define his cinema as an alternative practice, resistant to the industrial trends of the 1970s and 1980s. It is over and against the commedia all'italiana—the staple of midlevel Italian film production—that the author sets his own cinema, and it is Michele who constantly invokes examples of Italian comic film production in ways that establish Moretti's adversarial relationship to the genre. The filmmaker's rejection of this tradition is not unequivocal, however, for his impulse constantly to distance himself from the commedia all'italiana betrays a clear anxiety of influence and an urgent need to separate from a threatening parental presence.[12] Lina Wertmuller obviously represents the most oppressive of generic "mothers," for she comes under particularly withering attack in *Io sono un autarchico,* where her fictitious elevation to a chair in film studies at UC-Berkeley causes Michele literally to foam at the mouth (in technicolor green), while the inclusion of *Seven Beauties* in the newspaper's list of cinematic best bets prompts his repeated expressions of disbelief. In *Caro diario*, Wertmuller's *Swept Away* becomes the paradigm of authorial cynicism against which Moretti feels compelled to revolt, "where there's a man and a woman who hate each other, who beat each other's brains out on a desert island because the director doesn't believe in people." Alberto Sordi suffers similar abuse toward the end of *Ecce bombo*, when Michele can think of no better way to silence the reactionary pronouncements of a random acquaintance in a bar than to compare him to the quintessential *maschera* (stock character) of the commedia all'italiana. "Who's talking?" he storms. "Are we in an Alberto Sordi film? You deserve Alberto Sordi!" In *Sogni d'oro*, the opposition between Michele's film-in-progress entitled *La mamma di Freud* and the Vietnam musical being prepared by his rival, Gigio Cimino, exemplifies the generic tension between auteur cinema and commedia all'italiana and reveals Moretti's attempt to position himself somewhere between the two.

Besides expressing the author's animus against Italian film comedy through an internal system of allusions, Michele's role as agent of complicitous critique rescues this filmography from the bad faith of the comic genre, whose practitioners, according to Moretti, hold themselves aloof from the targets of their satiric attack. "The commedia all'italiana films considered most successful," he said in a 1983 interview,

> are those in which the authors have not staged themselves but, sometimes with affection and sometimes with racism, social categories far from them: the subproletariat, the proletariat that aspire to become the petty bourgeoisie. . . . I am interested in the opposite operation, and it is in this, I believe, that consists the blessed "self-irony" that is always spoken of with regard to my films. I found myself staging and poking fun at a group homogeneous with me (from a social, generational, political point of view), if not at myself directly.[13]

Caro diario, however, heralds a withdrawal from the social sphere into a far more private, introspective cinematic space. Implicit in the film's very title is Moretti's will to speak with an intensely personal voice, and the opening frames of *Cario diario*, in which a hand literally writes on a page the words that we hear on the soundtrack, make explicit his desire to forge a new kind of cinematic writing.[14] This writing will be impressionistic, paratactic, and spontaneous, lacking any obvious structuring principle that would bind it to a preestablished system of meaning. Accordingly, *Caro diario* is made up of three discrete essays, or minifilms, linked only by the continuous presence of Moretti himself onscreen: "In Vespa" (On My Motor Scooter), "Isole" (Islands), and "Medici" (Doctors).

Of the three episodes, the central one, "Isole," retains the closest ties with Moretti's earlier cinema in that it consists of a series of gags designed to satirize contemporary life. Seeking to escape the distractions of the city in order to write his next screenplay, the protagonist embarks on a journey through the Aeolians with his friend Gerardo. To his chagrin, Moretti finds that these islands present, on a microcosmic scale, all the social ills that he had hoped to leave behind in Rome. Lipari is a hotbed of traffic, Salina is dominated by families obsessed with raising their only children, Pannarea is an enclave of swinging singles, and Alicudi is an outpost of back-to-nature extremists. Despite this episode's obvious links to Moretti's earlier, satiric production, however, there is one crucial difference that announces *Caro diario*'s departure from its precedents. The social critique in "Isole" is not complicitous—Moretti does not inscribe himself as both focalizer and object of the satire. The ironic doubling operation that Michele afforded the filmmaker in earlier works is now displaced onto another character, Gerardo, played not by Moretti but by another actor, Renato Carpentieri. It is Gerardo who begins as a social critic—an avid reader of Hans Magnus Enzensberger and a boycotter of television for thirty years—only to end up as a slave of soap operas; Moretti, on the other hand, remains the detached observer, forever scribbling notes in his diary, untainted by the collective ills around him.

Caro diario also signals a departure from Moretti's earlier cinema in visual terms. The opening episode heralds this break in its very first frames, when the static and austere camera of Moretti's previous filmography gives way to a mobilized perspective that literally trails him, on his motor scooter, as he cruises through the neighborhoods of greater Rome.[15] Although cataloging his usual obsessions—his fascination with shoes, his love of dancing couples, his pastry fetish, his cinemania—the episode simply records the filmmaker's itinerant gaze as he rides through the streets of residential Rome in what amounts to a *flânerie in Vespa*.[16]

Two meta-cinematic moments in the first episode help us define, in contrast to other film practices, the new language that Moretti seeks to forge in *Caro diario*. "During the summer, in Rome, the movie theaters are all closed," Moretti tells us in voice-over. "Or there are films like *Sex, Love, and Shepherding* . . . or some horror film like *Henry,* or some Italian film." Then Moretti takes us into a movie theater that is showing, onscreen, a group of stylish middle-aged Italians taking stock of their generation: "By now I'm afraid to go back into circulation. I'm a coward. What has happened in all these years? You tell me. I don't know anymore"; "Your temples are turning white"; "Our defeats are beginning to weigh on us"; "A series of uninterrupted defeats"; "Our generation . . . what have we become? We've become advertisers, architects, stockbrokers, members of parliament, aldermen, journalists. . . . We're so changed. We've gotten worse. Today we're all accomplices, all compromised"; "We used to shout horrendous, violent things in our protest marches . . . and now look how we've all become so ugly." From his seat in the movie theater, Moretti-the-spectator disagrees: "You shouted horrendous, violent things and you became ugly. I shouted just things and now I'm a splendid forty-year-old!" With this exchange, Moretti's cinema takes a radical turn away from exemplarity, away from generational allegory, away from the impulses to tell the stories of all the potential Michele Apicellas droning on in the 1990s chic of this *Big Chill all'italiana*.[17] When Moretti disowns his generational counterparts onscreen and proclaims his identity as "a splendid forty-year-old," he signals a will to speak for no one but himself. In *Caro diario* he will forge a film language of authenticity and personal renewal, in marked contrast to the style of the film-within-a-film, which participates fully in the banality and pretentiousness of its characters' communal breast-beating.

A second meta-cinematic moment leads us closer, by antithesis, to Moretti's ideal of authentic film writing. As he walks out of the movie theater featuring *Henry: Portrait of a Serial Killer,* Moretti remembers having read a positive review of the film, and he fantasizes getting revenge on the critic, Carlo Mazzacurati, by appearing at his bedside and quoting the offending passages as the writer tries to escape into sleep. What emerges from this wonderfully parodic moment is a distaste for intellectual positions so abstract and self-important that they can find justification in the most repellent media spectacles: Henry might be a serial killer, argues the critic, but at least he experiences "a crazy solidarity with his victims, he is the blue-blooded prince of annihilation, he promises a compassionate death. Henry is perhaps the first to violate and revile with such lucidity the criminal philosophy of the Lombrosians of Hollywood." Here we are but one step away from the kind of poststructuralist criticism that justifies all cultural products, no matter how degraded, as long as they provide "settings for intertextual play," as long as they reveal some intimation of a self-reflexivity that, "by calling attention to themselves as art forms, call all works of art . . . into question." The above quotes come from a scholarly study of the splatter film that, as a genre, "portrays the postmodern condition as an optimistic vehicle for cultural transformation."[18]

In spoofing the intellectual connoisseurship of *Henry: Portrait of a Serial Killer,* Moretti is attacking a theoretical approach that operates at so many removes from the letter of the text that any story or spectacle becomes grist for the interpretive mill. For such critics, the literal level is a mere pretext for cultural allegory, for a play of meanings that denies the material reality of the profilmic world and dismisses the deleterious effects that such spectacles may have on audiences ill-equipped to decipher intertextual codes and indifferent to self-reflexivity. To celebrate the splatter film is to deny the body on screen, to dematerialize it, to make it a vehicle for allegory.[19] The antiliteralism of this approach is carried to absurd extremes in the intellectual enthusiasm for films that revel in degradation, horror, and pain. If the apotheosis of the splatter film in highbrow criticism coincides with the triumph of inauthenticity, then authentic film language must involve a return to the concrete, a recuperation of the body on screen, a recognition of film's referentiality.[20] In short, the quest for an authentic film language requires literalizing the body, which, after all the excesses of abstraction and *allegorici furori* of poststructuralist thought, will come to signify only itself.

The remainder of the first episode ("In Vespa") and all of episode three ("Medici") may be read as answers to the reviewer of *Henry.* Moretti ends episode one with a long, uninterrupted shot sequence of his pilgrimage *in Vespa* to the site of Pasolini's assassination. This act of homage is rich with personal significance for a filmmaker who traces his own lineage back to the committed cinema of the '60s and '70s.[21] Only in its juxtaposition with the *Henry* sequence, however, does the allusion to Pasolini reveal its full logic. If the defense of splatter films is predicated on the denial of their literal level—on the radical separation between viewer and spectacle and on the interpretive act that protects the intellectual from the personal consequences of the violence represented on screen—then Pasolini's death offers the most powerful of counterarguments: Pasolini was the victim of a splatter film.

As he makes his way *in Vespa* to the poet's assassination site, Moretti's quest for a film language of authenticity is conducted in Pasolinian terms. The camera simply trails Moretti's motor scooter as it courses down a seaside road, turns at what looks like a Pasolinian shanty town simply transplanted to the Idroscalo Ostiense, and circles back to a meadow, where he dismounts and walks to the unmarked monument. The sequence, three and a half minutes long and devoid of dialogue or cuts, represents Moretti's personal "translation" of Pasolini's essay "Osservazioni sul piano seguenza."[22] Inspired by the super-8 "home movie" of Kennedy's assassination, Pasolini argued that life is an infinite shot sequence, filmed from every imaginable camera angle, and that only from the perspective of death can we edit all those reels of biographical footage; to put it in the writer's own words, "La morte compie un fulmineo montaggio della nostra vita" (Death performs a lightning fast editing job on our life).[23] With the extended-shot sequence that leads Moretti to the site, the filmmaker offers his own enactment of Pasolini's ontology of film. Surprisingly, after the lengthy approach to the monument in Vespa, Moretti's camera lingers for only a brief thirty seconds on the object of his pilgrimage; perhaps this is out of disappointment or out of a desire to protect the privacy of the moment; or perhaps it is Moretti's technological approximation of death's final cut.

In response to the antiliteralism of contemporary intellectual discourse, in answer to the impulse to deny the body on screen its referent in a real body that suffers and dies, Moretti invokes Pasolini, victim of a splatter film, proponent of a realism that makes cinema *la lingua scritta della realtà* (the written language of reality).[24] Film, for Pasolini, will never coincide with life: it will always be a writing, a stylized transcription of the real. But he nonetheless insists on the primordial, barbaric truth of the *im-segni* (image signs) that make up its lexicon, giving film an unmediated, pregrammatical realism lacking in the highly codified *lin-segni* (linguistic signs) of verbal texts.[25]

Writing is also the theme of episode two, where Gerardo's journey through the Aeolians is as much literary as geographic. He has spent the last three decades studying Joyce's *Ulysses,* which suggests both the narrative structure of *Caro diario* (an odyssey through modern life) and an implied literary history, extending from its Homeric source to its postmodern corrective in a television series dedicated to tracking down missing persons, *Chi l'ha visto?* "Ulysses toured the Greek islands and no one looked for him," observes Gerardo in his attempt to rationalize his abandonment of high culture for television. "Telemachus didn't look for him, he didn't go around asking."

Just as Gerardo's voyage in "Isole" is meta-literary, Moretti's is meta-cinematic. The filmmaker's journey culminates in the sequence on the rim of the volcano—the setting for Rossellini's *Stromboli* (1949) that signaled the master's definitive break with neorealism and his foray into a new mode of interpersonal and psychological filmmaking. For both Rossellini's heroine and Moretti's protagonist, the ascent of the volcano brings a conversion and a revelation—Karen finally accepts her place in the filmmaker's Christian-humanist vision of the world and Gerardo comes to a recognition of his dependence on television. The smoking crater of the volcano, conduit of oracular truths, for Gerardo provides the most postmodern of prophecies: a glimpse of future plot developments in his favorite soap opera, provided by the sibylline presence of a knowledgeable American tourist.[26] The film's most important postmodern insight, however, comes as the two men leave Stromboli. The mayor sends them off with a description of his plans for regional improvement: he will hire film industry people—Ennio Morricone to compose a soundtrack for the entire island and Vittorio Storaro to oversee the lighting effects. In a Baudrillardian reversal of neorealist practice, island life will be made to simulate cinematic representations of it: the real will be tailored to fit its media image. Taken at its most cynical, the mayor's speech could be read as a postmodern parody of the neorealists' intent to use cinema as a privileged vehicle for national-popular renewal—"to rebuild Italy from scratch," the mayor proclaims. Reality itself will simply be replaced by its audio-visual simulacrum.

In episode three, Moretti uses medical writing as the foil for his own

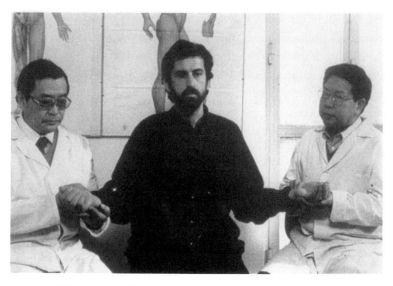

FIGURE 34 | After a long and futile odyssey through Rome's medical establishment, Moretti seeks an alternative approach to cure in *Caro diario*. Courtesy of the Museum of Modern Art/Film Stills Archive.

language of cinematic authenticity. Wandering from doctor to doctor in a vain attempt to find relief from the itching that keeps him awake at night, Moretti accumulates a prodigious number of prescriptions written for him over the course of a single year. These prescriptions serve as a counter diary, a series of entries compiled by the world of doctors, an exhaustive account of the pills, creams, serums, compresses, and emulsions that have come to dictate his daily routine. These medical jottings, though buttressed by all the authoritative terminology of the pharmacopoeia, become the most irrelevant of texts, both in their redundancy (the various doctors only duplicate and reduplicate the ineffectual efforts or their predecessors) and in their referential failure— the disease itself is never addressed (fig. 34).

What underlies the fiasco of this medical writing is, appropriately, a flawed practice of reading. The doctors simply misread Moretti's body —or to be more precise, their reading remains epidermal.[27] The constant itching that had led Moretti to seek medical help in the first place was never interpreted as a signifier of some deeply concealed signified—the disease of Hodgkin's lymphoma—but was treated as a local phenomenon of allergic or psychological origin. It is important to note here that Moretti's satire is not directed at the USL (the Italian national medical system); doctors in private practice, including the hallowed Prince of Dermatologists, are shown to be equally inept. Nor is his satire directed at the medical referral system, which Moretti adroitly circumvents, nor at the level of medical professionalism found in Italy, which is shown to be acceptably sophisticated. Moretti's critique is aimed at the arrogance and parochialism that authoritative discourse confers upon its users, who are thereby led to believe in the infallibility of their cognitive means. Indeed, the only accurate medical writing in the film is radiographic—the X ray and the CAT scan that finally reveal the internal cause of Moretti's symptoms. But even this writing is subject to misreading: the radiologist himself mistakes the tumor for an incurable variant, whereas only surgical removal of the mass reveals its true nature and its amenability to cure.

The quest for a film language of authenticity reaches its climax early in this final episode in a scene so shocking and destablizing that it has disconcerted more than one critic accustomed to the consoling notion that films are, after all, simulations.[28] Depriving us of this comfortable interpretive refuge, Moretti inserts documentary footage of his last chemotherapy session, recorded on super-8 stock that is reminiscent of the grainy and unsophisticated look of the flashback to his first film, *La sconfitta*, spliced into *Palombella rossa*. As a cloth band is tied around Moretti's head and a blue styrofoam cap is placed over the familiar mass of hair, the film-savvy spectator cannot help but think back to the fanciful haberdashery worn by the fictional Michele as the water-polo player in *Palombella rossa,* the penguin of *Sogni d'oro,* or the dapper Proust figure of *Bianca*—making this medically mandated headgear a poignant reminder of the difference between imaginary self-invention and testamentary self-documentation. This is a violent scene, not only because of what we know about the side effects of chemotherapy but also because it signals the breakdown of the sacrosanct critical distinctions between author and narrative persona, between the representing and represented body. I do not mean to conflate the documentary image with its real-life referent, for the filmed footage is still a transcription, a two-dimensional, technologically mediated rendering of the profilmic world. But here Moretti is neither performing nor reenacting—he is experiencing an event in a body whose suffering and mortality become the very theme of this *cinediario*.

Perhaps the most violent consequence of the chemotherapy session is that it augurs the death of Michele.[29] The internalized self-portrait and self-distancing device of the author as Apicella—the fictional identity that enabled Moretti to double and ironize his satiric vision and allowed him to make of his protagonist a generational emblem whose story traversed all the possible paths from 1968 to the present—is destroyed in chemotherapy. Several scenes later, the filmmaker will announce his identity as "Moretti, Giovanni, born 8/19/53 at Brunico, residing in Rome," while one of the doctors fills out his medical chart. No longer performing as his own alias, as *uomo-simbolo* whose body stood for the collective body of the *Ecce bombo* world, Moretti asserts his irreducible identity in the context of near-fatal disease. With the abandonment of his fictional alter ego, Moretti abandons fiction itself in "Medici," insisting that "nothing is invented," based as the episode is on the scores of prescriptions issued by doctors and the notes he took during a year of medical meanderings.

Having presented his brief documentary sequence, Moretti tells the rest of the story in flashback, simulating the rounds of medical visits and providing narrative continuity in voice-over. But we have witnessed the chemotherapy session in newsreel form, and this confers authority and gravity on the subsequent performance. For the body we see on the screen is the same body that went through the ordeal to which we bore documentary witness; the mimetic body carries the traces of the mortal struggle being replayed before us. Like Dante, who had to undergo the experience of Christian death and rebirth in order to be able to tell us his story, Moretti returns from chemotherapy to convey to us the mortal truth of his own particular human condition.

If *Caro diario* is about the quest for an authentic language of film, one that rejects the anti-literalism of contemporary critical jargon and insists on its referent in the world, then Moretti's answer is to return to the body in all its material specificity. His strategy is to represent the body as the single, indivisible unit that underwent chemotherapy—not as the double Michele/Moretti figure that could stand for an entire generation. With the inclusion of this documentary footage that brought together, at the moment of shooting, the representing and represented self, Moretti establishes the gold standard on which the linguistic coinage of his new cinema will be based. It is this body, in all its mortal certainty, that underwrites his quest for a new and distinct language of film, a *cinediario* of personal witness. In the film's final frames, he conveys his lesson to us in a classical Morettian understatement that cuts through all the pretense of authoritative medical jargon to arrive at the commonsense truth that "every morning, before breakfast, it's good to drink a glass of water." As he delivers this bit of homespun wisdom, Moretti looks straight into the camera with a gaze that seals a new pact with his audience, forging a link that is no longer generational, sociopolitical, or meta-cinematic but that implicates us in the most universal of all human struggles.

It should come as no surprise that Moretti's withdrawal from the social sphere would coincide with the end of the postwar order itself—the end of the hopes for national renewal sparked by the Resistance, enshrined in neorealism, and played out in the decades-long vicissitudes of the PCI and, in more acute form, the revolution of '68. With the disappointment of the Resistance promise for renewal came the withering of the social body dedicated to its fulfillment and the consequent waning of the impulse to make film "[the] mirror of the collective themes of national life." Equally significant is the fact that *Caro diario* was released in the very year of Fellini's death. Though by no means a direct commentary on the end of all that the great auteur had come to signify, *Caro diario* is nonetheless epochal in its attempt to forge a new relationship between the language of film and the experience to which it bears witness. As such, Moretti's film offers convincing proof that the contemporary Italian cinema is neither in its death throes nor mired in a condition of "afterness," but that it is poised to enter a season of surprising and life-giving fresh starts.

Appendix: Plot Summaries and Credits

Paisan, 1946

Title in Italian, *Paisà*
Directed by Roberto Rossellini
Produced by Roberto Rossellini, Rod Geiger
Subject by Roberto Rossellini, Sergio Amidei, Klaus Mann, Federico Fellini,
    Marcello Pagliero, Alfred Hayes, Vasco Pratolini
Screenplay by Sergio Amidei, Federico Fellini, Roberto Rossellini
Photography by Otello Martelli
Music by Renzo Rossellini
Edited by Eraldo Da Roma

The Cast:

Episode 1 (Sicily)
Carmela: Carmela Sazio; Joe from Jersey: Robert Van Loon

Episode 2 (Naples)
Joe: Dots M. Johnson; Pasquale: Alfonsino

Episode 3 (Rome)
Fred: Gar Moore; Francesca: Maria Michi

Episode 4 (Florence)
Harriet: Harriet White; Massimo: Renzo Avanzo

Episode 5 (Savignano di Romagna)
Capt. Martin: Bill Tubbs

Episode 6 (Po River)
Dale: Dale Edmonds; Cigolani: Cigolani

SYNOPSIS

Framing Narration: Accompanied by documentary footage, a voice-over commentary announces the Allied landing at Licata, Sicily, on July 10, 1943. Between subsequent episodes, the voice-over narrates the military progress of the liberation campaign until its completion in spring 1945.

Episode 1 (Sicily): A small group of U.S. soldiers arrives in an unnamed town and is mistaken for a German contingent. One intrepid young woman, Carmela, offers to lead the group through the bed of an old lava canal. In a "haunted" watchtower, Carmela is left alone with one of the soldiers, Joe from Jersey, while the others go off to reconnoiter. Drawn together by mutual sympathy, the young couple struggles to communicate; Joe is slain by German gunfire. Carmela avenges his death and is executed by Nazi soldiers, but her sacrifice is misunderstood by the returning GIs, who assume it was she who killed Joe.

Episode 2 (Naples): Joe, a black American MP in a drunken stupor, is "sold" into slavery by enterprising Neapolitan street urchins. One of them, Pasquale, leads Joe on an odyssey through the liberated city; when Joe passes out, Pasquale steals his boots. The boy is later caught by Joe, but the GI refuses to press charges when he sees the squalor of the orphan's living conditions in the teeming caves outside the city.

Episode 3 (Rome): Fred, one of the liberating troops in the Allies' triumphal entrance into Rome, meets Francesca. Six months later he returns to find her. In a drunken state, he is picked up by a prostitute whom he fails to recognize as the Francesca of his previous encounter. She leaves her name and address with him, hoping he will seek her out and she can revert to her earlier, "pre-fallen" self. Cynically, Fred crumples up the address; Francesca is left to wait in the rain.

Episode 4 (Florence): The city is divided in half. The part south of the Arno has been liberated by British troops; the northern part remains under Nazi-Fascist control. Two characters are desperate to cross the river: Massimo yearns to join his family on the other side; Harriet, a Red Cross nurse, longs to reunite with her former lover, who has become the legendary partisan leader Il Lupo. They succeed in crossing the river by passing through the Vasari corridor above the Ponte Vecchio. Massimo reaches his destination; Harriet discovers that Il Lupo has been mortally wounded.

Episode 5 (Savignano di Romagna): A Franciscan monastery in the hills of Romagna hosts three U.S. military chaplains: Captain Martin, a Catholic priest; Captain Jones, a Protestant minister; and Captain Feldman, a rabbi. The monks, scandalized to learn that they have two non-Catholics in their midst, decide to fast so that these lost souls may be redeemed. Their gesture of self-sacrifice is accepted as a gift by Captain Martin, but its meaning is lost on the two clergymen for whom the offering was made. *Episode 6 (Po River)*: Dale, an American officer of the OSS, is stationed with a band of Italian partisans, led by Cigolani, engaging in guerilla activity behind the German lines. Surrounded by Nazis, abandoned by Allied command, and heavily outnumbered, the partisans launch a last-ditch effort against the enemy. After the partisans' inevitable capture, Dale, protected as a prisoner of war, vainly tries to convince a German officer to extend such protection to Cigolani and his men. In protesting the partisans' execution, Dale, too, is slain.

Bellissima, 1951

Directed by Luchino Visconti
Subject by Cesare Zavattini
Screenplay by Suso Cecchi D'Amico, Francesco Rosi, Luchino Visconti
Photography by Piero Portalupi, Paul Ronald
Sets by Gianni Polidori
Costumes by Piero Tosi
Edited by Mario Serandrei
Music by Franco Mannino

The cast:
Maddalena Cecconi: Anna Magnani
Maria: Tina Apicella
Spartaco: Gastone Renzelli
Alberto Annovazzi: Walter Chiari
Alessandro Blasetti: Alessandro Blasetti
Tilde Sperlanzoni: Tecla Scarano
Iris: Liliana Mancini

SYNOPSIS

Dazzled by the myth of the cinema and eager for social mobility, Maddalena Cecconi drags her five-year-old daughter, Maria, to Cinecittà to audition for a part in Alessandro Blasetti's new movie *Oggi, domani, mai.* When Maria is chosen as a finalist, the working-class Maddalena makes tremendous sacrifices to finance the necessary acting lessons, ballet classes, photography sessions, and dressmaker services to give Maria the advantages enjoyed by her economically privileged peers. Her efforts cause strains in her marriage with Spartaco, whose priorities are far more realistic (and domestic) than those of his ambitious, starstruck wife. Maddelena, now a stage-door mother, gets into unsavory dealings with a small-time Cinecittà hustler, Alberto Annovazzi, who accepts Maddalena's bribe and nearly succeeds in seducing her in exchange for advancing Maria's prospects. Hidden in the projection booth during the viewing of Maria's screen test (in which the child does nothing but sob miserably), Maddalena witnesses the derision that Blasetti and his cronies heap upon her daughter's performance. In a fit of maternal outrage, she lambasts the director, accusing him of exploitation and inhumanity. Blasetti takes a second look at Maria's screen test and gives her the part. But Maddalena, by now morally awakened to the human needs of her daughter, steadfastly refuses to sign the contract.

The Last Emperor, 1987

Title in Italian, *L'ultimo imperatore*
Directed by Bernardo Bertolucci
Screenplay by Bertolucci and Mark Peploe, in collaboration with Enzo Ungari
Based on the autobiography of Aisin Gioro Pu Yi
Photography by Vittorio Storaro
Sets by Ferdinando Scarfiotti
Costumes by James Acheson
Edited by Gabriella Cristiani
Music by Ryuichi Sakamoto, David Byrne, Cong Su

The cast:
Pu Yi (age 3): Richard Wu
Pu Yi (age 8): Tiger Tsou
Pu Yi (age 17): Wu Tao
Pu Yi (adult): John Lone
Empress Wan Jung: Joan Chen
Reginald Johnston: Peter O'Toole
Governor of Fushun prison: Ying Roucheng
Amakasu: Ryuichi Sakamoto
Eastern Jewel: Maggie Han

SYNOPSIS

The Last Emperor starts in medias res with Pu Yi's journey to Fushun prison, where he will undergo a program of Communist "reeducation." Inserted into the film's narrative-present is a series of flashbacks that tell the story of Pu Yi's life up to his arrest. In 1908, at the age of three, the protagonist is taken from his mother and installed in the Forbidden City as emperor of the Ching dynasty. When China becomes a republic in 1912, Pu Yi remains ensconced within the protective confines of that world of privilege, shorn of any real political power. Infatuated with Western culture, Pu Yi assumes the tutorial services of a Scotsman, Reginald Johnston, and dreams of fleeing to Oxford. To distract the emperor from his escapist fantasies, at age sixteen he is pushed by the court into an arranged marriage. Some small battles are won—tutor "RJ" insists that his pupil's near-sightedness be corrected with glasses; Pu Yi cuts off his long, braided hair; an inventory of the storerooms is undertaken to control rampant thieving. When the eunuchs respond by setting fire to the storerooms, Pu Yi orders their expulsion from the Forbidden City. In 1924, after another government coup and with troubles raging in China, Pu Yi is forced to leave his palace; he chooses sanctuary with the Japanese embassy in Tiensin and there lives the life of a playboy until, in 1931, the Japanese invade Manchuria, setting up a puppet government headed by Pu Yi. The situation deteriorates and power devolves into the hands of Amakasu, the head of the motion-picture industry. The empress slips into opium addiction, becomes pregnant by her chauffeur, and goes insane after their newborn is killed at the behest of the Japanese. In 1945, Pu Yi is taken prisoner by the Soviets, who hand him over to the Chinese in 1950 for "reconditioning." After ten years in Fushun, he is released and becomes a gardener in Peking. During a parade celebrating Mao's cultural revolution, the prison governor (whose treatment of Pu Yi had been most humane) is held up to public ridicule as an unregenerate intellectual. Pu Yi makes a futile attempt to vindicate his kindly mentor. In the film's final sequence, the protagonist buys a sightseer ticket to visit the Forbidden City. Observed only by a young boy, he playfully mounts the throne again and proves his royal identity to the incredulous boy by retrieving a live cricket from a tiny cage he had hidden in the throne more than half a century before.

Mediterraneo, 1991

Directed by Gabriele Salvatores
Screenplay by Enzo Monteleone
Photography by Italo Petriccione
Sets by Thalia Istikopoulou
Costumes by Francesco Panni
Edited by Nino Baragli

Music by Giancarlo Bigazzi and Marco Falagiani

The cast:
Sergeant Lorusso: Diego Abatantuono
Lieutenant Montini: Claudio Bigagli
Farina: Giuseppe Cederna
Noventa: Claudio Bisio
Strazzabosco: Gigio Alberti
Colasanti: Ugo Conti
Felice Munaron: Memo Dini
Libero Munaron: Vasco Mirandola
Greek Orthodox priest: Luigi Montini
Vassilissa: Vanna Barba
Shepherd girl: Irene Grazioli
Italian aviator: Antonio Catania

SYNOPSIS

In the summer of 1941 a band of eight Italian soldiers is sent to patrol a tiny island in the Greek archipelago. When their ship is blown up and the radio disabled, they are cut off from the outside world. The island, which at first appeared to be deserted, turns out to have a thriving community of women, children, and elderly men (those of fighting age had been deported by the Germans). After a Turkish sailor introduces the Italians to the joys of hashish and absconds with their weapons, the men abandon their military mission altogether and assimilate to the native populace. Enjoying the island's abundant artistic, sexual, and recreational pleasures, each of the characters is able to live out a private wish-fulfillment fantasy. History enters when an Italian aviator lands on the island and informs the men that three eventful years have passed, during which time Mussolini has fallen, and Italy has now switched allegiances. When a British ship arrives to take the group home, one man stays behind with the former prostitute who has become his wife, and two others return later to escape the disappointments of the postwar era.

Pereira Declares, 1995

Title in Italian, *Sostiene Pereira*
Directed by Roberto Faenza
Screenplay by Roberto Faenza, Sergio Vecchio, in collaboration with
  Antonio Tabucchi

Based on the eponymous novel by Antonio Tabucchi (1993)
Sets by Giantito Burchiellaro
Costumes by Elisabetta Beraldo
Music by Ennio Morricone
Edited by Ruggero Mastroianni
Photography by Blasco Giurato

The cast:
Pereira: Marcello Mastroianni
Monteiro Rossi: Stefano Dionisi
Marta: Nicoletta Braschi
Dr. Cardoso: Daniel Auteuil
Manuel: Joaquim De Almeida
Ingeborg Delgado: Marthe Keller
Janitress: Teresa Madruga
Don Antonio: Nicolau Breyner
Editor-in-chief: Mario Viegas

SYNOPSIS

Lisbon, 1938. An aging and lonely journalist, Pereira, has recently been promoted from his paper's news desk to the editorship of the cultural page. In his search for an assistant to prepare obituaries of well-known writers, Pereira stumbles upon Monteiro Rossi, a young man whose love for the politically active Marta has led him into the struggle against Portugal's Salazar dictatorship and, in neighboring Spain, the Franco regime. Pereira, a long-time widower, and childless, takes a parental interest in the young couple, hires Rossi, and obligingly concedes to the young man's constant requests for monetary advances. After a brief stay in a spa, where he is disgusted by the cynical collaborationist position of his friend Silva, a university professor, Pereira returns to the city and agrees to help hide Monteiro Rossi's cousin Bruno, a political activist in trouble with Salazarist police. Advised to undertake a rest cure, Pereira meets the wise and politically progressive Dr. Cardoso, who ministers to the needs of both his patient's body and mind. Emboldened to translate and publish a short story by Alphonse Daudet, whose anti-German message will not sit well with the Salazarists, Pereira is called in by his editor and reprimanded for violating censorship laws. When Monteiro Rossi, who has sought refuge in Pereira's apartment, is tortured and killed by Salazarist police, the aged journalist is moved to action. He writes an obituary for the young man that denounces the regime for his murder, then tricks his paper's head printer into getting the piece published. As the newspaper hits the stands, Pereira heads for exile, armed with a false passport left in his safekeeping by the man whose death he has just avenged.

Three Brothers, 1981

Title in Italian, *Tre fratelli*
Directed by Francesco Rosi
Subject based on "The Third Son," by Andrei Platonov
Screenplay by Francesco Rosi, Tonino Guerra
Director of photography, Pasqualino De Santis
Set design by Andrea Crisanti
Costumes by Gabriella Pescucci
Special effects by Renato Agostini
Music by Piero Piccioni
Edited by Ruggero Mastroianni
Produced by Giorgio Nocella, Antonio Macrì

The cast:
Raffaele: Philippe Noiret
Rocco: Vittorio Mezzogiorno
Nicola: Michele Placido
The young Donato: Vittorio Mezzogiorno
The elderly Donato: Charles Vanel
Wife of Raffaele: Andrea Ferréol
Giovanna: Maddalena Crippa
Rosaria: Sara Tafuri
Marta: Marta Zoffoli
The young Caterina: Simonetta Stefanelli
The elderly Caterina: Gina Pontrelli
Son of Raffaele: Cosimo Milone

SYNOPSIS

It is the eve of the funeral of Caterina Giuranna, wife of Donato and mother of three sons. The sons have left their birthplace in the Murge area of Apulia for urban centers that represent the diversity and complexity of the Italian national situation on the threshold of the 1980s. One is Raffaele, a judge in Rome who is anxious about his assignment to a terrorist trial; another is Rocco, a social worker in Naples grappling with the problem of juvenile neglect; the third is Nicola, a factory worker in Turin who is involved in militant union activism against management. All three brothers are troubled by family and personal problems that arise from, or reflect significantly on, their professional lives. Raffaele's high-profile and dangerous position has caused deep tensions in his relationships with his wife and son; Rocco's selfless commitment to alleviating social ills has resulted in his inability to establish a family of his own; Nicola's confusion of identity as a transplanted southerner has spilled over into his domestic life, estranging him from his wife, Giovanna, and disrupting the childhood of their daughter, Marta. The return of the brothers to their ancestral home for the funeral becomes an occasion for them all to take stock of their personal and professional situations. It also offers Rosi the opportunity to take the pulse of the body politic in the midst of the tumultuous *anni di piombo* (years of lead).

La scorta, 1993

Directed by Ricky Tognazzi
Screenplay by Graziano Diana, Simona Izzo
Music by Ennio Morricone
Photography by Alessio Gelsini
Edited by Carla Simoncelli
Production designs by Mariangela Capuano
Costumes by Catia Dottori
Produced by Claudio Bonivento

The cast:
Michele De Francesco: Carlo Cecchi
Angelo Mandolesi: Claudio Amendola
Andrea Corsale: Enrico Lo Verso
Fabio Muzzi: Ricky Memphis
Raffaele Frasca: Tony Sperandeo
Polizzi: Leo Gullotta
Luigi Barresi: Angelo Infanti
Caruso: Benedetto Ranelli

SYNOPSIS

The film is set in Trapani in the wake of the assassinations of Judge Rizzo and Marshal Pietro Virzì. Carabiniere Angelo Mandolesi, a protégé of Virzì, vows to avenge the death of his mentor and asks to be transferred from his post in Rome to return to his native Trapani. There he is assigned to the escort *(la scorta)* of Judge Michele De Francesco, who has been appointed to take Rizzo's place. Included in the escort are Andrea Corsale, Fabio Muzzi, and Raffaele Frasca. When De Francesco begins to investigate criminal links between the building of a public dam that yields no water and the high prices charged by owners of private wells, his boss, Salvatore Caruso, takes him off the case. De Francesco has gotten dangerously close to exposing the hand of Mafia Don Giuseppe Mazzaglia. To increase De Francesco's isolation in pursing the matter, his friend and fellow magistrate Luigi Barresi refuses to consider possible connections between the murder of Rizzo, who was investigating the wells, and Mafia interest in keeping water prices high. Conflict arises between Mandolesi and Corsale, who has been secretly reporting De Francesco's activities to his boss. Corsale confesses to De Francesco, is pardoned, and reconciles with Mandolesi. De Francesco and his guards vow to continue the investigation in defiance of the boss's orders to stop and Mafia threats to their safety. Frasca is killed by a car bomb that was intended for De Francesco's daughter Roberta. De Francesco is ordered to move into an underground bunker, where he and his guards generate warrants for the arrest of a number of suspect officials. Nino Carabba, one of the men hired to kill Rizzo and Virzì, turns state evidence, naming Mazzaglia as the criminal mastermind operating behind the political cover of Senator Nestore Bonura. When Bonura and his bodyguard Marchetti are assassinated, De Francesco is transferred to the mainland and his guards are assigned to innocuous posts in other locations.

Stolen Children, 1992

Title in Italian, *Il ladro di bambini*
Directed by Gianni Amelio
Subject and screenplay by Gianni Amelio, Sandro Petraglia, Stefano Rulli
Sets by Andrea Crisanti
Costumes by Gianna Gissi, Luciana Morosetti
Music by Franco Piersanti
Edited by Simona Paggi
Photography by Tonino Nardi, Renato Tafuri

The cast:
Rosetta Scavello: Valentina Scalici
Luciano Scavello: Giuseppe Ieracitano

Antonio Criaco: Enrico Lo Verso
Antonio's sister: Vitalba Andrea
Commissioner: Renato Carpentieri
Martine: Florence Darel
Nathalie: Marina Golovine

SYNOPSIS

A Sicilian immigrant in Milan, abandoned by her husband, has forced her eleven-year-old daughter Rosetta into prostitution. On an insider tip (perhaps from nine-year-old brother Luciano), the household is raided by police. The mother is arrested and the children are taken into custody by two carabinieri who are to escort them to an orphanage in Civitavecchia. One of the carabinieri slips away to see his girl-friend, leaving his colleague Antonio Criaco to complete the mission. Because of Rosetta's past, however, the children are turned away from the orphanage to which they were assigned. Unwilling to contact headquarters for fear of getting his colleague in trouble, Antonio is forced to take full responsibility for the children, having to decide on his own where to take them. In Rome, Luciano has a severe asthma attack, requiring a temporary suspension of activity. Antonio takes the children to the apartment of a colleague in the city, and there Rosetta withdraws from an un-savory conversation with another carabiniere. After a painful quarrel between Rosetta and Antonio in a ladies' room in the station at Roma Ostiense, the trio takes the train to Reggio Calabria, where Antonio's sister runs a restaurant. There they join in the luncheon for the families of children celebrating their first Communion, until a vicious and hypocritical woman, Signora Papaleo, recognizes Rosetta and exposes her to public humiliation. The journey continues by car to Sicily, where the trio enjoys a euphoric afternoon by the sea and is joined by two French tourists. In Noto, the next stop on the journey, a camera thief is caught by the carabiniere and the group ends up in police headquarters. Antonio is reprimanded for helping the children on his own initiative, and the film ends just before the carabiniere delivers Rosetta and Luciano to their designated orphanage somewhere in Sicily.

Ginger and Fred, 1985

Directed by Federico Fellini
Screenplay by Federico Fellini, Tonino Guerra, Tullio Pinelli
Photography by Tonino Delli Colli, Ennio Guarnieri

Music by Nicola Piovani
Sets by Dante Ferretti
Costumes by Danilo Donati
Edited by Nino Baragli, Ugo De Rossi, Ruggero Mastroianni
Choreography by Tony Ventura

The cast:
Amelia Bonetti: Giulietta Masina
Pippo Botticella: Marcello Mastroianni
Aurelio: Franco Fabrizi
Transvestite: Augusto Poderosi
Admiral: Frederick Ledenburg
Assistant director: Martin Maria Blau
Flying friar: Jacques Henri Lartigue
Toto: Toto Mignone

SYNOPSIS

Amelia Bonetti and Pippo Botticella, former lovers and tap-dancing partners on the vaudeville stages of the 1940s and 1950s, are brought back together after many years to appear on a special Christmas installment of a TV show, *We Are Proud to Present*. Since they parted, Amelia had lived the staid life of a merchant's wife, while Pippo had suffered a nervous breakdown, followed by serial love affairs, career disappointments, and a struggle with alcoholism. The film follows the two through the twenty-four hours between their arrival in Rome and their climactic television appearance, providing a harrowing behind-the-scenes view of the hastily assembled, barely rehearsed, carnivalesque workings of televisual spectacle. The aged vaudeville couple, though completely unprepared for their performance, manage to pull it off with only a few minor missteps, but the expected romantic rapprochement does not occur. Their onstage rediscovery of the past and the symbolic reliving of their affair through dance does not carry over to life beyond the theater. The former lovers part, unable to bridge the gap of their loneliness and their lifelong failure of communication.

Cinema Paradiso, 1988

Title in Italian, *Nuovo cinema paradiso*
Directed by Giuseppe Tornatore
Subject and screenplay by Giuseppe Tornatore

Photography by Blasco Giurato

Music by Ennio Morricone, Andrea Morricone

Sets by Andrea Crisanti

Costumes by Beatrice Bordone

Edited by Mario Morra

Produced by Franco Cristaldi

The cast:

Salvatore Di Vita as a child: Salvatore Cascio

Salvatore Di Vita as an adolescent: Marco Leonardi

Salvatore Di Vita as an adult: Jacques Perrin

Maria (mother) as a young woman: Antonella Attili

Maria as an elderly woman: Pupella Maggio

Elena: Agnese Nano

Alfredo: Philippe Noiret

Anna (wife of Alfredo): Isa Danieli

Father Adelfio: Leopoldo Trieste

SYNOPSIS

The film chronicles three stages in the life of Salvatore Di Vita (nicknamed Totò): his grade-school years in the immediate postwar period; his late adolescence in the 1950s; and his midlife career as a successful filmmaker in the 1980s. Much of *Cinema Paradiso* is presented in flashback when the middle-aged Salvatore, living and working in Rome, learns that the projectionist of the old movie theater in his hometown of Giancaldo, Sicily, has just died. This news triggers Salvatore's return in memory to his boyhood in the town, where social life was organized around the parish church and, more importantly, its adjoining movie house. The parish is controlled by Father Adelfio, the priest who rigorously censors the films shown, taking out all love scenes deemed dangerous to public morality. Totò, son of Maria, a war widow whose husband was killed on the Russian front, conceives an early and transgressive love for the cinema and manages to insinuate himself into the projection booth by helping the illiterate Alfredo to pass his elementary-school equivalency test. Alfredo becomes the boy's surrogate father, mentor, teacher, and closest friend. When a fire destroys the old Cinema Paradiso, it is Totò who saves Alfredo and, because the old man is now blinded, takes over the job as projectionist of the rebuilt theater, the Nuovo Cinema Paradiso.

The film's second part is dedicated to Salvatore's romance with Elena, daughter of a wealthy banker who does not approve of their attachment. When Elena fails to show up for an appointment, Salvatore fears that the relationship is over. During his stint in the army, Elena's failure to answer his letters convinces Salvatore that he must give her up. Alfredo encourages his protégé to leave Sicily and pursue a career in Rome—advice that the young man reluctantly decides to follow.

In the film's third segment, the middle-aged Salvatore returns to Giancaldo for Alfredo's funeral, witnesses the demolition of the Nuovo Cinema Paradiso to make way for a parking lot, and receives Alfredo's posthumous gift to him—a reel of film. Upon returning to Rome, he screens the reel to find a montage of all the kisses edited out of the movies shown at the Cinema Paradiso.

The Icicle Thief, 1989

Title in Italian, *Ladri di saponette*
Directed by Maurizio Nichetti
Screenplay by Mauro Monti, Maurizio Nichetti
Sets by Ada Legori
Costumes by Mario Pia Angelini
Photography by Mario Battistoni
Music by Manuel De Sica
Edited by Rita Rossi, Anna Missoni

The cast:
Maurizio Nichetti: Played by himself
Antonio Piermattei: Maurizio Nichetti
Maria Caterina: Sylos Labini
Bruno: Federico Rizzo
Don Italo: Renato Scarpa
Heidi the model: Heidi Komarek

SYNOPSIS

The film begins in a television studio in Milan, where preparations are under way for the transmission of a black-and-white film made in homage to neorealism by an unknown director named Maurizio Nichetti. According to the plot summary that introduces the telecast, the film is to chronicle the misfortunes of Antonio Piermattei, his wife, Maria, and their sons, Bruno and Paolo, in the immediate aftermath of World War II; the unemployed father is to get a job in a chandelier factory but he will be paralyzed in a traffic accident, forcing his wife into prostitution and his sons to be consigned to an orphanage. This plot is sidetracked, however, due to a power failure in the TV studio that causes a commercial to spill over into the world of the inner film. When Heidi, a tall, blonde, scantily clad model, is catapulted from her Technicolored advertisement into the Piermatteis' black-and-white subsistence apartment, she manages to wreak havoc on the neorealist characters' family life. Convinced that her husband is having an affair with Heidi, Maria commits suicide; Antonio is accused of murder. The filmmaker, present in the studio as his film is mutilated by commercial intrusion, decides to enter into the neorealist world and try to get his plot back in order. As the film becomes more and more corrupted by televisual interference, a middle-class family of spectators remains unfazed. At the conclusion, the director manages to coax the characters of the film back into the impoverished 1940s setting of the original script with bribes of consumer goods from the prosperous 1980s. Trapped inside the TV screen, the desperate Nichetti appeals in vain to the viewing mother to free him from his imprisonment in the film's final frames.

To Die for Tano, 1997

Title in Italian, *Tano da morire*
Directed by Roberta Torre
Screenplay by Roberta Torre, Gianluca Sodaro, Enzo Paglino
Photography by Daniele Ciprì
Edited by Giogiò Franchini
Music by Nino D'Angelo
Sound by Glauco Puletti, Mauro Lazzaro
Choreography by Filippo Scuderi
Sets by Claudio Russo, Fabrizio Lupo
Costumes by Antonella Cannarozzi

The cast:
Tano Guarrasi: Ciccio Guarino
Narrator: Enzo Paglino
Tano's sisters:
    Franca: Mimma De Rosalia
    Caterina: Maria Aliotta
    Modesta: Anna Confalone
    Rosa: Adele Aliotta

Don Paliddu Billizza: Vincenzo Di Lorenzo
Salvo Lo Cicero: Lorenzo La Rosa
Anna (Tano's daughter): Francesca Di Cesare
Rapper: Filippo Teriaca
Widow Puglisi: Eleonora Teriaca

SYNOPSIS

On October 20, 1988, Mafia boss Gaetano (Tano) Guarrasi is gunned down in his butcher shop in the Vucciria, the vast and colorful food market of Palermo. The killer is a young man who has feigned a romantic interest in Anna, Guarrasi's over-protected daughter. The false suitor has used the young woman to gain access to the shop in order to carry out the crime. Flattered by the young man's attentions, Anna does not tell her father about her admirer, thus reducing Tano's chances of defending himself. Tano has also overprotected his four sisters, Franca, Caterina, Modesta, and Rosa, and his death is a liberation for them. They are now free to marry, and Franca is the first to take the opportunity. The wedding takes place two years after the death of Tano, but on that very occasion Franca is killed in what official reports call a Mafia vendetta. Local folk wisdom interprets the event otherwise, however: according to the narrator, spokesman for public opinion, the jealous brother has come back to claim his sister and to inveigh against the hypocrisy and ineptitude of those he left behind.

The Truce, 1997

Title in Italian, *La tregua*
Directed by Francesco Rosi
Based on the book by Primo Levi (1963)
Cinematic adaptation by Francesco Rosi, Tonino Guerra
Screenplay by Francesco Rosi, Stefano Rulli, Sandro Petraglia
Photography by Pasqualino De Santis, Marco Pontecorvo
Edited by Ruggero Mastroianni
Sets by Andrea Crisanti
Costumes by Alberto Verso
Music by Luis Bacalov

The cast:
Primo Levi: John Turturro
Cesare: Massimo Ghini

The Greek: Rade Serbedzija
Col. Rovi: Teco Celio
Unverdorben: Roberto Citran
Ferrari: Claudio Bisio
D'Agata: Andy Luotto
Galina: Agnieszka Wagner
Daniele: Stefano Dionisi
Flora: Lorenza Indovina
Marja Fiodorovna: Maryna Gerasymenko
Egorov: Igor Bezgin

SYNOPSIS

It is January 1945. Russian troops have just liberated Auschwitz. What Primo believes will be a brief and smooth journey from Poland to his home in Turin becomes a lengthy, convoluted odyssey through the Ukraine, Romania, Hungary, Austria, and Germany, and it takes more than nine months for him to arrive at his longed-for destination. His experiences amid the masses of other displaced persons floating about the war-ravaged landscapes provide a portrait of Europe in the throes of post-Nazi communal rebirth. Primo encounters vastly varied examples of humanity, including a Greek merchant who offers him lessons in survival and a lovely Russian nurse, Galina, with whom he becomes infatuated. But his most important relationships are with the motley group of returning Italian refugees—a microcosm of the homeland he so urgently seeks to reach. This is also very much a journey back to life for Primo, who comes to a progressively greater consciousness of both the pleasures of human concourse and the moral outrage of what he has suffered. At film's end, Primo's joyous reentry to his home is followed by the pain of having to bear witness to his ordeal through writing.

Life Is Beautiful, 1997

Title in Italian, *La vita è bella*
Directed by Roberto Benigni
Subject and screenplay by Roberto Benigni, Vincenzo Cerami
Photography by Tonino Delli Colli
Edited by Simona Paggi
Music by Nicola Piovani
Sets and costumes by Danilo Donati

The cast:
Guido Orefice: Roberto Benigni
Dora: Nicoletta Braschi
Giosuè: Giorgio Cantarini
Guido's uncle: Giustino Durano
Ferruccio: Sergio Bustric
Dr. Lessing: Horst Buchholz
Rodolfo: Americo Fontani

SYNOPSIS

It is 1939, and two exuberant country boys, Guido Orefice and his friend and aspiring writer Ferruccio, are on their way to the "big city" of Arezzo, where they
are about to relocate. Guido's dream is to open a bookstore; Ferruccio's is to become a published poet. On the way, they stop to fix a flat tire and chance to meet
Dora, who in trying to escape from a swarm of wasps falls from a window into
Guido's arms. In Arezzo, where Guido works as a waiter in the Grand Hotel under
the auspices of his uncle, a number of encounters with Dora occur, both by chance
and by the young man's design. Unhappily betrothed to Fascist party official
Rodolfo, Dora gladly lets Guido carry her away from her engagement party at the
Grand Hotel.

The second part of the film opens in 1944. Guido and Dora have a son, Giosuè. Guido is Jewish, and on Giosuè's fifth birthday Guido and the boy are carried
off for deportation. Dora joins them as the train pulls away and the family is trans-
ported to Auschwitz, along with the uncle, who is immediately sent to the gas
chambers. Guido keeps Giosuè's spirits up with the fiction that the concentration
camp experience is an elaborate game whose prize is an army tank, winnable by
the first contestant to earn one thousand points. Dora's morale is boosted several
times when Guido is able to send her messages of hope over the loudspeaker of the
camp. As the war ends, Giosuè emerges unscathed to behold the entrance of an
American tank into the camp; Dora, too, is alive. Although Guido has been killed
during the final camp evacuation, mother and son are reunited to proclaim the victory of Guido's strategy for their survival.

Caro diario, 1993

Directed by Nanni Moretti
Screenplay by Nanni Moretti

Photography by Giuseppe Lanci

Edited by Mirco Garrone

Sets by Marta Maffucci

Costumes by Maria Rita Barbera

Music by Nicola Piovani

The cast:

Nanni Moretti: Played by himself

Gerardo: Renato Carpentieri

Mayor of Stromboli: Antonio Neiwiller

First couple on Stromboli: Raffaella Lebboroni, Marco Paolini

Second couple: Claudia Della Seta, Lorenzo Alessandri

Jennifer Beals: Played by herself

Carlo Mazzacurati: Played by himself

First dermatologist: Valerio Magrelli

Second dermatologist: Sergio Lambiase

Substitute for Prince of Dermatologists: Gianni Ferraretto

Prince of dermatologists: Mario Schiano

Next dermatologist: Roberto Nobile

Reflexologist: Serena Nono

Chinese doctors: Yu Ming Lun, Tou Yui Chang Pio

SYNOPSIS

1. *"In Vespa"*: It is August and Moretti is cruising on his motor scooter through the abandoned streets of residential neighborhoods outside the center of Rome. During this fluid and picaresque sequence, narrated in voice-over by Moretti, the protagonist goes to the movies, watches a group of merengue dancers, assaults various passers-by with eccentric questions, harasses the writer of a positive review of the splatter film *Henry: Portrait of a Serial Killer,* and pays homage to the neglected monument to Pasolini at the Idroscala (seaplane basin) of Ostia.

2. *"Isole"*: Moretti travels to the Aeolian islands off the coast of Sicily in search of peace and quiet for the writing of his next screenplay. His host on the island of Lipari is Gerardo, who prides himself on having abstained from watching television for thirty years. Chased away from Lipari by the crowding and traffic, the two men embark on an odyssey throughout the archipelago, rejecting each island they visit as unconducive to their artistic and intellectual pursuits. In the process, however, Gerardo suffers toxic exposure to television; he becomes an incurable addict of soap operas.

3. "Medici": Afflicted with intolerable itching for many months, Moretti visits a series of dermatologists; they write out endless prescriptions for pills, balms, and shampoos that do nothing to relieve his symptoms. He turns to allergists, to New Age therapies, and finally to practitioners of oriental medicine, and the latter stumble on the true cause of Moretti's malaise—a tumor, which fortunately is amenable to cure.

Notes

Introduction

1. Daniel Singer, "Gatt and the Shape of Our Dreams," *Nation,* 17 Jan. 1994, 54. Fellini died on 31 Oct. 1993.
2. Clive James, "Mondo Fellini," *New Yorker,* 21 Mar. 1994, 164, and Alan Cowell, "Thousands of Italian Mourners File in Homage Past Fellini Bier," *New York Times,* 3 Nov. 1993, C22.
3. Tullio Kezich, *Fellini* (Milan: Rizzoli, 1988), 534. Unless otherwise noted, all translations from Italian sources are my own.
4. For the most eloquent and persuasive condemnation of '80s film production, see Lino Miccichè's much-cited "Gli eredi del nulla: Per una critica del giovane cinema italiano," in *Una generazione in cinema: Esordi ed esordienti italiani, 1975–88,* ed. Franco Montini (Venice: Marsilio, 1988), 251–58.
5. In the five-year period from 1970 to 1975, Italian films tallied 331 million tickets per year; the 1992 to 1996 period saw sales dwindle to 20.4 million per year. See Lino Miccichè, "Il lungo decennio grigio," in *Schermi opachi: Il cinema italiano degli anni '80,* ed. Lino Miccichè (Venice: Marsilio, 1998), 5.
6. The decision for the *libertà di antenna* was handed down by the Corte Costituzionale in the summer of 1976. See Miccichè, "Il lungo decennio grigio," 5. For the term *cine-disastro,* see ibid., 15, and for *cinecidio,* see 5.
7. Claudio Fava and Aldo Viganò, *I film di Federico Fellini* (Rome: Gremese, 1991), 174-75.
8. Giorgio Gosetti, "For an Italian Cinema of the '90s," in *Rai 2 Italy: The Other Cinema* (N.p: n.d.), 12.
9. Fabio Bo, "Dieci anni di solitudine: Dall'autobiografismo alla 'desistenza' narrativa," in *La "scuola" italiana: Storia, strutture, e immaginario di un altro cinema, 1988–96,* ed. Mario Sesti (Venice: Marsilio, 1996), 26.
10. Gosetti, "Italian Cinema of the '90s," 12-13.
11. Gian Piero Brunetta, "Il cinema italiano oggi," *Annali d'italianistica* 17 (1999) (*New Landscapes in Contemporary Italian Cinema* issue, ed. Gaetana Marrone): 18. Concurring is Felice Laudadio, president of Cinecittà Holding: "It [television] lowers the level of all films and flattens the imagination of filmmakers and audiences." See Alessandra Stanley, "So Few Fellinis," *New York Times,* 25 May 2000, B10.

12. Sandro Bernardi, "Una generazione suicidata: Sintomi del disagio e segnali per una rinascita," in *In nome del cinema: Quaderni del Ponte,* ed. Vito Zagarrio (Milan: Il Ponte, 1999), 148.

13. See Antonio Vitti, "Il cinema italiano alle soglie del duemila: Grande vitalità, poca esportazione e sprazzi di genialità: Una introduzione," *American Journal of Italian Studies* 22 (1999): 4. For commentary on the effects of rampant television consumption on Italian media culture, see Marcia Landy, *Italian Film* (Cambridge: Cambridge UP, 2000), 366–67.

14. Ibid. See also Manuela Gieri, "Landscapes of Oblivion and Historical Memory in the New Italian Cinema," *Annali d'italianistica* 17 (1999): 44.

15. Brunetta, "Il cinema italiano oggi," 18–19.

16. See Peter Bondanella, "Stolen Children," *Cineaste* 20 (1994): 38; Gosetti, "Italian Cinema of the '90s," 14; and Scola interview, in Aldo Tassone, *Parla il cinema italiano II* (Milan: Il Formichiere, 1980), 313.

17. *Webster's New World Dictionary: College Edition,* 1962; s.v. "Simulation."

18. Jean Baudrillard, *Simulations,* trans. Paul Foss, Paul Patton, and Philip Beitchman (New York: Semiotext(e), 1983), 4, 10.

19. Fredric Jameson, *Postmodernism, or, The Cultural Logic of Late Capitalism* (Durham, N.C.: Duke UP, 1991), 12.

20. See *Nuovo cinema italiano: Gli autori, i film, le idee* (Rome: Theoria, 1994), 9, 17, 12.

21. See Gianni Canova, "La commedia e il suo doppio," in *La "scuola" italiana,* 51.

22. Miccichè, "Il lungo decennio grigio," 13.

23. On the need for cinema to open itself to new technologies, see Paolo D'Agostini, "Un altro cinema: Voci e segnali del nuovo," in *La "scuola" italiana,* 43.

24. See Brunetta, "Il cinema italiano oggi," 30, and Vitti, "Il cinema italiano alle soglie del duemila," 3.

25. See the synthesis of Bruno Torri's findings in Vito Zagarrio, *Cinema italiano anni novanta* (Venice: Marsilio, 1998), 28.

26. Dissident voices include those of Mario Sesti, *Il nuovo cinema italiano: Gli autori, i film, le idee* (Rome: Theoria, 1994), and his various contributions to *La "scuola" italiana;* Gaetana Marrone, "Il nuovo cinema italiano: Pregiudizi, realtà e promesse," *Annali d'italianistica* 17 (1999): 7–14; Vitti, "Il cinema italiano alle soglie del duemila," 1–10; and Zagarrio, *Cinema italiano anni novanta.*

27. Sesti, *Il nuovo cinema italiano,* 13.

28. To do so, according to Marrone, "it is the function of the critic to venture into and participate in the mysterious process of invention." See "Il nuovo cinema italiano: Pregiudizi, realtà e promesse," 10.

29. Such a plea occurs in all of Sesti's writings on recent Italian cinema. See esp. "Tamburi lontani," in *La "scuola" italiana,* 66–67. See also Vito Zagarrio, "Elogio del cinema italiano," *Vivilcinema* 3 (May–June 2000): 9.

30. Ibid.

31. Mario Sesti, "Il nuovo cinema: Altre avventure," in *La "scuola" italiana,* 15–16.

32. This has been the subject of extensive critical comment. See, for example, Vitti, "Il cinema italiano alle soglie del duemila," 9, and Sesti's observations reported in Zagarrio, *Cinema italiano anni novanta,* 160.

33. See Vito Zagarrio et al., "Per un cinema-cinema," *Cinecritica* 11 (Jan.–June, 1988): 129. Further references to the manifesto can be found on this page of *Cinecritica.*

34. For a lively survey of the entire panorama of the Italian cinema of this period, see Zagarrio's *Cinema italiano anni novanta*, which despite the title dedicates generous coverage to the decade of the '80s.
35. See Sesti's introduction, xi, to *La "scuola" italiana*.
36. A videography is provided at the back of this volume.

Chapter 1. Roberto Rossellini's *Paisan*

For the screenplay of *Paisan*, see Roberto Rossellini, *The War Trilogy*, trans. Judith Green (New York, Grossman, 1973). Quotes from the screenplay are from this edition; page-number references are given in the text. For an account of the suppressed episodes and alterations from the original subject for *Paisan*, see Peter Bondanella, *The Films of Roberto Rossellini* (New York: Cambridge UP, 1993), 64–65, and P. Adams Sitney, *Vital Crises in Italian Cinema* (Austin: U of Texas P, 1995), 54–55.

1. André Bazin considers *Paisan* to be the highest achievement of neorealism. "We will arrange, by implication, the major Italian films in concentric circles of decreasing interest around *Paisan*, since it is this film of Rossellini that yields the most aesthetic secrets." See *What Is Cinema?* II, trans. Hugh Gray (Berkeley: U of California P, 1972), 30. Peter Bondanella sees *Paisan* as more groundbreaking than *Open City*, constituting a greater departure from the canons of Hollywood melodrama, and therefore coming closer to the orthodox definition of neorealism. See *Films of Roberto Rossellini*, 65–66.
2. It was Gramsci's belief that Risorgimento history in particular, and Italian history in general, is predicated on the myth that Italy has forever been a unified nation, and that foreign forces have simply suppressed the political manifestations of that unity. See *Il risorgimento* (Turin: Einaudi, 1952), 44.
3. See Peter Brunette, *Roberto Rossellini* (New York: Oxford UP, 1987), 62.
4. On the association between voice-over narration and "a position of superior knowledge . . . which superimposes itself 'on top' of the diegesis," see Kaja Silverman, *The Acoustic Mirror: The Female Voice in Psychoanalysis and Cinema* (Bloomington: Indiana UP, 1988), 48–49 ff.
5. As Roy Armes puts it, the six episodes provide a "kaleidoscope of incident" and "cover a wide range of mood from warm humor to bitter pessimism." See *Patterns of Realism* (London: Tantivy, 1971), 81. On the distinctness of each episode, see ibid., 76. See also Leo Braudy, "Rossellini: From *Open City* to *General della Rovere*," in *Great Film Directors*, ed. Leo Braudy and Morris Dickstein (New York: Oxford UP, 1978), 662. Similarly, Gianni Rondolino calls *Paisan* a "choral film," in *Roberto Rossellini* (Florence: La Nuova Italia, 1977), 58, as does Rossellini himself, in Carlo Lizzani, *Storia del cinema italiano, 1895–1961*, appendix, ed. Mino Argentieri and Giovanni Vento (Florence: Parenti, 1961), 436.
6. For an eloquent discussion of the ideological implications of the episode format, see Leo Braudy, "Rossellini: From *Open City* to *General Della Rovere*, 663 ff. On the link between the film's formal and ideological pluralism, see Gian Piero Brunetta, *Storia del cinema italiano dal 1945 agli anni ottanta* (Rome: Riuniti, 1982), 373.
7. This is the theme that recurs throughout Peter Brunette's excellent study of the relationship between *Paisan* and its national referent.

8. Geoffrey Nowell-Smith offers an excellent formulation of the codes of continuity editing. I quote it at length:

In Hollywood films, which have provided a conscious or unconscious model for filmmakers all over the world, the editing and matching of shots is carried out according to a set of rigidly codified norms which govern the matching of action proper and the angles and distances from which successive shots can be taken. The cumulative effect of these norms is to ensure a homogeneity of narrated action in time and space. The editing both relates the different parts of the action together and places the spectator in relation to it in such a way that (for the most part) the relationships thus established remain unquestioned for the duration of the film. Although the camera's physical vantage point is constantly changing, the transitions are carried out in a way that makes them so "natural" and so readily comprehensible as to pass unnoticed.

See G. Nowell-Smith, "Pasolini's Originality," in *Pier Paolo Pasolini,* ed. Paul Willemen (London: British Film Institute, 1977), 9.

9. Alexandra Wettlaufer, "Ruskin and Laforgue: Visual-Verbal Dialectics and the Poetics/Politics of Montage," *Comparative Literature Studies* 32 (1995): 515-16.

10. See, for example, V. I. Pudovkin, "Film Technique," in *Film: An Anthology,* ed. Daniel Talbot (Berkeley: U of California P, 1972), 190-93.

11. Gianni Rondolino, *Rossellini* (Florence: La Nuova Italia, 1977), 59. See also Rossellini's comments in *La table ronde* 149 (May 1960): 75.

12. See Brunette, *Roberto Rossellini,* 70. A number of critics have commented on the way this strategy precludes traditional dynamics of viewer identification. See ibid., 71, and Vernon Jarratt, *The Italian Cinema* (London: Falcon Press, 1951), 63. Bondanella considers this to be Rossellini's most powerful anti-Hollywood strategy. See *Films of Roberto Rossellini,* 81.

13. Robert Warshow eloquently formulates the implications of the film's pacing in *The Immediate Experience* (New York: Atheneum, 1974), 253-54. Mira Liehm, on the other hand, argues that "*Paisan* is explicitly and implicitly suffused with the theme of waiting." For her eloquent survey of this theme throughout the film's compilation of episodes, see *Passion and Defiance: Film in Italy from 1942 to the Present* (Berkeley: U of California P, 1984), 68.

14. Accordingly, Bondanella calls attention to Rossellini's "hybrid technique" in *Paisan*—his blend of documentary and simulation, of trained and nonprofessional actors, of on-location and studio sets, and so forth. See *Films of Roberto Rossellini,* 66-67. Leo Braudy relates the heterogeneity of *Paisan* to the notion of collage: "The presentation of settings and characters so juxtaposed as to give the spectator a sense of the wholeness of the world he is watching at the same time that he is keenly aware of its variety and disjunctures." See "Rossellini: From *Open City* to *General della Rovere,*" 657.

15. According to Armes, Rossellini's operation in *Paisan* is to present "war scaled down to a purely personal level." *Patterns of Realism,* 80.

16. On Rossellini's dedramatization of the landing, see ibid., 76. See also Armes's comments in *Film and Reality* (Harmondsworth, U.K.: Penguin, 1974), 67. On the ironic contrast between macro and micro levels of narration within the

film, see Angela Dalle Vacche, *The Body in the Mirror* (Princeton: Princeton UP, 1992), 215. Brunette comments on the strategy of juxtaposing documentary footage with fiction as a way of exposing the constructedness of realist filmmaking. See *Roberto Rossellini*, 71–73.

17. To account for the cave-like setting of this interaction, Brunette advances the intriguing hypothesis that Carmela and Joe's bond is less romantic than primeval, reverting to "some primitive ritual of connection—as though human history were beginning all over again." See *Roberto Rossellini*, 65.

18. On the reductiveness of Carmela's initial view of foreigners, which will be reflected later in Fred's reductive view of Roman women, see Bondanella, *Films of Roberto Rossellini*, 74.

19. P. Adams Sitney, *Vital Crises in Italian Cinema* (Austin: U of Texas P, 1995), 48.

20. See Warshow, *Immediate Experience*, 259.

21. On the episode's allusions to the classic horror genre and its use of lighting effects reminiscent of German expressionism, see Bondanella, *Films of Roberto Rossellini*, 70.

22. Sitney reads this as a reference to Don Quixote's destruction of Maese Pedro's puppets. See *Vital Crises*, 49. On Joe's confusion between fantasy and reality as an acute example of the tendency to accept appearances at face value throughout *Paisan*, see Ben Lawton, "Italian Neorealism: A Mirror Construction of Reality," *Film Criticism* 3 (winter 1979): 16. In this episode, according to Lawton, Rossellini makes explicit a meta-cinematic awareness that enjoins the viewer to consider the illusory basis of realist film.

23. On the bond between the American and the Neapolitan in their common plight of homelessness, see Sitney, *Vital Crises*, 49–50.

24. See "The Italian Body Politic Is a Woman: Feminized National Identity in Postwar Italian Film," *Sparks and Seeds: Medieval Literature and Its Afterlife: Essays in Honor of John Freccero* (Turnhout: Brepols, 2000), 336–37.

25. For Rossellini's critique of the British delay in entering Florence, see Pierre Sorlin, *European Cinemas/European Societies* (London: Routledge, 1991), 55. Another anti-U.K. dig, according to Sorlin, ibid., comes in the sixth episode, where the partisans and OSS are cut off from Allied support by order of Alexander, the British general.

26. Needless to say, this representation of the British soldiers caused a furor in the United Kingdom. The British critic Jarratt, however, refused to take umbrage at Rossellini's critique (*Italian Cinema*, 65 n.), but in doing so he indicated his obliviousness to the filmmaker's link between the British reverence for high culture and a stance of moral nonengagement.

27. Here I disagree with Sitney, who sees this character as a "military tourist," the equivalent of the British officers (*Vital Crises*, 52). As an informed observer, the major is able to relay important logistical information to Resistance forces and thus play a pivotal role in the defense of the city.

28. See his magisterial analysis of the sequence in *What Is the Cinema?* 37.

29. Peter Bondanella, *Italian Cinema from Neorealism to the Present* (New York: Continuum, 1990), 148.

30. I take issue with such critics as Armes (*Patterns of Realism*, 80) who see the execution of the Fascists as equal in horror to that of the partisans. Rossellini definitely takes a stand here. The killing of the snipers has nothing arbitrary

about it: these men were behind the random shootings of civilians, as the policeman informs Massimo and Harriet: "The Fascists are shooting just out of anger, even at the women going to get water from the fountains. Last night they killed two in Via Guelfa" (267–68). In the most immediate context, the three Fascists who were executed had been directly responsible for shooting at Massimo and for killing the partisan who dies in Harriet's arms.

31. Brunette offers an interesting comparison between the Red Cross nurse Harriet and the passive, propaganda-spouting nurse of *La nave bianca* (1941) as an index of how far Rossellini has traveled, in terms of both ideology and gender, since his days as a Fascist documentarist. See *Roberto Rossellini*, 66–67.

32. In one terse phrase, Carlo Lizzani summarizes this conversion: "The piazzas of Florence and their monuments had become macabre battlefields." See *Il cinema italiano* (Rome: Riuniti, 1992), 94.

33. *Fra Pacifico:* Nothing would ever grow here. Now it's become the most fertile part of our garden. A miracle of our Fra Raffaele's. . . . *Martin:* We've just been talking about miracles. *Jones:* I'm inclined to believe you. Where else could they happen but here? (304).

34. This argument recurs throughout Linda Hutcheon's *Theory of Parody: The Teachings of Twentieth-Century Art Forms* (New York: Methuen, 1985). See esp. 26, 57.

35. See Tom Conley's *Film Hieroglyphs* (Minneapolis: U of Minnesota P, 1991), 105.

36. This is one of the alternatives proposed by Bondanella in *Films of Roberto Rossellini,* 80. Ultimately, he argues that Martin's position supports both Rossellini's and Fellini's deinstitutionalized brand of Catholicism. See also Bondanella, *The Cinema of Federico Fellini* (Princeton: Princeton UP, 1992), 44–45. Sitney concurs: see *Vital Crises,* 53 and 56.

37. Brunette, *Roberto Rossellini,* 74.

38. Rossellini, *My Method: Writings and Interviews,* ed. Adriano Aprà (New York: Marsilio, 1995), 38–39.

39. On "the grim democracy of death" in this scene, see Sitney, *Vital Crises,* 52.

40. This is my direct translation of the Italian dialogue. The English dialogue in the published screenplay differs from this somewhat.

41. See, for example, Stefano Masi and Enrico Lancia, *I film di Roberto Rossellini* (Rome: Gremese, 1987), 28. Sitney acknowledges the futility of Dale's sacrifice but argues, convincingly, that "the film itself partially undoes that futility, keeping alive the stories of anti-Fascism in the immediate postwar years as the aspirations for a new kind of political organization were fading and even preserving those stories for the children of the war period." See *Vital Crises,* 54.

42. This is Armes's phrase in *Patterns of Realism,* 80.

43. The Resistance fighters were to have been portrayed as tall, blond, idealized physical types according to the iconography of socialist realism, and their ardor would have won over two Americans, parachuted in to convince them to cease operations. See Masi and Lancia, *I film di Roberto Rossellini,* 28.

44. According to Armes in *Patterns of Realism,* 79, this was an area where the young Rossellini had spent a great deal of time hunting and fishing.

45. On the activist aspirations of neorealism, see Armes, *Film and Reality,* 68–69. Similarly, Bazin calls neorealism "revolutionary humanism" in *What Is Cinema?* 21. Concerning neorealism's call to committed action on the part of its viewers, see Rondolino, *Rossellini,* 61.

Chapter 2. Luchino Visconti's *Bellissima*

1. Lino Miccichè, *Visconti e il neorealismo* (Venice: Marsilio, 1990), 194. Pio Baldelli concurs, arguing that *Bellissima* represents the abdication of cinema's commitment to engage in social reality, focusing instead on the illusory function of film, its parasitic nature, its narcotic effects and exploitative inclinations. See Baldelli, *Luchino Visconti* (Milan: Mazzotta, 1983), 123. On Visconti's abandonment of neorealist method for "his own critico-historical mode which would express his concern with human destinies enclosed within precise historical circumstances," see Mira Liehm, *Passion and Defiance: Film in Italy from 1942 to the Present* (Berkeley: U of California P, 1984), 125.

2. Carlo Lizzani claims that *Bellissima* is not an abdication but an accommodation to the new norms of the industry. By focusing on portraiture and on social mores, Visconti is returning to an interest already apparent in *Ossessione*. See Lizzani, *Il cinema italiano: Dalle origini agli anni ottanta* (Rome: Riuniti, 1992), 138. Giuseppe Ferrara sees a moral continuity between *La terra trema* and *Bellissima* in that both "express the judgment of History on our times." See Ferrara, *Luchino Visconti* (Paris: Seghers, 1963), 40–41.

3. Visconti's antipathy to the script is symptomatic of the general conflict, well documented by scholars, between Zavattinian and Viscontian approaches to realism. See Renzo Renzi, *Visconti segreto* (Bari: Laterza, 1994), 75–76. For the canonical treatment of the Zavattini/Visconti debate, see Guido Aristarco's "Esperienza culturale ed esperienza originale di Luchino Visconti," published as the introduction to the screenplay *Rocco e i suoi fratelli,* ed. G. Aristarco and G. Carancini (Bologna: Cappelli, 1960), 13–47.

4. "*Bellissima:* Storia di una crisi," in *Visconti: Il cinema,* ed. Adelio Ferrero (Modena: Comune di Modena, 1977), 42–43. This important interview with Michele Gandin (cited throughout my study) originally appeared in *Cinema* 75 (1 Dec. 1951).

5. Dominique Bluher comments on the patent irony of this moment in the scene. See "Cinéma dans le cinéma: L'acteur dans *Bellissima* ou Second Traité sur 'Le cinéma anthropomorphique,'" in *Théorème: Visconti, classicisme e subversion,* ed. Michele Lagny (Paris: Sorbonne Nouvelle, 1990), 152.

6. According to Bluher, *Bellissima* is, above all, a reflection on Anna Magnani and on her status as diva. See ibid., 140–41.

7. This is Gaia Servadio's excellent insight. See *Luchino Visconti: A Biography* (New York: Watts, 1983), 131.

8. For Pio Baldelli, the difference between the characterizations of Pina and Maddalena is also generic in origin since one hails from the world-historical stage of neorealism and the other from that of melodrama. See *Luchino Visconti,* 115.

9. "*Bellissima:* Storia di una crisi," 44.

10. See Baldelli, *Luchino Visconti,* 112. See also Henry Bacon, *Visconti: Explorations of Beauty and Decay* (Cambridge: Cambridge UP, 1998), 54.

11. "*Bellissima:* Storia di una crisi," 44.

12. This is Luciano De Giusti's useful term. For a detailed analysis of Visconti's visual technique in *Bellissima,* which favors unobtrusiveness over the "strong style" of an ostentatious *auteur,* see *I film di Luchino Visconti* (Rome: Gremese, 1985), 56.

13. The following analysis of "Anna" is a translated and revised version of sections

of my essay "Cane da grembo o carne in scatola? Il divismo in 'Anna' e 'La strega bruciata viva,'" in *Studi viscontiani,* ed. David Bruni and Veronica Pravadelli (Venice: Marsilio, 1997), 107-20.

14. For an overview of this film, see Henry Bacon, *Visconti: Explorations of Beauty and Decay,* 58-59.

15. Alessandro Bencivenni, *Luchino Visconti* (Florence: La Nuova Italia, 1982), 28.

16. *"Bellissima:* Storia di una crisi," 43.

17. On Visconti's criticism of "neorealist populism," on the one hand, and stodgy professionalism, on the other, see Geoffrey Nowell-Smith, *Visconti* (New York: Viking, 1973), 62.

18. Francesco Bolzoni, "Anna Magnani," in *Filmlexicon degli autori e delle opere: Sezione Italia, aggiornamenti e integrazioni, 1972–1991* (Rome: Nuova ERI, 1992), 599.

19. Bencivenni discusses the continuity between her successes on stage and off in *Luchino Visconti,* 28.

20. *"Bellissima:* Storia di una crisi," 43.

21. On Visconti's implication of the entire world of spectacle in his satire, see Bencivenni, *Visconti, 25.*

22. Bluher comments on the complexity of the relationships between man/actor and man/character—a relationship that "brings into play the origins of the person, his type, but equally his media-ized biography." See "Cinéma dans le cinéma," 153.

23. See ibid., 141.

24. On the representation of Blasetti, see Alfonso Canziani, *Visconti oggi* (Albano Terme: Piovan, 1984), 19.

25. De Giusti remarks on this bipolarity in *I film di Luchino Visconti,* 53-54.

26. On the apartment house as theater, see Bencivenni, *Visconti, 25.*

27. A great deal of critical attention has been devoted to the operatic aspects of *Bellissima.* See, for example, De Giusti, *I film di Luchiino Visconti,* 55, Nowell-Smith, *Visconti,* 57-58, and Baldelli, *Luchino Visconti,* 120.

28. For an amusing account of Blasetti's response to the satiric implications of this soundtrack, written by Visconti's musical composer and arranger Franco Mannino, see Mannino, *Visconti e la musica* (Lucca: Libreria Musicale Italiana, 1994), 21-22. Visconti does not exempt himself from this satire on filmmakers as peddlars of illusion. "We are all charlatans, we filmmakers. It is we who put illusions in the heads of mothers and little girls. It is we who take people in the street and it is our fault. We sell an elixir of love that is not the elixir as in the opera, it is the Bordeaux wine. This theme of the charlatan, is not just for you [Blasetti], but for me, too." From "Entretien avec Luchino Visconti," *Cahiers du cinéma* 93 (Mar. 1959), cited in Bluher, "Cinéma dans le cinéma," 143 (my trans.).

29. On the emotional displacement signaled by Maddalena's turning away from the mirror to the child, see De Giusti, *I film di Luchino Visconti,* 55.

30. Christian Metz, *The Imaginary Signifier: Psychoanalysis and the Cinema,* trans. Celia Britton, Annwyl Williams, Ben Brewster, and Alfred Guzzetti (Bloomington: Indiana UP, 1982), 51.

31. Ibid., 56; Laura Mulvey, "Visual Pleasure and Narrative Cinema," in *Visual and Other Pleasures* (Bloomington: Indiana UP, 1989), 18. This groundbreaking essay first appeared in *Screen* 16 (fall 1975): 6-18.

32. My use of the feminine pronoun here is both in polemic response to Lacan's translators and because I am applying the theory to a specifically female narrative context.

33. Jacques Lacan, *Écrits*, trans. Alan Sheridan (New York: Norton, 1977), 5 and 2.

34. Metz, *Imaginary Signifier*, 49. See also Jean-Louis Baudry, *L'effet cinéma* (Paris: Albatros, 1978), 24-25.

35. Miccichè sees this scene as "the true epicenter of *Bellissima*," in which Maddalena and Spartaco embody two opposed approaches to film spectatorship—one that accepts filmic illusion as truth and the other that acknowledges the "unreality of the representation." Miccichè views this dichotomy in more general terms as the opposition between the pleasure principle, on the one hand, and the reality principle, on the other. See *Visconti e il neorealismo*, 202-6.

36. See Metz's comments on the "paradoxical hallucination" engendered by the cinema situation in "The Fiction Film and Its Spectator: A Metapsychological Study," in *Imaginary Signifier*, 99-147.

37. Miccichè sees this resolution as a return to the proper gender hierarchy of "the patriarchal Italian family, authoritarian and phallocratic." *Visconti e il neorealismo*, 199.

38. I am using the term here as does Jessica Benjamin in *The Bonds of Love: Psychoanalysis, Feminism, and the Problem of Domination* (New York: Pantheon, 1988). For alerting me to Benjamin's work, I would like to thank Cinzia Sartini Blum, author of *The Other Modernism: F.T. Marinetti's Futurist Fiction of Power* (Los Angeles: U of California P, 1996).

39. Mulvey, *Visual and Other Pleasures*, 17.

40. Cited in Nancy Chodorow, *The Reproduction of Mothering: Psychoanalysis and the Sociology of Gender* (Berkeley: U of California P, 1978), 102.

41. Mulvey, *Visual and Other Pleasures*, 18.

42. On the link between psychological and cinematic projection, see Kaja Silverman, *The Acoustic Mirror: The Female Voice in Psychoanalysis and Cinema* (Bloomington: Indiana UP, 1988), 22-23.

43. Miccichè, *Luchino Visconti: Un profilo critico* (Venice: Marsilio, 1996), 26.

44. Miccichè, *Visconti e il neorealismo*, 201.

Chapter 3. Bernardo Bertolucci's *The Last Emperor*

1. "Silvia Bizio, "A Hollywood da infiltrato: Colloquio con Bernardo Bertolucci," *L'Espresso*, 24 Apr. 1988, 9.

2. Giovanni Buttafava, "Effetto Oscar," *L'Espresso*, 24 Apr. 1988, 6.

3. Alberto Moravia, "L'Ultima Cina," *L'Espresso*, 24 Apr. 1988, 9.

4. See Edward Said, *Orientalism* (New York: Random House, 1979).

5. Tony Rayns, "Model Citizen: Bernardo Bertolucci on Location in China," *Film Comment* 23 (Nov.-Dec. 1987): 35.

6. In her otherwise sympathetic reading of the film, Fatimah Tobing Rony objects to Bertolucci's orientalist approach, "which feeds into some dangerous myths about China." See her essay "The Last Emperor," in *Bertolucci's "The Last Emperor": Multiple Takes*, ed. Bruce Sklarew, Bonnie Kaufman, Ellen Spitz, and Diane Borden (Detroit: Wayne State UP, 1998), 144.

7. See Antonio Gramsci, *Il Risorgimento* (Turin: Einaudi, 1952), 100. For an intro-

duction to Gramsci's pervasive influence on Italian filmmakers, see Marcia Landy, *Italian Film* (Cambridge: Cambridge UP, 2000), 149-53.

8. Gramsci, *Il Risorgimento,* 46.

9. On Visconti's critique of *trasformismo,* see Geoffrey Nowell-Smith, *Visconti* (New York: Viking, 1973), 90.

10. *Scene madri di Bernardo Bertolucci,* ed. Enzo Ungari and Don Ranvaud (Milan: Ubulibri, 1987), 237.

11. See Bizio, "Hollywood da infiltrato," 11.

12. Rony suggests that Bertolucci was allowed to shoot the film in China in the mid-1980s with the full support of the government precisely because its unfavorable portrayal of the Maoist regime served the interests of the current Chinese ruling faction. "A critical perspective on the Cultural Revolution is welcome to the present government with its program of economic reforms, and it is only because of these reforms that a Western filmmaker like Bertolucci would be allowed to film in China at all." See her essay "The Last Emperor," 143.

13. On the way in which Pu Yi is used to construct a "model image" for promoting the agendas of the current holders of political power, see Robert Burgoyne, "The Stages of History," in *Bertolucci's "The Last Emperor,"* 224.

14. The term comes from Edward Behr, *The Last Emperor* (New York: Bantam, 1987), 322. I am much indebted to Behr for the historical portraits of Pu Yi, Johnston, and others; I refer to them throughout my study. (I note, however, that while praising Behr's book as "the fullest account available in English," reviewer John K. Fairbank advises us to take some of Behr's historical "facts" with a grain of salt. See "Born Too Late: *The Last Emperor," New York Review of Books,* 18 Feb. 1988, 15.) Film critics who see in Bertolucci's Pu Yi a true Communist convert include Pauline Kael, in her wittily titled "The Manchurian Conformist" *(New Yorker,* 30 Nov. 1987, 99); David Ansen ("The Emperor's New Clothes," *Newsweek,* 23 Nov. 1987, 82); Tony Rayns ("Model Citizen," 35); and Estelle and Morton Shane ("A Narrative of Psychological Rejuvenation," in *Bertolucci's "The Last Emperor"*), 106.

15. For variant interpretations of this rich and multilayered symbol, see three essays in *Bertolucci's "Last Emperor": Multiple Takes*: Estelle and Morton Shane ("A Narrative of Psychological Rejuvenation," 101-2), who see the image as key to a positive reading of Pu Yi's experience of psychological agency; Bonnie S. Kaufman ("Power Sublime and Dangerous: Self-analysis in the Filmcraft of *The Last Emperor,"* 132-33), who views the cricket as sign of the "creative power of metaphor" deriving from the early child developmental processes; and Ding Ning ("Solving Riddles and Concocting Riddles," 216), who finds in this motif "Bertolucci's conception of history—that is, its non-temporality."

16. *From Emperor to Citizen: The Autobiography of Aisin-Gioro Pu Yi,* trans. W.J.F. Jenner (Peking: Foreign Languages Press, 1964), 70.

17. Cinematographer Vittorio Storaro had a precise strategy for a thematically appropriate progression of the use of color and light throughout the film. For Storaro's description of this strategy, see Rayns, "Model Citizen," 36.

18. Critics of the stylized excesses of this sequence include Kael, "Manchurian Conformist," 100, and John Simon's review in *National Review,* 18 Dec. 1987, 55.

19. It would be no exaggeration to see in Bertolucci's own suggestively entitled

early film *Before the Revolution* (1964) a foreshadowing of the very Viscontian ambivalence that will lead him ideologically to welcome radical social change while sentimentally and stylistically regretting the passing of the old order.

20. Gramsci wrote voluminously about the role of literature in this process. On the need for a literature that addresses itself to popular sensibilities and on the need for writers to educate themselves in mass tastes by studying pulp novels and serialized literature, see Antonio Gramsci, *Quaderni del carcere,* ed. Valentino Gerratana (Turin: Einaudi, 1975), 3:1821-22. For a compilation of Gramsci's writings on literature, see Antonio Gramsci, *Marxismo e letteratura,* ed. Giuliano Manacorda (Rome: Riuniti, 1975), esp. 130-72. See also Luigi Bernardi, *Letteratura e rivoluzione in Gramsci* (Pisa: Editrice tecnico-scientifico, 1973), 23-27.

21. Georg Lukács, *Realism in Our Time: Literature and the Class Struggle,* trans. John and Necke Mander (New York: Harper & Row, 1964), 122.

22. Georg Lukács, *The Historical Novel,* trans. Hannah and Stanley Mitchell (London: Merlin Press), 63.

23. Ibid., 44.

24. See Robert Zaller, "After the Revolution," in *Bertolucci's "The Last Emperor,"* 246.

25. See Kael's criticism of Pu Yi's passivity and inertia in her "Manchurian Conformist," 98.

26. See Mulvey, "Visual Pleasure and Narrative Cinema," in *Visual and Other Pleasures* (Bloomington: Indiana UP, 1989), 14-26.

27. Bizio, "Hollywood da infiltrato," 11.

28. See, for example, Vittorio Spiga, "L'ultimo imperatore," in *In viaggio con Bernardo: Il cinema di Bernardo Bertolucci,* ed. Roberto Campari and Maurizio Schiaretti (Venice: Marsilio, 1994), 117-18, and Stefano Cocci, *Bernardo Bertolucci* (Milan: Castoro, 1996), 73.

29. Quoted in *Il cinema d'oggi,* ed. Franca Faldini and Goffredo Fofi (Milan: Mondadori, 1984), 142.

30. T. Jefferson Kline eloquently insists on the vital link that Bertolucci establishes between the psychoanalytic and ideological determinants of behavior: "No other filmmaker—and certainly no Italian filmmaker—has so single-mindedly pursued the relationship between Marxism and Freudianism in cinematic terms. . . . None has faced so dauntlessly the necessity of understanding the relationship between the unconscious forces that govern our individual lives and the larger historical forces that seem to legislate our collective life"; see "The Last Film Director in China: Repetition, Encapsulation, and Transformation in Bertolucci's Cinema," in *Bertolucci's "The Last Emperor,"* 149. Lynda Bundtzen is also attentive to the link between psychoanalytic phases and ideological constraints on Pu Yi; see "Bertolucci's Erotic Politics and the Auteur Theory: From *Last Tango in Paris* to *The Last Emperor,"* ibid., 190.

31. Robert Kolker, *Bernardo Bertolucci* (New York: Oxford, 1985), 187-88. I am indebted to Kolker's lucid and incisive discussion of the relevance of Lacan and Althusser to Bertolucci's thought.

32. Jacques Lacan, *The Language of the Self: The Function of Language in Psychoanalysis,* trans. Anthony Wilden (Baltimore: Johns Hopkins UP, 1968), 40-41.

33. See Louis Althusser, "Freud and Lacan," in the collection *Lenin and Philosophy and Other Essays,* trans. Ben Brewster (New York: Monthly Review Press, 1971), 215-16.

34. As Bundtzen put it, "There is, quite simply, no Oedipal conflict for the little boy . . . [and therefore] no maturity in a Freudian sense"; see "Bertolucci's Erotic Politics," 186–87.

35. This initial traumatic event sets up the principle of repetition compulsion that will govern Pu Yi's behavior, according to Kline's apt analysis in "Last Film Director in China," 157–58.

36. This is also a self-quotation. It refers back to the episode in *1900* when Attila, a demonic Fascist, hurls a kitten against a door and smashes it to death, foreshadowing the way in which later in the film he will brutalize and murder a young boy.

37. For an analysis of the mouse as a "transitional object" in the child's developmental journey toward autonomy from the mother, see Bruce H. Sklarew, "The Prison of Entitlement," in *Bertolucci's "The Last Emperor,"* 91–93.

38. Quoted in Francesco Casetti, *Bernardo Bertolucci* (Florence: La Nuova Italia, 1975), 14.

Chapter 4. Gabriele Salvatores' *Mediterraneo*

1. See Raffaella Grassi, *Territori di fuga: Il cinema di Gabriele Salvatores* (Alessandria: Edizioni Falsopiano, 1997), 60.

2. Quotes from the dialogue can be found in Enzo Monteleone, *Mediterraneo: Sceneggiatura del film diretto da Gabriele Salvatores* (Milan: Baldini & Castodi, 1992), 45 (page-number references to this work are hereafter included in main text). It should be noted that the screenplay includes a number of scenes that were cut from the version of the film distributed in Italy, and the English-language edition of the film cuts even more, being at least fifteen minutes shorter than the Italian version. In this chapter I refer to the Italian edition of the film, sometimes alluding to differences between it and Monteleone's screenplay.

3. Raffaella Grassi, in *Territori di fuga,* locates the film in the category of "commedia all'italiana vagamente impegnata" (vaguely engagé Italian film comedy), 60. Francesco Bolzoni claims in his review of the film that *Mediterraneo* belongs to the final phase of the commedia all'italiana genre; see *Rivista del cinematografo* 61 (Mar. 1991): 14.

4. As it appears in the screenplay, Lorusso's final speech simply reads, "Non siamo riusciti a cambiare niente" (We didn't succeed in changing anything) (124). The film's soundtrack adds a moralizing element to Lorusso's abdication.

5. "With Fascism, all good things are outlawed," says Strazzabosco, as he partakes of the pleasures of the hashish pipe.

6. See Lorenzo Pellizzari's review, in *Cineforum* 31 (Apr. 1991): 86, and Paolo Vernaglioni's in *Filmcritica* 42 (June 1991): 302.

7. For a detailed treatment of this topos, see my essay "The Italian Body Politic Is a Woman: Feminized National Identity in Postwar Italian Film," in *Sparks and Seeds: Medieval Literature and Its Afterlife: Essays in Honor of John Freccero,* ed. Dana Stewart and Alison Cornish (Turnhout, Belgium: Brepols, 2000), 329–47.

8. In this scene, there is a slight discrepancy between the dialogue of the published screenplay and that of the film. The latter omits the genetic allusions that I find of considerable interest in Salvatores' argument for a Mediterranean evolutionary source.

9. This scene, like the ones previously mentioned of Strazzabosco wearing chicken-feather wings astride his mule and of the shepherdess-turned-mermaid, was cut from the Italian version of the film.

10. See Roberto Silvestri's comments in "Dicono del film: Antologia dei pareri critici," in *Gabriele Salvatores*, ed. Flavio Merkel (Rome: Dino Audino, 1993), 49.

11. These lines from the screenplay were not included either in the Italian or the English cuts of the film.

12. See Raffaella Grassi's comments in *Territori di fuga*, 8, Pellizzari's review of the film for *Cineforum* 31 (Apr. 1991): 87, and Roberto Silvestri's remarks in "Dicono del film: Antologia dei pareri critici," in *Gabriele Salvatores*, ed. Merkel, 49.

13. *Contemporary Italian Filmmaking: Strategies of Subversion* (Toronto: U of Toronto P, 1995), 223.

14. For an in-depth analysis of *Night of the Shooting Stars*, see my *Italian Film in the Light of Neorealism* (Princeton: Princeton UP, 1986), 360-90. On *Mediterraneo's* characters' all seeming to find "their proper existential dimension," see Raffaella Grassi, *Territori di fuga*, 65.

15. Here the film's dialogue differs somewhat from the screenplay as Lorusso utters his wish to get on a ship and return to the world.

16. See Frye, *Anatomy of Criticism* (Princeton: Princeton UP, 1973), esp. 163-66.

17. For a more detailed development of this argument, see "Italian Body Politic Is a Woman," 337.

18. See Grassi, *Territori di fuga*, 62.

19. Riccardo Monni, "Nella forza dell'amicizia i segreti del successo," *La nazione*, 1 Apr. 1992, 5.

20. Ibid.

21. Quoted in Vittorio Spiga, "Uomini in fuga, lontani da sé," *La nazione*, 1 Apr. 1992, 5. Salvatores elaborates on his collaborative method as follows: "I consider it indispensable to involve actors in the writing of the film. They must themselves adapt the dialogue and characters. A time-tested, reciprocal understanding is therefore indispensable"; ibid.

22. Lorenzo Pellizzari, *"Mediterraneo,"* *Cineforum* 31 (Apr. 1991): 86.

23. Monni, "Nella forza dell'amicizia," 5.

24. See Frye, *Anatomy of Criticism,* 164 and 165.

Chapter 5. Roberto Faenza's *Pereira Declares*

1. Roberto Faenza, *Sostiene Pereira: Film Book* (Milan: Il Castoro, 1995), 15 (all references to the screenplay are to this edition; page-number references are given in the main text).

2. The reader is referred to my discussion of Gramsci's cultural theory in the context of Bertolucci's *The Last Emperor,* esp. 331, note 20.

3. In fact, in the introduction to the published screenplay Tabucchi himself uses the metaphors of transmigration, revival, and materialization to describe the process of cinematic adaptation. "Let's say that it has a curious effect: within those images there is your book, and, at the same time, it's not there, because it has become another language . . . and yet it is beautiful to see how one language transmigrates into another, how it relives under another form, how it materializes itself" (9).

4. This phrase appears on the back cover of the 1994 edition of the novel. See Antonio Tabucchi, *Sostiene Pereira* (Milan: Feltrinelli, 1994) (in the text, page-number references designated Tabucchi are to this edition).

5. For their magisterial study of the interpersonal mechanisms of bearing witness, see Shoshana Felman and Dori Laub, *Testimony: Crises of Witnessing in Literature, Psychoanalysis, and History* (New York: Routledge, 1992), esp. Laub's chapter "Bearing Witness or the Vicissitudes of Listening," 57–74. For the term *addressable other,* see 68.

6. Roy Menarini, "*Sostiene Pereira,*" *Segnocinema* (May–June 1995): 38. See also Luca Mosso's review in *Cineforum* 35 (Apr. 1995): 85.

7. On the decision to identify the voice-over with one of the film's characters, see the comments of Faenza's coscriptwriter Sergio Vecchio, published in the introduction to the screenplay, 17.

8. Mastroianni himself makes this link between Pereira's precarious health and that of the national body politic in "Il mio incontro con Pereira: Intervista a Marcello Mastroianni di Antonio Gnoli," published in the introduction to the screenplay, 13.

9. The most intricate system is that proposed by Christian Metz, who divides *voce narrante* into four categories:

1. extradiegetic voice-in: The narrator is a character who appears on-screen but does not participate in the story proper

2. homodiegetic voice-in: The narrator is a character who is part of the story

3. homodiegetic voice-off: The narrator, a character who is part of the story, narrates it, but in a time frame removed from that of the story

4. extradiegetic voice-off: The narrator is never onscreen and is not part of the story

On Metz's system, see Sandro Bernardi, *Introduzione alla retorica del cinema* (Florence: Casa Editrice Le Lettere, 1994), 83.

10. Gilles Deleuze, *Cinema 2: The Time-Image,* trans. Hugh Tomlinson and Robert Galeta (Minneapolis: U of Minnesota P, 1989), 236.

11. See Francesco Casetti and Federico di Chio, *Analisi del film* (Milan: Bompiani, 1990), 92.

12. This is actual footage from a film entitled *A revoluçao de Maio* that was made by Antonio Lopes Ribeiro in 1937.

13. Casetti and di Chio, *Analisi del film,* 93.

14. See Gian Luigi Rondi's review in *Rivista del cinematografo* 65 (June 1995): 17; Luca Mosso's review in *Cineforum* 35 (Apr. 1995): 85; and Lawrence Van Gelder, "Fascist Outrages Awaken a Death-Obsessed Editor," *New York Times,* 3 Apr. 1998, E26.

Chapter 6. Francesco Rosi's *Three Brothers*

1. See Gary Crowdus and Dan Georgakas, "The Audience Should Not Be Just Passive Spectators: An Interview with Francesco Rosi," *Cinéaste* 7 (fall 1975): 6.

2. Peter Bondanella, *Italian Cinema from Neorealism to the Present* (New York: Continuum, 1990), 170.

3. This is Francesco Bolzoni's term in *I film di Francesco Rosi* (Rome: Gremese, 1986), 129.

4. Quoted in Franca Faldini and Goffredo Fofi, *Il cinema italiano d'oggi, 1970–1984* (Milan: Mondadori, 1984), 531-32.

5. Quoted in Faldini and Fofi, *Il cinema italiano d'oggi*, 531.

6. See her review of *Three Brothers* in "The Current Cinema: Francesco Rosi," *New Yorker*, 22 Mar. 1982, 160.

7. On Piccioni's contributions to the soundtrack of *Three Brothers* and to Rosi's production in general, see Ermanno Comuzio, "Quando diventa esemplare il rapporto regista-compositore: La musica di Piccioni nei film di Rosi," in *Francesco Rosi*, ed. Sebastiano Gesù (Acicatena: Incontri con il Cinema, 1991), 65-73.

8. For a compilation of appreciative foreign reviews, see Bolzoni, *I film di Francesco Rosi*, 132.

9. Ibid. For other typical examples of such objections, see the comments of Mino Argentieri, M. Morandini, and Sauro Borelli, all quoted in the lineup or critical reactions in *Francesco Rosi*, ed. Gesù, 243-44.

10. See "The Current Cinema," *New Yorker*, 22 Mar. 1982, 160.

11. For Bolzoni's statements on the primacy of character in Rosi's cinema, see *I film di Francesco Rosi*, 14 and 9.

12. Cited in Bolzoni, *I film di Francesco Rosi*, 133. This label refers to the politics of Sandro Pertini, member of the Socialist Party and widely admired president of the republic from 1978 to 1985.

13. This is Bolzoni's position, ibid., 132.

14. As Pauline Kael notes in her review, the cinematography of this scene enables us to "*feel* the difference between North and South." See "The Current Cinema," *New Yorker*, 22 Mar. 1982, 161.

15. Quoted in *Francesco Rosi*, ed. Gesù, 244.

16. The writer of the English subtitles supplied this witticism, which is lacking in the Italian's more prosaic *Volevi un appartamento in questa posizione?* (lit., You wanted an apartment in this location?).

17. See Bolzoni, *I film di Francesco Rosi*, 132.

18. On Guerra's contribution to Rosi's screenplays, see Nino Genovese, "Le fonti letterarie del cinema di Rosi," in *Francesco Rosi*, ed. Gesù, 62.

19. Faldini and Fofi, *Il cinema italiano d'oggi*, 531.

20. Andrei Platonov, "The Third Son," trans. Cathleen Cook, in *Fro and Other Stories* (Moscow: Progress Publishers, 1972), 64 (page-number references hereafter given in the main text; all excerpts from the story are from this edition).

21. Faldini and Fofi, *Il cinema italiano d'oggi*, 531.

22. For his objection to this scene as eliciting an "easy heart tug," see Stanley Kauffmann, "Good Intentions," in *New Republic*, 21 Apr. 1982, 25.

23. Quoted in Aldo Tassone, *Parla il cinema italiano* (Milan: Il Formichiere, 1979), 282.

24. For this insight, see Peter Bondanella, *Italian Cinema from Neorealism to the Present*, 333. It should be noted that in the first episode of *Paisan*, an Italian American soldier, Tony Mascali, is included among the liberating forces. But the entire landing in Sicily is met with anxiety and suspicion by the local populace, and Tony's command of the Italian language does little to allay their fears. For an in-depth analysis of *Paisan*, see ch. 1.

Chapter 7. Ricky Tognazzi's *La scorta*

1. Quoted in Giona Nazzaro, *"La scorta,"* *Cineforum* 324 (May 1993): 50.
2. This is Gian Piero Brunetta's formulation. See his *Storia del cinema italiano dal 1945 agli anni ottanta* (Rome: Riuniti, 1982), 691.
3. Adelina Preziosi makes an important comparative assessment of audience responses then and now. See her review of *La scorta* in *Segnocinema* 13 (July-Aug. 1993): 49.
4. On Tognazzi's generic self-consciousness, see ibid.
5. Giona Nazzaro, *"La scorta,"* *Cineforum* 324 (May 1993): 50.
6. Maurizio Regosa, *"La scorta,"* *Cinema nuovo* 42 (July-Oct. 1993): 66.
7. By which "the film is freely inspired," according to the opening titles.
8. See Regosa's comments in *Cinema nuovo* 42 (July-Oct. 1993): 66. See also the reviews by Paolo D'Agostini in *Rivista del cinematografo* 63 (June 1993): 13, and Michele Picchi, in *Cinema nuovo* 42 (Nov.-Dec. 1993): 9.
9. Of the four men who stand on the dock to bid De Francesco farewell, three (Fabio Muzzi, Andrea Corsale, and Angelo Mandolesi) were part of the inner group that had supported the judge's anti-Mafia crusade from the very beginning. Replacing the slain Raffaele Frasca is Nicola, who had been one of the drivers of the two escort vehicles.
10. See Giona Nazzaro's review in *Cineforum* 324 (May 1993): 50. See also Manuela Gieri's comments on the film in *Contemporary Italian Filmmaking: Strategies of Subversion* (Toronto: U of Toronto P, 1995), 210.
11. These are Mino Argentieri's words. See his somewhat cynical review in "Le delusioni del ritorno al cinema civile," *Cinemasessanta* 34 (Mar.-June 1993): 38.

Chapter 8. Gianni Amelio's *Stolen Children*

1. On Amelio's debt to Italian film history, see Nino Siciliani de Cumis, "Il mestiere del critico," *Cinema nuovo* 41 (Nov.-Dec. 1992): 42, and Massimo Garritano, *"Ladro di bambini,"* *Cinemasessanta* 33 (Mar.-Apr. 1992): 27.
2. See Godfrey Cheshire, "The Compassionate Gaze of Gianni Amelio," *Film Comment* (July-Aug. 1993): 82.
3. So states Goffredo Fofi in his preface to the published screenplay of the film. See Gianni Amelio, *Il ladro di bambini* (Milan: Feltrinelli, 1992), vii (page-number references hereafter given in main text; all references to the film dialogue are from this edition). A number of other critics have also commented on the film's neorealist affinities. See, for example, Anna Maria Mori, "Un amaro viaggio nel Sud," *La repubblica,* 8 Apr. 1992, 33; Gary Crowdus and Richard Porton, "Beyond Neorealism: Preserving a Cinema of Social Conscience: An Interview with Gianni Amelio," *Cineaste* 21 (1995): 6, Peter Bondanella, "Stolen Children," *Cineaste* 20, nos. 1-4 (1994): 38, and Janet Maslin's review, excerpted in *Gianni Amelio,* ed. Mario Sesti and Stefanella Ughi (Rome: Dino Audino, 1994), 5.
4. *Amelio secondo il cinema: Conversazione con Goffredo Fofi* (Rome: Donzelli, 1994), 8.
5. On Amelio's preference for an improvisational directing style, see Cheshire, "Compassionate Gaze," 84, and Crowdus and Porton, "Beyond Neorealism," 13. The choice of Enrico Lo Verso, a professional actor, for the part of Antonio was based on his skill at improvisation. See Bruno Roberti and Edoardo Bruno, "Conversazione con Gianni Amelio," *Filmcritica* 43 (Apr. 1992): 162.

6. See Mori, "Un amaro viaggio nel Sud," 33. On the mix of nonprofessionals and professional actors and the latter being, in making the film, reimmersed "in a soil that was theirs," see *Amelio secondo il cinema,* 65.

7. On the film's refusal of dramaturgy, see Roger Ebert's comments quoted in *Gianni Amelio,* ed. Sesti and Ughi, 51.

8. See Cesare Zavattini, "Some Ideas on the Cinema," *Vittorio De Sica: Contemporary Perspectives,* ed. Howard Curle and Stephen Snyder (Toronto: U of Toronto P, 2000), 54 and 53.

9. Alessandro Cappabianca, "Il viaggio verso l'isola," *Filmcritica* 43 (Apr. 1992): 150. Stefano Salvetti sees in *Il ladro di bambini* a subcategory of "minimal-realist cinema" that privileges "the dimension of filmic temporality." See "Francesca Archibugi e il 'real minimalismo,'" *Ciem* 26 (Jan.-Mar. 1994): 37.

10. I am paraphrasing Massimo Garritano's technical analysis in *"Ladro di bambini,"* *Cinemasessanta* 33 (Mar.-Apr. 1992): 25.

11. Critics have invoked this label to describe Amelio's stylistic austerity. See, for example, Franco Prono, "Crisi di paternità e svolta nel cinema di Gianni Amelio," *Cinema nuovo* 41 (July-Oct. 1992): 41.

12. See Flavio De Bernardinis's review in *Segnocinema* 12 (May-June 1992): 41.

13. *Traduzione* is a technical term for the transporting of individuals under the custody of law-enforcement officers. In *"Il ladro di bambini,"* *Cineforum* 32 (June 1992): 73, Lorenzo Pellizzari sees this concept as an allegory for the contemporary Italian national condition in this time of perilous transition. Franco Prono considers Italy to be "orphaned of parents and devoid of culture"; see "Crisi di paternità e svolta nel cinema di Gianni Amelio," *Cinema nuovo* 41 (July-Oct. 1992): 41.

14. Amelio criticism abounds in references to the Italian "road movie" tradition; see, for example, Nino Siciliani de Cumis, "Il mestiere del critico," 42, and Massimo Garritano's review in *Cinemasessanta* 33 (Mar.-Apr. 1992): 26.

15. Peter Bondanella comments on Amelio's debt to *Paisan,* suggesting that he "may well intend *Stolen Children* as an ironic reversal of the positive emotional direction we encounter in Rossellini's epic journey from Sicily to northern Italy, a journey that promised both moral regeneration and national rebirth in a new Italian future." See his review in *Cineaste* 20, nos. 1-4 (1994): 37-38.

16. On the trajectories of Italian journey films, see Fofi's comments in *Gianni Amelio,* ed. Sesti and Ughi, 52-53.

17. In this unvarnished portrait of subproletarian squalor, Amelio avoids the trap of a sentimentalizing populism in favor of "an entomologist's gaze." See Massimo Garritano's review in *Cinemasessanta* 33 (Mar.-Apr. 1992): 25.

18. "Conversazione con Gianni Amelio," 153.

19. In his sensitive analysis of the film's perspective on gender, Godfrey Cheshire cites Amelio's goal of "feminizing male awareness." See "Compassionate Gaze," 88.

20. For Amelio's comments on Luciano's crisis of gender identity, see "Conversazione con Gianni Amelio," 153.

21. See Jennifer Hirsh's extremely insightful analysis of this scene in "Lo specchio, la luce, e l'ombra: Riflessioni stilistiche nel cinema di Gianni Amelio," *American Journal of Italian Studies* 22 (1999): 42.

22. See Mori, "Un amaro viaggio nel Sud," 33.

23. Quoted in ibid.

24. See Cappabianca, "Il viaggio verso l'isola," 150.

25. As Hirsch notes, photographs serve to fix and define the children's identity in the eyes of the world; see "Lo specchio, la luce, e l'ombra," 43.

26. According to Cheshire, "Amelio's purpose is to resist the media enforced impression that he [Rosetta's client] is literally everywhere, in every heart and adult gaze, by asserting what is seldom said: that innocence is as real as guilt, that the first and most enduring look between adult and child is one of love and compassion, not of passion and fear." See "Compassionate Gaze," 88.

27. Flavio De Bernardinis, "Il ladro di bambini," *Segnocinema* 12 (May–June 1992): 41.

28. According to Bondanella, the photo represents the "privileged life they will never enjoy." See his review of the film in *Cineaste* 20, nos. 1–4 (1994): 38.

29. Amelio sees in the Zorro image another sign of victimization. Southern families, he explains, look with great pride on their carabinieri sons, who bear the weight of highly unrealistic expectations for a social heroism obstructed by the south's own corruption of the judicial ideal. See *Amelio secondo il cinema,* 26.

30. In Luciano's identification with the photo, see Hirsh, "Lo specchio, la luce, e l'ombra," 42. In Amelio's own words:

> He identifies with that funny photo . . . and there [occurs] a first moment of sympathy that brings him then to speak. But also in that photo, there is the idea of the hero, the carabiniere as a child is dressed up as Zorro, the avenger. And if indeed a child [the young Antonio] is able to bring justice, even he [Luciano] can triumph over all that has happened. Thus there is an identification, on the level of a shared childhood, above all on the level of "role," of "uniform."

See "Conversazione con Gianni Amelio," 153.

31. See Cappabianca, "Il viaggio verso l'isola," 149.

32. For a fascinating account of the way this scene was modified from its original conception, see *Amelio secondo il cinema,* 61–64.

33. Fofi interprets the restaurant scene as a mirror of contemporary Italian decadence. See his introduction to the screenplay, ix–x.

34. In Flavio De Bernardinis's insightful analysis, this unfinished dwelling offers "the limiting case of an interior that is at the same time exterior, an apartment that does not separate, a house just built, brand new in its clamorous precariousness and already dilapidated and in ruins." See his review in *Segnocinema* 12 (May–June 1992): 41.

35. In Amelio's words: "I know that the south isn't this way because there is a north, but the south is south because there is also a mistaken south." See *Amelio secondo il cinema,* 43.

36. On the restorative function of this scene, see Fofi's introduction to the screenplay, x–xi.

37. Ibid., vii.

38. See Crowdus and Porton, "Beyond Neorealism," 12. On the relevance to Amelio's film of Antonioni's use of architecture in general, see Bondonella's review in *Cineaste* 20, nos. 1–4 (1994): 38.

39. See Fofi's preface to the screenplay, v.

40. In Amelio's words, the film is "a story of poverty and marginalization, in which the characters recount the life of Italy today without raising their voices, with-

out any desire or pretension to being emblematic." See Nino Siciliani di Cumis, "Gianni Amelio e il suo *Ladro di bambini,*" *Cinema nuovo* 41 (Mar.-Apr. 1992): 18.

41. See "Conversazione con Gianni Amelio," 155.

42. Jessica Benjamin, *Psychoanalysis, Feminism, and the Problem of Domination* (New York: Pantheon, 1988), 43. Benjamin bases her challenge to Freudian thinking on recent scientific evidence that proves newborns enter the world with a distinct perception of self, not with the sense of undifferentiated, oceanic oneness with the world that Freud proposed. This means that whereas orthodox psychoanalysis posited psychic development in the child's separation and individuation from the mother, the infant instead forms his or her identity through outreach and rapprochement.

43. This is Amelio's phrase. See "Conversazione con Gianni Amelio," 161.

44. See Edoardo Bruno, "L'epica e la riflessione," *Filmcritica* 43 (Apr. 1992): 147. In the same essay, Bruno develops a convincing analogy between Amelio's gaze in *Il ladro di bambini* and Rossellini's "poetics of the gaze" (147) in *Voyage in Italy.*

45. "Conversazione con Gianni Amelio," 154.

46. These are Amelio's words as reported in "'La regia è come un iceberg, la parte importante sta sotto': Intervista a Gianni Amelio a cura di Dino Audino e Gino Ventriglia," *Script* 5 (May 1994): 37. For his account of how this ending differed from the one originally written (Luciano was to have killed Antonio, but the boy actor refused to comply), see ibid.

47. Bondanella, instead, sees *Il ladro di bambini* as a critique of neorealism's optimistic use of children to signal hope for social renewal. See his review in *Cineaste* 20, nos. 1-4 (1994): 38.

48. Quoted in Mori, "Un amaro viaggio nel Sud," 33. In this ending, Amelio acknowledges a debt to Antonioni's *L'avventura,* specifically to Claudia's gesture of reconciliation with Sandro in the film's final frames. See "Conversazione con Gianni Amelio," 157.

Chapter 9. Federico Fellini's *Ginger and Fred*

1. Fellini discusses the work of expansion in the prefatory sections of the screenplay, published in Federico Fellini, *Ginger e Fred,* ed. Mino Guerrini (Milan: Longanesi, 1985). All translations of these introductory materials and of the film dialogue are mine (page-number references are given in the text; all are to this 1985 edition).

2. Much of the film's critical reception has hinged on the perceived compatibility or imbalance between the love story and the satire of contemporary video culture. Thus, Giulio Cattielli faults *Ginger and Fred* for its "disequilibrium" (for this comment, see Claudio G. Fava and Aldo Viganò, *I film di Federico Fellini* [Rome: Gremese, 1991], 178), and Tullio Kezich argues that "the pharaonic frame—that is, the mega-show in which the two protagonists participate—does not detract from the story and above all does not disturb the delicate half tones" (see Kezich, *Fellini* [Milan: Rizzoli, 1988], 520). Critical disagreement goes beyond the question of structural balance, however, to the very nature of the film's core dichotomy. For Catielli and Giovanni Grazzini (see Fava and Viganò, at 178 and 176, respectively) the opposition is generic, involving the tension between satire and parody, on the one hand, and romance tinged with irony, on

the other. For Alberto Moravia (Fava and Viganò, 177), Edoardo Bruno (in "Ciao Pippo," *Filmcritica* 37 [1986]: 94), and Kezich (see his *Fellini,* 521), the film is traversed by a nostalgia for a past perceived as authentic and irretrievable in the face of a brutal and mechanized present. For Peter Bondanella (*The Cinema of Federico Fellini* [Princeton: Princeton UP, 1992], 222), Andrea Zanzotto ("Critica dossier," *Cinemasessanta* 227 [Mar.-Apr. 1986]: 51), and Silvana Cielo ("Qualche minuto al buio," *Filmcritica* 37 [1986]: 95), *Ginger and Fred* represents a struggle between competing types of spectacle, wherein such older and more "innocent" forms as vaudeville and cinema are pitted against the corrupt, all-devouring medium of contemporary TV.

3. I am very grateful to my student Dorothée Bonnigal, whose many conversations with me on the subject of the hyperfilm have helped enormously in the elaboration of the idea. Her own contributions to the notion may be found in "Federico Fellini's *Amarcord:* Variations on the Libidinal Limbo of Adolescence," in *Federico Fellini: Contemporary Perspectives,* ed. Frank Burke and Marguerite Waller (Toronto: Toronto UP, 2002), and "Fellini's *Casanova:* Exorcising the Loss of the Baroque Circle," *Il Veltro* (1996): 58-62 nn. 1-2.

4. For the term *mitobiografia,* see Kezich, *Fellini,* 17.

5. Ibid., 515.

6. See Fava and Viganò, *I film di Federico Fellini,* 180. On the occurrence of a number of Fellinian commonplaces in *Ginger and Fred,* see ibid., 175.

7. This is Bondanella's observation in *Cinema of Federico Fellini,* 223.

8. Numerous critics have remarked on the status of Pippo as Fellinian self-projection. See, for example, Vittorio Giacci, "Ballo. Non solo," *Filmcritica* 37 (1986): 95; Francesco Tornabene, *Federico Fellini: The Fantastic Vision of a Realist* (Berlin: Benedikt Taschen, 1990), 122; Pauline Kael, "Lost Souls," *New Yorker,* 21 Apr. 1986, 100.

9. See Carolyn Geduld, *"Juliet of the Spirits:* Guido's Anima," in *Federico Fellini: Essays in Criticism,* ed. Peter Bondanella (New York: Oxford, 1978), 137-51. In *Amelia,* Masina exhibits that combination of "shyness, curiosity, vulnerability, tolerance, impatience, anger, and resolve" that mirrors an aspect of Fellini's own psychology, according to Kezich in *Fellini,* 522. On the roles of Masina and Mastroianni as twin alter egos of the director, see ibid., as well as Kezich's comments in "Federico Fellini *Ginger e Fred:* Critica dossier," *Cinemasessanta* 227 (Mar.-Apr. 1996): 54, and Jack Kroll, "Last Waltz in Roma," *Newsweek,* 31 Mar. 1986, 72.

10. See Bruno, "Ciao Pippo," Stefano Reggiani, in *Cinemasessanta* 227 (Mar.-Apr. 1986): 50, and Pauline Kael, "Lost Souls," *New Yorker,* 21 Apr. 1986, 97. Frank Burke notes that Fellini's own tirades against television are couched in the very language found in so many reviews of his own film aesthetic. See *Fellini's Films* (New York: Twayne, 1996), 267.

11. What emerges from the actress's own account of the collaboration is that any attempt on her part actively to formulate a reading of her character is perceived by her husband as a usurpation of his authorial control.

With other directors it is easier for me to have a dialogue. With him, instead, perhaps because I know that he doesn't listen to me (nor does he listen to anyone else), I have a greater, almost inexplicable shyness. With Federico I know that one must not talk, that it's useless to ask explanations, I know that he seeks the character 'upon you' *[te lo cerca addosso]* on set, and thus, at the beginning of the film, the things that I feel that I need to tell him, well, I get some paper and think and I write them down for him. (61)

12. For the way in which the problematic relationships between director-husbands and actress-wives are internalized in the cinema of two prominent auteurs, see Dorothée Bonnigal, "Restrained Women and Artistic Emancipation: Authority and Resistance in Federico Fellini's *Giulietta degli spiriti* and John Cassavetes' *A Woman under the Influence*," *Romance Languages Annual* 7 (1995): 204-11.

13. From a feminist point of view, this erasing of the identity of Masina is disturbing, as is Fellini's assertion (above) that he, and not his wife, understands the effectiveness of her facial expressions.

14. In this sequence, Fellini may be making a grotesque allusion to the television program on eye exercises that Giulietta watches with her maids, where a beautiful young model demonstrates ocular movements that "helped your favorite actresses to achieve their success." See the screenplay, published in English as Federico Fellini, *Juliet of the Spirits,* trans. Howard Greenfeld (New York: Ballantine, 1965), 211. I am grateful to Marguerite Waller for calling my attention to this analogy.

15. On the "shrinking world" of televisual representation, see Marcia Landy, *Italian Film* (Cambridge: Cambridge UP, 2000), 371.

16. On television's subordination of serious journalism to the overriding goal of entertainment, see Federico Fellini, *Fare un film* (Turin: Einaudi, 1980), 142.

17. For the satiric implications of Fellini's Dante allusion, see Bondanella, *Cinema of Federico Fellini,* 225. Landy wittily labels this practice "cultural vandalism" in her critique of *Ginger and Fred;* see *Italian Film,* 397.

18. See Fava and Viganò, *I film di Federico Fellini,* 174. For an extended treatment of this development, see my introduction.

19. See René Girard, *Deceit, Desire, and the Novel,* trans. Yvonne Freccero (Baltimore: Johns Hopkins UP, 1965).

20. Jean Baudrillard, *Simulations,* trans. Paul Foss, Paul Patton, and Philip Beitchmann (New York: Semiotext(e), 1983), 10-11. On Fellini's portrait of television as a medium dedicated to self-representation, see Mino Argentieri, "No, non è di T.V. che si tratta," *Cinemasessanta* 227 (Mar.-Apr. 1986): 51, and Riccardo Rosetti, "La fuga dalle cose," *Filmcritica* 37 (1986): 99-101. Frank Burke has provided a number of valuable insights into the way in which Fellini's television works by simulation. For Burke, *Ginger and Fred* occupies an important step in Fellini's signifying itinerary, as in his later work the filmmaker moves ever farther from the nonproblematic representation of his early filmography to an every more deeply felt loss of the referent and consequent focus on processes of self-signification. See "Federico Fellini: From Representation to Signification," *Romance Languages Annual* 1 (1989): esp. 38-39.

21. Fredric Jameson, *Postmodernism, or, The Cultural Logic of Late Capitalism* (Durham, N.C.: Duke UP, 1991), 37.

22. On the essential *ripetitività* and indistinguishability of television messages, see Umberto Eco's remarks in *Cinemasessanta* 227 (Mar.-Apr. 1986): 50; Riccardo Rosetti, "La fuga dalle cose," *Filmcritica* 37, 101; and Fellini's own comments in Tornabene, *Federico Fellini,* 121. As a result of the semiotic indistinguishability of the video process, interpretation is rendered impossible by the failure of any privileged element to "occupy the position of 'interpretant.'" See Jameson, *Post-*

modernism, or, The Cultural Logic of Late Capitalism, 90. On the significance of Fellini's many impersonators and the centrality of imitation to TV epistemology, see Burke, *Fellini's Films*, 260.

23. See Mario Giusti's review for *Il Manifesto* excerpted in *Cinemasessanta* 227 (Mar.-Apr. 1986): 50.

24. See Kezich, *Fellini*, 512.

25. For example, see ibid. and the reviews of Stefano Reggiani and Mino Argentieri in *Cinemasessanta* 227 (Mar.-Apr. 1986): Reggiani at 50; Argentieri at 52.

26. On the filmographic consequences of this casting choice, see Bondanella, *Cinema of Federico Fellini*, 222.

27. See Federico Fellini, *Essays in Criticism*, ed. Peter Bondanella (New York: Oxford, 1978), 15.

28. See Bondanella, *Cinema of Federico Fellini*, 225, and Riccardo Rosetti, "La fuga dalle cose," *Filmcritica* 37, 101.

29. To add yet another step to this process of deferred reference, Burke notes that Fred Astaire and Ginger Rogers are themselves "'imitations,' having effaced their identities of Frederick Austerlitz and Virginia Catherine McMath." See *Fellini's Films*, 262.

30. See Marian Hannah Winter, "Juba and American Minstrelsy," in *Chronicles of the American Dance*, ed. Paul Magriel (New York: Holt, 1948), 40.

31. Quoted in Jerry Ames and Jim Siegelman, *The Book of Tap: Recovering America's Long Lost Dance* (New York: David McKay, 1977), 57. See also Mary Clarke and Clement Crisp, *The History of Dance* (New York: Crown, 1981), 238.

32. See Paolo Vernaglione's excellent discussion of Fellini's mimesis of television aesthetics in "Variazioni minime sul sonoro," *Filmcritica* 37 (1986): 107. Silvana Cielo and Pauline Kael both remark that *Ginger and Fred* was shot like a made-for-TV film; see Cielo, "Qualche minuto al buio," *Filmcritica* 37 (1986): 95, and Kael, "Lost Souls," 97.

33. On the televisual interference in the sentimental plot, see Burke, "Federico Fellini: From Representation to Signification," 39.

34. Burke predicates the failure of this gesture on its very basis in simulation. "Their farewell turns into a recreated piece of business from their televised Ginger and Fred routine: now an imitation of an imitation of an imitation," ibid.

35. For Burke, this ending proves Fellini's case against the self-referentiality of television: "Unable to refer, it can only signify its will to ceaselessly signify," ibid.

36. It is interesting to note that Fellini sought to exaggerate the pathos of the performance by having Amelia and Pippo dance far below their level of training and expertise. See Masina's comments in the preface to the screenplay for *Ginger and Fred*, 62.

37. Burke concurs on the irrelevance of the Hollywood resolution-through-dance to the sentimental lives of Fellini's protagonists. See *Fellini's Films*, 260.

Chapter 10. Giuseppe Tornatore's *Cinema Paradiso*

1. See Jameson, *Postmodernism, or, The Cultural Logic of Late Capitalism* (Durham: Duke UP, 1991), 19–22 (page-number references to Jameson hereafter given in the main text). Manuela Gieri suggests the relevance of this label to Tornatore's film; see *Contemporary Italian Filmmaking: Strategies of Subversion* (Toronto: U of Toronto P, 1996), 220.

2. Ermanno Comuzio, *"Nuovo cinema paradiso," Cineforum* 29 (May 1989): 81, 82, 84.
3. See Patrick Rumble, "Tornatore e l'America: Il cinema dell'anamnesi," *Sicilia e altre storie: Il cinema di Giuseppe Tornatore,* ed. Valerio Caprara (Naples: Edizioni Scientifiche Italiane, 1996), 11–20.
4. See, for example, Tom Milne's review in *Monthly Film Bulletin* 57 (Mar. 1990): 72.
5. Rosario Lizzio, "Intervista a Giuseppe Tornatore," *Cineforum* 29 (May 1989): 85.
6. Marcello Walter Bruno, "Meta in Italy," *Segnocinema* 11 (Sept.–Oct. 1991): 13.
7. Tornatore comments on the deliberateness of these stylistic choices in his interview with Rosario Lizzio in *Cineforum* 29 (May 1989): 86.
8. Giuseppe Tornatore, *Nuovo cinema paradiso* (Palermo: Sellerio, 1990), 63 (page-number references hereafter given in the main text; all quotes from the screenplay are from this edition; the English translations are mine).

Chapter 11. Maurizio Nichetti's *The Icicle Thief*

1. See the interview with Jean Gili in *Le cinéma italien* (Paris: Union Générale d'Editions, 1978), 291–92.
2. This beautiful formulation is André Bazin's. See *What Is Cinema?* trans. Hugh Gray (Berkeley: U of California P, 1971), 54.
3. "It was the Golden Age of Italian cinema," states Nicola, "when films were the only innovative cultural force: Rossellini, Zavattini, Visconti, Amidei, De Sica."
4. Manuela Gieri, *Contemporary Italian Filmmaking: Strategies of Subversion* (Toronto: U of Toronto P, 1995), 219.
5. On the function of this allusion, see also Marguerite Waller, "Decolonizing the Screen: From *Ladri di biciclette* to *Ladri di saponette,"* in *Designing Italy: Italy in Asia, Africa, the Americas, and Europe,* ed. Beverly Allen and Mary Russo (Minneapolis: U of Minnesota P, 1997), 257.
6. Frank Kermode, *The Sense of an Ending: Studies in the Theory of Fiction* (New York: Oxford UP, 1975).
7. "It is not the concern of an artist to propound solutions," wrote Cesare Zavattini. "It is enough, and quite a lot, I should say, to make an audience feel the need, the urgency for them. . . . At least, in my work, I leave the solution to the audience." See "Some Ideas on the Cinema," in *Vittorio De Sica: Contemporary Perspectives,* ed. Howard Curle and Stephen Snyder (Toronto: U of Toronto P, 2000), 56. Fellini aptly explained the way in which open-endedness invests viewers with responsibility for completing the film and carrying its meaning into their lives. "My films don't have what is called a final scene. The story never reaches its conclusion. . . . I feel that a film is the more moral if it doesn't offer the audience the solution found by the character whose story is told. . . . My films, on the contrary, give the audience a very exact responsibility. . . . If the film has moved us, and troubled us, we must immediately begin to have new relationships with our neighbours." Federico Fellini, *Fellini on Fellini,* trans. Isabel Quigley (New York: Dell, 1976), 150–51.
8. For the Viscontian allusion, see Marco Pistoia, *Maurizio Nichetti* (Milan: Il Castoro, 1997), 63.
9. Because Nichetti had no money to pay for electronic special effects, his staff worked on the sequence frame by frame, in the way cartoons are processed. The sequence was printed first in color, then in black and white with a hole where Heidi was, and a third composite print was struck. See Annette Insdorf,

"In *The Icicle Thief* Parody Turns into a Tour de Force," *New York Times*, Sunday, 19 Aug. 1990, H26. See also Nuccio Orto, *Maurizio Nichetti: Un comico, un autore* (Chieti: Métis, 1990), 65-66.

10. See Raymonde Borde and André Bouissey, "Le miserabilisme romain," in *Le nouveau cinéma italien* (Lyon: Serdoc, 1963), 18-33.

11. This is Waller's felicitous term; see "Decolonizing the Screen," 268.

12. I am grateful to my student Bruce Snider at the University of Texas for this insight.

13. Roberto Rossellini, *The War Trilogy*, trans. Judith Green (New York: Grossman, 1973), 69-70.

14. For this observation I am indebted to Angela Tran, who took my Italian cinema course in fall 1995.

15. I am grateful to the students in my Italian cinema class who pointed out this reference.

16. Quoted in Insdorf, "Parody Turns into a Tour de Force."

17. Ibid. For further statements by Nichetti on the subject of commercial interruptions, see Robert Seidenberg, "*The Icicle Thief*: Maurizio Nichetti Brings His Slapstick to America," *American Film* 15 (June 1990): 51.

18. Waller sees this mode of viewing as an example of "a kind of faux rhizome of discontinuous, narrative and non-narratively based" discourse in which—to use the terminology of Gilles Deleuze and Felix Guattari ("Decolonizing the Screen," 264-65)—rhizome metaphorically signifies a nonhierarchical and therefore nonauthoritarian organization of space.

19. I am grateful to my student Aaron Tucker ("Italian Cinema," fall 1996, University of Texas) for this insight and for the idea, mentioned above, that Anna creates her own entertainment by means of channel surfing. For further comments on the televisual editing of films by viewers armed with remote controls, see Marcia Landy, *Italian Film* (Cambridge: Cambridge UP 2000), 367-68.

20. I am indebted to my student Kristin Organ ("Italian Cinema," fall 1995) for this idea.

21. Though she does not use the term *postmodernity*, Susan Sontag anticipates the concept in describing our contemporary culture as based on the activity of "producing and consuming images, when images that have extraordinary powers to determine our demands upon reality and are themselves coveted substitutes for firsthand experience become indispensable to the health of the economy, the stability of the polity and the pursuit of private happiness." See *On Photography* (New York: Dell, 1973), 153.

22. On the inertia of this family, which perhaps is not so much better off than its neorealist predecessors, see Stanley Kauffmann's "Fine Italian Hands," *New Republic*, 1 Oct. 1990, 26.

23. Carlina's comment is an in-joke. The Splash ad and Carlina's experiences sharing an apartment with Angela and Luisa are references to the plot of Nichetti's 1980 film *Ho fatto splash*. The actress who played Carlina in the 1980 film (Carlina Torta) plays the role of the pregnant mother, also named Carlina, in the viewing family of *The Icicle Thief*.

24. According to Robert DiMatteo, "Nichetti grasps what other postmodernists do: that the omnipresence of television and movies in our lives has managed to wreak havoc on that thing called 'old fashioned reality'"; see "Who Framed Maurizio Nichetti," *Film Comment* (Sept.-Oct. 1990): 57.

25. For details of Nichetti's past experience with mime as student, actor, and teacher, see Orto, *Maurizio Nichetti*, 9-27, passim.
26. On Fava's auteurism, see Waller, "Decolonizing the Screen," 267.
27. I am indebted to my students at the University of Texas for making these points in class discussion.
28. Pistoia notes Nichetti's Pirandellian affinities in *The Icicle Thief*; see *Maurizio Nichetti*, 66.
29. On Nichetti's fondness for doubling in this scene and in other contexts throughout *The Icicle Thief* and his previous filmography, see Pistoia, *Maurizio Nichetti*, 66-67.
30. For her comments on the implications of the film's ending for the future of media culture, see Landy, *Italian Film*, 370.
31. See Linda Hutcheon, *The Politics of Postmodernism* (London: Routledge, 1989), 2 ff.
32. On Nichetti's complicitous relationship with television, see DiMatteo, "Who Framed Maurizio Nichetti," 54. For insights into the way in which Nichetti's experience in television has enriched his cinematic language and streamlined his modus operandi, see Orto, *Maurizio Nichetti*, 23 and 68-70.
33. On Nichetti's hybrid art, see ibid., 127.
34. De Sica made this claim for his first neorealist film, *Sciuscià* (1946); see his comments in *La table ronde* 149 (May 1960): 80.
35. See Cristina Degli-Esposti, "Recent Italian Cinema: Maniera and Cinematic Theft," *Canadian Journal of Italian Studies* 20 (1997): 20.
36. Jim Collins, "Television and Postmodernism," in *Channels of Discourse, Reassembled*, ed. Robert C. Allen (Chapel Hill: U of North Carolina P, 1992), 335.
37. This is Manuela Gieri's term. See *Contemporary Italian Filmmaking*, 210.

Chapter 12. Roberta Torre's *To Die for Tano*

1. Gleaned from a speech delivered at the conference "La letteratura in 101 anni di cinema," Gabinetto Viesseux, Florence, 6-7 June 1997. My thanks to Isabella Panero for giving me the benefit of her excellent notes on the proceedings, some of which I was not able to attend.
2. Goffredo Fofi, "Una nota," in Roberta Torre, *Tano da morire, un film: Soggetto e appunti di regia* (Palermo: Edizioni della Battaglia, 1995), 25.
3. This phrase, in Italian, appears prominently on the cover of the commercial videocassette version of the film.
4. Emanuela Martini, "Tano e gli altri," *Cineforum* 37 (Sept. 1997): 6.
5. Ibid.
6. Fofi, "Una nota," 25.
7. Luca Mosso, "Una milanese a Palermo: Intervista a Roberta Torre," *Cineforum* 37 (Sept. 1997): 7.
8. Luchino Visconti, writing in 1941:

> To me, a Lombard reader—accustomed by traditional conditioning to the limpid rigor of the Manzonian fantasy—the primitive and gigantic world of the fishermen of Aci Trezza and of the shepherds of Marineo always seemed elevated in an imaginative and violent tone of epic: to my Lombard eyes, happy even with the sky of my land that is "so beautiful when it is beautiful," Verga's Sicily really seemed the island of Ulysses, an island of adventures and

fervid passions, situated immobile and proud against the breakers of the Ionian Sea.

See Luchino Visconti, "Tradizione e invenzione," in Adelio Ferrero, *Visconti: Il cinema* (Modena: Comune di Modena, 1977), 38.

9. Mosso, "Una milanese a Palermo," 7.

10. See Vito Zagarri's analysis of the film in *Cinema italiano anni novanta* (Venice: Marsilio, 1998), 81.

11. See the interview by Mary Cappello, Wallace Sillanpoa, and Jean Walton, "Roberta Torre: Filmmaker of the *Incoscienza*," *Quarterly Review of Film and Video* 17, no. 4 (2000): 324.

12. Mario Sesti, "Tamburi lontani," in *La "scuola" italiana: Storia, strutture, e immaginario di un altro cinema, 1988–1996,* ed. Mario Sesti (Venice: Marsilio, 1996), 63.

13. Mosso, "Una milanese a Palermo," 8–9.

14. Ibid. For further commentary on Torre's subversion of the Mafia's stereotype as perpetuated by mainstream cinema, see the Cappello, Sillanpoa, and Walton interview, "Roberta Torre," 317, 325.

15. For the well-known and exceedingly useful interpretive concept of carnival, see Mikhail Bakhtin, *Rabelais and His World,* trans. Hélène Iswolsky (Bloomington: Indiana UP, 1984). Michael Holquist's introduction (ibid., 1–58) offers an especially helpful entrée to Bakhtin's thought.

16. The inconsistencies and contradictions in the popular accounts of Tano's legend are what dictated Torre's unconventional choice of genre for the telling of his story. "So with all these elements, the film started to become like an operetta, a musical, because there were multiple realities to Tano." See "Roberta Torre; Filmmaker of the *Incoscienza,* 320.

17. For these allusions, see Torre, *Tano da morire,* 24.

18. Mosso, "Una milanese a Palermo," 8.

19. For the published version of Caruso's account, see Torre, *Tano da morire,* 5.

20. On Torre's origins in documentary cinema, see the Cappello, Sillanpoa, and Walton interview, "Roberta Torre," 320.

21. See Martini, "Tano e gli altri," 6. Salvatore Riina, the "boss of bosses," masterminded the Sicilian Mafia's violent campaign against the state. He was arrested in 1993 and is serving eleven consecutive life sentences in a maximum security prison.

22. "Una milanese a Palermo," 8. For a brilliant and exhaustive treatment of the history and genre of the sceneggiata, see Giuliana Bruno, *Streetwalking on a Ruined Map: Cultural Theory and the City Films of Elvira Notari* (Princeton: Princeton UP, 1993).

23. See interview, "Roberta Torre," 317.

24. Mosso, "Una milanese a Palermo," 8l.

25. Martini, "Tano e gli altri," 6. These skulls also allude to the Capuchins' mausoleum in Palermo. See interview, "Roberta Torre," 324.

26. Don Fabrizio's long disquisition to Chevalley on Sicily's penchant for voluptuous oblivion is the best literary explanation of this syndrome. See Giuseppe Tomasi di Lampedusa, *The Leopard,* trans. Archibald Colquhoun (New York: Pantheon, 1960), 204-8.

27. In Mosso, "Una milanese a Palermo," 7.

Chapter 13. Francesco Rosi's *The Truce*

1. Primo Levi, *I sommersi e i salvati* (Turin: Einaudi, 1991), 10.
2. On the theoretical issues raised by cinematic renditions of literary texts, see my "Umbilical Scenes: Where Filmmakers Foreground Their Relationships to Literary Sources," *Romance Languages Annual* 10 (1998): xix–xxiv, and my introduction to *Filmmaking by the Book: Italian Cinema and Literary Adaptation* (Baltimore: Johns Hopkins UP, 1993), 1–24.
3. Shoshana Felman and Dori Laub, *Testimony: Crises of Witnessing in Literature, Psychoanalysis, and History* (New York: Routledge, 1992), 5.
4. Primo Levi, *I sommersi e i salvati*, 8. For an insightful analysis of the problem of the Holocaust survivor as a witness manqué, see Gian Paolo Biasin, *Le periferie della letteratura* (Ravenna: Longo, 1997), 112.
5. Levi, *I sommersi e i salvati*, 65.
6. See Felman and Laub, *Testimony*, 68, 69.
7. Primo Levi, *La tregua* (Turin: Einaudi, 1997), 61 (page-number references hereafter given in main text, all to this edition; the English translations are mine).
8. Or, in the words of Elena Cantoni, "Levi, deprived of hope and faith, had at bottom the courage to . . . take upon himself—with great calmness and sobriety—the terrible, but necessary, burden of testifying to the ultimate evil. Today, Francesco Rosi has, in a certain sense, committed himself to doing the same." See "Scrittore per necessità," in *Supplemento a New Age Music and New Sounds* 70 (summer 1997): 17. See the related comments by Raffaello Carabini in the introduction to the same issue: 1.
9. Reprinted in Primo Levi, *Se questo è un uomo e La tregua* (Turin: Einaudi, 1989), 330.
10. The decision to end this sequence with the prisoners' dance is one of Rosi's several original, medium-specific additions to Levi's written account. See Cantoni, "Scrittore per necessità," 17.
11. Quoted in Beatrice Cattaneo, "Francesco Rosi," in *Supplemento a New Age Music and New Sounds* 70 (summer 1997): 19. For Turturro's own comments on his effort to get into character, see Isabella Fava, "Un lungo viaggio incontro alla vita," in *Supplemento a New Age Music and New Sounds* 70 (summer 1997): 13.
12. I therefore disagree with Fernaldo Di Giammatteo, who sees in the film's third-person visualization of Levi an eclipse of "[the] 'us' of whom Levi is the spokesman," with the result that "the thickness of the story-testimony . . . is considerably diminished." See "Al centro del nulla grigio," *Rivista del cinematografo* 67 (Mar. 1997): 35. Some of the film's negative critics have focused on the infidelity of Turturro's performance to Levi's self-presentation in the text. Cf. Cesare Segre's review, exhaustively titled "Confronti: Incomprensioni ed errori: Alcune soluzioni del film tradiscono il libro di Levi. Ma soprattutto disturbano. *La tregua?* Caro Rosi, proprio non ci siamo," in *Corriere della sera* (28 Feb. 1997): 31. Edoardo Bruno's defense of the performance as a reinvention of the character, by the actor, through a process of internalization and reexternalization of the first-person experience of the author goes far toward dispelling the force of such "fidelity criticism." See "Il percorse dell'erranza," *Filmcritica* 47 (Apr. 1997): 188–89.
13. Quoted in Fava, "Un lungo viaggio incontro alla vita," 9.

14. See Fernaldo Di Giammatteo, "Al centro di un nulla grigio," 34.
15. Levi, *Se questo è un uomo,* 7.
16. Francesco Rosi, "La tregua non è rosa," *La repubblica,* 6 June 1997, 47.
17. For a sensitive discussion of the meaning of Levi's title, see Alessandro Cappabianca, "Allegria di naufragi," in *Filmcritica* 47 (Apr. 1997): 191. Nicholas Patruno offers valuable insights into the irony of the title given to the English edition of the memoirs, *The Reawakening,* lifted from the title of the final chapter of the volume, "Il risveglio." See *Understanding Primo Levi* (Columbia: U of South Carolina P, 1995), 29 and 52.
18. The use of such regional stereotypes has formed the basis of much criticism of the film, bringing down charges of Rosi's descent to a commedia all'italiana level inappropriate to the dignity of the subject matter. See, for example, Marco Balbi's review of *La tregua* in *Ciak* 13 (Mar. 1997): 33; Francesco Pitassio's review in *Cineforum* 37 (Mar. 1997): 73; and Bruno, "Il percorso dell'erranza," 188. What such criticisms ignore is the dynamic interchange that Rosi establishes between the epic register of his film and its parodic, mirror opposite in the commedia all'italiana—a dialectic that translates into cinematic terms the literary relationship between Cesare's use of *romanesco* to organize his world and Levi's high-cultural attempt to contain and order the chaos of experience through an elevated language in the writing of his memoirs.
19. According to Bruno, *The Truce* is "a film woven on symbologies that we considered obsolete but that, in the locomotive that moves in the acrid smoke of the steam engine, finds an ideological recall, a symbol, or, better, the allegory of an unrepeatable season"; see "Il percorso dell'erranza," 188.
20. For my study of this topos in the Italian context, see "The Italian Body Politic Is a Woman: Feminized National Identity in Postwar Italian Film," in *Sparks and Seeds: Medieval Literature and Its Afterlife: Essays in Honor of John Freccero,* 329–47.
21. On the colossal scale of the film, which Di Giammatteo construes in purely negative terms, see "Al centro del nulla grigio," 35. For accounts of the way in which the process of filming *The Truce* became mimetic—reproducing, in the material difficulties of shooting on location in Poland and the Ukraine (in weather conditions ranging from 30 above to 30 below zero C), the physical and psychological ordeal of the characters in the story—see Isabella Fava, "Un lungo viaggio incontro alla vita," 10.
22. "There are two complementary, but different, aspects: on the one hand, the individual, on the other, the masses, chorality," explains Luis Bacalov, describing his logic in composing the music for *The Truce.* See Marco Fullone, "Luis Bacalov," in *Supplemento a New Age Music and New Sounds* 70 (summer 1997): 24.
23. Carlo Dansi, "La tregua," *Ciak* 13 (Mar. 1997): 61.
24. See Fullone, "Luis Bacalov." Similarly, Bruno sees the film as a recall "to a past, between culture and nature in the filmic fiction—memorable in and of itself— a cinema that by now has become 'classic'"; see "Il percorso dell'erranza," 188.

Chapter 14. Roberto Benigni's *Life Is Beautiful*

1. Umberto Eco, *The Limits of Interpretation* (Bloomington: Indiana UP, 1990), 165.
2. The enthusiasm generated by the film needs no documentation, as the results

at Cannes and the Academy Awards testify. Typical of negative reactions are David Denby's two reviews in the *New Yorker* (16 Nov. 1998, 114-16, and 15 Mar. 1999, 96-99) and Stuart Liebman's "If Only Life Were So Beautiful," in *Cineaste* 24, nos. 2-3 (1999): 20-22. My thanks to Ruth Perlmutter for bringing Liebman's article to my attention.

3. Luigi Pirandello, *L'umorismo* (Milan: Mondadori, 1986), 135 (page-number references to Pirandello's essay hereafter given in the main text).

4. See Benigni's comments in preface to the screenplay, published as Roberto Benigni and Vincenzo Cerami, *La vita è bella* (Turin: Einaudi, 1998), vii (page-number references hereafter given in the main text; all quotes from the screenplay are from this edition).

5. On Benigni's decision not to document or describe the Holocaust but to evoke it imaginatively, see his comments in the screenplay preface, x.

6. Primo Levi, *Survival at Auschwitz,* trans. Stuart Woolf (New York: Touchstone, 1996), 66.

7. This was the substance of Barbie Zelizer's talk at the colloquium "Documenting the Holocaust," held at the National Museum of American Jewish History, Philadelphia, 15 Apr. 1999.

8. On the need for alternative approaches to Holocaust representation, see Marcia Landy, *Italian Film* (Cambridge: Cambridge UP, 2000), 120.

9. This framing narration is not present in the original Italian version of the film. Harvey Weinstein, the president of Miramax, suggested to Benigni the need for such a framework for the American version. The framework was then included in the Italian version of the Miramax video. Here I have decided to consider the frame as an element of what Gérard Genette terms the "paratext," and therefore an integral part of the way in which viewers are positioned with respect to the work. For his comprehensive study of paratextual devices in literature, see Genette, *Paratexts: Thresholds of Interpretation,* trans. Jane Lewin (Cambridge: Cambridge UP, 1997).

10. Stuart Liebman, "If Only Life Were So Beautiful," *Cineaste* 24, nos. 2-3 (1999): 22.

11. Landy also notes the association between Benigni's framing and that of the Taviani brothers' film; see *Italian Film,* 120.

12. For an extended analysis of the Taviani brothers' film, see my chapter *"Night of the Shooting Stars:* Ambivalent Tribute to Neorealism," in *Italian Film in the Light of Neorealism* (Princeton: Princeton UP, 1986), 360-90.

13. Maurizio Viano comments on the reemergence of this framing fragment in *"Life Is Beautiful:* Reception, Allegory, and Holocaust Laughter," *Annali d'Italianistica* 17 (1999): 165.

14. According to Giorgio Cremonini, the image of mass death "is necessary, among other things, to remind us that Guido does not escape into a dream but is conscious of what is happening to him and of what he is doing"; see "Uno, due, tre, oggi si ride (storto)," *Cineforum* 370 (Dec. 1997): 10.

15. This phrase comes from "The Syntax of Death in the European Cinema," a paper presented by Dudley Andrew at the "European Cinemas/European Societies, 1895-1995" conference held at Indiana University, 29 Sept. 1995.

16. Quoted in Alexandra Stanley, "The Funniest Italian You've Probably Never Heard Of," *New York Times Magazine,* Sunday, 11 Oct. 1998, 44.

17. Morandino Morandini, "Il bello di Benigni," *Cineforum* 370 (Dec. 1997): 3.
18. For a probing analysis of the implications of the film's dichotomous structure, which amounts to a veritable "architectural allegory," see Viano, "*Life Is Beautiful:* Reception, Allegory, and Holocaust Laughter," 163 ff.
19. On the Grand Hotel as signifier in Italian cinema of the 1930s, see James Hay, *Popular Film Culture in Fascist Italy* (Bloomington: Indiana UP, 1987), ch. 1, "Castelli in Aria: The Myth of the Grand Hotel," 37-63. See also Landy, *Italian Film,* 117.
20. In an interview reported by Edward Rothstein ("Using Farce to Break the Dark Spell of Fascism," *New York Times,* 18 Oct. 1998, 28), Benigni explained that *Amarcord's* representation of Fascism as a circus world, presided over by the "big, big face of Mussolini," was an important influence on *Life Is Beautiful.*
21. This information was gleaned from an unpublished article by Stefania Parigi: "Un telefono bianco per comunicare con i sogni."
22. Edward Rothstein makes an excellent argument for the general way in which Fascism invites the critical assaults of satire; see "Using Farce," 28.
23. My thanks to Manuela Gieri, whose *Contemporary Italian Filmmaking: Strategies of Subversion, Pirandello, Fellini, Scola, and the Directors of the New Generation* (Toronto: Toronto UP, 1995) brought to my attention the central importance of Pirandello to the postwar cinematic imagination.
24. In my thinking about translation, I am indebted to Lina Insana for her numerous insights on the subject, growing out of the research for her dissertation "Translation 'alla rovescia': The Metaphor and Practice of *Translatio* in Primo Levi's Holocaust Writings," University of Pennsylvania, 2001.
25. "Che errore la regia," *Rivista del cinematografo* 12 (Dec. 1997): 15.
26. See Sigmund Freud, *Jokes and Their Relation to the Unconscious,* trans. James Strachey (New York: Norton, 1963), 90.
27. On Benigni's desire to make us see through the eyes of Giosuè, the reader is referred to his comments in the screenplay preface, x.
28. When Benigni improvised this scene in a trattoria with Vincenzo Cerami, it became the germ of what would develop into the full-fledged story of *Life Is Beautiful.* See Alessandra Stanley, "The Funniest Italian You've Probably Never Heard Of," 44.
29. In complaining that Guido "is forced to dismiss—perhaps a bit too strenuously—as absurd the rumors Giosuè hears about prisoners being made into buttons," Stuart Liebman has pinpointed the rhetorical mechanism by which Benigni's dismissal, and the energy that goes into it, only heighten the effect of the horror. See Liebman, "If Only," 21.
30. *Jokes and Their Relation to the Unconscious,* 151.
31. Primo Levi, *I sommersi e I salvati* (Turin: Einaudi, 1991), 10.
32. See Cremonini, "Uno, due, tre," 10.
33. On this audience response, see Leonard Pitts Jr., "A Movie about the Holocaust Reminds Viewers that Laughter Is Often an Act of Faith," *Philadelphia Inquirer,* 14 Nov. 1998, A10. See also Gian Luigi Rondi, "Il riso amaro del nuovo Chaplin," *Rivista del cinematografo* 12 (Dec. 1997): 7.
34. On the complexity of the film's ending, see Sander Gilman, "Is Life Beautiful? Can the Shoah Be Funny? Some Thoughts on Recent and Older Films," *Critical Inquiry* 20 (winter 2000): 303-4.

Chapter 15. Nanni Moretti's *Caro diario*

1. See Francesco Rosi, "C'era una volta il cinema," in *La repubblica,* 20 Apr. 1994, 33. My thanks to Carlo Testa for bringing the article to my attention.
2. See Clive James, "Mondo Fellini," *New Yorker,* 21 Mar. 1994, 164.
3. Angela Dalle Vacche, *The Body in the Mirror: Shapes of History in Italian Cinema* (Princeton: Princeton UP, 1992), 254, 277.
4. Mario Sesti, "Storia naturale del cinema di Moretti," in *Facciamoci del male: Il cinema di Nanni Moretti,* ed. Paola Ugo and Antioco Floris (Cagliari: CUEC Editrice, 1990), 135.
5. On the representativeness of his cinema, see Moretti's comments quoted in Flavio De Bernardinis, *Nanni Moretti* (Pavia: Il Castoro, 1993), 3. In his review of *Io sono un autarchico,* Alberto Moravia pointed out the way in which the young, countercultural members of the viewing public recognized themselves in Moretti's satire. See Moravia's "Come eravamo? Da ridere," reprinted in Ugo and Floris, eds., *Facciamoci del male,* 135.
6. This is Moretti's phrase, quoted from the interview in Mimmo Giovannini, Enrico Magrelli, and Mario Sesti, *Nanni Moretti* (Naples: Edizioni Scientifiche Italiane, 1986), 16.
7. On Michele's status as grapheme of his generation, see Sesti, "Storia naturale," 14.
8. In the words of De Bernardinis, *Nanni Moretti,* 47.
9. Sesti comments on the importance of this juxtaposition of self-images in "Ritorno al futuro: Ritratti dell'artista da personaggio," in Giovannini, Magrelli, and Sesti, *Nanni Moretti,* 51.
10. See Linda Hutcheon, *The Politics of Postmodernism* (London: Routledge 1993), 2 ff.
11. On this doubled and ironized gaze, see Sesti, "Storia naturale," 16-20, passim. Sesti considers the inscription of Moretti's perspective as both subject and object of satiric attack to be the very hallmark of the filmmaker's vision; see "Ritorno al futuro," 47-48. Fellini's self-implicating satire rests on similar grounds, where the displaced autobiographism of Titta/Moraldo/Marcello/Guido/Snaporaz allows the filmmaker the freedom both to recognize and reproach his protagonist. Because Moretti plays the role of his own autobiographical stand-in, his complicitous critique is less mediated than Fellini's but more coy, constantly calling our attention to the shifting degrees of identification and ironic distance that stand between author and narrative persona.
12. On the commedia all'italiana antecedents of *Ecce bombo,* see Ugo Casiraghi's review reprinted in *Facciamoci del male,* 143.
13. Quoted in De Bernardinis, *Nanni Moretti,* 6.
14. For a meditation on the way in which the diary format liberates Moretti to seek a language of pure cinematic expressivity, see ibid., 131.
15. According to Landy, the first episode of *Caro diario* documents Moretti's process of "shaking loose from the prison house of conventional images and words." See *Italian Film* (Cambridge: Cambridge UP, 2000), 374.
16. Moretti gave the following account of the visual novelty of this segment:

In the first episode I cruise through the streets on my Vespa in a deserted Rome, followed only by a jeep on which there were the cameraman and the director of photography. A joy—I felt free just as when I shot my first short subjects. Even the style reflects this: there's the novelty that the camera moves in continuous dolly shots on things . . . it performs evolutions where before I preferred fixed frames and a certain kind of internal montage. In short, here, there's more air, more breathing space, more music, and a bit of improvisation because I shot starting from a treatment, more than on the basis of a hard and fast screenplay.

From the interview with Ermanno Comuzio, "Moretti a tu per tu con il pubblico," *Cineforum* 93 (Nov. 1993): 62.

17. I am indebted to Roberto Ellero for this apt analogy to *The Big Chill*. See his review in *Segnocinema* 14 (Jan.-Feb. 1994): 41.

18. See Michael A. Arzen, "Who's Laughing Now? The Postmodern Splatter Film," *Journal of Popular Film and Television* 21 (winter 1994): 179, 180, and 178. I am grateful to my student Jennifer Breen for bringing this article to my attention.

19. Or, as Emanuela Martini puts it, Moretti takes issue with the critic who puts together words without worrying about their literal or ethical meaning. See her review in *Cineforum* 33 (Nov. 1993): 60.

20. In this, we may find the key to the "moral gaze" that Moretti is seen to share with his predecessors Rossellini and Pasolini. See Comuzio interview, "Moretti a tu per tu con il pubblico," 63.

21. Moretti has often cited the Taviani brothers, Bertolucci, Bellocchio, Pasolini, Olmi, and Ferreri as his cinematic forebears. See, for example, the interviews in Giovannini, Magrelli, and Sesti, *Nanni Moretti,* 38, and in *Cineforum* 93: 62-63, and the quotes appearing in *Nanni Moretti,* ed. Georgette Ranucci and Stefanella Ughi (Rome: Dino Audino Editore, 1994), 13, and in De Bernardinis, *Nanni Moretti,* 8.

22. See Pier Paolo Pasolini, *Empirismo eretico* (Milan: Garzanti, 1981), 237-41. For the English translation of this important collection of essays, see *Heretical Empiricism,* trans. Louise Barnett and Ben Lawton (Bloomington: Indiana UP, 1988). It was De Bernardinis's comments in *Nanni Moretti,* 125, and Roberto Ellero's review in *Segnocinema* 14 that alerted me to the relevance of Pasolini's film theory to this sequence in *Caro diario.*

23. Pasolini, *Empirismo eretico,* 241.

24. See the essay of this title, ibid., 198-226.

25. For Pasolini's suggestive but highly controversial semiotics of the cinema, see his pioneering essay "Cinema di poesia," ibid., 167-87. Moretti, seeking to balance the claims of referentiality with the need for avant-garde experimentation, models his art on the auteur cinema of the 1960s, a cinema that, in his own words, "seeks to elaborate a new expressive language, but always keeping itself bound to reality." See his interview with Comuzio in *Cineforum* 33 (Nov. 1993): 63.

26. To compound the intertextual humor of this scene, the soap-opera plot reverses the denouement of Rossellini's film. Where Karen resolves to try to salvage her marriage with Antonio after her attempted escape, we learn that in *The Bold and the Beautiful* Nancy has no intention of returning to her husband, Thorn.

27. According to Landy, in this episode Moretti represents his body as a "text to be read"; see *Italian Film,* 375.

28. See, for example, the unease expressed in Emanuela Martini's review in *Cine-forum* 33 (Nov. 1993): 61.

29. Moretti's dismissal of his *maschera* has been the subject of much critical commentary with respect to *Caro diario*. See, for example, Landy, *Italian Film*, 375, Emanuela Martini's review in *Cineforum* 33 (Nov. 1993): 59, Roberto Ellero's in *Segnocinema* 41, Stanley Kauffmann's "Fine Italian Hand," in *New Republic*, 17 Oct. 1994, 38, and De Bernardinis's comments in *Nanni Moretti*, 125.

Bibliography

Althusser, Louis. *Lenin and Philosophy and Other Essays.* Trans. Ben Brewster. New York: Monthly Review Press, 1971.

Amelio, Gianni. *Amelio secondo il cinema: Conversazione con Goffredo Fofi.* Rome: Donzelli, 1994.

———. *Ladro di bambini.* Milan: Feltrinelli, 1992.

Ames, Jerry, and Jim Siegelman. *The Book of Tap: Recovering America's Long Lost Dance.* New York: David McKay, 1977.

Ansen, David. "The Emperor's New Clothes." *Newsweek,* 23 November 1987, 81–82.

Argentieri, Mino. "Federico Fellini *Ginger e Fred:* Critica dossier." *Cinemasessanta* 227 (March–April 1986): 51.

———. "*La scorta.*" *Cinemasessanta* 34 (March–June 1993): 38–40.

Aristarco, Guido. "Esperienza culturale ed esperienza originale di Luchino Visconti." In *Rocco e i suoi fratelli,* ed. G. Aristarco and G. Carancini, 13–47. Bologna: Cappelli, 1960.

Armes, Roy. *Film and Reality.* Harmondsworth, U.K.: Penguin, 1974.

———. *Patterns of Realism.* London: Tantivy, 1971.

Arzen, Michael A. "Who's Laughing Now? The Postmodern Splatter Film." *Journal of Popular Film and Television* 21 (winter 1994): 176–85.

Audino, Dino, and Gino Ventriglia, eds. "'La regia è come un iceberg, la parte importante sta sotto': Intervista a Gianni Amelio." *Script* 5 (May 1994): 33–37.

Bacon, Henry. *Visconti: Explorations of Beauty and Decay.* Cambridge: Cambridge University Press, 1998.

Bakhtin, Mikhail. *Rabelais and His World.* Trans. Hélène Iswolsky. Bloomington: Indiana University Press, 1984.

Balbi, Marco, "*La tregua.*" *Ciak* 13 (March 1997): 33.

Baldelli, Pio. *Luchino Visconti.* Milan: Mazzotta, 1983.

Baudrillard, Jean. *Simulations.* Trans. Paul Foss, Paul Patton, and Philip Beitchman. New York: Semiotext(e), 1983.

Baudry, Jean-Louis. *L'effet cinéma.* Paris: Albatros, 1978.

Bazin, André. *What Is Cinema? II.* Trans. Hugh Gray. Berkeley: University of California Press, 1972.

Behr, Edward. *The Last Emperor.* New York: Bantam, 1987.

Bencivenni, Alessandro. *Luchino Visconti.* Florence: La Nuova Italia, 1982.

Benigni, Roberto, and Vincenzo Cerami. *La vita è bella.* Turin: Einaudi, 1998.
Benjamin, Jessica. *The Bonds of Love: Psychoanalysis, Feminism, and the Problem of Domination.* New York: Pantheon, 1988.
Bernardi, Luigi. *Letteratura e rivoluzione in Gramsci.* Pisa: Editrice Tecnico-scientifico, 1973.
Bernardi, Sandro. "Una generazione suicidata: Sintomi del disagio e segnali per una rinascita." In *In nome del cinema,* ed. Zagarrio, 147-52.
———. *Introduzione alla retorica del cinema.* Florence: Le Lettere, 1994.
Bertolucci, Bernardo. "A Hollywood da infiltrato: Colloquio con Bernardo Bertolucci." Interview by Silvia Bizio. *L'Espresso,* 24 April 1988, 9-11.
———. *Scene madri di Bernardo Bertolucci.* Interviews by Enzo Ungari and Don Ranvaud. Milan: Ubulibri, 1987.
Biasin, Gian Paolo. *Le periferie della letteratura.* Ravenna: Longo, 1997.
Bluher, Dominique. "Cinéma dans le cinéma: L'acteur dans *Bellissima* ou Second Traité sur 'Le cinéma anthropomorphique.'" In *Théorème: Visconti, classicisme, e subversion,* ed. Michele Lagny, 137-53. Paris: Sorbonne Nouvelle, 1990.
Blum, Cinzia Sartini. *The Other Modernism: F. T. Marinetti's Futurist Fiction of Power.* Los Angeles: University of California Press, 1996.
Bo, Fabio. "Dieci anni di solitudine: Dall'autobiografismo alla 'desistenza' narrativa." In *La "scuola" italiana,* ed. Sesti, 25-38.
Bolzoni, Francesco. "Anna Magnani." In *Filmlexicon degli autori e delle opere: Sezione Italia, aggiornamenti e integrazioni, 1972–1991,* 599-601. Rome: Nuova ERI, 1992.
———. *I film di Francesco Rosi.* Rome: Gremese, 1986.
———. "Mediterraneo." *Rivista del cinematografo* 61 (March 1991): 14.
Bondanella, Peter. *The Cinema of Federico Fellini.* Princeton: Princeton University Press, 1992.
———. *The Films of Roberto Rossellini.* New York: Cambridge University Press, 1993.
———. *Italian Cinema from Neorealism to the Present.* New York: Continuum, 1990.
———. "Stolen Children." *Cineaste* 20 (1994): 37-38.
Bonnigal, Dorothée. "Federico Fellini's *Amarcord:* Variations on the Libidinal Limbo of Adolescence." In *Fellini: Contemporary Perspectives,* ed. Burke and Waller.
———. "Fellini's Casanova: Exorcising the Loss of the Baroque Circle." *Il veltro,* nos. 1-2 (1996): 58-62.
———. "Restrained Women and Artistic Emancipation: Authority and Resistance in Federico Fellini's *Giulietta degli spiriti* and John Cassavetes' *A Woman under the Influence.*" *Romance Languages Annual* 7 (1995): 204-11.
Borde, Raymonde, and André Bouissey. "Le miserabilisme romain." *La nouveau cinéma italien.* Lyon: Serdoc, 1963.
Braudy, Leo. "Rossellini: From *Open City* to *General della Rovere.*" In *Great Film Directors,* ed. Leo Braudy and Morris Dickstein, 655-73. New York: Oxford University Press, 1978.
Brunetta, Gian Piero. "Il cinema italiano oggi." In *Annali d'italianistica,* ed. Marrone, 16-30.
———. *Storia del cinema italiano dal 1945 agli anni ottanta.* Rome: Riuniti, 1982.
Brunette, Peter. *Roberto Rossellini.* New York: Oxford University Press, 1987.
Bruno, Edoardo, "Ciao Pippo." *Filmcritica* 37 (1986): 93-95.
———. "L'epica e la riflessione." *Filmcritica* 43 (April 1992): 147-48.

———. "Il percorso dell'erranza." *Filmcritica* 47 (April 1997): 188-89.

Bruno, Giuliana. *Streetwalking on a Ruined Map: Cultural Theory and the City Films of Elvira Notari.* Princeton: Princeton University Press, 1993.

Bruno, Marcello Walter. "Meta in Italy." *Segnocinema* 11 (September-October 1991): 10-13.

Bundtzen, Lynda. "Bertolucci's Erotic Politics and the Auteur Theory: From *Last Tango in Paris* to *The Last Emperor.*" In *Bertolucci's "The Last Emperor,"* ed. Sklarew et al., 175-99.

Burgoyne, Robert. "The Stages of History." In *Bertolucci's "The Last Emperor,"* ed. Sklarew et al., 223-33.

Burke, Frank. "Federico Fellini: From Representation to Signification." *Romance Languages Annual* 1 (1989): 34-40.

———. *Fellini's Films.* New York: Twayne, 1996.

Burke, Frank, and Marguerite Waller, eds. *Federico Fellini: Contemporary Perspectives.* Toronto: University of Toronto Press, 2002.

Buttafava, Giovanni. "Effetto Oscar." *L'Espresso,* 24 April 1988, 6-9.

Canova, Giovanni. "La commedia e il suo doppio." In *La "scuola" italiana,* ed. Sesti, 49-56.

Cantoni, Elena. "Scrittore per necessità." *Supplemento a New Age Music and New Sounds* 70 (summer 1997): 14-17.

Canziani, Alfonso. *Visconti oggi.* Albano Terme: Piovan, 1984.

Cappabianca, Alessandro. "Allegria di naufragi." *Filmcritica* 47 (April 1997): 190-91.

———. "Il viaggio verso l'isola." *Filmcritica* 43 (April 1992): 149-50.

Cappello, Mary, Wallace Sillanpoa, and Jean Walton. "Roberta Torre: Filmmaker of the *Incoscienza.*" *Quarterly Review of Film and Video* 17 (2000): 317-31.

Casetti, Francesco, and Federico di Chio. *Analisi del film.* Milan: Bompiani, 1990.

———. *Bernardo Bertolucci.* Florence: La Nuova Italia, 1975.

Casiraghi, Ugo. *"Ecce Bombo."* In *Facciamoci del male,* ed. Ugo and Floris, 142-44.

Cattaneo, Beatrice. "Francesco Rosi." *Supplemento a New Age Music and New Sounds* 70 (summer 1997): 18-21.

Cheshire, Godfrey. "The Compassionate Gaze of Gianni Amelio." *Film Comment* (July-August 1993): 82-85, 88.

Chodorow, Nancy. *The Reproduction of Mothering: Psychoanalysis and the Sociology of Gender.* Berkeley: University of California Press, 1978.

Cielo, Silvana. "Qualche minuto al buio." *Filmcritica* 37 (1986): 95-96.

Clarke, Mary, and Clement Crisp. *The History of Dance.* New York: Crown, 1981.

Cocci, Stefano. *Bernardo Bertolucci.* Milan: Il Castoro, 1996.

Collins, Jim. "Television and Postmodernism." In *Channels of Discourse, Reassembled,* ed. Robert C. Allen. 327-53. Chapel Hill: University of North Carolina Press, 1992.

Comuzio, Ermanno. "Moretti a tu per tu con il pubblico." *Cineforum* 33 (November 1993): 62-63.

———. *"Nuovo cinema paradiso."* *Cineforum* 29 (May 1989): 81-84.

———. "Quando diventa esemplare il rapporto regista-compositore: La musica di Piccioni nei film di Rosi." In *Francesco Rosi,* ed. Gesù, 65-73.

Conley, Tom. *Film Hieroglyphs.* Minneapolis: University of Minnesota Press, 1991.

Cowell, Alan. "Thousands of Italian Mourners File in Homage Past Fellini Bier." *New York Times,* 3 November 1993, C22.

Cremonini, Giorgio. "Uno due tre, oggi si ride (storto)." *Cineforum* 370 (December 1997): 9-11.

Crowdus, Gary, and Dan Georgakas. "The Audience Should Not Be Just Passive Spectators: An Interview with Francesco Rosi." *Cineaste* 7 (fall 1975): 2-8.

Crowdus, Gary, and Richard Porton. "Beyond Neorealism: Preserving a Cinema of Social Conscience: An Interview with Gianni Amelio." *Cineaste* 21 (1995): 6-13.

D'Agostini, Paolo. "Un altro cinema: Voci e segnali del nuovo." In *La "scuola" italiana*, ed. Sesti, 39-47.

————. "La scorta." *Rivista del cinematografo* 63 (June 1993): 13.

Dalle Vacche, Angela. *The Body in the Mirror.* Princeton: Princeton University Press, 1992.

Dansi, Carlo. "La tregua." *Ciak* 13 (March 1997): 61.

De Bernardinis, Flavio. "Ladro di bambini." *Segnocinema* 12 (May-June 1992): 41-42.

————. *Nanni Moretti.* Pavia: Il Castoro, 1993.

De Giusti, Luciano. *I film di Luchino Visconti.* Rome: Gremese, 1985.

Degli-Esposti, Cristina. "Recent Italian Cinema: Maniera and Cinematic Theft." *Canadian Journal of Italian Studies* 20 (1997): 19-36.

DeLeuze, Gilles. *Cinema 2: The Time-Image.* Trans. Hugh Tomlinson and Robert Galeta. Minneapolis: University of Minnesota Press, 1989.

Denby, David. "Darkness Out of Light: Looking for Salvation in *The Siege, Elizabeth,* and *Life Is Beautiful.*" *New Yorker,* 16 November 1998, 114-16.

————. "In the Eye of the Beholder: Another Look at Roberto Benigni's Holocaust Fantasy." *New Yorker,* 15 March 1999, 96-99.

De Sica, Vittorio. "Vittorio De Sica." *La table ronde* 149 (May 1960): 78-82.

Di Giammatteo, Fernaldo. "Al centro del nulla grigio." *Rivista del cinematografo* 67 (March 1997): 34-37.

DiMatteo, Robert. "Who Framed Maurizio Nichetti." *Film Comment* (September-October 1990): 53-57.

Eco, Umberto. "Federico Fellini *Ginger e Fred: Critica dossier.*" *Cinemasessanta* 227 (March-April 1986): 50.

————. *The Limits of Interpretation.* Bloomington: Indiana University Press, 1990.

Ellero, Roberto. "Caro diario." *Segnocinema* 14 (January-February 1994): 41-42.

Faenza, Roberto. *Sostiene Pereira: Film Book.* Milan: Il Castoro, 1995.

Fairbank, John. "Born Too Late: *The Last Emperor.*" *New York Review of Books,* 18 February 1988, 14-16.

Faldini, Franca, and Goffredo Fofi, eds. *Il cinema d'oggi, 1970–1984.* Milan: Mondadori, 1984.

Fava, Claudio. *I film di Federico Fellini.* Rome: Gremese, 1991.

Fava, Claudio, and Aldo Viganò. "Che errore la regia." *Rivista del cinematografo* 12 (December 1997): 14-15.

Fava, Isabella. "Un lungo viaggio incontro alla vita." *Supplemento a New Age Music and New Sounds* 70 (summer 1997): 6-13.

Fellini, Federico. *Fare un film.* Turin: Einaudi, 1980.

————. *Fellini on Fellini.* Trans. Isabel Quigley. New York: Dell, 1976.

————. *Ginger e Fred.* Ed. Mino Guerrini. Milan: Longanesi, 1985.

————. *Juliet of the Spirits.* Trans. Howard Greenfeld. New York: Ballantine, 1965.

Felman, Shoshana, and Dori Laub. *Testimony: Crises of Witnessing in Literature, Psychoanalysis, and History.* New York: Routledge, 1992.

Ferrara, Gisueppe. *Luchino Visconto.* Paris: Seghers, 1963.

Ferrero, Adelio, ed. *Visconti: Il cinema.* Modena: Comune di Modena, 1977.

Freud, Sigmund. *Jokes and Their Relation to the Unconscious.* Trans. James Strachey. New York: Norton, 1963.

Frye, Northrop. *Anatomy of Criticism.* Princeton: Princeton University Press, 1973.

Fullone, Marco. "Luis Bacalov." *Supplemento a New Age Music and New Sounds* 70 (summer 1997): 22–24.

Garritano, Massimo. *"Il ladro di bambini." Cinemasessanta* 33 (March–April 1992): 25–27.

Geduld, Carolyn. *"Juliet of the Spirits:* Guido's Anima." In *Federico Fellini: Essays in Criticism,* ed. Peter Bondanella, 137–51. New York: Oxford University Press, 1978.

Genette, Gérard. *Parataexts:Thresholds of Interpretation.* Trans. Jane Lewin. Cambridge: Cambridge University Press, 1997.

Genovese, Nino. "Le fonti letterarie del cinema di Rosi." In *Francesco Rosi,* ed. Gesù, 55–63.

Gesù, Sebastiano, ed. *Francesco Rosi.* Acicatena: Incontri con il Cinema, 1991.

Giacci, Vittorio. "Ballo: Non solo." *Filmcritica* 37 (1986): 96–99.

Gieri, Manuela. *Contemporary Italian Filmmaking: Strategies of Subversion.* Toronto: University of Toronto Press, 1995.

———. "Landscapes of Oblivion and Historical Memory in the New Italian Cinema." In *Annali d'italianistica,* ed. Marrone, 39–54.

Gili, Jean. *Le cinéma italien.* Paris: Union Générale d'Editions, 1978.

Gilman, Sander. "Is Life Beautiful? Can the Shoah Be Funny? Some Thoughts on Recent and Older Films." *Critical Inquiry* 20 (winter 2000): 279–308.

Giovannini, Mimmo, Enrico Magrelli, and Mario Sesti, eds. *Nanni Moretti.* Naples: Edizioni Scientifiche Italiane, 1986.

Girard, René. *Deceit, Desire, and the Novel.* Trans. Yvonne Freccero. Baltimore: Johns Hopkins University Press, 1965.

Giusti, Mario. "Federico Fellini *Ginger e Fred:* Critica dossier." *Cinemasessanta* 227 (March–April 1986): 50.

Gosetti, Giorgio. "For an Italian Cinema of the '90s." *Rai 2 Italy:The Other Cinema* (n.d.): 12–14.

Gramsci, Antonio. *Marxismo e letteratura.* Ed. Giuliano Manacorda. Rome: Riuniti, 1975.

———. *Quaderni del carcere,* III. Ed. Valentino Garratana. Turin: Einaudi, 1975.

———. *Il risorgimento.* Turin: Einaudi, 1952.

Grassi, Raffaella. *Territori di fuga: Il cinema di Gabriele Salvatores.* Alessandria: Edizioni Falsopiano, 1997.

Hay, James. *Popular Film Culture in Fascist Italy.* Bloomington: Indiana University Press, 1987.

Hirsch, Jennifer. "Lo specchio, la luce e l'ombra: Riflessioni stilistiche nel cinema di Gianni Amelio." *American Journal of Italian Studies* 22 (1999): 38–51.

Hutcheon, Linda. *The Politics of Postmodernism.* London: Routledge, 1989.

———. *Theory of Parody: The Teachings of Twentieth-Century Art Forms.* New York: Methuen, 1985.

Insana, Lina. "Translation 'alla rovescia': The Metaphor and Practice of *Translation* in Primo Levi's Holocaust Writings." Dissertation, University of Pennsylvania, 2001.

Insdorf, Annette. "In *The Icicle Thief* Parody Turns into a Tour de Force." *New York Times,* 19 August 1990, 26H.

James, Clive. "Mondo Fellini." *New Yorker,* 21 March 1994, 154-65.

Jameson, Fredric. *Postmodernism, or, The Cultural Logic of Late Capitalism.* Durham: Duke University Press, 1991.

Jarrett, Vernon. *The Italian Cinema.* London: Falcon Press, 1951.

Kael, Pauline. "The Current Cinema: Francesco Rosi." *New Yorker,* 22 March 1982, 160-64.

———. "Lost Souls." *New Yorker,* 21 April 1986, 97-100.

———. "The Manchurian Conformist." *New Yorker,* 30 November 1987, 98-101.

Kaufman, Bonnie. "Power Sublime and Dangerous: Self-Analysis in the Filmcraft of *The Last Emperor.*" In *Bertolucci's "The Last Emperor,"* ed. Sklarew et al., 121-34.

Kauffmann, Stanley. "Fine Italian Hand." *New Republic,* 17 October 1994, 38-39.

———. "Fine Italian Hands." *New Republic,* 1 October 1990, 26-27.

———. "Good Intentions." *New Republic,* 21 April 1982, 24-25.

Kermode, Frank. *The Sense of an Ending: Studies in the Theory of Fiction.* New York: Oxford University Press, 1975.

Kezich, Tullio. "Federico Fellini *Ginger e Fred:* Critica dossier." *Cinemasessanta* 227: 54.

———. *Fellini.* Milan: Rizzoli, 1988.

Kline, T. Jefferson. "The Last Film Director in China: Repetition, Encapsulation, and Transformation in Bertolucci's Cinema." In *Bertolucci's "The Last Emperor,"* ed. Sklarew et al., 147-72.

Kolker, Robert. *Bernardo Bertolucci.* New York: Oxford University Press, 1985.

Kroll, Jack. "Last Waltz in Rome." *Newsweek,* 31 March 1986, 72.

Lacan, Jacques. *Écrits.* Trans. Alan Sheridan. New York: Norton, 1977.

———. *The Language of the Self: The Function of Language in Psychoanalysis.* Trans. Anthony Wilden. Baltimore: Johns Hopkins University Press, 1968.

Landy, Marcia. *Italian Film.* Cambridge: Cambridge University Press, 2000.

Lawton, Ben. "Italian Neorealism: A Mirror Construction of Reality." *Film Criticism* 3 (winter 1979): 8-23.

Levi, Primo. *Se questo è un uomo e La tregua.* Turin: Einaudi, 1989.

———. *I sommersi e i salvati.* Turin: Einaudi, 1991.

———. *Survival at Auschwitz.* Trans. Stuart Woolf. New York: Touchstone, 1996.

———. *La tregua.* Turin: Einaudi, 1997.

Liebman, Stuart. "If Only Life Were So Beautiful." *Cineaste* 24 (1999): 20-22.

Liehm, Mira. *Passion and Defiance: Film in Italy from 1942 to the Present.* Berkeley: University of California Press, 1984.

Lizzani, Carlo. *Il cinema italiano: Dalle origini agli anni ottanta.* Rome: Riuniti, 1992.

———. *Storia del cinema italiano, 1865-1961.* Florence: Parenti, 1961.

Lizzio, Rosario. "Intervista a Giuseppe Tornatore." *Cineforum* 29 (May 1989): 85-86.

Mannino, Franco. *Visconti e la music.* Lucca: Libreria Musicale Italiana, 1994.

Marcus, Millicent. "Cane da grembo o carne in scatola? Il divismo in 'Anna' e 'La strega bruciata viva.'" In *Studi viscontiani,* ed. David Bruni and Veronica Pravadelli, 107-20. Venice: Marsilio, 1997.

———. *Filmmaking by the Book: Italian Cinema and Literary Adaptation.* Baltimore: Johns Hopkins University Press, 1993.

———. "The Italian Body Politic Is a Woman: Feminized National Identity in

Postwar Italian Film." In *Sparks and Seeds: Medieval Literature and Its Afterlife: Essays in Honor of John Freccero,* ed. Dana Stewart and Alison Cornish, 329-47. Turnhout, Belgium: Brepols, 2000.

———. *Italian Film in the Light of Neorealism.* Princeton: Princeton University Press, 1986.

———. "Umbilical Scenes: Where Filmmakers Foreground Their Relationship to Literary Sources." *Romance Languages Annual* 10 (1998): xix-xxiv.

Marrone, Gaetana, ed. *Annali d'italianistica* 17, *New Landscapes in Contemporary Italian Cinema* (1999).

———. "Il nuovo cinema italiano: Pregiudizi, realtà e promesse." In *Annali d'italianistica,* 7-13.

Martini, Emanuela. "Caro diario." *Cineforum* 33 (November 1993): 58-61.

———. "Tano e gli altri." *Cineforum* 37 (September 1997): 3-6.

Masi, Stefano, and Enrico Lancia. *I film di Roberto Rossellini.* Rome: Gremese, 1987.

Menarini, Roy. "*Sostiene Pereira.*" *Segnocinema* (May-June 1995): 37-38.

Merkel, Flavio, ed. *Gabriele Salvatores.* Rome: Dino Audino, 1993.

Metz, Christian. *The Imaginary Signifier: Psychoanalysis and the Cinema.* Trans. Celia Britton, Annwyl Williams, Ben Brewster, and Alfred Guzzetti. Bloomington: Indiana University Press, 1982.

Miccichè, Lino. "Gli eredi del nulla: Per una critica del giovane cinema italiano." In *Una generazione in cinema,* ed. Montini, 251-58.

———. *Luchino Visconti: Un profilo critico.* Venice: Marsilio, 1996.

———. "Il lungo decennio grigio." In *Schermi opachi,* ed. Miccichè, 3-16.

———. *Visconti e il neorealismo.* Venice: Marsilio, 1990.

———, ed. *Schermi opachi: Il cinema italiano degli anni '80.* Venice: Marsilio, 1998.

Milne, Tom. "*Cinema Paradiso.*" *Monthly Film Bulletin* 57 (March 1990): 72-73.

Monni, Riccardo. "Nella forza dell'amicizia i segreti del successo." *La nazione,* 1 April 1992, 5.

Monteleone, Enzo. *Mediterraneo: Sceneggiatura del film diretto da Gabriele Salvatores.* Milan: Baldini & Castodi, 1992.

Montini, Franco, ed. *Una generazione in cinema: Esordi ed esordienti italiani, 1975–1988.* Venice: Marsilio, 1988.

Morandini, Morandino. "Il bello di Benigni." *Cineforum* 37 (December 1997): 3-5.

Moravia, Alberto. "Come eravamo? Da ridere." In *Facciamoci del male,* ed. Ugo and Floris, 134-35.

———. "L'ultima Cina." *L'Espresso,* 24 April 1988, 8-9.

Mori, Anna Maria. "Un amaro viaggio nel Sud." *La repubblica,* 8 April 1992, 33.

Mosso, Luca. "Una milanese a Palermo: Intervista a Roberta Torre." *Cineforum* 37 (September 1997): 7-9.

———. "*Sostiene Pereira.*" *Cineforum* 35 (April 1995): 84-85.

Mulvey, Laura. "Visual Pleasure and Narrative Cinema." In *Visual and Other Pleasures,* 14-26. Bloomington: Indiana University Press, 1989.

Nazzaro, Giona. "*La scorta.*" *Cineforum* 324 (May 1993): 49-51.

Ning, Ding. "Solving Riddles and Concocting Riddles." In *Bertolucci's "The Last Emperor,"* ed. Sklarew et al., 213-20.

Nowell-Smith, Geoffrey. "Pasolini's Originalilty." In *Pier Paolo Pasolini,* ed. Paul Willemen, 4-20. London: British Film Institute, 1977.

———. *Visconti.* New York: Viking, 1973.

Orto, Nuccio. *Maurizio Nichetti: Un comico, un autore.* Chieti: Métis, 1990.

Pasolini, Pier Paolo. *Empirismo eretico.* Milan: Garzanti, 1981.

————. *Heretical Empiricism.* Trans. Louise Barnett and Ben Lawton. Bloomington: Indiana University Press, 1988.

Patruno, Nicholas. *Understanding Primo Levi.* Columbia: University of South Carolina Press, 1995.

Pellizzari, Lorenzo. *"Il ladro di bambini."* *Cineforum* 32 (June 1992): 72-76.

————. *"Mediterraneo."* *Cineforum* 31 (April 1991): 85-87.

Picchi, Michele. *"La scorta."* *Cinema nuovo* 42 (November-December 1993): 9-10.

Pirandello, Luigi. *L'umorismo.* Milan: Mondadori, 1986.

Pistoia, Marco. *Maurizio Nichetti.* Milan: Il Castoro, 1997.

Pitassio, Francesco. *"La tregua."* *Cineforum* 37 (March 1997): 73.

Pitts, Leonard, Jr. "A Movie about the Holocaust Reminds Viewers that Laughter Is Often an Act of Faith." *Philadelphia Inquirer,* 14 November 1998, A10.

Platonov, Andrè. "The Third Son." In *Fro and Other Stories,* trans. Cathleen Cook, 64-72. Moscow: Progress Publishers, 1972.

Preziosi, Adelina. *"La scorta."* *Segnocinema* 13 (July-August 1993): 49-50.

Prono, Franco. "Crisi di paternità e svolta nel cinema di Gianni Amelio." *Cinema nuovo* 41 (July-October 1992): 38-41.

Pudovkin, V. I. "Film Technique." In *Film: An Anthology,* ed. Daniel Talbot, 189-200. Berkeley: University of California Press, 1972.

Pu Yi, Aisin-Gioro. *From Emperor to Citizen: The Autobiography of Aisin-Gioro Pu Yi.* Trans. W. J. F. Jenner. Peking: Foreign Languages Press, 1964.

Ranucci, Georgette, and Stefanella Ughi, eds. *Nanni Moretti.* Rome: Dino Audino, 1994.

Rayns, Tony. "Model Citizen: Bernardo Bertolucci on Location in China." *Film Comment* 23 (November-December 1978): 31-36.

Reggiani, Stefano. "Federico Fellini *Ginger e Fred:* Critica dossier." *Cinemasessanta* 227 (March-April 1986): 50.

Regosa, Maurizio. *"La scorta."* *Cinema nuovo* 42 (July-October 1993): 66-67.

Renzi, Renzo. *Visconti segreto.* Bari: Laterza, 1994.

Roberti, Bruno, and Edoardo Bruno, eds. "Conversazione con Gianni Amelio." *Filmcritica* 43 (April 1992): 151-63.

Rondi, Gian Luigi. "Il riso amaro del nuovo Chaplin." *Rivista del cinematografo* 12 (December 1997): 7-10.

————. *"Sostiene Pereira."* *Rivista del cinematografo* 65 (June 1995): 17.

Rondolino, Gianni. *Roberto Rossellini.* Florence: La Nuova Italia, 1977.

Rony, Fatimah Tobing, "The Last Emperor." In *Bertolucci's "The Last Emperor,"* ed. Sklarew et al., 137-45.

Rosetti, Riccardo. "La fuga dalle cose." *Filmcritica* 37 (1966): 99-101.

Rosi, Francesco. "C'era una volta il cinema." *La repubblica* 20 April 1994, 33.

————. *"La tregua* non è rosa." *La repubblica,* 6 June 1997, 47.

Rossellini, Roberto. *My Method: Writings and Interviews.* Ed. Adriano Aprà. New York: Marsilio, 1995.

————. "Roberto Rossellini." *La table ronde* 149 (May 1960): 74-78.

————. *The War Trilogy.* Trans. Judith Green. New York: Grossman, 1973.

Rothstein, Edward. "Using Farce to Break the Dark Spell of Fascism." *New York Times,* 18 October 1998, 28.

Rumble, Patrick. "Tornatore e l'America: Il cinema dell'anamnesi." In *Sicilia e altre storie: Il cinema di Giuseppe Tornatore,* ed. Valerio Caprara, 11-20. Naples: Edizioni Scientifiche Italiane, 1996.

Said, Edward. *Orientalism.* New York: Random House, 1979.

Salvetti, Stefano. "Francesca Archibugi e il 'real minimalismo.'" *Ciem* 26 (January-March 1994): 36-40.

Segre, Cesare. "Confronti: Incomprensioni ed errori." *Corriera della sera,* 28 February 1997, 31.

Seidenberg, Robert. "*The Icicle Thief:* Maurizio Nichetti Brings His Slapstick to America." *American Film* 15 (June 1990): 51.

Servadio, Gaia. *Luchino Visconti: A Biography.* New York: F. Watts, 1983.

Sesti, Mario. "Il nuovo, il cinema. Altre avventure." In *La "scuola" italiana,* ed. Sesti, 3-24.

———. *Nuovo cinema italiano: Gli autori, i film, le idee.* Rome: Theoria, 1994.

———. "Ritorno al futuro: Ritratti dell'artista da personaggio." In *Nanni Moretti,* ed. Giovannini, Magrelli, and Sesti, 41-51.

———. "Storia naturale del cinema di Moretti." In *Facciamoci del male,* ed. Ugo and Floris, 11-27.

———. "Tamburri lontani." In *La "scuola" italiana,* ed. Sesti, 59-67.

———, ed. *La "scuola" italiana: Storia, strutture, e immaginario di un altro cinema, 1988-1996.* Venice: Marsilio, 1996.

Sesti, Mario, and Stefanella Ughi, eds. *Gianni Amelio.* Rome: Dino Audino, 1994.

Shane, Estelle, and Morton Shane. "A Narrative of Psychological Rejuvenation." In *Bertolucci's "The Last Emperor,"* ed. Sklarew et al., 101-6.

Siciliani de Cumis, Nino. "Il mestiere del critico." *Cinema nuovo* 41 (November-December 1992): 41-46.

Silverman, Kaja. *The Acoustic Mirror: The Female Voice in Psychoanalysis and Cinema.* Bloomington: Indiana University Press, 1988.

Simon, John. "For Your Eyes Only." *National Review,* 18 December 1987, 54-57.

Singer, Daniel. "Gatt and the Shape of Our Dreams." *Nation,* 17 January 1994, 54.

Sitney, P. Adams. *Vital Crises in Italian cinema.* Austin: University of Texas Press, 1995.

Sklarew, Bruce, Bonnie Kaufman, Ellen Spitz, and Diane Borden, eds. *Bertolucci's "The Last Emperor": Multiple Takes.* Detroit: Wayne State University Press, 1998.

———. "The Prison of Entitlement." In *Bertolucci's "The Last Emperor,"* 85-99.

Sontag, Susan. *On Photography.* New York: Dell, 1973.

Sorlin, Pierre. *European Cinemas / European Societies.* London: Routledge, 1991.

Spiga, Vittorio. "L'ultimo imperatore." In *In viaggio con Bernardo: Il cinema di Bernardo Bertolucci,* ed. Roberto Campari and Maurizio Schiaretti, 112-19. Venice, Marsilio, 1994.

———. "Uomini in fuga, lontani da sé." *La nazione,* 1 April 1992, 5.

Stanley, Alessandra. "So Few Fellinis." *New York Times,* 25 May 2000, B10.

———. "The Funniest Italian You've Probably Never Heard Of." *New York Times,* 11 October 1998, magazine, 42-45.

Tabucchi, Antonio. *Sostiene Pereira.* Milan: Feltrinelli, 1994.

Tassone, Aldo. *Parla il cinema italiano* II. Milan: Il Formichiere, 1980.

Tomasi di Lampedusa, Giuseppe. *The Leopard.* Trans. Archibald Colquhoun. New York: Pantheon, 1960.

Tornabene, Francesco. *Federico Fellini: The Fantastic Vision of a Realist.* Berlin: Benedikt Taschen, 1990.

Tornatore, Giuseppe. *Nuovo cinema paradiso*. Palermo: Sellerio, 1990.

Torre, Roberta. *Tano da morire, un film: Soggetto e appunti di regia*. Palermo: Edizioni della Battaglia, 1995.

Ugo, Paola, and Antioco Floris, eds. *Facciamoci del male: Il cinema di Nanni Moretti*. Cagliari: CUEC, 1990.

Ungari, Enzo, and Don Ranvaud, eds. *Scene madri di Bernardo Bertolucci*. Milan: Ubulibri, 1987.

Van Gelder, Lawrence. "Fascist Outrages Awaken a Death-Obsessed Editor." *New York Times*, 3 April, 1998, E26.

Vernaglione, Paolo. *"Mediterraneo." Filmcritica* 42 (June 1991): 301-2.

———. "Variazioni minime sul sonoro." *Filmcritica* 37 (1986): 106-7.

Viano, Maurizio. "*Life Is Beautiful:* Reception, Allegory, and Holocaust Laughter." *Annali d'Italianistica* 17 (1999): 155-71.

Visconti, Luchino. "*Bellissima:* Storia di una crisi." Interview with Michele Gandin, in *Visconti: Il cinema*, ed. Adelio Ferrero, 42-46. Modena: Comune di Modena, 1977.

———. "Tradizione e invenzione." In *Visconti: Il cinema*, ed. Ferrero, 38.

Vitti, Antonio. "Il cinema italiano alle soglie del duemila." *American Journal of Italian Studies* 22 (1999): 1-10.

Waller, Marguerite. "Decolonizing the Screen: From *Ladri di biciclette* to *Ladri di saponette.*" In *Designing Italy: Italy in Asia, Africa, the Americas, and Europe*, ed. Beverly Allen and Mary Russo, 253-74. Minneapolis: University of Minnesota Press, 1997.

Warshow, Robert. *The Immediate Experience*. New York: Atheneum. 1974.

Wettlaufer, Alexandra. "Ruskin and Laforgue: Visual-Verbal Dialectics and the Poetics/Politics of Montage." *Comparative Literature Studies* 32 (1995): 514-35.

Winter, Marian Hannah. "Juba and American Minstrelsy." In *Chronicles of the American Dance*, ed. Paul Magriel. New York: Holt, 1948.

Zagarrio, Vito. *Cinema italiano anni novanta*. Venice: Marsilio, 1998.

———. "Elogio del cinema italiano." *Vivilcinema* 3 (May-June 2000): 8-9.

———, ed. *In nome del cinema: Quaderni del ponte*. Milan: Il Ponte, 1999.

Zagarrio, Vito, et al. "Per un cinema-cinema." *Cinecritica* 11 (January-June 1988): 129.

Zaller, Robert. "After the Revolution." In *Bertolucci's "The Last Emperor,"* ed. Sklarew et al., 235-50.

Zanzotto, Andrea. "Federico Fellini *Ginger e Fred:* Critica dossier." *Cinemasessanta* 227 (March-April 1986): 51.

Zavattini, Cesare. "Some Ideas on the Cinema." In *Vittorio De Sica: Contemporary Perspectives*, ed. Howard Curle and Stephen Snyder, 50-61. Toronto: University of Toronto Press, 2000.

Videography

Unless otherwise noted, the videos listed are in NTSC (American system) and are in Italian with English subtitles. The phone number for Facets, which distributes many of these videos, is 1-800-331-6197. Because the video distribution industry is quite volatile, some of the information listed below may have changed since the time it was compiled.

Amelio, Gianni. *Stolen Children (Il ladro di bambini)*. Curzon Video. Distributed by Fox Video, U.K. Tel: 071-753-8686. PAL (Italian) system.

Benigni, Roberto. *Life Is Beautiful (La vita è bella)*. Facets.

Bertolucci, Bernardo. *The Last Emperor (L'ultimo imperatore)*. English. Facets.

Faenza, Roberto. *Sostiene Pereira*. Mondadori Video. FAX: 02-75423230. Italian. PAL system.

Fellini, Federico. *Ginger and Fred (Ginger e Fred)*. Facets.

Moretti, Nanni. *Caro diario*. Facets.

Nichetti, Maurizio. *The Icicle Thief (Ladri di saponette)*. Facets.

Rosi, Francesco. *Three Brothers (Tre fratelli)*. TLA Video. 1-800-333-8521.

Rosi, Francesco. *The Truce (La tregua)*. English. Facets.

Rossellini, Roberto. *Paisan (Paisà)*. Facets.

Salvatores, Gabriele. *Mediterraneo*. Facets.

Tognazzi, Ricky. *The Escort (La scorta)*. Tartan Video. Distributed by Sony Music Operations, U.K. PAL system.

Tornatore, Giuseppe. *Cinema Paradiso (Nuovo cinema paradiso)*. Facets.

Torre, Roberta. *Tano da morire*. Lucky Red Home Video. Italian. PAL (Italian) system.

Visconti, Luchino. *Bellissima*. Facets.

Index

Page numbers in italics refer to film stills.

8 ½ (Fellini), 182, 184, 197, 246
1968: and disillusionment, 86; and
  Moretti, 286–287, 299; and PDUP, 122

Accaio (Ruttmann), 218
Activism, 285
Adaptation: in *The Last Emperor,* 65–66; in
  Pereira Declares, 94–105; in *Three Broth-*
  ers, 128–132, 137; in *The Truce,* 253–268
Advertising, 6, 187–189, 196, 222, 224,
  226, 227
Aisin-Gioro Pu Yi. *See* Pu Yi, Aisin-Gioro
Allegory: in *Caro diario,* 291–293; in
  Three Brothers, 118, 129, 134
Allonsanfan (Taviani brothers), 111
Althusser, Louis, 71–72
Altman, Robert, *The Player,* 215–216
Amarcord (Fellini), 273
Amelio, Gianni, 7, 11, *172; Stolen Children,*
  11, 154–177. See also *Stolen Children*
Amendola, Claudio, *142*
Anachronism, 68, 86
Andrew, Dudley, 271
Anna (Lattuada), 206
"Anna" (Visconti), 43–47, 327n13. See
  also *Siamo donne*
Antonioni, Michelangelo, 3; *Il grido,* 206;
  L'avventura, 173
Apocalypse Now (Coppola), 79
Ariosto, Ludovico, 207
Astaire, Fred, 194, 257. See also *Ginger*
  and Fred; tap dancing

Auteuil, Daniel, *102*
Auteurism, 227–231

Bacalov, Luis, 267
Bakhtin, Mikhail, 22, 236
Balzac, Honoré de, 95
Baudrillard, Jean, 6, 188, 295
Bazin, André, 323n1
Bellissima (Visconti), 10, 39–58, 222; cam-
  era work in, 43, 57; credits, 303; and
  divismo, 40–47; and film history, 47;
  and the gaze, 53–58; and gender roles,
  52–53; and improvisation, 42–43; and
  Lacan's mirror phase, 54–56; and
  melodrama, 50, 58; and opera, 45,
  50–51; plot summary, 303–304; and
  projection, 40–41, 51, 56–57; and the
  spectator, 329n35; and utopia, 58. *See*
  also Theater acting
Bellocchio, Marco, 4
Benigni, Roberto, 7; biography of, 271;
  Life Is Beautiful, 7, 11–12, 268–284; *The*
  Monster, 278. See also *Life Is Beautiful*
Benjamin, Jessica, 175. *See also* Feminism;
  Psychoanalysis
Berlusconi, Silvio, 187, 285
Bernardi, Sandro, 5
Bertolucci, Bernardo, 4, 267; aestheticism
  of, 66–67; *The Conformist,* 81; *The Last*
  Emperor, 7, 10–11, 61–75; and psycho-
  analysis, 70–74; *Spider Stratagem,* 119.
  See also *Last Emperor, The*

Bianca (Moretti), 286
Bicycle Thief (De Sica), 156, 160-161, 175-176, 278; and the church, indictment of, 155; as cinematic "superego," 214-216; in *The Icicle Thief* pastiche, 218-226, 229; as topos, 215-216
Bitter Rice (De Santis), 177
Blasetti, Alessandro, *46*, 47, 57, 322n28
Blood Feud, A (Wertmuller), 111
Body, the: of dead partisan in *Paisan*, 35-36, 38; female and fetishized in *The Icicle Thief*, 219, 229; and forced prostitution, 230; guarded in *La scorta*, 149, 152; Nazi harvest of, 279; and performance, 246; and plenitude in *To Die for Tano*, 235; pregnant, 227; as referent in *Caro diario*, 294, 296, 298-299, 325n24; on screen as reflection of national self, 286; as social metaphor in Moretti, 12, 287-288; of the spectator in *Cinema Paradiso*, 202
Body politic: allegorized by marital relationship, 123; and the body erotic, 267; in *Caro diario*, 12; and the disease of terrorism, 116; family as allegory of, 118, 122, 129; feminized, in *Mediterraneo*, 91; and *Life Is Beautiful*, spoof of Fascism in, 274; the marketplace as its stomach, 236; personified by Pereira in *Pereira Declares*, 102-103; as Salazarist propaganda ploy, 105
Bolzoni, Francesco, 44, 119, 120
Bondanella, Peter, 6, 29, 323n1
Borsellino, Paolo, 140
Brandt, Willy, 260
Brunetta, Gian Piero, 5
Brunette, Peter, 15, 34
Bruno, Edoardo, 174
Bruno, Marcello Walter, 205
Buttafava, Giovanni, 61

Cadaveri eccellenti (Rosi), 115
Camera work: in *Bellissima*, 43, 57; in *Caro diario*, 294; in *La scorta*, 150; in *Mediterraneo*, 77; in *Paisan*, 27-29; in *Starmaker*, 205-206; in *Stolen Children*, 156-157, 160, 175-176; in *Three Broth-*

ers, 124, 132, 136-137; in *To Die for Tano*, 240-241; in *The Truce*, 256, 260. See also De Santis, Pasqualino; *Mise-en-scène*; Projection
Cammino della Speranza (Germi), 157
Caprara, Valerio, 121
Carnival: in *Ginger and Fred*, 191; in *The Icicle Thief*, 232; in *Paisan*, 22; in *Stolen Children*, 168; in *To Die for Tano*, 236, 247
Caro diario (Moretti), 9, 11-12, 285-299; and allegory, 291-293; and the body, 286, 287-288, 294, 296, 298-299, 325n24; camera work in, 294; and Christian humanism, 295; and *commedia all'italiana*, 289-290; credits, 318-319; and documentary, 297, 298; and the gaze, 291, 299; and genre, 289-290; and Pasolinian semitoics, 293-295; plot summary, 319-320; and spectacle, 293, 294; and the splatter film, 293; and television, 291, 295
Casanova (Fellini), 182
Cascio, Salvatore, *210*
Casetti, Francesco, 103
Catene (Amadio), 206
Cavalleria rusticana (Zeffirelli), 139
Censorship, 201-202
Children Are Watching Us, The (De Sica), 154
Christ Stopped at Eboli (Rosi), 115, 117
Christian humanism: in *Caro diario*, 295; and Rossellini, 34; in *Three Brothers*, 128
Church, the: *Bicycle Thief* indictment of, 155; Catholic kitsch, 248-249; in *Cinema Paradiso*, 207-208; in *The Icicle Thief*, 218; and *La messa è finita*, 287; and *Mediterraneo* frescoes, 89-90; and *Paisan*, fifth episode, 31-34; in *Stolen Children*, 160-161; in *Three Brothers*, 128
Cinema Paradiso (Tornatore), 7, 199-213; and the church, 207-208; credits, 312-313; and escapism, 200; and film history, 200-201; films and actors included in, 200-201; and the gaze, 206; and pastiche, 199-201; and pleasure,

208–213; plot summary, 313–314; and postmodernism, 199–200, 207; and projection, 209; and reception, 199, 200–201; and the spectator, 202, 205–207; and sublimation, 211. *See also* Psychoanalysis

Cinema politico, 4, 115–117, 127; as generic influence on *La scorta*, 138–139, 140–141; origin of, 138

Cinematography. *See* Camera work

City of Women (Fellini), 184

Clift, Montgomery, 48

Collins, Jim, 233

Commedia all'italiana, 4; in *Caro diario*, 289–290; in *Life Is Beautiful*, 284; in *Mediterraneo*, 76, 78, 90, 93

Commedia dell'arte, 22

Commercials, 187–188. *See also* Advertising

Complicitous critique, 231, 290

Conformist, The (Bertolucci), 81

Contrappasso, 57

Conversion: in *The Last Emperor*, 64; in *Pereira Declares*, 112

Coppola, Francis Ford, 139; *Apocalypse Now*, 79; *Godfather Part II*, 139, 244, 245

Costa-Gavras, 115, 139; *Z*, 139

Cowell, Alan, 3

Credits, 301–320

Croce, Benedetto, 96, 119–120

Crosby, Bing, 65

Dalle Vacche, Angela, 285–286

Damiani, Damiano, 139

Daniele, Pino, 127

D'Annunzio, Gabriele, 111

Dansi, Carlo, 267

Dante Alighieri, 57, 84, 187, 298

Daudet, Alphonse, 95

De Chirico, Giorgio, 124

Degli-Esposti, Christina, 233

Deleuze, Gilles, 103. *See also Pereira Declares;* Voice-over

De Rougemont, Denis, 212

De Santis, Giuseppe, 177, 267; *Bitter Rice*, 177

De Santis, Pasqualino (cinematographer), 124, 136–137

De Sica, Vittorio, 3, 49, 267; *Bicycle Thief*, 154–156, 160–161, 214–226, 229, 278; career of, 214–215; *The Children Are Watching Us*, 154; *Shoeshine*, 154; *Umberto D*, 217

Desire, 188

Destiny, 241–243

Di Chio, Federico, 103

Dionisi, Stefano, *264*

Director's Notebook, A (Fellini), 190

Divismo, 40–47

Divorce Italian Style (Germi), 139

Documentary: as antecedent of neorealism, 218; in *Caro diario*, 297, 298; and Fellini, 190; heroic German, 260; and *Life Is Beautiful*, 281; *Paisan*, opening footage, 18; pro-Salazarist, in *Pereira Declares*, 104; and Rosi, 115; and Sicilian history in *La scorta*, 140; in *To Die for Tano*, 243; in *The Truce*, 260

Donizetti, Gaetano, 45, 50–51

Dream, in *Three Brothers*, 126–128

Ecce bombo (Moretti), 286, 287

Eco, Umberto, 268

Enzensberger, Hans Magnus, 291

Epic, 266–267

Epitaph, 36

Er Piotta, 246

Escapism, 91, 186, 200, 258

Ethiopia, 272–273

Euripides, 239

Europa Europa (Holland), 274

Fabrizi, Franco, 183, *189*

Faenza, Roberto, *Pereira Declares*, 10–11, 94–114. See also *Pereira Declares*

Falcone, Giuseppe, 140

Fascism: in *Life Is Beautiful*, 272–275; in *Mediterraneo*, 82–83; in *Paisan*, 35–36; in *Pereira Declares*, 95

Fava, Claudio, 4, 277; in *The Icicle Thief*, 227, 228, 231, 233

Fegatelli, 190

Feldman, Elmer, 33

Fellini, Federico, 3, 30, 31; *8 ½*, 182, 184, 197, 246, 285; *Amarcord*, 273; *Casanova*, 182; *City of Women*, 184; *A Director's Notebook*, 190; and documentary, 190; *Ginger and Fred*, 11, 181-198, 232, 246; "hyperfilm" of, 182-184, 198; *I clowns*, 183, 190; *I vitelloni*, 182; *Juliet of the Spirits*, 183, 191; *La dolce vita*, 182, 184; *La strada*, 158, 161-162, 185; *La voce della luna*, 191; *Nights of Cabiria*, 183, 185; *Roma*, 182; Rosi's tribute to, 285; *Satyricon*, 191; television films of, 190; *Variety Lights*, 183; *The White Sheik*, 183. See also *Ginger and Fred*

Felman, Shoshana, 253-254

Feminism, 45, 174-175, 240. *See also* Gender roles

Ferrara, Giuseppe, 139

Ferreri, Marco, 4

Film history: and Bertolucci's aestheticism, 66; Blasetti as personification of the film industry, 47; and *Cinema Paradiso*, 200-201; and film scholarship, 7-12; and *Ginger and Fred*, 182-183, 185; and *The Icicle Thief*, 214-220; and *La scorta*, 138-141; and *Life Is Beautiful*, 269-270; in *Mediterraneo*, 87-88; and Mastroianni in *Pereira Declares*, 111; of Noto in *Stolen Children*, 173; in *Three Brothers*, 135

Firemen of Viggiù, The (Mattoli), 206

Fofi, Goffedo, 234

Follow the Fleet (Sandrich), 194, 198

Forster, E. M., 26

Foscolo, Ugo, 36

Franciolini, Gianni, 43

French Connection, The (Friedkin), 39

Freud, Sigmund, 279. *See also* Benjamin, Jessica; Jokes; Lacan, Jacques; Mulvey, Laura; Narcissism; Projection; Psychoanalysis; Sublimation

From Emperor to Citizen (Pu Yi), 63

Frye, Northrop, 90, 93

Garbo, Greta, 48

Gaze: in *Bellissima*, 53-58; in *Caro diario*, 291, 299; and childish curiosity in *Three Brothers*, 136-137; collective, in *Cinema Paradiso*, 206; in *La scorta*, 141; in *The*

Last Emperor, Pu Yi as object of, 70; in *Paisan*, 26-31; in *Pereira Declares*, 105-110; in *Stolen Children*, 167-168, 174-176; of surveillance in *Mediterraneo*, 77; and television in *The Icicle Thief*, 231; in *The Truce*, 258-262

Gender roles: in *Bellissima*, 52-53; in *La scorta*, 148-150; in *The Last Emperor*, 69-70; in *Mediterraneo*, 90; in *Stolen Children*, 163-165; in *Three Brothers*, 123-126; in *To Die for Tano*, 239-240

Generational comedy, 286, 292

Genre: and comedy in *Life Is Beautiful*, 281, 283, 284; and dreams in *Three Brothers*, 127; and Holocaust representation, 269; and the journey-of-Italy film, 157-158; in *La scorta*, 139-141; and *The Last Emperor*, 69, 75; of Mafia films, 234; *Mediterraneo*, 90, 92-93; and the miracle tale in *Paisan*, 32; and Moretti, 289-290; and neorealist requirements, 219; the spectrum of, in *The Icicle Thief*, 223-224; and the splatter film, 293; and the thriller in *To Die for Tano*, 243-244; and the variety of *Paisan*, 22. See also *Cinema politico; Commedia all'italiana*

Germany, Year Zero (Rossellini), 135

Germi, Pietro, 139; *Cammino della Speranza*, 157; *Divorce Italian Style*, 139; *Nel nome della legge*, 201; *Seduced and Abandoned*, 139

Gerusalemme liberata (Tasso), 207

Gilda (Vidor), 218

Ginger and Fred (Fellini), 11, 181-198, 232; and carnival, 191; and commercials, 187-188; credits, 311-312; and critique of spectacle, 188-198; and desire, 188; and escapism, 186; and film history, 182-183, 185; and hyperfilm, 182-184; and mirror, 188-190; plot summary, 312; and postmodernism, 182, 188-190, 196-198; and projection, 184; and tap dancing, 193-194; and television, 181, 184-187, 188-193, 195; and television montage, 185; and utopia, 197. *See also* Baudrillard, Jean; Jameson, Fredric

Girard, René, 188
Giusti, Mario, 190
Godfather Part II (Coppola), 139, 244, 245
Gone with the Wind (Fleming), 204-205
Gosetti, Giorgio, 4, 6
Grable, Betty, 48
Gramsci, Antonio, 62, 68, 75, 97-98, 323n2; and national-popular culture, 40, 58, 68, 83, 98, 285; and organic intellectual, 97; and trasformismo, 62
Great War, The (Monicelli), 87
Guarini, Alfredo, 43

Hawks, Howard, Red River, 48
Hayworth, Rita, 219
Heaven Can Wait (Lubitsch), 227
Holland, Agnieszka, Europa Europa, 274
Holocaust, 11-12, 253-284
Homer, 89, 235, 266, 295
Homosexuality, 86
Hutcheon, Linda, 231
Hyperconsciousness, 233
Hyperfilm, 182-184, 198. See also Fellini, Federico

Icicle Thief, The (Nichetti), 11, 214-233; and auteurism, 227-231; and body, 219, 227, 230; and carnival, 232; and chandelier, 221; and the church, 218; credits, 314; and documentary, 218; and film history, 214-220; and the gaze, 231; and genre, 223-224; and miserablism, 220; narrative structure of, 216; and pastiche, 217-219; plot summary, 314-315; and postmodernism, 216, 225, 226-227, 231-233; and reception, 224, 233; and television, 225-233. See also Mise-en-scène; Neorealism
I clowns (Fellini), 183, 190
Ideology: and 1950s retrenchment in Bellissima, 42, 48; and auteurist abuse in The Icicle Thief, 230; of the characters in Bicycle Thief, 229; and cinema politico in Rosi, 115, 116; debates on, in Three Brothers, 128; evolution in the journey film, 157; the intellectual's withdrawal from, 97; and L'umorismo of Pirandello, 268; and moral engagement in Paisan, 33-34; in Pereira Declares, the gaze of Pereira, 106; —, Salazarist propaganda film, 104-106; —, and voice-over, 101; and psychoanalysis, 71; and the splitting of audiences in Life Is Beautiful, 279; and the spoof of Fascism in Life Is Beautiful, 272; in "The Third Son," 130, 132
Ieracitano, Giuseppe, 154, 171, 172
Il postino (Radford), 7
Il posto (Olmi), 226
Il sistema periodico (Levi), 254
Image: and advertising in The Icicle Thief, 222, 224; chain of, on television, 185; of the chandelier in The Icicle Thief, 221; and channel surfing, 187, 225; cinematography of North vs. South in Three Brothers, 124; in conflict with sound in La scorta, 150; and crime photography in Three Brothers, 121; and documentary in Caro diario, 297; of false glamour in Fascism, 274; of Fascist Italy in Pereira Declares, 95; and Fellini's televisual transformation, 192; in framing of Life Is Beautiful, 271; frozen in photo portrait in Pereira Declares, 109, 110; generative, 34; of Italian national self, 285, 286; and Lacan's mirror phase, 54-56; in La scorta, 141, 143; of locomotive in The Truce, 266; of the Mafia, 236; in the mirror, 40, 58, 163-164; of mother in Three Brothers, 134-136; and orientalism, 62; and Pasolini's semiotics of cinema, 294; in a postmodern economy, 226; and postmodern simulation, 6, 295; projected onto the audience in Cinema Paradiso, 205; projected on screen, 56-57; and the Salazarist propaganda film in Pereira Declares, 105; of the Soviet state, 103; in Stolen Children finale, 176; tabloid, 165-166; televised image of bourgeois affluence in Stolen Children, 159; of train in Life Is Beautiful, 281; of wedding ring in Three Brothers, 132, 137; of World War II in neorealism, 90; and Zorro photo in Stolen Children, 168

Improvisation, 42-43
Intersubjectivity, 174-176
Io sono un autarchico (Moretti), 286, 287
I sommersi e i salvati (Levi), 254
I vitelloni (Fellini), 182, 205
Italianità: in *The Last Emperor*, 62, 68; in
  Mediterraneo, 76, 78, 83-84; in *The
  Truce*, 263-265

James, Clive, 3
Jameson, Fredric: and architecture/
  television, 188-189; and nostalgic
  postmodernism in *Cinema Paradiso*,
  199-200, 207; and simulation, 6
Johnson, Dots, 25
Jokes (joke work), 279-281
Jones, Nowell, *33*
Juliet of the Spirits (Fellini), 183, 191

Kael, Pauline, 69, 74, 117, 119
Kapo (Pontecorvo), 276, 281, 283
Kermode, Frank, 216
Kezich, Tullio, 3
Kolker, Robert, 71

Laborit, Henri, 76
Lacan, Jacques, 54-55, 73
La cieca di Sorrento (Malasomma), 41
La dolce vita (Fellini), 182, 184
La messa è finita (Moretti), 286, 287
Lancaster, Burt, 48
Lanzmann, Claude, *Shoah*, 281
La presa di Roma (Alberini), 285
La sconfitta (Moretti), 288
La scorta (Tognazzi), 11, 138-153; and the
  body, 149, 152; camera work in, 150;
  and *cinema politico*, 138-139, 140-141;
  credits, 309; and documentary, 140;
  and film history, 138-141; and the
  gaze, 141; and genre, 139-141; and the
  Mafia, 140, 142-144, 147-148; plot
  summary, 309-310; and religious processions, 139-140; and the spectator,
  152; and utopia, 141, 143, 152; and
  voice-over, 148. See also *Mise-en-scène*
La sfida (Rosi), 115
Last Emperor, The (Bertolucci), 7, 10-11,
  61-75; and adaptation, 65-66; and

conversion, 64; credits, 304; and film
  history, 66; and the gaze, 70; and gen-
  der roles, 69-70; and genre, 69, 75; and
  Italianità, 62, 68; and Marxism, 64-69;
  plot summary, 304-305, and projec-
  tion, 71; and the spectator (as theo-
  rized by Mulvey), 70; and utopia, 64.
  See also Psychoanalysis; Spectacle;
  Theater acting
La strada (Fellini), 158, 161-162, 183, 185
La terra trema (Visconti), 39, 201, 204, 220
Laub, Dori, 254-255
La voce della luna (Fellini), 191
L'avventura (Antonioni), 173
Lemmon, Jack, 245
Leonardo da Vinci, 34
Leopard, The (Visconti), 62, 204
Levi, Carlo, 117
Levi, Primo, 12, 99, 253-267
Liebman, Stuart, 269
Life Is Beautiful (Benigni), 7, 11-12,
  268-284; and body politic, 274; and
  commedia all'italiana, 284; credits,
  317-318; and Ethiopia, 272-273; and
  Fascism, 272-275; and film history,
  269-270; and genre (comedy), 281,
  283, 284; and genre (Holocaust repre-
  sentation), 269; and image of train,
  281; and "joke work," 278-279; plot
  summary, 318; and reception, 278-281;
  and testimony, 269, 272; and *toscanità*,
  277; and translation, 275-278; and
  L'umorismo, 268, 275, 278. See also
  Spectacle
Literary tradition, 36, 38, 84, 207, 267
Lone, John, *64*
Lo Verso, Enrico, *142, 146, 171, 172*
Love in the Western World (Rougemont), 212
Luchetti, Daniele, *Portaborse*, 287
Luhrmann, Baz, *Romeo + Juliet*, 248
Lukács, Georg, 62, 68-69. See also
  Realism
L'umorismo, 268, 275, 278

Maccheroni (Scola), 245
Mafia: in *Ginger and Fred*, 186; in *La
  scorta*, 140, 142-144, 147-148; in *To Die
  for Tano*, 234-249

Magnani, Anna, 40–47. *See also* Neorealism
Malasomma, Nunzio, *La cieca di Sorrento*, 41
Mankiewicz, Herman J., *A Woman's Secret*, 48
Marrakech Express (Salvatores), 76, 91
Marriage, in *Three Brothers*, 132–134, 137
Martini, Emanuela, 234
Marxism, 64–69
Masina, Giulietta, 183, *183*, 185, 197
Masked reference, 272
Mastroianni, Marcello, *102*, *109*, 110–112, 183, *183*, 197
Mauriac, François, 97
Mediterraneo (Salvatores), 7, 10–11, 76–93; and body politic, 91; camera work in, 77; and the church, 89–90; and *commedia all'italiana*, 76, 78, 90, 93; credits, 305–306; and escapism, 91; and Fascism, 82–83; and film history, 87–88; and the gaze, 77; and genre, 90, 92–93; and national identity, 76, 78, 82–84; plot summary, 307; and projection, 91; and reception, 92; and the spectator, 77, 92; and translation, 88–89; and utopia, 91–93. *See also* Neorealism; Theater acting
Melodrama: in *Bellissima*, 50, 58; and the *sceneggiata* in *To Die for Tano*, 244–245; on television in *The Icicle Thief*, 225
Memphis, Ricky, *142*
Meta-performance, 40–44, 58, 112
Metaphor: and body politic/erotic, 267; in *Caro diario*, 287; of the chandelier in *The Icicle Thief*, 221; of the circle in *Three Brothers*, 132; contrasted with allegory in *Three Brothers*, 118; of the family in *La Scorta*, 143, 150, 152; and Holocaust testimony, 256; and interpretive displacement in *Pereira Declares*, 95; and journey narratives in *Stolen Children*, 157; and maternity in *Three Brothers*, 136; in *Mediterraneo*, 78, 91; and political revolution in *Pereira Declares*, 102–103; and subjective camera in *Three Brothers*, 117
Metz, Christian, 54

Mezzogiorno, Vittorio, 128, *133*
Miccichè, Lino, 4, 7, 39, 58, 329n35
Mirror: in *Bellissima*; 40–41, 53–58; cinema as, 285, 299; in *Cinema Paradiso*, 206; in *Ginger and Fred*, 188–190; in *Stolen Children*, 163–164
Mise-en-abyme, 92, 104–106
Mise-en-scène: in *The Icicle Thief*, 229; in *La scorta*, 150; in *Pereira Declares*, 110; in *Stolen Children*, 156, 159, 169, 170, 174; in *Three Brothers*, 124, 131
Miserablism, 220
Monicelli, Mario: *The Great War*, 87; *The Organizer*, 111
Monni, Riccardo, 91
Monster, The (Benigni), 278
Montage: defined, 16; and false impression in *Mediterraneo*, 77; internal, 43; in *Paisan*, 22, 34, 38; and television in *Ginger and Fred*, 185
Monumental history, 18
Morandini, Morandino, 272
Moravia, Alberto, 61–62, 69, 71, 74, 75
Moretti, Nanni, 7, 9, 86; *Bianca*, 286; *Caro diario*, 9, 11–12, 285–299; *Ecce bombo*, 286–290; *Io sono un autarchico*, 286, 287, 289; *La messa è finita*, 286, 287; *La sconfitta*, 288; *Palombella rossa*, 286, 287, 288; *Sogni d'oro*, 286, 287, 290. *See also Caro diario*
Morricone, Ennio, 110, 295
Mulvey, Laura, 54–56
Music: in *La scorta*, 142; in *The Last Emperor*, 65; in *Pereira Declares*, 110; in *Stolen Children*, 167; in *Three Brothers*, 117, 134; in *To Die for Tano*, 235–236, 244–246; in *The Truce*, 267

Narcissism, 53–58, 208, 274
National identity: and agrarian past in *Three Brothers*, 119; in *Caro diario*, 286; and Gramsci, 68; Greek and Italian, in *Mediterraneo*, 76, 78, 82–84; and journey narrative in *Stolen Children*, 157; in *La scorta*, 138; in *Paisan*, 15–17, 19; and television, 5–6; in *The Truce*, 263, 265; and *toscanità* in *Life Is Beautiful*, 277

Nationalism, 95

Nazzaro, Giona, 140, 153

Nel nome della legge (Germi), 201

Neorealism: compared to *cinema politico,*
139; demise of, 39-41, 58; film endings
of, 176, 215-216; generic requirements
of, 220-221; as Golden Age, 215; and
The Icicle Thief, 215-233; and Italy, renewal of, 285, 299; and Liberation,
135; Magnani as visual trademark of,
41, 45; and *Mediterraneo,* 76, 87, 90; and
national identity in *Paisan,* 16, 157;
and non-professional actors in *Bellissima,* 44; and *pedinamento* in *Bellissima,*
43; referential function of, 5-6, 11,
157, 200; "second phase" of, 115; and
Stolen Children, 154-157, 176; subject
matter of, 270; techniques of, 154; and
Three Brothers, 135. See also *Pedinamento;* Realism; Zavattini, Cesare

Nichetti, Maurizio, 7; *The Icicle Thief, The*
214-233. See also *Icicle Thief, The*

Night of the Shooting Stars (Taviani brothers), 87, 270

Nights of Cabiria (Fellini), 183, 185; in *The
Icicle Thief* pastiche, 217, 218

Noiret, Philippe, *210*

Nostalgia, 199-201, 206-207

Novelized history, 61, 68-69, 74

Nowell-Smith, Geoffrey, 324n8

O'Hara, Maureen, 48

Olden, Christine, 56

Olmi, Ermanno, 226, 234; *Il posto,* 226

Open City (Rossellini), 15, 16, 32, 33, 41,
176, 222, 283; in *The Icicle Thief* pastiche, 217, 220

Opera, 50-51

Organizer, The (Monicelli), 111

Orlando furioso (Ariosto), 207

Oscar prize, 7, 61, 92

Ossessione (Visconti), 218

Paisan (Rossellini), 10, 15-38, 87, 93, 135,
157, 245; camera work in, 27-29; and
carnival, 22; and Christian humanism,
34; and the church, 31-34; credits, 301;
and documentary, 18; and the gaze,
26-31; and genre, 22; and montage, 22,
34, 38; and national identity, 15-17, 19;
and partisan's corpse/epitaph, 35-36,
38; plot summary, 302-303

Palombella rossa (Moretti), 286, 287

Pasca, Alfonsino, 25

Pasolini, Pier Paolo, 3; semiotics of cinema, 293-295

Pastiche: in *Cinema Paradiso,* 199-201; in
The Icicle Thief, 217-219; in *To Die for
Tano,* 243, 244

Peck, Gregory, 247

Pedagogy, 119

Pedinamento, 43, 155. See also Neorealism;
Zavattini, Cesare

Peploe, Mark, 61

Pereira Declares (Faenza), 10-11, 94-114;
and adaptation (of Tabucchi), 94-105;
and body politic, 102-103, 105; and
conversion, 112; credits, 306-307; and
Fascism, 95; and film history, 111; and
the gaze, 105-110; and ideology of the
Salazarist propaganda film, 104-106;
and *mise-en-abyme,* 104-106; plot summary, 307-308; and reception, 100; and
testimony, 99-100; and translation, 95-
96; and voice-over, 101-104. See also
Metaphor; *Mise-en-scène;* Psychoanalysis

Pesaro manifesto, 9-10

Petri, Elio, 4, 115

Piccioni, Piero, 117

Pirandello, Luigi, 230; *L'umorismo,* 268,
275, 278

Platonov, Andrei, 128-132, 137

Player, The (Altman), 215-216

Pleasure, 208-213

Plot summaries, 301-320 (appendix)

Pontecorvo, Gillo, 276; *Kapo,* 276, 281, 283

Portaborse (Luchetti), 287

Postmodernism, 6-7, 11; in *Cinema Paradiso,* 199-200, 207; in *Ginger and Fred,*
182, 188-190, 196-198; in *The Icicle
Thief,* 216, 225, 226-227, 231-233. See
also Baudrillard, Jean; Jameson,
Fredric; Nostalgia; Simulation

Poststructuralism, 46, 293

Projection: in *Bellissima,* 40-41, 51,
56-57; Bertolucci's cinema criticized

as, 71; in *Cinema Paradiso*, 209; and
Fellini in *Ginger and Fred*, 184; in
Mediterraneo, 91; and performance in
To Die for Tano, 246; in *Stolen Children*,
163
Psychoanalysis: in *Cinema Paradiso*, and
the primal scene, 202; —, and projection, 209; —, and sublimation, 211; —,
and wish-fulfillment fantasies, 208;
and intersubjectivity in *Stolen Children*, 174-176; and "joke work" in
Life Is Beautiful, 278-279; and maternity in *Bellissima*, 53-58; and *medécin-
philosophes* in *Pereira Declares*, 102-103;
and oedipal drama in *The Last Emperor*, 65, 70-75. *See also* Benjamin, Jessica; Bertolucci, Bernardo; Feminism;
Freud, Sigmund; Lacan, Jacques;
Mulvey, Laura; Mirror; Narcissism;
Projection
Pudovkin, V. I., 17
Pu Yi, Aisin-Gioro, 61, 63-65

Rapagnetta, Gabriele, 111
Realism, 115, 200, 217, 221. *See also* Neo-
realism; Socialist realism
Reception: and generations of testimony
in *Life Is Beautiful*, 272; and *The Icicle
Thief*, 224, 233; and "joke work" in
Life Is Beautiful, 278-281; and *Mediter-
raneo*, 92; in *Pereira Declares*, 100; privi-
leged object of *Cinema Paradiso*, 199,
200-201; and television, 5-7; and
Three Brothers, 119. *See also* Spectator
Red River (Hawks), 48
Referential function, 5-6, 157, 200, 216,
271-272, 293
Regosa, Maurizio, 140
Religious processions, 139-140, 247
Resurrection, 94, 99
Risorgimento, 62, 76, 83-84
Road films, 157-158
Roberti, Bruno, 174
Rocco and His Brothers (Visconti), 158
Rogers, Ginger, 257
Roma (Fellini), 182
Romantic love, 208-213
Romeo + Juliet (Luhrmann), 248

Rondi, Gian Luigi, 124
Rondolino, Gianni, 17
Room with a View (Merchant/Ivory), 26
Rosi, Francesco, 4, 139, 285; *Cadaveri
eccellenti*, 115; *Christ Stopped at Eboli*,
115, 117; *La sfida*, 115; *Salvatore Giu-
liano*, 115; *Three Brothers*, 11, 115-137;
The Truce, 11-12, 253-267. *See also
Three Brothers; Truce, The*
Rossellini, Roberto, 3, 43, 49, 176, 217,
267; *Germany, Year Zero*, 135; *Open
City*, 15, 16, 32, 33, 41, 135, 217, 218,
222, 283; *Paisan*, 10, 15-38, 87, 93, 135,
157, 218; *Stromboli*, 295. *See also Paisan*
Rumble, Patrick, 199
Russia, as portrayed by Rosi in *The Truce*,
266-267
Ruttmann, Walter, *Acciaio*, 218

Said, Edward, 62
Salvatore Giuliano (Rosi), 115
Salvatores, Gabriele, 7; *Marrakech Express*,
76, 91; *Mediterraneo*, 7, 10-11, 76-93;
Turné, 76, 91. *See also Mediterranao*
Sandrich, Mark, 194
Satyricon (Fellini), 191
Saving Private Ryan (Spielberg), 78
Sazio, Carmela, *21*
Scalici, Valentina, 154, *171*, *172*
Sceneggiata, 245-246
Schindler's List (Spielberg), 281, 283
Sciascia, Leonardo, 204
Scola, Ettore, 4; *Maccheroni*, 235; *A Special
Day*, 107, 111; *Trevico-Torino, viaggio nel
Fiatnam*, 123; *We All Loved Each Other
So Much*, 87, 91, 214
Seduced and Abandoned (Germi), 139
Seduction of Mimi (Wertmuller), 158
Semiotics. *See Caro diario;* Jameson,
Fredric; Pasolini, Pier Paolo
Senso (Visconti), 50, 62
Sesti, Mario, 7, 8-9, 236, 286
Seven Beauties (Wertmuller), 283
Shakespeare, William, 239
Shoah (Lanzmann), 281
Shoeshine (De Sica), 154
Siamo donne (Visconti et al.), 43-45
Sicily, 139-140

Simon, John, 74
Simulation, 6, 7, 188, 192, 226, 274
Singer, Daniel, 3
Six Characters in Search of an Author
 (Pirandello), 230
Socialist realism, 67-69
Sogni d'oro (Moretti), 286, 287, 290
Sordi, Alberto, 290
Special Day, A (Scola), 107
Spectacle: and Bertolucci's aesthetics in
 The Last Emperor, 66-69, 75; in *Caro
 diario*, 293, 294; of Fascism as style,
 273; Fellini's critique of, in *Ginger and
 Fred*, 188-198; in *La scorta*, 139; in *Life
 Is Beautiful*, 271; of martyrdom in
 Open City, 176; of militarized youth in
 Pereira Declares, 106; of Pereira's shrine
 dedicated to his wife, 109; in *To Die
 for Tano*, 236, 242, 247, 248
Spectator, the: in *Caro diario*, 286, 292,
 297; and exemplarity in *La scorta*, 152;
 and *Mediterraneo*, 77, 92; as metaphori-
 cal body in *Cinema Paradiso*, 202; and
 Miccichè's interpretation of *Bellissima*,
 329n35; Mulvey's idea of, in *The Last
 Emperor*, 70; and the *sceneggiata* in *To
 Die for Tano*, 245; and testimony in *The
 Truce*, 261-262; as "viewed" by film in
 Cinema Paradiso, 205-207. *See also* Re-
 ception
Spider Stratagem (Bertolucci), 119
Spielberg, Steven, 78, 281; *Saving Private
 Ryan*, 78; *Schindler's List*, 281, 283
Splatter film, 293
Stanno tutti bene (Tornatore), 158
Starmaker (Tornatore), 203-205; camera
 work in, 205-206;
Stefanelli, Simonetta, *133*
Stolen Children (Amelio), 11, 154-177,
 215, 310; camera work in, 156-157; and
 carnival, 168; and the church, 160-161;
 credits, 310-31; and the gaze, 167-168;
 and gender roles, 163-165; and image
 of tabloid, 165-166; and journey narrative, 154-157; and mirror, 163-164;
 and *mise-en-scène*, 156, 159, 169, 170,
 174; and neorealism, 154-157, 176; and
 Noto in film history, 173; plot sum-

mary, 311; and projection, 163; and tel-
 evision, 167; and utopia, 156, 171-173;
 and voyeurism, 165-166, 174; and
 Zorro photo, 168. *See also* Neorealism
Storaro, Vittorio, 295
Stromboli (Rossellini), 295
Sublimation, 211
Supercafone (Er Piotta), 246
Swept Away (Wertmuller), 290
Synopses, 301-320 (appendix)

Tabloid journalism, 165
Tabucchi, Antonio, 94-101
Tap dancing, 193-194
Tasso, Torquato, 207
Taurisano, Francesco, 140
Taviani brothers, 4; *Allonsanfan*, 111;
 Night of the Shooting Stars, 87, 270
Television, 4-7, 11, 94, 159, 167; in *Caro
 diario*, 291, 295; in *Ginger and Fred*,
 181, 184-187, 188-193, 195; in *The
 Icicle Thief*, 225-233; privatization of,
 187; in *Stolen Children*, 167; in *To
 Die for Tano*, 243; and triangulation
 of desire, 188
Temple, Shirley, 48
Terrorism, 115-116, 120-121
Testimony, 12, 99-100, 253-268, 269,
 272. *See also Life Is Beautiful; Pereira
 Declares; Spectator, the; Truce, The*
Theater acting: in *Bellissima*, 44-45; in
 The Last Emperor, 63, in *Mediterraneo*,
 78
"Third Son, The" (Platonov), 128-132,
 137
Thomas, Jeremy (producer), 61
Three Brothers (Rosi), 11, 115-137; and
 adaptation (of Platonov), 128-132, 137;
 and allegory, 118, 129, 134; and body
 politic, 116, 118, 122, 123, 129; camera
 work in, 124, 132, 136-137; and the
 church, 128; and *cinema politico*,
 115-117, 127; credits, 308; dream,
 126-128; and film history, 135; and the
 gaze, 136-137; and gender roles,
 123-126; North vs. South in, 124; plot
 summary, 308-309; and reception, 119;
 and terrorism, 115-116, 120-121. *See*

also Image; Metaphor; *Mise-en-scène;* Neorealism; "Third Son, The"

To Die for Tano (Torre), 11, 234-249; and body politic, 236; camera work in, 240-241; and carnival, 236, 247; and Catholic kitsch, 248-249; and Christian humanism, 128; credits, 315-316; and destiny, 241-243; and documentary, 243; flashbacks, 242-243; and gender roles, 239-240; and genre, 243-244; and Mafia, 243-249; and melodrama, 244-245; and pastiche, 243, 244; plot summary, 316; and projection/performance, 246; and religious processions, 247; and spectacle, 236, 242, 247, 248; and television, 243; and tragedy, 239-240

Tognazzi, Ricky, 11; *La scorta*, 11, 138-153. See also *La scorta*

Tornatore, Giuseppe, 7; *Cinema Paradiso*, 7, 11; *Stanno tutti bene*, 158; *Starmaker*, 203-205

Torre, Roberta, 11; *To Die for Tano*, 11, 234-249. See also *To Die for Tano*

Tourist gaze (in *Paisan*), 26-31

Tragedy, 239-240, 284

Translation: in *Caro diario*, 294; in *Life Is Beautiful*, 275-278; in *Mediterraneo*, 88-89; in *Pereira Declares*, 95-96; in *The Truce*, 259

Trevico-Torino, viaggio nel Fiatnam (Scola), 123

Truce, The (Rosi), 11-12, 253-267; and adaptation (of Levi), 253-268; and body politic/erotic, 267; camera work in, 256, 260; credits, 316-317; and documentary, 260; and epic, 266-267; and escape, 258; and the gaze, 258-262; and *Italianità*, 263-265; plot summary, 317; and testimony, 253-268; title of, 262-263; and translation, 259

Tubbs, William, *33*

Turné (Salvatores), 76 , 91

Turner, Lana, 48

Turturro, John, 256, 258, *264, 265*

Umberto D (De Sica), in *The Icicle Thief* pastiche, 217

Utopia: in *Bellissima*, 58; in *Ginger and Fred*, 197; in *La scorta*, 141, 143, 152; in *The Last Emperor*, 64; in *Mediterraneo*, 91-93; in *Stolen Children*, 156, 171-173

Van Loon, Robert, *21*

Variety Lights (Fellini), 183

Verdi, Giuseppe, 50, 186, 187

Verdone, Carlo, 7

Viganò, Aldo, 4

Visconti, Luchino, 3, 62, 67, 235, 267; *Bellissima*, 10, 39-58; *The Leopard*, 62, 204; *Ossessione*, 218; *Rocco and His Brothers*, 158; *Senso*, 50, 62; *Siamo donne*, 43-45; *La terra trema*, 39, 201, 204, 220. See also *Bellissima*

Voice-over: in *Pereira Declares*, 101-104; in *La scorta*, 148

Voyeurism, 165-166, 174

Vu, Richard, 67

Warshow, Robert, 21

We All Loved Each Other So Much (Scola), 87, 91, 214

Wertmuller, Lina, 4, 289; *A Blood Feud*, 111; *Seduction of Mimi*, 158; *Seven Beauties*, 283, 289; *Swept Away*, 290

Wettlaufer, Alexandra, 16

White Sheik, The (Fellini), 183

White-telephone comedies, 217

Woman's Secret, A (Mankiewicz), 48

Z (Costa-Gavras), 139

Zagarrio, Vito, 8

Zaller, Robert, 69

Zampa, Luigi, 43

Zavattini, Cesare, 40-42, 49, 155. See also Neorealism; *Pedinamento*

Zeffirelli, Franco, *Cavalleria rusticana*, 139